FACING TEXTS

Printed in the United States of America
on acid-free paper ∞
Library of Congress Cataloging in
Publication Data appear on the last prin
page of this book.

William H. Gass
homini fabro

CONTENTS

CHAPTERS FROM NOVELS

POSTLECTURE

PREFACE

Some time ago William Gass talked with Joanne Ferguson of Duke University Press about my putting together a collection of pieces by contemporary American writers. When Joanne Ferguson asked me if I liked the idea, I immediately recognized that in effect I was being offered the opportunity to realize one of my pet ideas: to bring together, in one book and between two covers, unpublished pieces by authors as well as critics that would, in a sense, defy the chronological secondariness of critical interpretation. Such a book would make the relationship between author and critic an unmediated encounter, with authors and critics becoming one another's ideal readers.

For this book, two things seemed to be necessary. One: if possible, the pieces offered by the authors should indeed be hitherto unpublished so as to give the critics a sense of the exclusiveness, even privacy of their work and thus convey to them the impression of a close encounter with the respective author. I refrained from stipulating that the authors' texts be of any special kind or given length; in fact, they didn't even have to be fictional. Two: the authors should choose their own critics in order to ensure that the close encounter I had in mind would not, unintentionally, be hostile, and thus destroy the possibility of mutual ideal readership. Most authors did. In the other cases I suggested the critic. I particularly sought to bring in European critics (though by no means all the European critics in this volume were selected by me) in order to ensure an international and thus more general basis for what I hoped these encounters would become—a metaphor for contemporary writing that rested on a shared literary tradition. As with the authors, I made no attempt to constrict the critics' approach to their text: it was up to them to choose whether to do a close reading of that text or relate it to the other works of the author or, perhaps, see it as exemplary for a larger literary development.

The writers and critics in this volume constitute a group. Yet I would like to contend that their congruity is not brought about by their adherence to any special concept, say, the concept of postmodernism, but by their common deference to what I would call the anthological principle, the conviction that one's own text is always framed by others to the point where the identity of one's own text is defined through its context. There are, of course, other contemporary American writers who would fit into this group. My choice, although not random, was at times dictated by the willingness of the authors and critics to participate in this venture, and this inclination was in turn mostly influenced by mutual esteem. However, in contemplating the result of my often complicated, and at times discouraging, editorial endeavors, I feel content. To my mind, this volume contains many outstanding pieces—both fictional and critical. I also find that the aesthetic principle I try to define in the introduction has been convincingly demonstrated in the texts, a principle that presupposes the absence of both enmity and self-love in both authors and critics.

It remains for me to thank the Duke University Press and especially Joanne Ferguson for patience, trust, and support. I thank all the critics for responding so conscientiously to the confidence placed in them. Finally and above all, I want to thank the authors for their contributions, hoping that, as in a Platonic symposium, they will enjoy the company in which they find themselves.

Heide Ziegler
Stuttgart, March 1987

INTRODUCTION

HEIDE ZIEGLER

......

Facing Texts

Anthologies have always served many functions. Their traditional importance, continuing to this day, can be detected when we survey the history of the genre. From the beginning, the etymological meaning of the word points up this importance. The Greek words *ánthos,* flower, and *légein,* to gather together, combine to describe, like the Latin equivalent *florilegium,* a collection of selected texts or excerpts that—as each flower is the epitome of the plant—the editor considers representative of the works of one or a number of authors, of a literary school or a genre, of an epoch, or of the literature of a whole nation. An anthology can also become the means to variously illustrate a special topic or theory. Initially anthologies served the special purpose of saving texts of otherwise unpublished authors from being forgotten. Thus they could inspire subsequent works whose authors claimed originality. Only later, that is, during late antiquity, the Middle Ages, and especially the Renaissance, did anthologies assume the didactic function we tend to connect with them today. They were used in Latin schools to convey to the pupils a sense of *studium generale,* a basic education in the sciences, ethics, and aesthetics. During the nineteenth and the twentieth centuries the number of anthologies published to serve various purposes became countless; yet the conserving and didactic heritage to some degree still informs even the wildest offshoots of the genre—even in cases where the act of gathering together the separate texts becomes more important than the individual selections themselves, that is, where the anthological effect as such becomes paramount. The oldest known anthology (no longer extant) was called *Stephanos,* "wreath." The very fact that from this anthology, a collection of epigrams, everything was lost to later generations but its name enhances the meaning of *anthology:* since we no longer know the aspect or the scent of any single flower, the very process of their having been gathered into a wreath gains importance. Through a whim of literary history, the anthology as we find it in the beginning coincides with its most advanced contemporary expressions.

In the beginning, anthologies tended to gather together epigrams or poems. This, of course, was due to quantitative rather than qualitative considerations, since the pieces chosen had to be complete (especially when their authors were anonymous) and therefore short. Only later did prose pieces gain entry into anthologies, and not before the eighteenth century were essays collected into one book. Anthologies of "secondary" criticism have an even shorter tradition. Gathering together fictional pieces in order to face them with critical pieces therefore demanded previous editorial reflection upon the function of such a juxtaposition, especially since the fictional pieces were in no case culled from existing books or short-story collections. Instead, they were elicited from each author, who chose the piece for this anthology—just as each critic was to write the accompanying essay as a response to the author's choice. The choice demanded of the editor, therefore, was not among eligible texts, but among representative authors and critics, not violating, but at least departing from the traditional process of anthologizing. Thus it was only after reflection upon the origins of anthology that the structural features of the genre could be reapplied to the present anthology, *Facing Texts*.

Since the relationship that generically has to be established between the anthologizing editor and the anthologized texts was transferred to the relationship between editor and each author and critic, the didactic and the conserving qualities of the anthology are redefined. The traditional didactic quality on the one hand, that is, the quality resulting from any encounter between mentor and pupil, surfaced in the relationship between author and critic, in that the critic not only had to read a given text for evaluative purposes but had to respond personally and privately to the actual author of that text. This is not the same as when a critic reviews a published work by a living author. The traditional conserving quality, on the other hand, shifted to the collecting of the texts themselves. The critical texts might not have been written otherwise. And the fictional texts, although unlikely to become literally forgotten otherwise (in the sense that they could or would not have been published elsewhere), have been saved from a different kind of submergence: the effect achieved both through the encounter between each fictional and each critical text and the relationship constituted among all the fictional texts could not have come into existence, could not be recognized and remembered, had they not been anthologized. This effect can indeed be compared to a gathering together of flowers to form a wreath. The flowers do not lose their respective individuality in being thus assembled, yet a general aura might have gone unnoticed were it not for the arrangement of which they have become part. In other words, each flower seems to take on the general structuring principle of the whole wreath.

At first glance it might seem that the anthological principle employed in this collection is not all that innovative, but that the gathering together of the present texts rather derives from the desire to illustrate a special literary epoch, the epoch that has come to be known as postmodernism. Yet not only is the term *postmodernism* more often employed by its detractors than by its defenders or simple chroniclers—to the point where doubts seem justified even about the unmistakable contours of such an epoch, let alone about its correct designation—but the question whether or not the term *postmodernism* should be applied to the authors or fiction texts assembled in this collection need not even concern us. For even if the ten fictional pieces faced with ten critical responses together enact what might be called postmodernist strategies, then those strategies are transcended by the texts' independence from them as reasons for being. Although conscious of their historical position after the age of modernism, the authors, by employing experimental or neorealistic or ironic modes of writing, question the unifying term *postmodernism* as an appropriate designation of the present literary age. And the critics, by reacting in poststructuralist or deconstructive or idiosyncratic fashion to the authors' texts, further scotch any implicit need for a uniform label.

These pieces relate to each other—on the one hand each fictional and accompanying critical piece, on the other hand each pair of texts to the other pairs of texts—so as to effect the transcendence of each text's individual historical conditions without denying the need for such conditions in the name of a generalizing theory. Instead, the collection furthers the idea of anthology as such by defying closure and perpetuating the notion of a gathering together of exemplary specimens. This is obviously true for chapters from novels, that is, from larger contexts, by Walter Abish, William Gass, John Hawkes, and Joseph McElroy; but it is also true for the stories by Donald Barthelme, Robert Coover, Guy Davenport, and Susan Sontag; and it is still true for the two lectures by Stanley Elkin and John Barth. In the group of stories, for instance, even the title of Susan Sontag's short story, "Description (of a Description)," conveys a sense of metafiction or interplay of two distinct levels, which is taken up and intensified by Richard Howard's critical response, metatitled "A Description of 'Description (of a Description).'" And Elkin's lecture "What's in a Name?" does not ask the question implied in the title in order to answer it; nor does Barth call his lecture "The Limits of Imagination" in order to define those limits, but rather in order to refine them out of existence. Finally, with regard to the critics and readers, the etymological meaning of the word *anthology* should once more be taken into consideration. Both the Greek verb *légein* and the Latin verb *legere* mean "to read" as well as "to gather together." The process of reading what has been arranged in order to constitute a whole can be seen as precluding the intended closure at the same time. The critics, who through their interpretation of the authors' texts defy the closure of those texts, define the texts' exemplary status at the same time. Yet every reader also extends the anthological principle in that he or she continues what the editor and the authors and the critics have already attempted to do: add to the imaginary space in which all texts may be woven together.

Reflecting upon the structure of this anthology then meant relaying the principle of openness from one text-related stage to the next. This process turned out to imply an increasing applicability of this principle of openness that can serve as metaphor for the changing nature of any latter-day encounter with one's own literary tradition. The initial encounter between the editor and each author defied closure, because it had to result in the author's turning away toward the text that he wanted to provide for the anthology while yet trying to meet the editor's requirements. The ensuing encounter between author and critic also defied closure, because by attempting to place the author's text within a larger literary context, the critic had to reach out in two different directions while also trying to meet the editor's requirements: toward the general reader and back to the author, whom he had to conceive of as his special or ideal reader. In *Facing Texts* the reader's encounter, finally, is with the author *and* with the critic, and with their multiplying, past- and future-oriented encounters. The reader alone can connect, and interpret the relationship among, all the texts assembled in this collection. Since the reader may further relay as well as increase the applicability of the principle of openness by becoming, for instance, a reviewer of this anthology, the anthological principle would appear infinite, if the anthology did not present a text in itself. In other words, the principle of openness has a counterpart in the text as it is published. However, that principle of openness infiltrates even the published text, representing its historical as opposed to its literary dimension. Attempting to find a link between these two dimensions, the historical and the literary, we shall have recourse to what can be called the "spirit of the text" since, whatever that spirit may turn out to be, it can be defined as something both inside and outside the text, capable of being an interface of the text's historical (or open) and its literary (or closed) character. Moreover, since this particular text not only constitutes itself—as that of any anthology—through a succession of separate texts created by the interstices between those texts, that is, as a succession of words and silences that frame each other; but since it does, moreover, represent the anthological principle microcosmically, so to speak, in each pair of texts, the spirit of the text should also be discernible within each of those pairs of texts, since each—on a smaller scale—mirrors the interrelationship noted between the historical and the literary dimensions.

In his essay "The Fate of Reading" Geoffrey Hartman says that often "a critical discourse based on the criterion of adequation (of vehicle to tenor, for example), even when as complex as that of organic form, disappoints. We feel that structures, norms, techniques, and so forth, are important, but only as they are broken or breaking does the spirit leap forth."[1] Hartman seems to see the spirit of the text as something hidden in the text, something that appears only when its "structures, norms, techniques, and so forth" are broken down or dissolve. Then the spirit leaps forth like something that has been kept under pressure for a long time or, more metaphysically, like something that has longed to be liberated. Still, although it seems to substantiate that spirit, Hartman's is too reader-oriented a definition. "As they *are broken* or *breaking*" could, of course, mean that the structures, norms, techniques, and so forth are either actively broken by the reader or dissolving on their own accord during the encounter between text and reader. In the latter case the spirit can apparently leap forth because it is no longer textually confined and may now exist independently in the space of time between the text as it was written and the text as it is being read; in the former case the spirit—being yet confined within the limits of the text—all of a sudden seems to defy that very text with the help of the reader by destroying that which shapes it: structures, norms, and techniques. In other words, either the reader is merely confronted with the rebellious spirit of the text or actively participates in its liberation. In both cases, however, this spirit of the text seems to be lurking in the prison house of language like a sleeping beauty, waiting to come to life from the kiss of the reader as each happens to come along. Even when Hartman later on defines the spirit of the text as a tension between wonder and enlightenment, his spirit still does not answer the question as to what actually causes that excitement: its discovery? its nature? the mere fact that it exists? The undefined character of this spirit also causes a lack of differentiation between various kinds of texts—although it may be exactly this lack that makes Hartman's definition enticing in the first place. But what the evocation of a reader-oriented spirit of the text fails to help us understand is why certain texts create a tension in the reader's soul and others do not; or why those texts create a tension for some readers and not for others. In other words, the fact that it remains unclear where exactly the spirit of the text has to be located and how it can be defined, undermines even Hartman's general argument.

The foregoing argument with Hartman's deconstructive reception theory does not imply a denial of the "existence" of a spirit of the text; I rather want to contend that what could be called the spirit of the text constitutes itself as the interplay between words and silences, texts and frames, that is, as the principle of textuality itself, which implies that each text is distinct yet inseparable from the "context" in which it is situated. The contention implicitly illustrated by *Facing Texts* is that the constitution of this context is not primarily dependent on the reader reception of any given text. Instead, it is established through a series of metaphorical leaps between texts and, by analogy, within a text. These leaps between words and across silences, texts and frames, are metaphorical, because they defy, on principle, the referential function of the language employed in each of the texts. Although *Facing Texts* is the result of a series of historically conditioned referential situations—historically conditioned because of the marketing and advertising procedures that had to be considered by the publisher; because of compromises between the initial theoretical concept and necessary practical decisions made by the editor; because of time limits on the authors' creativity; and because of the idiosyncratic literary inclinations of each critic—these presuppositions are no longer part of the anthology as it now stands. Instead, two different kinds of situations prevail in which texts relate to one another before they relate to any outer reality. First, the juxtaposition of each fictional text with a critical one; second, the grouping of lectures, stories, chapters from novels, which may develop common features derived from their correlation.

Metaphor, then, is understood here as a nonreferential device, since it totally depends on the imagination for its constitution. It is, moreover, understood as a combination of static and dynamic elements, and its concretization, the image in a text, as the epitome of that combination

—just as the flower, *ánthos,* is the epitome of the plant. This understanding of metaphor seems to me to relate back to James Joyce's concept of epiphany as it is implicitly found in *A Portrait of the Artist as a Young Man.* We remember that for Stephen Dedalus, in his interpretation of Aquinas's theory of the beautiful, the *quidditas* or "whatness" of a beautiful object can appear only after the two previous stages, *integritas* or "wholeness," and *consonantia* or "harmony," have been fully grasped and, more importantly, are kept constantly in mind by the beholder. The phases that precede the apprehension of beauty are not left behind in the act itself. For this reason Stephen says on the one hand that the beautiful is apprehended in an "instant" while on the other hand likening that instant, in which the mind has been "arrested by its [the image's] wholeness and fascinated by its harmony," to "the luminous silent *stasis* of esthetic pleasure" (my italics).[2] It follows that, for Joyce, the apprehension of the beautiful is an ultimate state within the mind depending on the individual's capacity for a suspension of time. The conditions for this suspension of time, however, are constituted by the image itself, which is apprehended in an instant, that is, in nontime, "that mysterious instant Shelley likened beautifully to a fading coal."[3] How Joyce's theory of the beautiful as a dynamic process culminating in stasis can inform the anthological principle shall be shown by comparing "Sunday Drive," an excerpt from Gass's novel-in-progress *The Tunnel,* and Tony Tanner's interpretation of it.

In "Sunday Drive" we find the sentence: "In this part of the country autumn is the only season one can celebrate." The four characters attempt to celebrate the season in traditional fashion: they go on a Sunday drive and have a picnic. Tony Tanner celebrates Gass's description of this celebration of autumn by evoking another dimension that has been added to the nature depicted: that of Gass's art. Thus, in Tanner's text, a tension is created between nature and culture that he relates to the picnic as metaphor, the appropriate climax of a Sunday drive as well as the artistic drive: "Labour and rest; contrivance and indolence; tending and neglect; conviviality and separation; harmony and discord; consummation and loss; permanence and transience; ripeness and rottenness; gratification and melancholy; sociability and loneliness; sexual abandon and decorous civility: in two words, nature and art—their mutual encroachments and exclusions, blendings and oppugnancies, consonances and dissonances." Using general instead of specific terms, Tanner first diminishes the tension between nature and art that he has discovered in Gass's text. Then, by organizing his own language rhythmically, as in a litany, he syntactically dissolves this tension altogether, letting his own text become a metaphorical mirror of that autumnal ripeness that Gass's narrator finds alone worth celebrating. In this part of the century, language's is the only autumn one *can* celebrate. Thus Tanner's essay represents the third step of stasis in the apprehension of the beautiful, the first two steps having been constituted by the dynamic sequence, in Gass's text, of nature and art.

Later in his essay Tanner substitutes the term *desire* for *nature,* thus moving another step in the direction of writing into his own text the tension between nature and art that he has observed in Gass. Desire can be defined as nature (that is, instinct or impulse) without a hold on the things of nature and is hence a proper quality of a text. However, a text inspired by desire to the point where the text's perpetual quality of lack constitutes its art will never be able to arouse in the reader that Joycean moment of silent stasis provoked by the wholeness and harmony of an image. Hence Tanner's concentration on the epiphany of the picnic, Gass's description of how his narrator's Sunday drive culminates in a central image: the vision of three unused barns in an abandoned barnyard. For, as the narrator observes, "these barns have been abandoned, but they have been abandoned to beauty. They are no longer barns. They are themselves." The abandonment of the barns means that they have been divested of their economic function; they no longer serve. Being no longer a shelter for anything else, they have been freed to become themselves. They are objects that could even defy the name *barn*. Their static self-sufficiency is beauty because their wholeness and harmony are no longer being questioned in the "name" of function.

Instead, they can become part of a literary tradition. In Herman Melville's story "The Piazza" the narrator formulates an idea of beauty that seems to connect with Joyce's and—via the image of an abandoned barn—with Gass's. Ruminating upon beauty, Melville's narrator comes to the conclusion that "beauty is like piety—you cannot run and read it; tranquillity and constancy, with, now-a-days, an easy chair, are needed."[4] From this easy chair he notices in the faraway distance something like a glen, or grotto, in the mountainside: "but a work-a-day neighbor said, no doubt it was but some old barn—an abandoned one, its broadside beaten in, the acclivity its background. But I, though I had never been there, I knew better."[5] Melville's Romantic narrator can still believe—although as it turns out, mistakenly—that what he seems to detect in the distance belongs to some kind of fairyland. He desires a fictional object. Desire for

Gass's narrator, however, is directed toward the real thing. It has no longer recourse to "speculation" (whose connotations in this case should be both *speculative* and *specular*) as a guarantee for "tranquillity and constancy," but is content with what can truly be seen. The apparent modesty, however, is deceptive, because for Gass, in contrast to Melville, reality needs to comply to an idea—not vice versa—if the beautiful is to be experienced. His is a Joycean secularization of Melville's concept of beauty in that it attempts to defeat, not to escape, a functionally distorted reality.

Literature as metaphor can liberate things from such distortion. And like things, language that is no longer employed primarily for information can become beautiful. The question of literary aesthetics is not whether a word in the text refers to an existing thing or not, whether an obvious relationship between signifier and signified is established or not, but whether words combine to produce the text as an image. Inducing this process—Joyce's first and second steps toward the epiphany of the beautiful—is as important as its result, but—as has been shown—the three steps cannot be taken separately, the first and second referring to writing, the last one to reading. Again, the image *in* the text, in order to become beautiful, first has to be separated from the context that defines its place in the narrative. In Gass's example the narrator comes upon the barns by surprise, after having crossed "an *artificial* rise" (my italics). The rise has been consciously created by the author in order to enable his narrator to separate the barns from a landscape dominated by the road that functions as a means of travel. The word *artificial* calls attention to this fact. Next, the image's inner harmony, that which makes it special, has to be recognized. The three barns are described as varying in size and design. Thus the observer is induced—again surprisingly—to relate them to one another; for he has already inadvertently separated them from the context and set them aside as being the same in kind—barns in the plural. Finally, when the image has become itself in the narrator's eye, beauty is achieved. This beauty presupposes the abandonment to the present, the timeless moment when the observer fully concentrates on the image, suspending any reflection upon the context that would force him to participate in the narrative flux, past or future words. Yet the image has arisen from just this narrative flux. "A calm elation has come over me," Gass's narrator says, "and the barns are the cause. I understand that much, although I am unable to explain why I am elated or why I am calm." This is Joyce's "luminous silent stasis of esthetic pleasure" that is identical with the experience of the spirit of the text. That is, the spirit of the text, though dependent on its context, becomes recognizable only when it is being separated from that context as an image of the whole text whose parts correspond and fall harmoniously into place. The definition of this process, however, can be performed only by the critic. Although the spirit of "Sunday Drive" exists in the text and can be intuited by the reader, it needs a critical reading like "On Reading 'Sunday Drive'" to make it known.

Just as the tradition of a well-known image may serve to separate its present version from its contemporary function by supplying a literary context instead, the literary text itself, which repeats the metaphorical process leading to the ultimate stasis of aesthetic pleasure on a larger scale, requires the separation from a referential context for the spirit of the text to appear. The interrelationship between fictional and critical pieces proves this point in the present anthology. Thus an anthology like *Facing Texts* may well be a metaphor for the state of writing. The image *in* the text becomes the image *of* the text. Even when it aspires to a metafictional status, that is, to the level of critical discourse, the fiction text can name but its own central image; it can never name the image it itself represents. In naming that image, the critic is framing the fiction text—like a picture. In this anthology fictional and critical texts face one another, but they also face the reader like a picture in a frame. Therefore, literary tradition not only serves as a treasure house of images to be remembered and reused, but, even more importantly, as it is kept alive by critical readers, this tradition can change an image into the image of a text by providing its contextual framework. Be it Donald Barthelme's basil or Robert Coover's Aesopian lion, Guy Davenport's steam balloon or John Hawkes's French equestrienne, in each case the central image created by the author's imagination constitutes the focus of the text itself; but, as the accompanying essays demonstrate, the impact of these images transcends the margins of that text; they are in need of further contextualization. Thus they instigate a further accretion of literary tradition that in turn imaginatively attempts to frame them, creating new images of the text.

Notes

1 Geoffrey H. Hartman, *The Fate of Reading and Other Essays* (Chicago and London: University of Chicago Press, 1975), p. 256.

2 James Joyce, *A Portrait of the Artist as a Young Man* (Harmondsworth: Penguin, 1960 [1916]), p. 213.

3 Ibid.

4 Herman Melville, *Selected Writings* (New York: Random House, 1952), p. 438.

5 Ibid., p. 442.

PRELECTURE

STANLEY ELKIN

......

The 1987 Elizabeth and Stewart Credence Memorial Lecture: What's in a Name?

Professor Adams, thank you for your kind introduction. You're very generous.

Chancellor Jones, Dean Smith, members of the faculty, students, ladies and gentlemen . . . .

As Professor Adams has already told you, my name is Stanley. Could you be mugged by a Stanley? Could a Stanley rape you? Tops, I might molest your kid, but *you'd* never know it, and neither would she. What, a little suntan lotion rubbed along the bottom of her swimsuit like a piping of frosting around a birthday cake? What, a spot of spilled tea on the sunsuit, my finger in the bespittled handkerchief moist from what it wouldn't even occur to you was drool before it was saliva, and vigorously brushing across what won't be breasts for another half dozen years yet, my grunt the two- or three-tone guttural hum of deflection, nervous and oddly dapper as the tugs, pats and twitches of a stand-up comic, distracting as the shot cuffs of magicians and cardsharps, all random melody's tangential rove? Because how could you ever even guess at my intentions and interiors, my inner landscapes and incisor lusts, the thickening at my throat like hidden shim, the ponderous stirrings of my ice-floe blood, deep as resource, buried as oil in my gnarled and knotty groin, my clotted sexual circuits? Could put it past you plenty, believe me, holding the kid's shoulder, the little girl's, for the leverage, drawing her within the fork of my white old thighs, a pervert like a master artisan, fixing her there like a piece of carpentry. Or violating her in absentia, my eyes on her kindergarten picture, my snoot in her laundry, in her eight-year-old grimes. All

According to the terms of their bequest, the Elizabeth and Stewart Credence Memorial Lecture is given in odd-numbered years of even-numbered decades of odd-numbered centuries. The 1987 lecture was delivered on March 24, 1987, at Case Western University.

contacts troubled, gone off, amok but deceptive, accidental, clever as a pickpocket's.

Protected by reputation, see, my triumph of the human-spirit spirit, that heart of gold which I don't possess but people attribute to me anyway, mistaking cholesterol for karats, hypertension for love, innocence by association, by stereotype, dismissing me finally, all the world waving me through Customs like that guy in the audience at the night club whose lap the chanteuse sits in, kissing his bald spot, pinching his cheek, and telling folks what a good sport he is, leading the applause.

Protected finally by all my grotesque cuddlies— the limp, the cane, my toothless, grampsy ways, my fatty's belly and threatless aura, my ducky's waddle and feeble's klutz, my *Stanleyness* on me like a wimp heraldrics. Hey, I'm kidding. Only offering credential here, only flashing badge, showing my hand, franked under the ultraviolet like a kid's at the dance.

Stanley is as Stanley does and you are what you're called.

Stanley is your brother-in-law, your CPA, your cousin in Drapes. He collects stamps, washes his car, belongs to Triple A, and keeps a weather eye on the gas mileage. He is, that is, as all of us are, the fiction of his sound, all his recombinant glottals, labials, fricatives and plosives. He's his flaps and trills. He's his spirants, I mean. He is, I mean, the vibrations of his name.

For great characters demand great names. (Of writers I admire, only Henry James—itself a fine name—lumbers his characters with bad ones. I'm thinking of Henrietta Stackpole, I'm thinking of Ralph Touchett, of Fleda Vetch and Milly Theale. I'm thinking of Madam Merle, of Casper Goodwood, Pansy Osmond, and Hyacinth Robinson. I'm thinking of Margaret Thatcher.) Here's a roll call for you. Beowulf and the Wife of Bath. King Lear but not Titus Andronicus. Hamlet but not Garp. Snow White, Pinocchio, and Mary Poppins but not Cinderella. Peter Pan but not Captain Hook. R2D2, Han Solo, C3PO, and Obi-wan (Ben) Kenobi but not Princess Leia. Leopold Bloom but not Stephen Dedalus. (Who can explain it, who can tell you why? Fools give you reasons, wise men never try. Rodgers and Hammerstein but not Weber and Rice.) Harry Morgan, Harry Bailey, Harry Angstrom, Harry Lime. J. R. Phil Esterhaus. Babbitt. Mr. Toots. John Jarndyce. Mr. Tulkinghorn. Flem Snopes. Will Varner. V. K. Ratliff. Dick Diver, Jay Gatsby. My Uncle Toby. Dorothea Brooke and Mr. Casaubon. Jiminy Cricket. Tom Jones, Humphrey Clinker. Hazel Motes. Becky Sharp. Captain Dobbin like a reliable horse. Emma Bovary, Emma Woodhouse, Julian Sorel. Swann and the Guermantes. Vautrin. Hans Castorp. Levin. Father Zossima. Bartleby. Hester Prynne and Arthur Dimmesdale. Angel Clare, Old Goriot, Elizabeth Bennett and her four sisters. All the not-to-be-pronounced names of God.

I want to speak to you this evening about Louis Paul Pelgas, the first Director of Admissions at any school in the Thirteen Colonies Conference, but before I begin it will be necessary to provide you with some sometimes dense, and often apparently trivial, historical background.

Clifton College is, as many of you may know, a small liberal arts college in what are, quite literally, the outer edges of Pennsylvania. It is out of the way even for Norbiton, Pennsylvania, even for Chapel County. Look at a map. Surrounded on two sides by West Virginia in the extreme southwestern corner of what—it's that close to the West Virginia line, that close to the Ohio one—is referred to by its inhabitants as the "state" rather than the "commonwealth" of Pennsylvania (possibly to lend a little aura of the average to what is uncompromisingly an atypical part of the nation), Norbiton, like a heel in an old shoe, exactly snugs the perfect right angle in the tight corner where its western and southern borders meet.

This tiny portion of Pennsylvania had been unofficially a "state" since ante-bellum days when, feeling itself both physically and spiritually closer to the gravitational pull—Chapel County was the only county in Pennsylvania where it was legal to keep slaves although, due to the impossibility of cultivating crops in its harshly alkaline soil, except for the handful of "house niggers," exchanged as a sort of gag gift between one local merchant and another, there was never any appreciable slave population there—of its Virginian and West Virginian anti-abolitionist neighbors than it was to Harrisburg, 357 miles distant, or Philadelphia 369 miles off, or even to Pittsburgh, which though less than 100 miles away was, for 80 of those 100, accessible only through what John James Audubon himself has described in his notes as "wilderness so cluttered and remote that its very sky is uninhabitable by the birds of the air, wilderness so cluttered and remote that that sky is itself wilderness." "A dry hole," he remarks in an 1847 journal entry,

> which for all its varied vegetation, succulent berries, meaty nuts and abundant fruit, is as zoologically lifeless as the moon. I cannot sketch there. My inks, oils and water colors go off like stale milk and lose their ability to congeal or adhere to paper. My pencil leads liquefy and my lines melt and run. There is a liquorish rifeness in the air so profound it lasts the autumn and can burn holes in the snow,

> or make—so viable is the halflife of the fermented spirits of all its fierce flora, its growth and undergrowth, its leaves and barks—an illusion of its "frozen" streams and lakes, of ice apparently 2 and even 3 inches thick which is not only impossible to stand upon but worth your hat to set down on its obdurate-seeming surface. It is a wilderness so impregnable that no jack rabbit, dog, possum, coon, turkey or even insect, let alone any animal as fragile and exotic as a bird, could possibly get close enough to it to thrive.

Nor is any of this typical John Audubon hyperbole. After a failed late-nineteenth-century attempt to survey the 1,000 or so square miles of this "queer, thick country"—Audubon's phrase—Phil and Pembler Roberts released foxes, dogs, and other small mammals at the margins of The Thicket. (Called "The Thicket" at the Chapel County end and "The Woody" at the Pittsburgh one, one recalls Pembler Roberts's famous comment: "Viewing the unspoiled, unnibbled trees, leaves and grasses in 'The Thicket' is as different from viewing them in 'ordinary' nature, a sylvan woodland or forest, say, as gazing at the defined, beautifully articulated stars in the country is from looking up at them in town.") Seeing them founder and return to their release points they seemed, in Phil Roberts's analogy, "like confused, guilty hunting dogs who have lost the scent." (The experiment has been successfully repeated for seventeen years in Professor Roger Barr's Psychology 101 classes. Julia Rayburton, while still a junior at Clifton College, devised a variant of the Pembler and Barr experiments. Wishing to test the very letter of Captain Audubon's 1847 journal entry, Ms. Rayburton stood at the edge of The Thicket—now, with the advent of bulldozers, trenchers, and the introduction of other heavy earth-moving equipment, reduced to a plot no larger than a decent-sized park in a medium-sized city—and scattered kernels of white corn, the favored food of all agrarian birds, into it in full view of three hungry bluejays who'd been kept in cages and deprived of food for more than eight hours. The jays who had carefully and even rather slavishly followed the short trajectory of the corn—Rayburton is lefthanded but tosses corn with her right hand—were unable to retrieve any of the kernels. They flew up and around but never entered the air space above "The Thicket," thus offering proof of Professor Barr's speculations regarding "Density theory," the psychological-cum-sociological postulate that "All bodies repudiate areas smaller than the space required to provide their egress!" The implications this has for America's crowded prison system are, of course, immense. Professor Barr's and Julia Rayburton's findings have already been cited in four court rulings and must be *sub judice* in who knows how many more.)

If this isolated and somewhat remarkable edge of the commonwealth had unofficially chosen to think of itself as a state since, you'll recall, the mid-nineteenth century, it ought to be said that no one really knows why the citizens of Chapel County preferred one designation over another. (What's in a name, eh?) Even as late as 1837, when Chapel and Green counties split off from each other (for reasons, incidentally, which had more to do with the close identification of The Thicket with the town of Norbiton than they did with slaver or anti-slaver sentiments), the term *commonwealth*, not *state*, was the legal nomenclature in each of the seventeen articles of incorporation. In fact, Chapel County has only *officially* been designated part of the "state of Pennsylvania" since Maurdon Legurney, both Mayor of Norbiton and County Supervisor, was chosen to represent Chapel County at the Pennsylvania Constitutional Convention of 1878, about a year after the Congress of the recently reunited states of America had put an end to the period of reconstruction. The Convention, referred to in the newspapers of the day—even Horace Greeley sent a correspondent to cover it for the old *New York World-Examiner*—as "The New Reconstruction," was convened at the instigation of the people of Chapel County but was equally the brainchild of Legurney's political protégé, Governor Lamar White, a native of Norbiton who, when Legurney put his name into nomination at the Democratic Convention in St. Louis in 1880, was the first politician ever referred to as a "favorite son," though his family had removed from Norbiton when White was only two years old.

Reconstruction had been, of course, a time of *ad hoc* law, a period of makeshift legislation when some of the most bizarre laws in the history of this or any other nation were passed, almost, it seemed, as a kind of willed whim. It's largely forgotten now, but from 1865 to 1877 when this odd chapter in our history closed, Congress forbade the raising of orchids and carnations. It prohibited the sale of calves' liver in quantities under three pounds and made it a Federal offense, punishable by a mandatory seven years in prison, for women to fish from a pier. The statute was vaguely worded, perhaps deliberately, and in the five years it was on the books, no one was actually sent to prison. Ironically, it was the vagueness and unenforceability of the law which gave rise, during the period, to its public flouting and introduced the term *fishwife* into the American vocabulary. (Less whimsical, but far more dangerous, was a peculiar law of evidence introduced just after the Civil War. This, of course, was the infamous "Mixed Race Witness Rule," which, when crimes were alleged against persons of one race by persons of another, made it obligatory for prosecutor and defense alike to produce witnesses of *both races* to the crime. The rule was obviously directed against the defeated South—it did not apply in non-slave states on the dubious grounds that Negroes were less populous in the North—by a piqued, if victorious, Union. What is perhaps more astonishing than the rule itself is the fact that during the dozen years before its repeal it was five times sent up to the Supreme Court for "challenging," and five times adjudged constitutional!)

As indicated earlier, the Pennsylvania Constitutional Convention was convened in 1878 by a governor who, though he'd been a mere toddler when he left and had never been back, was born in Norbiton. As was also indicated, this was barely a year after the nation had junked the notion of Reconstruction, that queer period of back-scratch law when all that was necessary to get a law passed was a quorum of cronies who would do unto each other what they would have each other do unto them. As in all periods to which there is an inevitable reaction, that reaction, when it finally came, was a lulu. What were demanded now were unarbitrary and entirely righteous rules of order, logic and sequentiality— a return, if you will, to 1837, when Chapel County quietly signed seventeen articles of incorporation, each of which designated the new county as continuing to belong to the "Commonwealth" rather than to the "*State* of Pennsylvania." (That people in Chapel County held slaves was merely a fact of home rule, of little more significance at the time, really, than the local option that governs the sale of alcohol or is responsible for the blue laws.)

Now, however, there was, at least on the parts of the people of Chapel County, Governor White, and Maurdon Legurney, White's political guru and hand-picked emissary from Chapel County to the Pennsylvania Constitutional Convention, a reaction to the reaction to the reaction. If America wanted sequentiality again, some apostolic succession of convention and right reason, Chapel County, on the very verge of The Thicket, that then still 1,000 square miles of all waivered, rebuffed, exempt and repudiate Nature's lush and pointless, extended bramble, wanted, yearned for, and actually *demanded* the return of the random, even if they had to invent a legitimate, legal, due-processed pandect of *de jure* and prescribed code under the fiction of a rigged Constitutional Convention.

Here's what happened:

The people of Chapel County got to Maurdon Legurney, Maurdon Legurney got to Lamar White, and Governor White got a Constitutional Convention for his commonwealth that was in all respects (save for that first cause like a wicked itch that convened it in the first place) splendid, making Pennsylvania a paradigm of justice and good sense that became a model of high democracy. With this exception—the little legalistic eye-teaser buried in the middle of chapter VII, article 42, section 12, subsection 9, paragraph 19, line 5: "All territory south of 79°, 30′ longitude, 39°, 45′ latitude, and north of 80°, 30′ longitude, 40°, 45′ latitude, and all peoples residing within said territory, shall henceforth, to the contrary notwithstanding, upon receipt of a vote of the majority in any constitutionally convened poll or public plebiscite as defined in chapter III, article 18, section 34, paragraph 1, line 1, not to be interpreted as incorporating the provisions of chapter IV, article 9, paragraph 1, line 16, in accordance with the doctrine '*inclusio unius est exclusio alterius*,' have the right to designate itself, and themselves citizens *of*, in perpetuity, subject to no contingent remainders or to conditional limitations or any other encumbrances, the State of Pennsylvania."

What, quite simply, this did was permit Norbiton, Pennsylvania, and all of Chapel County, and *only* Norbiton and *only* Chapel County, since only Norbiton and Chapel County were to the south and north of all those degrees like a temperate zone, and all those minutes like so many conveniently bunched quarters of an hour, all that mathematical, seaborne geography of that inland commonwealth, to (once the plebiscite passed) unsubjugate itself to all the laws then on the books, and all the laws that might henceforth be written to join them, of that only *Commonwealth* of Pennsylvania!

I've already told you. The soil was alkaline. They were only local merchants, only small businessmen. But what Maurdon Legurney, Governor White, and the people of Chapel County had given themselves up to was the return of the random, permission to wallow in muddle and romp in their carefully legislated labyrinthine, skimble-skamble, higgledy-piggledy, helter-skelter, harum-scarum anarchy.

They opened whore houses, and nobody came.

They beat their horse stables into gaming casinos and their horses stood in the rain while the local merchants stood high and dry inside, forlorn at the craps tables, which, despite all the spit, polish, elbow grease and good honest effort that the remaining house niggers now emancipate-proclamated into ordinary domestics at the stroke of the presidential pen could put into them, still smelled faintly of crap. And nobody came.

"I tell you, boys," Legurney, back from all he'd accomplished for them at the Constitutional Convention at the capitol in Harrisburg, told them, "the world's our oyster. Norbiton, Pennsylvania, could be a regular Sin City, U.S.A. It's just too bad we're so far off the beaten track."

"Think of it, boys," said Oldham Broom, a pretty fair country tailor in his time, but now the kingpin numbers runner for all Chapel County, or, more precisely, numbers walker, or, yet more precisely still, not numbers runner, or walker, or any kind of numbers mover at all, or even just any common, ordinary, garden-variety arithmetician, but full-fledged Theoretical Mathematician, each day drawing the lottery and picking what would have been the winning combinations if only somebody had put down the two, four, six bits or buck other side of the ante, and solemnly contemplating the mysterious and elegant laws of chance, "double sixes three days running. What do you suppose the odds against something like *that* are?"

"It's just too bad we're so far off the beaten track," Maurdon Legurney said.

And at first moved their stills out from their old hole-and-corner hiding places into direct sunlight, and then—advertising was coming into its own about then—out onto the public sidewalks, and then, if they were tipsy enough from sampling their own brew, or maybe even just still sober enough to manage it, might carry a few bottles over to the empty Norbiton jail and offer to put them up against the sheriff's own, going from tipsy to cockeyed, cockeyed to maudlin, and maudlin to philosophical over the course of another slow, businessless, lazy afternoon.

"Folks in this part of the state couldn't get themselves arrested if they tried," Ed Flail, former operator of Norbiton's leading drygoods store and now one of the town's most prominent dealers in stolen goods, remarked to Sheriff Leon Edgers.

"That's a fact," agreed Billy Slipper, poacher, sports fisherman, and hunter out-of-season of other people's trout and game.

And got an Amen from the county's rustlers, pimps, pickpockets, and other scoundrels.

Because it was true. Crime *didn't* pay. Not in Norbiton, not in Chapel County.

They were sitting on the porch of the Norbiton Inn. Maurdon Legurney, now a broken and melancholy man, nominal lame duck Mayor and County Supervisor with just a scant five-and-a-half years left to run on one or the other of his overlapping terms, started to say "I tell you, boys, it's just too bad we're so . . ."

"Again with the beaten track," Ed Flail said.

"Yeah, shut up about that damn beaten track already," Sheriff Edgers told His Honor.

But it was true. They were. And who knew this better than Legurney himself, who had not only been to the capitol in Harrisburg within the year but had come back from it as well, making not the giant but expeditious swing from Norbiton at the bottom, western limits of Pennsylvania the 100 miles up to Pittsburgh and then, by rail, from Pittsburgh on a more or less straight easternly shot to Harrisburg two-thirds across the commonwealth, but the long, piecemeal, switchbacked, drawn-out, up-hill-and-down-dale, down-hill-and-up-dale, zig-zag journey through woodland and across farms where there were no roads, an honest-to-God, on-foot trespasser slash poacher far from the beaten and unbeaten track either when he wasn't an out-and-out, horsebackride hitchhiking beggar? Practically slaloming himself the length and breadth of the all-but-Commonwealth-of-Pennsylvania. A Pennsylvania which near where he was was still only this fits-and-starts civilization, borrowing even its placenames from all the tamed cities and myths of place, towns, and villages tinier than towns, tinier than villages, calling themselves Paris, Rome, London, Vienna, calling themselves Athens, Cairo, Istanbul, even Chicago. The better part of two entire weeks until he even got to the part where the spur started where you waited for the freight train that brought you to the whistle stop that took you to the place where if you managed to get there by a Tuesday you had only to wait till Thursday or Friday till you could catch the train to Harrisburg.

So it was true. Off the beaten track. Off the beaten path. Off, for all practical purposes, the very goddamn compass itself. So they knew that, who were only these local merchants and small businessmen and gentlemen alkaline farmers. Whose feathered, attenuate world had been shaped, though they'd forgotten this, were too close to it, who couldn't see the forest for the trees or any of those 1,000 or so thorny square miles of difficult bramble that somebody on the Norbiton side had once thought to call The Thicket. (Which hadn't been surveyed, hadn't been mapped, and which, for all any of them knew, might contain somewhere within its tough terrains lost, fabled cities of the Indians, tall mountains, vast deserts, gritty sand dunes, deep inland seas.) Suddenly reminded only then, by Legurney's lugubrious account of his long and epic but boring odyssey, despondent, failed and failing criminals manqué on the porch of the Norbiton Inn. And who (the fellow who suddenly reminded them lost too) mentioned that he'd heard tell that, speaking of Pittsburgh, it was an oddity of geographical history that though they was off the beaten track now, in the old days a right smart of folks had come down all the way from Philadelphia and Harrisburg and the Poconos and just all over, even from out of state, to see it.

"Speaking of Pittsburgh?"

"Well from all over except Pittsburgh."

"Ex*cept* Pittsburgh."

"Well they had their *own* half. Where'd they get any call to go traipsing all over hell and gone if all they wanted to look at The Woody was to—"

"The Woody?"

"Well ain't that what they call it up there? I thought they called it by a different name. I thought they called it The Woody."

"Yeah? Well?"

"Well, all I was going to say was that if they wanted to see it all they ever had to do was just turn their heads back over their shoulders and there she'd be."

And someone else remembered that Norbiton had been practically a boom town in those days, and that wasn't it funny the way things changed, that why even this porch we're standing on wasn't always the porch of just any old country inn but was once part of a regular hotel.

"The Hotel Norbiton?"

"Thicket House," said Oldham Broom, who till now hadn't opened his mouth.

"Oh yeah, Thicket House. I recollect hearing talk of that now."

And then all of them began to pitch in with their memories. And collectively remembered that The Thicket had been a sight, even a tourist attraction, years before there was a railroad in Pennsylvania, let alone national or state parks.

"Commonwealth parks," Billy Slipper said.

"Yeah," said Ed Flail, "commonwealth parks."

Somebody remembered reading somewhere that the first picture postcard was of The Thicket, and someone else that the first hotel in America named for its view, or proximity to a point-of-interest, was in 1792 when Thicket House was built. They recalled all manner of things.

It was Maurdon Legurney himself who recalled all the old talk about slaves in The Thicket.

"Maurdon!" Sheriff Edgers said.

"Gettysburg's only the largest and most famous of Pennsylvania's battlefields," Legurney said.

"Maurdon!" the sheriff said.

"Shit," Legurney said, "if the citizens of a community ain't entitled to the use of their own legatee'd and birthrighted natural resources, I'd like to know who is then?"

"Maurdon, damn it to hell, shut up."

"Well who? Who is?"

"I'm warning you, Maurdon," the sheriff told his mayor. "Maurdon, I'm warning you."

"Why'd God put it here then? Can somebody tell me that? Why'd the good Lord give us a sense of humor to appreciate it in the first place? Why'd—"

"Maurdon, I'm not telling you again!"

"—He teach folks to plant and farm or dig up all the precious metals deep down in the mines? Why'd He stock the rivers and seas with fish and give us our rifles and our shells and our abiding, manly instinct to hunt?"

"Maurdon—"

"He makes some good points there, Leon," Ed Flail said.

"It's briars, god damn it!" Legurney went on. "It's all pins-and-needled, barbed-wired, saw-toothed, razor's edgery. It's all spiked, prickly and pointy, stinging bristliosity. And what don't bite, nail, and sharp you to death would rash your skin clear off your bones. Because what ain't briars is all itchweed, poison oak and poison ivy, poison sumac allergens!

"*Why'd He inspire us to come up with chapter VII, article 42, section 12, sub-section 9, paragraph 19, line 5, and all the godgiven, goddamn, chickenshit, loophole rest of it?*"

"What?" the sheriff asked. "What's that?"

"What if it *is* tacky? What if it *is*? Because if we ain't subject to the strict letters of the laws of the Commonwealth, we ain't liable to being sued neither, Leon."

"Aw, Maurdon," the sheriff said. "Maurdon, aww."

So the whore houses came down, and the stills were silenced, and all the energies of the people of Chapel County were redirected into beating the old Norbiton Inn back into its original avatar. It became Thicket House again.

The Thicket opened for business in the Spring of 1881. It had taken two-and-a-half years to build the thirty-seven miles of great wooden wall, the wide, tall planked platform, accessible by ladder, that rose around the perimeter of The Thicket and sent off cantilevered shoots deep into that queer and lifeless jungle.

They came from all over the Commonwealth, from Ohio and West Virginia and Maryland and up and down the entire eastern seaboard, from Kentucky and the border states and the states of the Confederacy that was, and from the west and even from foreign lands and it became, you might say, America's first theme park.

The people of Chapel County were famous for their sense of humor, those gag-gift slaves they had once exchanged with each other, the "house niggers" whose trust they'd patiently cultivated in the years immediately preceding the Civil War, the abolitionist sympathies they faked, the underground railroad mythology they perpetuated.

"Follow," they'd said, drawing a slave aside and whispering to him, pointing to The Thicket and seducing him with the dream of freedom, "the drinking gourd!" And steer or lead him in the direction of the infrequent, illusory clearing or occasional false trail.

Or *I* say they said. As I've attributed to Legurney and Slipper and Oldham Broom and Sheriff Leon Edgers and the others *most* of the dialogue I've put down here. Because, except for Audubon's journal entries and Phil and Pembler Roberts's remarks, which are documented, we'll never really know who actually said what. The beginnings of a conspiracy are often smoky and seldom known, and all this was over one hundred years ago. But we know who was there and, because of the attendant publicity, have a pretty good idea of their personalities. The New York, Wheeling, Philadelphia, Harrisburg, and even Pittsburgh papers tell us what happened. So it had to be *something* like the way I've put it down. It *had* to be.

The rest is quickly told.

After the sawmill went up and the logging teams arrived, after the estimated million trees had been cut down, and the two-and-a-half years of construction was completed, and The Thicket officially opened, and the public came to climb the ladders that led to the exalted overview atop the high planks set on a wooden scaffolding like the jerrybuilt crisscrosses of condemnation, the thirty-seven miles of braided grid like a rough cat's cradle of loosely crocheted timber, after the first tentative, trepidatious, dread weight they put on the reinforced railing, after their first rubberneck gawk, *after the first remains of the runaways had been spotted*—remember: there were no signposts to lead them to them, no plaques; the carpenters who were the first to walk these planks, or get any sort of view at all from them, never told what they'd seen, and anyway it was advertised in the newspapers as a sort of "treasure hunt" even though there was no treasure, no prize, and all it ever really was was only this crazy sort of bird watching—not clumps of the skeletal dead—or at least not ordinarily—although there is the odd photograph of dead slaves huddled together for warmth or comfort or solace, embracing each other in loving, awful, open death, their twining elbows and ulnas, their back bones and collar bones, their flanges and humeruses, their scapulas, their sternums, their rib cages, their carpals and frontals, their cheek bones just touching—home at last the house niggers— *after* all this, they waited for more than two years—this would have been the summer of 1883—letting word of mouth do its job, the reports in the press, suckering them in, building the tip, specific about the summer—timing was everything—because they had to choose a season not just when the park was sure to be crowded—the idea of the two-week paid vacation had begun to catch on at about the same time that work was begun on the great wooden wall—but a time when the weather was dependable, when they could rely upon the long spells of hot, dry weather, when the rain, if it came, was likely to be the sort of fierce, brief deluge of which all traces are gone one or two hours after it has ceased.

They kept their counsel and agreed on July 18, 1883, which fell on a Saturday that year, not just a time when a lot of folks—there was a railroad in Norbiton now—would be enjoying their summer vacations but was part of a weekend, too—timing was *every*thing—so that even those folks *not* on vacation would be in town to take advantage of the generous weekend discounts offered by Thicket House. They were quite lucky. The weather had been splendid for upwards of three weeks, no rain—they weren't farmers in Chapel County; the soil was too alkaline; no corn was ruined, no soybeans or tomatoes or greens—the temperatures hot but bearable, and the wall filled with holiday makers all along its great, winding wooden length. Pelgas and the others were ready. The wall was a tinder box. When Louis Paul and the other domestics, after first preparing the most strategic struts, pilings, and braces with oil, finally ignited it, it went off like a firework. Two hundred and fourteen tourists and holiday makers either burned or fell to their deaths on the thorns and briars, the burning brambles and bushes, incinerated and drowned in the lake of blazing liquors of the primed, fermenting fruits forty feet below them.

By law, there were no laws in this corner of the state. There was no conspiracy. There was no arson. There was no murder. There were not even any courts, and the jail, unused for years, was only another curiosity on the tour. As honorary as Maurdon Legurney's titles, as emptily symbolic as the badge the sheriff still wore. So they *had* to lynch them.

Who knew if, in defense of what they'd done—the domestics were all dead; they had no defense—the claim of the citizens of Norbiton and Chapel County, that The Thicket had merely been "salted," was true? That they'd dug up the graves of white men and Negroes already legitimately dead and slowly, careful as puppeteers, lowered their bones into The Thicket? There could be no lawsuits so nothing was ever proven. And, at the time, the records were simply unavailable to the hordes of yellow journalists who descended on Norbiton to investigate what had happened. Indeed, they didn't even know if there *were* records.

For the record, there were records.

Here is a partial list of slaves encouraged to believe they could escape into The Thicket:

The Emmas Woodhouse and Bovary. The Harrys Morgan, Bailey, Angstrom, and Lime. Tom Jones. John Jarndyce. Phil Esterhaus. Dick Diver. V. K. Ratliff. Dorothea Brooke. Flem Snopes. Becky Sharp. A Titus and a Hamlet. A Cricket and a White. C3PO. A Dobbin. Someone else, whether male or female has never been ascertained, known as J. R. A Tulkinghorn. A person named Gatsby, initial J. Henrietta Stackpole. Elizabeth Bennett, Hester Prynne, Arthur Dimmesdale. A Babbitt, a Toots, a slave girl named Leia. A group of blacks probably from the Caribbean: Julian Sorel. Swann, Cassaubon, Vautrin, an old man known only as Goriot, and all the members of the Guermantes family. Hazel Motes, Angel Clare, Hyacinth Robinson. Uncle Toby.

I've not told you yet about that Director of Admissions named Louis Paul Pelgas and my hour is just about up. You will be thinking, of course, that he is descended from the Louis Paul Pelgas who led his fellow domestics to torch the wall. And probably have surmised that because he studied American History at the University of Minnesota and did his doctoral dissertation on the terrible incidents of the commonwealth turned state, that he accepted the Directorship of Admissions in order to exclude whites and turn Clifton College into what, under his tenure, would probably have become an all-black school. But you would be wrong. This particular Louis Paul Pelgas is white and no relation. Coincidence. Nothing but coincidence. Because of his name and the associations it has for the people of Norbiton, you might suppose he takes a lot of ribbing. He doesn't. The fact of the matter is, he's not all that interested in administration. He's looking for another post, has sent out several dozen letters, half a hundred *curricula vitae*. No takers so far, though he's promised his wife he'll keep trying. Well it's the job market. The job market stinks. It's a lousy time for historians. And he hasn't published.

Gee, I haven't told you that much about names at all, have I? Unless detail functions, as perhaps it does, as a kind of noun, and a menu of proper names as a sort of register of fact. What I suppose I've been talking about is connection. Connection, invention, and all the enumerate links, synapses, and lovely nexuses of fiction.

Oom boom!

Esmiss Esmoor!

Only connect!

Thank you, drive carefully, and goodnight.

PATRICK O'DONNELL

......

The Thicket of Writing: On Stanley Elkin's Fiction

Stanley Elkin is a celebrant of the particular, a writer of many parts. Whatever can be named, listed, or anatomized is of interest to him, and the more heterogeneous the assortment to be included in a given metaphorical category (i.e., "the body," "clothing," "systems of communication," "interior space") the better.[1] Here, for example, is a list of particulars from *A Bad Man*:

> He pushed the revolving doors, feeling, as he always did, heavier, and waiting, as he shoved slowly on the door's metal rungs to feel himself thicken with opulence, to become wider, gravid. The door spun him out onto the main floor, and he smelled at once the perfumes and face powders, the mascaras and polishes bright as sodas. By the high glass cases he knew himself some glamour mogul; by the lipstick cartridges like golden bullets a grand armorer, love's field marshall among those shiny warheads. Art, art, thought Feldman, impresario of deep disks of red rouge, pastel as flesh, of fine-grained dusting powders like soft, fantastic sand, of big plush puffs and cunning brushes. He stood by the lotions in bottles, by cylinders of deodorant in a female climate of balmy aromatics, in a scent of white gardens, thinking of dreamy debauches in palatial bathrooms, of comic blows, cutie-pie spankings with big fluffy puffs. Here, where other men might have felt intimidated, Persian Feldman lingered, feeling the very *texture* of his wealth, his soft, sissy riches, the unctuous, creamy, dreamy dollars.
>
> I am master of all I purvey.[2]

Several of Elkin's concerns are revealed in a passage such as this one describing the cosmetic department in Leo Feldman's store. There are forced comparisons ("mascaras and polishes bright as sodas"), circular in form, which shed no light on the nature of the paralleled elements (is there anything added to our knowledge of nail polishes or sodas by the insertion of "bright as"?) but which enlarge the associative qualities of phenomena from two dissociated realms of being. The description of sodas as "bright" confers upon confection an added range of reference beyond that of color and flavor—an *intensity* of light that lends gravity to the passage. There is, by extension, the "thickness" of the description, a linguistic layering and richness that matches the opulence Feldman senses as he opens the door to "feel himself thicken," becoming "wider, gravid." Rather trite abstractions (the parallels between love and war) are grounded in assonance ("glamour mogul" / "grand armorer" / "love's field marshall") so that the age-old cliché connecting "amor" with "armor" is renewed through the sonorities of language where, by implication, the connection originated in the first place. The text becomes a "texture"; the sinuosities of the passage promote an "erotics of reading" that coincides with the intention of the encompassing referent of the description ("cosmetics") used for purposes of seduction and concealment. The passage, in essence, is at once come-on and commodity, a purveyance of language and a poetic enhancement of consumerism, sound teased out for those resonances which, made grammatical, become meaning, metaphor.

Such passages are typical of Elkin's fiction only in the sense provided by their reduction to the form of "catalogue," yet it is their typicality that, for the moment, I will dwell upon. For, to use the imagery provided by "What's in a Name?" these long, layered, sonorous descriptions might be viewed as linguistic "thickets" that the reader feels compelled to encompass or to penetrate in search of the "deep meanings" and coherencies contained within. Reading Elkin's fiction, one is seduced into the view that to make sense of the world is to make a world of sense—a seduction that Elkin vends and unmasks at every opportunity. The urge to quote is irresistible:

> Where has he seen these men? Their sport coats are the nubby textures and patterns of upholstery from credit furniture supplements in Sunday newspapers. They are crosshatched, double knits, drapery, checks like optical illusions, designs like aerial photographs of Kansas wheat fields, Pennsylvania pastureland, or the russets of erosion in western national parks. The pockets of their blazers are slashed, angled as bannister. Change would fall out of them, he thinks. The

> flaps are mock, shaped like the lower halves of badges. Their notched, pointed collars ride their shoulders like the conferral of wide, mysterious honors, the mantles of secret orders—and Flesh supposes they belong to these. He has never seen such shoes. Many are glossy white loafers, the color and sheen of wet teeth in ads. Gratuitous, useless buckles vault the white piping that rises from their shoes like welts. The jewelry and fixtures in the center of their false straps could be I.D. tags, or metal tablets, or slender sunken scutcheons. He sees no belts in the tight cuneiform-print trousers, in the plaids like colored grids, like cage, windowpanes, that climb their legs like ladders. The pants hold themselves up, self-supportive, a flap of fabric buttoned to a rim of itself like flesh sealed to flesh in operations. He marvels at their bump-toe shoes, their thick fillets of composition heels like shiny mignon or rosy cross sections of pressed geology. At their shirts like Christmas ties.[3]

Ben Flesh, the entrepreneurial protagonist of *The Franchiser*, answers a question that connects place, memory, and perception ("Where has he seen these men?") with a list of particulars wherein "the human" is broken down into its sartorial components. The illusion rendered by the passage—the impresario's trick—is that the secret of being may be known by the signs of these habiliments. Flesh is attending a convention when he witnesses this covey of businessmen walking through a hotel lobby; thus, the passage linguistically "conventionalizes" what occurs spatially at an event where individuals are homogenized by common interests and desires. This evocation of sameness is underscored by the assimilative imagery of the passage: the collars of the men's shirts "ride their shoulders like the conferral of wide, mysterious honors, the mantles of secret orders"; the flaps of their jackets are "shaped like the lower halves of badges"; their shoe buckles appear as "I.D. tags" or "scutcheons." To what masonic secret order or mercantile knighthood do these men belong? Everything in the passage suggests that there is a hidden design underlying these particularities that confers upon each "individual"—each manifestation of The Same—history, class, identity. The implication extends beyond the men to the descriptive language that names and identifies them by noting, in a contagion of resemblance, that they are not only identical to themselves, but to other, larger, more archaic orders of being—those of geography and agriculture. It is not even necessary (and this is part of the illusion) for Elkin to designate the order or pattern that the passage refers to; it is enough that the presence of such orders is implied by the activity of the language itself, which, again, appears to resonate with the similarities of scattered particulars and, seemingly, disparate points of reference. How does the heel of a shoe resemble the marblings of a steak ("shiny mignon") or a cross-section of the earth ("pressed geology")? All are "patterned," all signify a design in process or a series of evolving connections which it is the work of these signs to identify. The seduction of the passage resides in its centripetal energy where, potentially, ever-expanding referential categories are sucked into the assimilatory vortex of language.

To franchise "reality" in this manner is certainly one of the linguistic tasks of Elkin's fiction, yet one matched by its antiseductive impulses, its evocation of difference and the random. Elkin wishes, by turns, both to bring forth and deface these signs that point toward an interpretable pattern that lies behind, or is the assimilatory medium for the scattered particularities of existence. At once, the language of his fiction is hermeneutic, as it alludes to the interpretability of its patterns, and "genealogical," in Foucault's sense of genealogy as a form of historical knowledge which reveals that "there is 'something altogether different' behind things: not a timeless and essential secret, but the secret that they have no essence or that their essence was fabricated in a piecemeal fashion from alien forms."[4] For Foucault, genealogy, which "must record the singularity of events outside of any monotonous finality," unmasks the quest for the secret of truth "behind things" as a quest for identity and origins. Oppositely, "where the soul pretends unification or the self fabricates a coherent identity, the genealogist sets out to study the beginning—numberless beginnings whose faint traces and hints of color are readily seen by an historical eye."[5] Ultimately, the genealogical vision recognizes "the events of history, its jolts, its surprises, its unsteady victories and unpalatable defeats—the basis of all beginnings, atavisms, and heredities."[6] In *The Franchiser*, only a dozen pages after Flesh's list of clothing conventions, we encounter a description of the Finsberg family, eighteen in all, four sets of triplets and three sets of twins, each suffering from the effects of a unique, exotic disease: all

> were freaks, and carried in their bloodstreams and pee, in their saliva and fundament and the tracings of their flesh, all the freak's ruined genetics, his terrible telegony and dark diathetics. It was Julius, set in his ways, throwing himself like an ocean into Estelle's coves and kyles, till all that was left of his genes and chromosomes was the

> sheath, the thread of self like disappearing chesire garments resolved at last to their stitching. Obsessive, worn-out, he had made hemophiliacs of the self-contained and self-centered. Julius's progeny—that queer wall of solidarity and appearance, that franchise of flesh—were husks, the chalices in which poisoners chucked their drops and powders.[7]

Such are the offspring of a betraying, obsessive seduction; such is Elkin's genealogy, the heritage of the self "resolved at last to its stitching." The threads of the businessmen which, apparently, conceal selves united in the mysterious order of common desire and purpose are unraveled here as the "chesire garments" that clothe an identity whose beginnings in gene and chromosome are already frayed, multiple. *This* language, the language delineating Julius Finsberg's "self" and its reproductions, is entropic and centrifugal though, of course, he would have it be just the opposite: it is the other of that seductive, centered discourse of the convention and the cosmetic counter; it is blemished, unnatural, freakish; it proceeds from the language of origins, which attempts to cover up and contain all difference within its "self-centered," assimilatory movements. Yet the language of genealogy and difference will out. Elkin's fiction, which often takes as its subject the body and its history of illness, insists that the story of identity is a travesty, revealing as history "the systematic dissociation of identity. This is necessary because this rather weak identity, which we attempt to support and to unify under a mask, is in itself only a parody; it is plural; countless spirits dispute its possession; numerous systems intersect and compete."[8] To revert, once again, to the analogy provided by the work at hand, if Elkin's writing is a "thicket," it is also that which denatures the thicket by attacking its boundaries and revealing the artificiality of those conventions whereby its "naturalness" would be viewed as coterminous with the beginnings of things.

I have been discussing in detail a few passages from Elkin's fiction as allegories of language and authorship; it is in this light that I wish to assess the curious essay/story we have before us, "What's in a Name?" As its interrogative title suggests, there is an immediate question regarding what kind of writing this is. This example of Elkin's fiction (since, heuristically, it must bear some generic label) is deprived of a name by the very title that queries the contents of nomination; it also seems to lack clear generic cues that would allow us to place it as an essay, autobiography, or short story. While "What's in a Name?" begins as a fugue on the hidden scandal of the author's first name, it soon purports to be a story about another name, Paul Louis Pelgas, though not, indeed, about him either, in what turns out to be a dark historical fiction about "America's first theme park." Elkin refuses to make any transitions between the nominal beginnings and the "real story" behind "What's in a Name?" And even here, in the realm of what is obviously a red herring, things are not so clear. Elkin wishes to convert the "wimp heraldrics" of an apparently harmless "Stanley" into a more powerful name, one that would scandalize the reader, as would be the case if his name was Charles Manson or Sirhan Sirhan instead of Stanley Elkin. So, Elkin reveals "the intentions and interiors" of the man behind the Stanley, the "clotted sexual circuits" of the pervert as he declares himself to be a secretive child molester, "undercover." Are we supposed to be shocked? Is this a confession by "the inner man" regarding the hidden motives and desires concealed by the public name of the writer?

Here is the beginning of another fiction, published almost thirty years before "What's in a Name?" was originally read at the 1984 Bread Loaf Writers' Conference: "Lolita, light of my life, fire of my loins. My sin, my soul. Lo-lee-ta: the tip of the tongue taking a trip of three steps down the palate to tap, at three, on the teeth. Lo. Lee. Ta."[9] Like Elkin's fiction, Nabokov's novel begins with a reflection on a name, though in the case of the latter we have the scandalous confessor vocalizing the name of his beloved instead of probing the perversities that lie behind his own ugly, doubled name—Humbert Humbert. Elkin's opening is an example of intertextual humbuggery as he transforms himself into a parodic reflection of a famous fictional character whose name may well be a cover for one possible author-behind-the-author, the shadowy John Ray, Jr. ("genre" junior). While Elkin's Stanley may appear a monstrous double of Nabokov's Humbert ("What, a spot of spilled tea on the sunsuit, my finger in the bespittled handkerchief moist from what it wouldn't occur to you was drool before it was saliva and vigorously brushing across what won't be breasts for another half dozen years yet . . . ?"), he is really a junior version, "just kidding": "Only offering credential here, only flashing badge, showing my hand, franked under the ultraviolet like a kid's at the dance." This Stanley is a counterfeit, a rescinded version of the original whose ordinary name must be set aside so that the "character" it identifies can be revealed by—can gain identity through—its reference to the more infamous "author" of the confession entitled *Lolita*. Here, it appears that there is nothing in a name except hot air: "He [Stanley] is, that is, as all of us are, the fiction of his sound, all his recombinant glottals, labials, fricatives and plosives. He's his flaps and trills. He's his spirants, I mean. He is, I mean, the vibrations of his name." So why dwell upon the uninspiring "Stanley," and not the more majestic "Elkin," with its animalistic associations to a regal beast and its reference to "god-kin"? For Elkin, the name is arbitrary, yet when it is encountered in a fiction, it, by chance or design, gains a significant quality generated by its own sound: it *becomes* character, identity. In this opening Elkin transforms himself, without changing his name, into a literary character in order to speculate upon the resonances and functions of a nominative language in the history of fiction, and the fiction of history.

The parody and scandal of naming that initiates "What's in a Name?" can be seen, according to Roland Barthes, as an enactment of the text's achieving significance, its hermeneutic labor: "to find meanings is to name them; but these named meanings are swept toward other names; names call to each other, reassemble, and their grouping calls for further naming: I name, I unname, I rename: so the text passes: it is a nomination in the course of becoming, a tireless approximation, a metonymic labor."[10] For Barthes, language in its essence is a nominative process, constantly in motion, which calls attention to its own evocations and the arbitrary nature of referential systems. Using sleight-of-hand, Elkin "renames" himself at the beginning of the fiction as he becomes a character in a story that will mock the preserve of authorship. In a parallel fashion, "genre," which is the name we confer upon a kind of discourse in order to identify it, is also parodied as the narrator of the story changes his role from mock confessor to mock literary critic. The nominative impresario calls the roll of a most heterogeneous list of names: "Harry Morgan, Harry Bailey, Harry Angstrom, Harry Lime. J. R. Phil Esterhaus. Babbitt." The names come from places high and low, from generic categories ordinarily separated by borders distinguishing the literary from the nonliterary, serious from popular fiction. Harry Morgan (at least one of them) plays the commander of a medical corps in the television series, "MASH." Harry Bailey is the proprietor of a tavern in *The Canterbury Tales*. Harry Angstrom is the hero of *Rabbit, Run*; Harry Lime the hero of *The Third Man*. J. R. is the villain of a nighttime television soap opera; Phil Esterhaus a former roll-call sergeant and father-figure on the more "serious" soap, "Hill Street Blues." Babbitt is, of course, the protagonist of the novel that bears his name. The effect of this list is to break down the barriers between the classic and the ephemeral, and to contaminate the purity of generic categories by bringing all these names together in one place, as if a character from Chaucer could end up playing a cop on an American television series.

It is significant, I think, given Elkin's dismantling of the authorial name, that some of these works are signed by famous authors, while others are multiauthored, products of a collaboration that potentially involves dozens of "authors." Elkin goes on: "Hamlet but not Garp. Snow White, Pinocchio, and Mary Poppins but not Cinderella. Peter Pan but not Captain Hook. R2D2, Han Solo, C3PO and Obi-wan (Ben) Kenobi but not Princess Leia. Leopold Bloom but not Stephen Dedalus. (Who can explain it, who can tell you why? Fools give you reasons, wise men never try. Rodgers and Hammerstein but not Weber and Rice)." The assumption that the name of a character in a fiction automatically bears some special significance—that there must be a connection between the name, "being," and actions of a character—is here deflated. The distinction between the names of great characters as opposed to those that won't do is purely arbitrary, though Elkin encourages us to engage in the "foolishness" of that difference. Is "Hamlet" better than "Garp" because the latter sounds ugly, or because the former is clearly a more important character than the hero of John Irving's novel? Is "Bloom" better than "Dedalus" because the flat-footed name of the artist called after a Greek hero rings dead in our ears, while that of the modern ad canvasser flowers in the imagination? Even though many of the protagonists of Elkin's own fiction bear rather obvious names (Ben Flesh, Perlmutter, Op and Glyp, Alexander Main), just as many have most unpromising handles: George Mills, Dick Gibson, Marshall Preminger. In short, there is nothing in a name save its placement by authors and readers within a context where its significance is a matter of the expectations created by sound, genre, and literary history. There is nothing in a name or in a genre, Elkin implies, that necessitates its right to meaning or form.

Yet, knowing this, writers insist on naming and making worlds, investing them with purpose and significance, relying upon the reader's compliance for the success of the illusion. Indeed, Elkin counts upon our awareness of the artificiality of genre and of the synthetic history of novelistic namings to bring the whole thing off. Slipping into the role of historian ("I want to speak to you this evening about Paul Louis Pelgas") Elkin finally discovers his own métier, that of the storyteller. Thus ensues the fiction, initially told in the voice of the historical scholar (only the footnotes are missing) of Chapel County, The Thicket, and "America's first theme park." Historical scholarship is transformed into historical fiction when Elkin coyly admits of the dialogue he has recounted between the citizens of Norbiton: "I've attributed to Legurney and Slipper and Oldham Broom and Sheriff Leon Edgers and others *most* of the dialogue I've put down here. Because, except for Audubon's journal entries and Phil and Pembler Roberts's remarks, which are documented, we'll never know who actually said what. The beginnings of a conspiracy are often smoky and seldom known, and all this was over one hundred years ago." With this admission, Elkin relies on the fact that readers need only a little credible detail to enable them to indulge in the fiction of historical reconstruction. We will readily attribute to the names of fiction and history actions, motivations, and conversations that occur in the realm of probability as long as we are assured that certain "facts"—literary or historical—have been established: a war, a constitutional convention, the conventionalizing of a Quixote or a Madame Bovary. Elkin means to undermine this fragile illusion for, if as he suggests, we take out our maps (something the members of the audience to whom Elkin originally delivered "What's in a Name?" couldn't have done), we discover that there is no Chapel County in southwestern Pennsylvania, no Norbiton, no Clifton College. As far as I can discover, Audubon never wrote the words Elkin attributes to him, and certainly there is no "Density Theory" attributable to a Professor Robert Barr. There is, of course, a Pennsylvania, a John James Audubon, but they simply recede into their names when Chapel County disappears from the map. Elkin could have arranged matters differently, either by locating his story more firmly within a network of real places, names, and facts, as he does in *The Franchiser* (there is a Ringgold, Georgia, a Baskin-Robbins in every town), or less so, by allegorizing the mundane, as he does in *The Living End*. Instead, by maintaining the tone of the fabulist/historian in "What's in a Name?" while purposefully skewing the facts, Elkin complicates the connection to be made between allegory and history; he questions the "truth of the imagination" by partially severing the link between the historical, generic, and intertextual contingencies of a fiction and its "names," the language of its nominations and references.

The strange history of "The Thicket," then, can be seen as the story of Elkin's writing and its allegorization as a form of enslavement. The very obverse of Wallace Stevens's anecdotal jar that "did not give of bird or bush, / Like nothing else in Tennessee," Elkin's thicket is a form of nature that will admit neither bird nor man: it is a "natural" yet bounded labyrinth; it lacks both the order of cultural mazes (gardens, puzzles, mysteries) and the openness of a true wilderness.[11] The Thicket is entropic; in its present state it is "reduced to a plot not larger than a decent-sized park in a medium-sized city," yet even in decline it is, as the spurious Julia Rayburton's experiments prove, still impenetrable. We discover that The Thicket may contain the remains of runaway slaves bearing the names of all those fictional characters Elkin has named, though the attempts to transform the dry bones of the betrayed "house niggers" into a spectacle worthy of a "theme park" are disastrous. Finally, we are told that the disenchanted domestics who may well be the descendants of the lost runaways massacre the white spectators viewing "the Woody" as a perverse source of amusement. The domestics are, themselves, lynched, leaving behind no record of these events save the names of the runaway slaves inscribed, as we know, in the annals of fiction.

A "theme park"? A boneyard for runaway characters? An impenetrable wilderness which, nevertheless, decreases in size and is temporarily surrounded by a construction allowing the spectator an "exalted overview atop the high planks set on a wooden scaffolding like the jerry built criss-crosses of condemnation, the thirty-seven miles of braided grid like a rough cat's cradle of loosely crocheted timber"? The fictional history of Chapel County posing as the explanation for this construction and its demise? These are the metaphors Elkin presents and discards as conceptualizations of "the craft of fiction" or "the scene of writing." One of the false seductions of fiction is that it may be thematically organized, its meanings named and categorized; another is that fiction can be viewed "from above," its hidden treasures spotted from the "scaffolding" of form. Yet the allegory of Elkin's thicket implies something much more unsettling than the mockery of these accepted truisms regarding fiction's semantic or generic traits. The repository of writing—the thicket—contains the "remains" of characters who purportedly have been transported there from proper burial sites. This scene of historical transgression encompasses the auto-da-fé of its own form and content. Its transgressional nature is allied with its intertextuality in several senses: petty theft, grave robbing, enslavement, fraud, arson, murder—all are the crimes recorded within this metaphor of writing disguised as history. For Elkin, fiction making is a "criminal" activity that involves the disruption of proper generic boundaries and the dissimulation of the author as the beneficent deity of the world he makes. Here, the author is at once a pitchman, a thief, and a hangman. Characters from other texts are enslaved and renamed in the service of writing, then lost in the entanglements of its false history; authors and readers are, themselves, sundered by their attempts to "domesticate" the form or import of what they write and read. This is a lawless country, where the Barthesian "plaisir du texte" is transformed into an apocalyptic immolation, and where those "constructions" that would support the safety of our overviews or interpretations collapse: "The wall was a tinder box. When [Pelgas] and the other domestics, after first preparing the most strategic struts, pilings, and braces with oil, finally ignited it, it went off like a firework. Two hundred and fourteen tourists and holiday makers either burned or fell to their deaths on the thorns and briars, the burning brambles and bushes, incinerated and drowned in the lake of blazing liquors of the primed, fermenting fruits forty feet below them." If the thicket can be viewed as the work of fiction where deluded, enslaved characters seek escape from their white, pandering masters, then writing proves treacherous to all; it is both a trap and a consummation; it is the writing of difference which, in the form of a revolt, turns against itself.

It may appear that there are few connections to be made between the metaphor of writing Elkin constructs in "What's in a Name?" and his own writing as I have described it. Yet there are, indeed, links between the allegory of writing and its productions, for all writing, Elkin concludes, is a form of "connection": "What I suppose I've been talking about is connection. Connection, invention and all the enumerate, lovely links, synapses, and nexuses of fiction." There is some relation, Elkin suggests, between historical events, the aesthetics of fiction, and the names of characters, just as there is the connection Elkin makes *in writing* between slavery in the North, an absurdist tale portraying a domestic revolt, and the name of Paul Louis Pelgas. Thematically, Elkin's work reveals a concern with "connection" as the sign of genetic determinism, or paranoia, or the labyrinthine intricacies of a system of communication. The elaborate descriptions of a dry-cleaning shop, a cosmetic counter, a pharaoh's tomb, a power grid, or a radio network all convey the sense that "what Elkin is talking about" is connection—that his fiction assumes the task of making the connection between the manifestations of a disparate, heterogeneous reality and the artful metaphors by which it may be assimilated. Writing, then, is the tracing out of these connections, almost as if the penstrokes themselves (or the printed characters) signified the "synapses and nexuses." Yet the allegory of writing presented in "What's in a Name?" suggests the fragility of connections and suggests further that, even while making them, writing fractures "these lovely links," even as the "cat's cradle" construction of the wall in Norbiton is consumed by the act of arson in the thicket. "Detail," Elkin writes, can be seen "as a kind of noun, and a menu of proper names . . . a register of fact." So the "fact" of fiction resides in its assemblage of name and detail into recognizable shapes or venues. Yet the edifice of this fact is built on shaky ground, for it is equally the work of the language of fiction to skew the facts, pervert its own history, and rob its own treasury when it scatters names across texts, or becomes opaque, or breaks form. This is the dialectic of fiction which, I believe, Elkin finely perceives.

The caves of Marabar that Elkin refers to in the last line of "What's in a Name?" are, in Forster's novel, a place of defamiliarization, where the ordinary is converted into the strange. "Esmiss Esmoor" (the proper name of Mrs. Moore skewed and echoed) understands these caves only because she can accept them as utterly alien, then escape them, then die at sea. Elkin, too, hollows out the language of the commonplace—the jingo, the sales pitch, everyday speech—in order to reveal the deformed estrangements that lie hidden beneath forms of convention. Just as often, Elkin's fiction reverses itself when the exotic is made into the ordinary: the symptoms of the rare diseases suffered by the children of *The Magic Kingdom* are the most dependably observable phenomena in a pandemonious, intensely claustrophobic "Disney World." Elkin's writing continually wavers between the registers of ordinariness and otherness, the familiar and the alien. The energy of his work can be explained by the fact that he refuses to settle his language down into either the category of the conventional or the anarchic; rather, he uses the effects of each to explode the other. Ultimately, this movement of language is the sign of the comic writer, who uses his language to parody the forms and intonations of conventional discourse while, at the same time, preserving these altered forms and accents in metaphor, catalogue, and speech.[12] But this characterization of Elkin's writing does it justice only in the most general sense, from the overview provided by the critic's place on the parapet. There remain the discontents of analysis that only a plunge into the thicket, itself, will absolve.

Notes

1 For discussions of metaphor as the primary stylistic and structural element of Elkin's fiction, see Peter Bailey, *Reading Stanley Elkin* (Urbana: University of Illinois Press,

1985), pp. 1–20, 41–47; and Marc Chénetier, "MS, or 'The IMP of OSSIBILITY': Reflexions on the Work of Stanley Elkin and Gilbert Sorrentino," forthcoming in *Making Sense*, ed. Gerhard Hoffman.

2 Stanley Elkin, *A Bad Man* (1967; rpt. New York: Warner Books, 1980), p. 226.

3 Stanley Elkin, *The Franchiser* (1976; rpt. Boston: David Godine, 1980), p. 73.

4 Michel Foucault, "Nietzsche, Genealogy, History," in *Language, Counter-Memory, Practice: Selected Essays and Interviews*, ed. Donald F. Bouchard; trans. Donald F. Bouchard and Sherry Simon (Ithaca, N.Y.: Cornell University Press, 1977), p. 142.

5 Ibid., p. 145.

6 Ibid., pp. 144–45.

7 Elkin, *The Franchiser*, p. 85.

8 Foucault, "Nietzsche, Genealogy, History," p. 161.

9 Vladimir Nabokov, *Lolita* (1955; rpt. New York: Berkeley Medallion Books, 1966), p. 5.

10 Roland Barthes, *SZ: An Essay* (New York: Hill and Wang, 1974), p. 11.

11 Wallace Stevens, "Anecdote of the Jar," in *The Collected Poems of Wallace Stevens* (New York: Alfred A. Knopf, 1972), p. 76.

12 This conception of the comic writer issues from Mikhail Bakhtin's discussion of the comic novel since Rabelais, with whom Elkin bears some interesting comparisons. See "Discourse in the Novel," in *The Dialogic Imagination: Four Essays by M. M. Bakhtin*, ed. Michael Holquist; trans. Caryl Emerson and Michael Holquist (Austin: University of Texas Press, 1981), especially pp. 308–12.

STORIES

DONALD BARTHELME

......

Basil from Her Garden

A—In the dream, my father was playing the piano, a Beethoven something, in a large concert hall that was filled with people. I was in the audience and I was reading a book. I suddenly realized that this was the wrong thing to do when my father was performing, so I sat up and paid attention. He was playing very well, I thought. Suddenly the conductor stopped the performance and began to sing a passage for my father, a passage that my father had evidently botched. My father listened attentively, smiling at the conductor.

Q—Does your father play? In actuality?

A—Not a note.

Q—Did the conductor resemble anyone you know?

A—He looked a bit like Althea. The same cheekbones and the same chin.

Q—Who is Althea?

A—Someone I know.

Q—What do you do, after work, in the evenings or on weekends?

A—Just ordinary things.

Q—No special interests?

A—I'm very interested in bow-hunting. These new bows they have now, what they call a compound bow. Also, I'm a member of the Galapagos Society, we work for the environment, it's really a very effective—

Q—And what else?

A—Well, adultery. I would say that that's how I spend most of my free time. In adultery.

Q—You mean regular adultery.

A—Yes. Sleeping with people to whom one is not legally bound.

Q—These are women.

A—Invariably.

Q—And so that's what you do, in the evenings or on weekends.

A—I had this kind of strange experience. Today is Saturday, right? I called up this haircutter that I go to, her name is Ruth, and asked for an appointment. I needed a haircut. So she says she has openings at ten, ten-thirty, eleven, eleven-thirty, twelve, twelve-thirty— On a Saturday. Do you think the world knows something I don't know?

Q—It's possible.

A—What if she stabs me in the ear with the scissors?

Q—Unlikely, I would think.

A—Well, she's a good soul. She's had several husbands. They've all been master sergeants, in the Army. She seems to gravitate toward NCO Clubs. Have you noticed all these little black bugs flying around here? I don't know where they come from.

Q—They're very small, they're like gnats.

A—They come in clouds, then they go away.

A—I sometimes think of myself as a person who, you know what I mean, could have done something else, it doesn't matter what particularly. Just something else. I saw an ad in the Sunday paper for the CIA, a recruiting ad, maybe a quarter of a page, and I suddenly thought, It might be interesting to do that. Even though I've always been opposed to the CIA, when they were trying to bring Cuba down, the stuff with Lumumba in Africa, the stuff in Central America. . . . Then here is this ad, perfectly straightforward, "where your career is America's strength" or something like that, "aptitude for learning a foreign language is a plus" or something like that. I've always been good at languages, and I'm sitting there thinking about how my résumé might look to them, starting completely over in something completely new, changing the very sort of person I am, and there was an attraction, a definite attraction. Of course the maximum age was thirty-five. I guess they want them more malleable.

Q—So, in the evenings or on weekends—

A—Not every night or every weekend. I mean, this depends on the circumstances. Sometimes my wife and I go to dinner with people, or watch television—

Q—But in the main—

A—It's not that often. It's once in a while.

Q—Adultery is a sin.

A—It is classified as a sin, yes. Absolutely.

Q—The Seventh Commandment says—

A—I know what it says. I was raised on the Seventh Commandment. But.

Q—But what?

A—The Seventh Commandment is wrong.

Q—It's wrong?

A—Some outfits call it the Sixth and others the Seventh. It's wrong.

Q—The whole Commandment?

A—I don't know how it happened, whether it's a mistranslation from the Aramaic or whatever, it may not even have been Aramaic, I don't know, I certainly do not pretend to scholarship in this area, but my sense of the matter is that the Seventh Commandment is an error.

Q—Well if that was true it would change quite a lot of things, wouldn't it?

A—Take the pressure off, a bit.

Q—Have you told your wife?

A—Yes, Grete knows.

Q—How'd she take it?

A—Well, she *liked* the Seventh Commandment. You could reason that it was in her interest to support the Seventh Commandment for the preservation of the family unit and this sort of thing but to reason that way is, I would say, to take an extremely narrow view of Grete, of what she thinks. She's not predictable. She once told me that she didn't want me, she wanted a suite of husbands, ten or twenty—

Q—What did you say?

A—I said, Go to it.

Q—Well, how does it make you feel? Adultery.

A—There's a certain amount of guilt attached. I feel guilty. But I feel guilty even without adultery. I exist in a morass of guilt. There's maybe a little additional wallop of guilt but I already feel so guilty that I hardly notice it.

Q—Where does all this guilt come from? The extra-adulterous guilt?

A—I keep wondering if, say, there is intelligent life on other planets, the scientists argue that something like two per cent of the other planets have the conditions, the physical conditions, to support life in the way it happened here, did Christ visit each and every planet, go through the same routine, the Agony in the Garden, the Crucifixion, and so on. . . . And these guys on these other planets, these life forms, maybe they look like boll weevils or something, on a much larger scale of course, were they told that they shouldn't go to bed with other attractive six-foot boll weevils arrayed in silver and gold and with little squirts of Opium behind the ears? Doesn't make sense. But of course our human understanding is imperfect.

Q—You haven't answered me. This general guilt—

A—Yes, that's the interesting thing. I hazard that it is not guilt so much as it is inadequacy. I feel that everything is being nibbled away, because I can't *get it right*—

Q—Would you like to be able to fly?

A—It's crossed my mind.

Q—Myself, I think about being just sort of a regular person, one who worries about cancer a lot, every little thing a prediction of cancer, no I don't want to go for my every-two-years checkup because what if they find something? I wonder what will kill me and when it will happen and how it will happen, and I wonder about my parents, who are still alive, and what will happen to them. This seems to me to be a proper set of things to worry about. Last things.

A—I don't think God gives a snap about adultery. This is just an opinion, of course.

Q—So how do you, how shall I put it, pursue—

A—You think about this staggering concept, the mind of God, and then you think He's sitting around worrying about this guy and this woman at the Beechut TraveLodge? I think not.

Q—Well, He doesn't have to think about every particular instance, He just sort of laid out the general principles—

A—He also created creatures who, with a single powerful glance—

Q—The eyes burn.

A—They do.

Q—The heart leaps.

A—Like a terrapin.

Q—Stupid youth returns.

A—Like hockey sticks falling out of a long-shut closet.

Q—Do you play?

A—I did. Many years ago.

Q—Who is Althea?

A—Someone I know.

Q—We're basically talking about Althea.

A—Yes. I thought you understood that.

Q—We're not talking about wholesale—

A—Oh Lord no. Who has the strength?

Q—What's she like?

A—She's I guess you'd say a little on the boring side. To the innocent eye.

Q—She appears to be a contained, controlled person, free of raging internal fires.

A—But my eye is not innocent. To the already corrupted eye, she's—

Q—I don't want to question you too closely on this. I don't want to strain your powers of—

A—Well, no, I don't mind talking about it. It fell on me like a ton of bricks. I was walking in the park one day.

Q—Which park?

A—That big park over by—

Q—Yeah, I know the one.

A—This woman was sitting there.

Q—They sit in parks a lot, I've noticed that. Especially when they're angry. The solitary bench. Shoulders raised, legs kicking—

A—I've crossed both major oceans by ship—the Pacific twice, on troopships, the Atlantic once, on a passenger liner. You stand out there, at the rail, at dusk, and the sea is limitless, water in every direction, never-ending, you think *water forever,* the movement of the ship seems slow but also seems inexorable, you feel you will be moving this way forever, the Pacific is about seventy million square miles, about one-third of the earth's surface, the ship might be making twenty knots, I'm eating oranges because that's all I can keep down, twelve days of it with thousands of young soldiers all around, half of them seasick— On the Queen Mary, in tourist class, we got rather good food, there was a guy assigned to our table who had known Paderewski, the great pianist who was also Prime Minister of Poland, he talked about Paderewski for four days, an ocean of anecdotes—

Q—When I was first married, when I was twenty, I didn't know where the clitoris was. I didn't know there was such a thing. Shouldn't somebody have told me?

A—Perhaps your wife?

Q—Of course, she was too shy. In those days people didn't go around saying, This is the clitoris and this is what its proper function is and this is what you can do to help out. I finally found it. In a book.

A—German?

Q—Dutch.

A—A dead bear in a blue dress, face down on the kitchen floor. I trip over it, in the dark, when I get up at 2 A.M. to see if there's anything to eat in the refrigerator. It's an architectural problem, marriage. If we could live in separate houses, and visit each other when we felt particularly gay— It would be expensive, yes. But as it is she has to endure me in all my worst manifestations, early in the morning and late at night and in the nutsy obsessed noontimes. When I wake up from my nap you don't *get* the laughing cavalier, you get a rank pigfooted belching blunderer. I knew this one guy who built a wall down the middle of his apartment. An impenetrable wall. He had a very big apartment. It worked out very well. Concrete block, basically, with fibre-glass insulation on top of that and sheetrock on top of that—

Q—What about coveting your neighbor's wife?

A—Well on one side there are no wives, strictly speaking, there are two floors and two male couples, all very nice people. On the other side, Bill and Rachel have the whole house. I like Rachel but I don't covet her. I could covet her, she's covetable, quite lovely and spirited, but in point of fact our relationship is that of neighborliness. I jump-start her car when her battery is dead, she gives me basil from her garden, she's got acres of basil, not literally acres but— Anyhow, I don't think that's much of a problem, coveting your neighbor's wife. Just speaking administratively, I don't see why there's an entire Commandment devoted to it. It's a mental exercise, coveting. To covet is not necessarily to take action.

Q—I covet my neighbor's leaf blower. It has this neat Vari-Flo deal that lets you—

A—I can see that.

Q—I am feverishly interested in these questions.

Q—Ethics has always been where my heart is.

Q—Moral precepting stings the dull mind into attentiveness.

Q—I'm only a bit depressed, only a bit.

Q—A new arrangement of ideas, based upon the best thinking, would produce a more humane moral order, which we need.

Q—Apple honey, disposed upon the sexual parts, is not an index of decadence. Decadence itself is not as bad as it's been painted.

Q—That he watched his father play the piano when his father could not play the piano and that he was reading a book while his father played the piano in a very large hall before a very large audience only means that he finds his roots, as it were, untrustworthy. The father imagined as a root. That's not unusual.

Q—As for myself, I am content with too little, I know this about myself and I do not commend myself for it and perhaps one day I shall be able to change myself into a hungrier being. Probably not.

Q—The leaf blower, for example.

A—I see Althea now and then, not often enough. We sigh together in a particular bar, it's almost always empty. She tells me about her kids and I tell her about my kids. I obey the Commandments, the sensible ones. Where they don't know what they're talking about I ignore them. I keep thinking about the story of the two old women in church listening to the priest discoursing on the dynamics of the married state. At the end of the sermon one turns to the other and says, "I wish I knew as little about it as he does."

Q—He critiques us, we critique Him. Does Grete also engage in dalliance?

A—How quaint you are. I think she has friends whom she sees now and then.

Q—How does that make you feel?

A—I wish her well.

Q—What's in your wallet?

A—The usual. Credit cards, pictures of the children, driver's license, forty dollars in cash, Amex receipts—

Q—I sometimes imagine that I am in Pest Control. I have a small white truck with a red diamond-shaped emblem on the door and a white jumpsuit with the same emblem on the breast pocket. I park the truck in front of a subscriber's neat three-hundred-thousand-dollar home, extract the silver cannister of deadly pest killer from the back of the truck, and walk up the brick sidewalk to the house's front door. Chimes ring, the door swings open, a young wife in jeans and a pink flannel shirt worn outside the jeans is standing there. "Pest Control," I say. She smiles at me, I smile back and move past her into the house, into the handsomely appointed kitchen. The cannister is suspended by a sling from my right shoulder, and, pumping the mechanism occasionally with my right hand, I point the nozzle of the hose at the baseboards and begin to spray. I spray alongside the refrigerator, alongside the gas range, under the sink, and behind the kitchen table. Next, I move to the bathrooms, pumping and spraying. The young wife is in another room, waiting for me to finish. I walk into the main sitting room and spray discreetly behind the largest pieces of furniture, an oak sideboard, a red plush Victorian couch, and along the inside of the fireplace. I do the study, spraying the Columbia Encyclopedia, he's been looking up the Seven Years' War, 1756–63, yellow highlighting there, and behind the forty-five-inch RCA television. The master bedroom requires just touches, short bursts in her closet which must avoid the two dozen pairs of shoes there and in his closet which contains six to eight long guns in canvas cases. Finally I spray the laundry room with its big white washer and dryer, and behind the folding table stacked with sheets and towels already folded. Who folds? I surmise that she folds. Unless one of the older children, pressed into service, folds. In my experience they are unlikely to fold. Maybe the au pair. Finished, I tear a properly made out receipt from my receipt book and present it to the young wife. She scribbles her name in the appropriate space and hands it back to me. The house now stinks quite palpably but I know and she knows that the stench will dissipate in two to four hours. The young wife escorts me to the door, and, in parting, pins a silver medal on my chest and kisses me on both cheeks. Pest Control!

A—Yes, one could fit in in that way. It's finally a matter, perhaps, of fit. Appropriateness. Fit in a stately or sometimes hectic dance with nonfit. What we have to worry about.

Q—It seems to me that we have quite a great deal to worry about. Does the radish worry about itself in this way? Yet the radish is a living thing. Until it's cooked.

A—Grete is mad for radishes, can't get enough. I like frozen Mexican dinners, Patio, I have them for breakfast, the freezer is stacked with them—

Q—Transcendence is possible.

A—Yes.

Q—Is it possible?

A—Not out of the question.

Q—Is it really possible?

A—Yes. Believe me.

ALAN WILDE

......

Barthelme His Garden

Q: Are you bored with the question-and-answer form?

A: I am bored with it but I realize that it permits many valuable omissions: what kind of day it is, what I'm wearing, what I'm thinking. That's a very considerable advantage, I would say.

Q: I believe in it.

—Donald Barthelme, "The Explanation"

Otherwise unnamed, Q and A, the interlocutors of "Basil from Her Garden," appear elsewhere in Barthelme's work (most notably, in "Kierkegaard Unfair to Schlegel"); and they will serve, in all their alphabetic purity, as convenient emblems of what that body of work intends. To begin with, Barthelme, like one of the characters in "The Leap," is "a double-minded man. H[as] always been a double-minded man,"[1] which no doubt explains the attraction for him of various dialogic forms—forms that, by their structure alone, tend to suggest doubt or division and that invite a dialectical, ongoing apprehension of both self and world.[2] The recurrence of such stories is interesting enough in itself.[3] More significant, however, if also more problematic, is Barthelme's attitude toward the comedy or frustration of double-mindedness that he enacts in many of these dialogues. Thus, in "The Leap," to quote from that pivotal story once again, one of the speakers responds to the statement that "Purity of heart is to will one thing," by asserting his own, apparently more Barthelmean credo: "No. Here I differ with Kierkegaard. Purity of heart is, rather, to will several things, and not know which is the better, truer thing, and to worry about this, forever" (p. 384). No doubt, there are dangers in assuming that this character—or any character, for that matter—speaks for Barthelme, but in this case there are compelling reasons for the identification. In a recent essay (actually, a talk), Barthelme sets forth his own eminently postmodern belief that "Problems are a comfort. Wittgenstein said of philosophers that some of them suffer from 'loss of problems,' a development in which everything seems quite simple to them, and what they write becomes (I'm quoting) 'immeasurably shallow and trivial.' The same can be said of writers."[4]

And of the character in "The Leap" whom I have now twice cited. What is at issue in both that story and the essay is a willingness to live with and in the untidiness of existence: to abide, even to welcome, the problematic; to see it, indeed, as "a comfort," if also—possibly a distinction without a difference—as a source of fertile worry. In any case, the contrast between the desire for "one thing" and the acceptance of "many things" is central to the dialectic of Barthelme's work and, arguably, nowhere more so than in "Basil from Her Garden," where Q and A sinuously and ironically explore the possibilities that define the world in which his characters live, act, and talk. I say "ironically" because, despite what appears to be a psychiatric encounter, it is A, the "patient," who emerges not only as the more resilient and independent but, finally, as the comforter of his interlocutor. (On the other hand, in "Kierkegaard Unfair to Schlegel" an earlier avatar of Q, speaking from within a similar situation, reminds A that "I'm not your doctor."[5]) At any rate, whatever the precise roles we are meant to attribute to the two, it is clear that Q's movement is from heuristic prompter to worried and aggravated participant in the dialogue, while A's is from generally willing and sometimes expansive respondent to increasingly assured and confident affirmer of the ordinary.

The effect, needless to say, is to destroy the *apparent* modality of the question-and-answer situation, to make it, in every possible way, ironic. But that is to get ahead of Barthelme and his story. Anterior to our awareness of how his characters reposition themselves in the course of their exchange is the more fundamental recognition that "Basil from Her Garden," like "The Leap," bases itself on the clash of two opposing cosmologies, each of which has, at one time or another, its attractions for the speakers. The first, represented by the jumpy, disjunctive, paratactic structure of the story, by its distractable, associative characters, and, perhaps, more graphically, by the clouds of "little black bugs flying around here" that A irrelevantly notices at one point, suggests the irredeemable messiness and contingency of the (postmodern) world. The second, opposing view reveals itself in a sense of something lost and regretted, something *other* than the world Q and A inhabit—a prelapsarian Garden of coherence and order and wholeness, as it might appropriately be called—whose emblems include flying, dreams, the "limitless," "never-ending" ocean, religion, and, of course, as the ultimate source of them all, God. This heterocosmic desire—the longing for an alternative, if merely imaginable, elsewhere—is, as stories like "A Shower of Gold," "The President," "Paraguay," and, especially, "Florence Green is 81" demonstrate, nothing new in Barthelme's fiction; and in A's ruminations on the possibility of "starting completely over in something completely new, changing the very sort of person I am" one hears echoes of Florence Green's wish "to go to some *other* place. . . . Somewhere where *everything is different*"—a remark the narrator of that story glosses as follows: "A simple, perfect idea. The old babe demands nothing less than total otherness."[6]

Familiar too, as the cause of the desire for the entirely different, are the feelings that A, continually prompted by Q, acknowledges in his meditations on adultery, the central, or at least the most obsessive, concern of the dialogue:

> A—There's a certain amount of guilt attached [to adultery]. I feel guilty. But I feel guilty even without adultery. I exist in a morass of guilt. There's maybe a little additional wallop of guilt but I already feel so guilty that I hardly notice it. . . .
> Q—You haven't answered me. This general guilt—
> A—Yes, that's the interesting thing. I hazard that it is not guilt so much as it is inadequacy. I feel that everything is being nibbled away, because I can't *get it right*—
> Q—Would you like to be able to fly?
> A—It's crossed my mind.

But, as I've already intimated, A does eventually *get it right*, manages, that is, to accommodate his guilt and inadequacy and to forgo the temptation of flying; and it is at that point that the differences, not only between the story's cosmological choices but between Q and A, assert themselves unmistakably.

And yet, to phrase things in this way may suggest too dramatic a series of changes in "Basil from Her Garden." The fact is that throughout the story we come increasingly to recognize a real, if unsteady, modulation in A's responses and, equally, to question Q's role as Socratic facilitator and guide—to see mirrored in the relative strengthening of one ego the commensurate disintegration of the other. Thus, even before we reach the final section, we become aware that, of the two, it is Q, the ostensible cicerone, who is the more depressed ("only a bit depressed, only a bit"), the more naive and unsure, and, above all, the more theoretical and utopian in his hopes and aspirations. Or, as he puts it himself: "A new arrangement of ideas, based upon the best thinking, would produce a more humane moral order, which we need." Nevertheless, it is only in the tenth and closing scene of the story that the full dimensions of what has transpired become clear. "I sometimes imagine that I am in Pest Control," Q tells A and proceeds to relate a cheerful fantasy of himself as the agent of domestic order, a fantasy that ends as the young wife of the house "pins a silver medal on my chest and kisses me on both cheeks." Two things signify in Q's tale: first, that the emphasis falls on Control and not on the unseen Pests (though it is tempting to recall the contingent "little black bugs" of an earlier section) and, second, that rehearsing the conceit does nothing whatever to allay his worries about "Last things."

Indeed, as "Basil from Her Garden" comes to its end and as A contemplates what he has already called "ordinary things," Q continues to fret about the unsatisfactoriness of life with a self-protective humor that reveals more than it conceals ("Does the radish worry about itself in this way? Yet the radish is a living thing. Until it's cooked") and that finally protects nothing, as the lines that close the story make abundantly clear:

Q—Transcendence is possible.
A—Yes.
Q—Is it possible?
A—Not out of the question.
Q—Is it really possible?
A—Yes. Believe me.

The easiest way to read these lines is to see in them Q's almost despairing need for reassurance and A's willingness to console and cajole. But it is more productive to recognize that the key word of the exchange means very different things to the two speakers—that for Q transcendence implies an ordering of the world (as well as a removal from it), a ridding it, as in the tale of the Pest Controler, of everything that makes life uneven, unpredictable, and recalcitrant, whereas for A it is a matter of coming to terms with guilt, anxiety, and thoughts of inadequacy *in the world* as it is and as it offers itself to consciousness. Like Mad Moll of "The Emerald," with her "memories of God who held me up and sustained me until I fell from His hands,"[7] A (and Barthelme, on this reading) accepts what follows from inhabiting a postlapsarian world; or, as A puts it in response to

Q's Pest Control story: "It's finally a matter, perhaps, of fit. Appropriateness. Fit in a stately or sometimes hectic dance with nonfit." The orderly and harmonious suggestions of a dance are qualified, appropriately, by "hectic," as well as by the double-minded adverb "perhaps," and, most of all, by the acknowledgment of the "nonfit," that is, whatever stubbornly refuses Q's dreams and parables of order. Which is to say, too, that the story's apparent closure, its emphatic "Yes. Believe me," is anything but final, is, instead, a momentary halt in what must be a continuing dialogue with the world.

Up to this point, it might be argued, I have deliberately ignored, even contravened, Barthelme's contention that "the paraphrasable content of art is rather slight";[8] and it might further be said that I have been of Q's party in imposing on the story an orderliness that the story itself expressly aims to frustrate. Let me admit, then, that much of "Basil from Her Garden" remains, at least in the discursive context I've so far established for reading it, puzzling in the extreme and that, again in these specific terms, it is almost impossible to account for much that goes on in it. Which is, no doubt, why so many critics have been anxious to claim Barthelme as a metafictionist, to define his concerns as, exclusively, language and play. To be sure, some of the stories, earlier ones like "Sentence" especially, seem to fit naturally into this category. And, given the loosely assorted, willfully inconsequent, episodic structure of "Basil from Her Garden"; given the "many valuable omissions" to which an earlier A refers in the epigraph I've used;[9] and given, finally, the fact that most of its sections end, as often as not, with a sense of the apparently irrelevant or mysterious, it would be less than surprising to find this story swept into the metafictional bin as well. Furthermore, Barthelme has on occasion helped to promote such readings of his work by speaking, through his characters or *in propria persona,* of the "objecthood" of the work of art, as in "Kierkegaard Unfair to Schlegel," where yet another A objects "that Kierkegaard fastens upon Schlegel's novel [*Lucinde*] in its prescriptive aspect—in which it presents itself as a text telling us how to live—and neglects other aspects, its objecthood for one" (p. 165).[10] On the other hand, Barthelme has recently offered an ambiguous and partial recantation of that position in "Not-Knowing": "Twenty years ago I was much more convinced of the autonomy of the literary objects than I am now, and even wrote a rather persuasive defense of the proposition that I have just rejected, that the object is itself world. . . . The proposition's still attractive. What's the right answer? Bless Babel" (p. 49). But it hardly required such a statement to make the point that many of his stories —among them, some of his very best, stories like "Rebecca," "The Great Hug," "Engineer-Private Paul Klee," or "Overnight to Many Distant Cities" —not to mention *The Dead Father,* are, whatever their playfulness, nothing if not moral: studies in smallness and risk that endorse an ethic of tentative, provisional pleasures against a background of daily life that frequently remains as frustrating as it is drab.

Which brings us back to "Basil from Her Garden." Ludic or moral? I would agree, happily, with those who, rejecting the choice as an unreal one, see the story as both, and would agree still more readily with those for whom the story is both and, in addition, something different still. The fact is that, to do justice to the variety of Barthelme's work, one needs to add to this raggedly taxonomic scheme yet another kind of fiction; and to describe it no one comes more snugly to hand than Susanne Langer. Langer's famous description of "the forms of feeling" in *Philosophy in a New Key* has more to do, of course, with music, ritual, and myth than with fiction. Its applicability to the last of these should, however, be apparent; and the notion of literature that resists discursive paraphrase but that conveys knowledge nevertheless (knowledge, precisely, of the morphology of feeling) helps at once to make sense of a story like "Basil from Her Garden" and to distinguish it from those of other writers who march under the reflexive, nonreferential banner of poststructuralist theory and who arrogate to themselves too exclusively the designation of postmodern.

My point is that we would do well to read various of the episodes in "Basil from Her Garden" (A's soliloquy on the ocean, Q's fantasy of Pest Control, to mention only two) neither as conventionally symbolic nor as allegorical but as emblematic: to seek in them such information about the forms of feeling as we require to make sense of what Barthelme is telling us about human beings living in a puzzling and quandarous world. If all of this sounds as if I'm obliquely trying to rescue Barthelme for realism, it is not what I intend. Clearly, the time has come to recognize that contemporary fiction does not lend itself to the kinds of binary oppositions that are the subject of Thomas Pynchon's anathematizations and that, in mapping the literary present, all too easily divide the field between the realistic and the metafictional. What has been excluded in this division of spoils is a middle ground where many of today's best writers—Stanley Elkin, Max Apple, Thomas Berger, Grace Paley, Pynchon, and, I'm suggesting, Barthelme—position themselves. Neither taking the world for granted nor regarding it as so impenetrable as to place it, effectively, hors de combat, "midfiction," as I have called it elsewhere,[11] negotiates the extremes of realism and metafiction and carves out for itself a more equivocal but also a more various space in which to bring the world into being.

That Barthelme is not a realist, no one, I think, will deny. As for his putative reflexiveness, a statement made in the latest interview with him—"I don't have any great enthusiasm for fiction-about-fiction"[12]—says all that probably needs to be said about Barthelme's aims and interests. My suggestion, then, is that, thematically, stylistically, and structurally, Barthelme's work, or much of the best of it, belongs with the tertium quid of midfiction; and although the terms I've been using are mine, not his, he has recently acknowledged as much in "Not-Knowing," the spirited and vivid essay from which I've been quoting. As playful and serious as "Basil from Her Garden," as associative in its logic, the essay can be viewed as a companion piece to the story, and, because of the light it sheds on its fictional brother, I want briefly to examine what it has to say about literature and its relation to the world it has traditionally been thought to represent.

The thesis of the essay, as its title suggests, is that "writing is a process of dealing with not-knowing, a forcing of what and how" (p. 38) and, further, that "the not-knowing is crucial to art, is what permits art to be made. Without the scanning process engendered by not-knowing, without the possibility of having the mind move in unanticipated directions, there would be no invention" (p. 38). Invention is the key word here, although in its older sense of "finding" rather than in the more usual (and metafictional) sense of "making up." What is being invented or found, as well as how, becomes clear later on, but first Barthelme deals with the various pressures of language (and of attitudes toward language) on literature during the last hundred years or so. Citing the growing complexity in "the effort toward mimesis" (p. 42), "the political and social contamination of language" (p. 41), and "a loss of reference . . . a world of reference to which all possible readers in this country can respond" (p. 43), Barthelme offers a still stronger assertion of the belief I've already noted, namely, that "problems, in part, define the kind of work the writer chooses to do, *and are not avoided but embraced*" (p. 44; my italics).

This assent to the complexities of writing (and of much else) leads, in turn, to the essay's central question: "In what sense is the work 'about' the world" (p. 46). The two related answers that Barthelme provides are, first, that "the world enters the work as it enters our ordinary lives, not as a world-view or system but in sharp particularity" (p. 47) and, second, "that art is always a meditation upon external reality rather than a representation of external reality" (p. 49). These propositions are fleshed out in a wonderfully inventive anecdote that is worth quoting:

> Let us suppose that I am the toughest banjulele player in town and that I have contracted to play "Melancholy Baby" for six hours before an audience that will include the four next-toughest banjulele players in town. . . . There is one thing of which you may be sure: I am not going to play "Melancholy Baby" as written. Rather I will play something that is parallel, in some sense, to "Melancholy Baby," based upon the chords of "Melancholy Baby," made out of "Melancholy Baby," having to do with "Melancholy Baby"—commentary, exegesis, elaboration, contradiction. (p. 49)

The passage does not end quite yet, and I will return in a moment to its close; but already certain things are clear. Despite the fact that what we have here may seem to be a meditation on intertextuality, on art's (the banjulele player's) response to, and only to, art ("Melancholy Baby"), the opposite—or nearly the opposite—is true. For, as Barthelme argues elsewhere in the essay, "the prior history of words [and I take it that, in Langer's sense, music and words equally express that prior history] is one of the aspects of language the world uses to smuggle itself into the work" (p. 48). "Melancholy Baby" functions, in other words, not only as an aesthetic limit but, more broadly, as any "reality" that exists outside us. It follows that, although Barthelme doesn't broach directly the question that haunts the poststructuralist imagination—whether we can in any way know the world or, to phrase it alternatively, whether we are irretrievably caught, and caught up, in a web of language—the tale of the banjulele player nonetheless implies both that the world (in a manner of speaking) leans on us and that we, in our turn, reciprocate the pressure: commenting, elaborating, contradicting, in short, *referring* to whatever that world is or may be. More succinctly, as Pierre Thévenaz writes, "the world gives itself to consciousness which confers on it its meaning."[13]

My invocation at this point of a phenomenological philosopher is altogether deliberate. Barthelme has, at various times in his career, acknowledged a debt of sorts to phenomenology. Thus, for example, in his interview with Klinkowitz, he says: "As to 'deeper cultural sources' [Klinkowitz's phrase], I have taken a certain degree of nourishment (or stolen a lot) from the phenomenologists: Sartre, Erwin Straus, etc." (*The New Fiction*, p. 52); while in "Not-Knowing," he writes, in confirmation of the views I've been attributing to him: "Art is a true account of the activity of mind. Because consciousness, in Husserl's formulation, is always consciousness *of* something, art thinks ever of the world, cannot not think of the world, could not turn its back on the world even if it wished to. This does not mean that it's going to be honest as a mailman; it's more likely to appear as a drag queen" (p. 50).[14] But sources, even deeper sources, are not the issue here. At stake is the fact that Thévenaz's account of consciousness as a locus of both reception and "invention" coincides so neatly with Barthelme's own sense of art's limits and possibilities: "The interest of my construction, if any," he notes in concluding his story of the banjulele player, "is to be located in the space between the new entity I have constructed and the 'real' 'Melancholy Baby,' which remains in the mind as the horizon that bounds my efforts" (p. 49). As emblem of the world, "Melancholy Baby" suggests the "reality" that constrains the artist who imagines or invents it into significative existence; and as the prototypically phenomenological word "horizon" intimates, not-knowing depends as much upon the fluid boundaries of consciousness (what "bounds my efforts") as upon consciousness itself, so that Barthelme's space or gap becomes, precisely, the middle ground I spoke of earlier, where the world, neither steady and immutable nor opaque and irrelevant, offers itself to interrogation rather than re-presentation, even as it asserts (above all, to the artist as drag queen) its equivocal but undeniable presence.

If I appear to have digressed, it has only been so as to circle back, now with theoretical provisions, to a reconsideration of what Barthelme is about in his unsettling and problematic story. What, then, can we now say about "Basil from Her Garden" in the light of Barthelme's apologia? To begin with, the fiction is obviously, richly, and precisely concerned with the "ordinary things" A speaks of—bow-hunting, haircuts, television, cancer, adultery, not to mention the contents of A's wallet: "Credit cards, pictures of the children, driver's license, forty dollars in cash, Amex receipts—." More to the point, it is concerned with how these things, the world, seep into or impinge on consciousness "in sharp particularity." No doubt, the world in question is, from Q's psychiatric interpretation of the dream with which the story opens to A's ruminations about God's intentions, to a large degree a cultural and linguistic construct, a matter, as poststructuralists would argue, of codes that interpose themselves between us and what we naively persist in regarding as reality. But, as Barthelme argues in "Not-Knowing": "If words can be contaminated by the world they can also carry with them into the work trace elements of world which can be used in a positive sense" (p. 48). Furthermore, the story is not only about the specific, linguistically determined systems that cause A's guilt and anxiety. There is, too, the object of A's covetousness, Althea: the solicitation of a world that is, whatever else we say about it, palpably there.

This is not, however, to suggest that either adultery in general or Althea in particular embodies the answer to A's dilemma. On the contrary, the tensions that make Althea at once desirable and forbidden remain to the end; and the question, perhaps, is more nearly one of defining what attitudes A (and, by extension, human beings) need to adopt in order to deal with life's inevitable contradictions, the "hectic dance [of fit] with nonfit," as they appear to "poor lapsarian futiles whose preen glands are all out of kilter" ("The Leap," p. 384). The choices that the story offers are, it seems to me, three. There is, first of all, the residual sense of the genuinely extraordinary that leads Q down the dangerous and impossible path of a perfect and irrefrangible order. But as A argues throughout and as even Q acknowledges ("He critiques us, we critique Him"), God's commandments are no longer gospel. In the second place, the story offers the consequences of acquiescence in life's dailiness, a possibility that Barthelme has mooted from time to time, and nowhere more effectively than in "City Life," which ends with Ramona's comically dreary and defeated words: "I accepted. What was the alternative?"[15] In "Basil from Her Garden" A's thoughts are equally occupied with the quotidian, as, intermittently, he contemplates his wife, Grete: "It's an architectural problem, marriage. If we could live in separate houses, and visit each other when we felt particularly gay— It would be expensive, yes. But as it is she has to endure me in all my worst manifestations, early in the morning and late at night and in the nutsy obsessed noontimes. When I wake up from my nap you don't *get* the laughing cavalier, you get a rank pigfooted belching blunderer." But A's self-awareness is something different from Ramona's resignation, less monolithic, more elastic; and in the story as a whole, A both confronts and contests the sources of his predecessor's weariness, accepting her version of dailiness but moving beyond it as well.

The clue to this third and final attitude, which seems to me Barthelme's too, is embedded in the story's title or, rather, in the episode to which it refers. Q has asked him about coveting his neighbor's wife, and A's answer brings us to the unobtrusive center of the fiction: "I like Rachel but I don't covet her, she's covetable, quite lovely and spirited, but in point of fact our relationship is that of neighborliness. I jump-start her car when her battery is dead, she gives me basil from her garden, she's got acres of basil, not literally acres but—." Nothing, in fact, is changed by this description—not the architecture of marriage, nor the guilt of adultery, and still less A's felt inadequacy in the face of life. But in Rachel and her basil, and in A's neighborly relationship with her, there is imaged another, postlapsarian garden that celebrates—amidst all the angst and tension, in the face of Q's desirous reaching for transcendence—the *ordinary.* More than the daily (but incorporating it), Barthelme's garden is populated by characters who are, as he described them in one of his interviews, "knitting lively lives—perhaps in subdued tones" (*Anything Can Happen,* p. 40).

Double-minded though it is, Barthelme's witty assertion nevertheless contrives to stress the liveliness and activity of his characters and, in so doing, designates the traits that mark his own fictional grasp of the world, his intentionality, as well. Thus, to have A say of Rachel that "she's got acres of basil, not literally acres but—" is to open up to us unimaginable (or only imaginable) visions of abundance, even though he and Barthelme, inevitably, pinch back this figurative excess and, it is implied, settle for the perceptible and the finite. But what matters is that we are given the movement of the imagination *before* it is vaguely and regretfully cut to size (forms of feeling indeed!), which is also to say that, as much as his conception of *la vie quotidienne,* this movement continues to inform his sense of what "ordinary" life has to offer. As does his choice of spice. Functional and unexotic, adding flavor and delight nonetheless to the world's otherwise insipid stew, basil, itself part of that world, figures the exact purpose and rewards of a garden, that enclave of nature and cultivation, which, like Candide's and like Barthelme's own writing, borrows the world to find and *make* pleasure in it. In short, the ordinary, here and elsewhere in Barthelme's work, is the ground, the middle ground, of whatever possibilities A's uneven progress evokes: a garden of earthly anxieties and delights, where one lives not, as in *The Waste Land,* between memory and desire but in an acceptance (more vigorous, riskier, than Ramona's passive response) of all the contradictions, the "problems," that inhabiting a fallen and imperfect world entails.

It is perhaps worth insisting that Rachel's garden promises no easy answers, no solutions or resolutions (as I suggested earlier, the story's ending ironically contests its own closural gestures), nothing extraordinary except the ordinary itself. If, nevertheless, this reading seems unduly moral and extravagant in its claims for the referential function of Barthelme's literary enterprise, it may be best to give the last word to Barthelme himself, who ends "Not-Knowing" in the following way:

> It's our good fortune to be able to imagine alternative realities, other possibilities. We can quarrel with the world constructively. . . . "Belief in progress," says Baudelaire, "is a doctrine of idlers and Belgians." Perhaps. But if I have anything unorthodox to say, it's that I think art's project is fundamentally meliorative. The aim of meditating about the world is finally to change the world. It is this meliorative aspect of literature that provides its ethical dimension. We are all Upton Sinclairs, even that Hamlet, Stéphane Mallarmé. (p. 50)

One final note: it's unlikely that anyone will confuse Barthelme with Upton Sinclair; it may be time, however, to recognize just how different he is from either Hamlet or Mallarmé—or, indeed, from the metafictional standard-bearer he is, even now, too often taken to be.

Notes

1 Donald Barthelme, "The Leap," *Sixty Stories* (New York: G. P. Putnam's Sons, 1981), p. 379. Subsequent references to this story (and to other works after their first citation) are given parenthetically in the text.

2 This is true even, or especially, of the question-and-answer stories, which might, on the face of it (that is, because of their formulaic quality), seem to inhibit genuine dialogue. Barthelme's use of the form plays against and disrupts the notion of speakers fixed in static, unchanging roles.

3 They are clustered most thickly in *Great Days,* but there are dialogues in *Sadness, City Life,* and the "previously uncollected" section of *Sixty Stories,* as well as in *The Dead Father.*

4 Donald Barthelme, "Not-Knowing," in *Voicelust*, ed. Allen Wier and Don Hendrie, Jr. (Lincoln: University of Nebraska Press, 1985), pp. 40–41.

5 Donald Barthelme, "Kierkegaard Unfair to Schlegel," *Sixty Stories*, p. 167.

6 Donald Barthelme, "Florence Green is 81," *Come Back, Dr. Caligari* (Boston: Little, Brown, 1964), pp. 14–15.

7 Donald Barthelme, "The Emerald," *Sixty Stories*, p. 410.

8 The statement appears in an interview with J. D. O'Hara, "Donald Barthelme: The Art of Fiction LXVI," *Paris Review* 80 (Summer 1979): 199.

9 Donald Barthelme, "The Explanation," *City Life* (New York: Bantam Books, 1971), p. 80.

10 See too, Barthelme's comment in an interview with Jerome Klinkowitz in *The New Fiction: Interviews with Innovative American Writers,* ed. Joe David Bellamy (Urbana: University of Illinois Press, 1974), p. 52: "This new reality [he is speaking of collage], in the best case, may be or imply a comment on the other reality from which it came, and may be also much else. It's an *itself*, if it's successful."

11 See my book, *Middle Grounds: Studies in Contemporary American Fiction* (Philadelphia: University of Pennsylvania Press, 1987).

12 The statement appears in an interview conducted by Larry McCaffery and included in *Anything Can Happen: Interviews with Contemporary American Novelists,* ed. Tom LeClair and Larry McCaffery (Urbana: University of Illinois Press, 1983), p. 38.

13 Pierre Thévenaz, *What is Phenomenology? and Other Essays,* ed. James M. Edie (Chicago: Quadrangle Books, 1962), p. 50.

14 See too "The Catechist," a quasi-dialogic story, in *Sadness* (New York: Bantam Books, 1974), with its reference to "the works of Scheler, who holds that love is an aspect of phenomenological knowledge" (p. 121).

15 Donald Barthelme, "City Life," *Sixty Stories,* p. 159.

ROBERT COOVER

. . . . . .

Aesop's Forest

Deep in the gloom of the forest, the old lion lies dying in his cave. His ancient hide drapes the royal bones like a worn blanket, rheum clots his warm nose, his eyes are dimmed with cataracts. Yet, even in such decline, the familiar hungers stir in him still, rippling in tremors across his body from time to time like mice scurrying under a tattered carpet, his appetite for power outlasting his power to move, his need for raw flesh biting deeper than his decaying teeth. "I would be king!" he rumbles wheezily, his roar muddied with catarrh.

"Eh? Eh?" asks the fox insolently from the mouth of the cave.

"Damn your eyes. Bring me meat."

He does not trust the fox, of course, but on the other hand he has never trusted anyone, and the fox at least is useful. It is a wise policy, he knows, to keep potential enemies where you can either watch them or eat them. Unfortunately, that now means keeping them pretty close (even now, though the mouth of the cave seems empty of his scrawny silhouette, he cannot be sure the devil's gone) and so, fearing seditious alliances just beyond the reach of his shriveling senses, he has reduced his court to one, this fox, whose very notoriety for wiliness has isolated the wretch from any serious contenders for his power. The fox, a likely victim of any new regime, serves him because it is in the fox's own best interest to do so, though such bitter truths—and his helpless reliance on them—sadden the old lion. He has roared against them all his life, knowing that some truths are just not worth having, and now they have returned to haunt him, as though the instinct for survival were itself the ultimate disgrace. A sigh rips through him like the windy echo of some half-remembered rage: his hatred of duplicity.

There was a time when such treacherous lickspits, leading him to trapped prey, would have served him as prior savories: dispassionately he would have slit their bellies with his fierce claws, nuzzled in the hot wound as though to caress them with their own culpability, and, staring resolutely into their craven eyes already glazing over, his cool majestic gaze the last thing on this earth their fading sight would see, would have eaten their still-pulsing hearts, just appetizers for the feast to follow, juicy morals for the hunchback's fables. He who plots against another, the fabler would say then, plots his own destruction, and if this was a truth the world felt it could depend upon, it was a truth founded upon his own powerful claws and sharp white teeth, his incorruptible detachment. It is this—his sovereign independence, his lonely freedom—that he now misses most. As must all. For if he was once the source of all their truths, now, crippled, sinking into dry rot, reduced to begging from a thieving liar, he still is: it is truth itself that is changing. Yes, yes, he thinks, we take *everything* with us when we go.

"Who, *what—?!*" Ah. That dumb stag. Vainglory in the flesh. The more or less succulent flesh. The old king, tired eyes asquint, lies low, settling his jowls behind his paws. He's seen this one before, smelled him before. That funk: the poor fool must still have his stripes, and yet here he is, serving himself up again, will wonders never cease. "I tell you, when he caught hold of your ear last time," he hears the fox whispering, nudging the stag forward, "it was to give you his last advice before he died." Such big eyes he has: eyes for looking where forbidden . . . . "It is you he wants as our next king: your horns scare the snakes, he told me so!" Inwardly, waiting patiently, the old lion grins. Have to admire the sly bastard: in his way, he's an artist. "You see? He's smiling! He's pleased you're here! Now lean forward and tell him that you accept your great responsibilities!"

Death is everywhere in Aesop's dark forest. Asses are drowning under sodden loads, vixens are being torn to pieces by maddened dogs, swans sacrificed for the sake of their songs. Cats are eating cocks. Kites frogs. "What an unexpected treat has come our way!" they cry, descending. All have butcher's work to do. Eagles and vixens devour each other's young, newborn apes are murdered by their mothers, hens by serpents they themselves have hatched. Partridges, goats, doves betray their own to preying men, nannies are butchered to doctor asses. At the request of horses, boars are slaughtered: yet happiness is elusive. Snakes are driven to suicide by the stinging of wasps, elephants by gnats in their ears, hares by their own weariness, as though it were time's way of solving difficult problems. "The moral is that it is too late to be sorry after you have let things go wrong," the fabler explains, but the fact is it is always too late. Lambs are being devoured by wolves, mice by weasels, fawns by bears, nightingales by hawks, and all by the patient intransigent vultures. Even lions.

The news of the old despot's decline, spread by the fox, stirs ambition in some (a lot of empty-headed people rejoice over the wrong things, needless to say) but provokes skepticism in most: with that fox things are not always what they seem, most here in the forest know that all too well, having learned from painful experience, once bitten and all that, no, seeing is believing. Not too close, though: there are a lot of bones around the cave mouth, and tracks leading up but none leading away.

The fabler watches the watchers watch. It is comforting to the wretched, he knows, to see others worse off than themselves. The victor vanquished, the mighty fallen—it's a kind of narcotic, this pageant, numbing for the cowardly their common wound of mortality. The fabler envies them this easy consolation. In him, something more fundamental is dying with the dying lion, and just when he needs it most, his own death approaching inexorably and apace. Not so much the courage, no, for though his is not so lofty perhaps, being that bitter grit of the misfit, the freak, the taunted cripple, it is no less mettlesome. Not the fabled power either, far from it, he has often reveled in forcing humiliating compromise upon the old tyrant, throwing him into bad company, jamming thorns in his paws and enfeebling love in his heart, snatching him up in nets and cages to spoil his appetite with a moral lesson or two, chiding him with avarice and brutality. Sour grapes? Perhaps, especially now at life's and wit's end when he could use a little last-minute clout, but political power as such has never held the fabler's fancy. Hasn't he turned his crooked back on it all his life, abandoning the court life again and again for his dark uncivil forest? Yes, freedom has been his one desire, freedom and—and this is what the old lion's death means to him, this is what he fears to lose, even as he's losing it—his ruthless solitude.

As though to dramatize his sense of loss, the fox, that cartload of mischief, emerges from the cave mouth now, swaggering presumptuously, his red tail on high, a bloody heart between his jaws. Not the lion's heart, of course—a consumptive rumble from the cave behind the charlatan attests irritably to that—yet it might as well be. That lion's kingly roar once caused havoc at three hundred miles, women miscarried, men's teeth fell out; now it flutters thinly from the cave mouth like wisps of dirty fleece. In the end, crushed by fortune, even the strongest become the playthings of cowards: this is the message of the dripping heart in the fox's grinning jaws. And it enrages him. Not the message, but the grin. It is his, the fabler's, own.

There is a grisly tension building in the forest, he can feel it as he stalks the cave mouth, the stag's heart in his jowls like a gag, bitter foretaste of the impending disaster. Well, foretasted, forearmed, he reminds himself with a giddiness that brings a grimace to his clamped jaws—for how *does* one arm himself against the sort of nightmare about to descend here? Eyes blink and glitter behind tree trunks, clumps of grass, leaves, heavy stones: in them he sees avarice, panic, vanity, distrust, lust for glory and for flesh, hatred, hope, all the fabled terrors and appetites of the mortal condition, drawn together here now for one last demented frolic. The louring forest is literally atwinkle with that madness that attends despair.

Two eyes in particular absorb his gaze: the dark squinty lopsided orbs of the little brown humpback, come to hurl himself like a clown into the final horror—for isn't it the cripple who always wants to lead off the dance? The grotesque grotesqued. That loathsome monstrosity now huddles swarthily behind a pale boulder, hugging it as if afraid it might fly away from him, his knee-knobs stuck out like a locust's. A turnip with teeth, he's been fairly called, a misshapen pisspot. His hump rises behind his flapping ears like a second head, but one stripped of its senses as though struck mute and blind with terror. Or wisdom, same thing. What that snub-nosed bandy-legged piece of human garbage has never appreciated is how much they're two of a kind, and how much the fraud owes him for his bloated reputation. The fox has been the butt of too many horseshit anecdotes not to have grasped a moral the fabler seems to have missed: that we ridicule in others what we most despise in ourselves.

The humpback lets go the boulder now and hops, toad-like, behind a stunted laurel. Headed this way, it seems. Can't leave well enough alone. Or ill enough. Perhaps he dreams still of some last-minute escape from the calamity that awaits him, awaits them all in this airless stinkhole of a so-called forest. Well, if he hopes for help from the sorehead behind him, still grumbling in his tubercular senility about the missing heart ("You can stop looking, he didn't have one," he'd told the motheaten old geezer, talking with his mouth full, "anybody who'd come twice into a lion's den and within reach of his paws has to be ninety percent asshole, and that's what you just ate . . ."), then the fool's in for a bitter experience.

As the fabler advances through the penumbral forest, creeping, bounding, stumbling over roots, crouching under bushes, zigging and zagging in the general direction of the lion's den, he stirs a wide commotion. There are scurryings, flutterings, rustlings all around. Twigs pop, pebbles scatter, leaves and feathers float on the air like the tatters of muffled rumors, stifled panic, as though the forest were beset on all sides—and from within as well—by strange and unexpected dangers. Wild rumors. Hopes. Mad ambitions.

Much of this the fabler reads in all the shit he squats and tumbles in: the hard nuggets of avidity and pride, puddled funk, noisome pretense, the frantic scatter of droppings unloosed on the run in uncertainty and confusion—that eloquent text of the forest floor. He knows it well, he's had his nose in it since the day he was born. "Has he lost something?" people would ask. "He's like a hog rooting in mud." He was pretending to be studying the ground, of course, in order to pretend he could straighten up if he wanted to, an imposter twice over. But out of adversity, wisdom. Once a famous Hellenic philosopher, his master in the dark days of his enslaved youth, had asked him why it was, when we shat, we so often turned around to examine our own turds, and he'd told that great sage the story of the king's loose-living son who one day, purging his belly, passed his own wits, inducing a like fear in all men since. "But you don't have to worry, sire," he'd added, "you've no wit to shit." Well, cost him a beating, but it was worth it, even if it was all a lie. For the real reason we look back of course is to gaze for a moment in awe and wonder at what we've made—it's the closest we ever come to being at one with the gods.

Now what he reads in this analecta of turds is rampant disharmony and anxiety: it's almost suffocating. Boundaries are breaking down: eagles are shitting with serpents, monkeys with dolphins, kites with horses, fleas with crayfish, it's as though there were some mad violent effort here to link the unlinkable, cross impossible abysses. And there's some dejecta he's not sure he even recognizes. That foul mound could be the movement of a hippogriff, for example, this slime that of a basilisk or a harpy. His owns bowels, convulsed by all this ripe disorder, fill suddenly with a plunging weight, as though heart, hump, and all might have just descended there: he squats hastily, breeches down (well, Zeus sent Modesty in through the asshole, so may she exit there as well), to leave his own urgent message on the forest floor. Ah! yes! a man must put his hand to his wealth and use it, example is—grunt!—better than precept. Just so . . . . But quality, not quantity. Inconsistency is harmful in everything, though no forethought, of course, can prevail against destiny. Oof! Easy. Accomplishments are not judged by speed but by completeness. With what measure you mete shall it be measured to you again, and so on. That's better. He wipes himself with his soiled breeches, leaves them behind. Doesn't need them here anyway. When in Delphi, as they say . . .

Not all here in Aesop's troubled forest are pleased, of course, to have their miserable excrement read so explicitly. It makes many of them feel vulnerable and exposed, especially at a time when all the comforting old covenants are dissolving, and no one knows for certain who they are anymore, or who they're supposed to fuck or eat. Can one not even take a homely shit without worrying about the consequences, they ask, are there no limits? But of course that's just the point, there *are* no limits any longer, that's the message of the old king's desperate condition, this pointy-headed freak's intrusion here, his frantic bare-ass bob through these dark brambly thickets at the core. Though he talks wolfy enough at times, he rarely comes this deep, skirting the edges mostly where the shepherds keep their sheep, plummeting in here only when lust or terror overtakes him. What beast here wouldn't raise its tail for the hunchback, painful as the experience can be, if that's all it would take to resume the old peaceful carnage? But, alas, it's plain to see it's not rut that's brought the fabler back—that heavy wattle he's dragging through the pine needles and dead leaves between his crooked shanks is, by itself in its gross wilt, cause enough for panic here.

So it is that birds screech, beetles scurry, moles burrow in blind desperation, as Aesop makes his way toward the lion's den. Stupidity, fear, deceit, carnality, treason break out in the forest like scabies. There is the sharpening of tusks, the popping of toads, breath-sucking, the casting of long shadows. Suicidal hares and frogs hurl themselves out of their element, elephants eat their own testicles, worms blind themselves so as not to see the approaching catastrophe. As Aesop reaches the cave mouth, the fox slinks aside, lips curled back, baring his teeth above the stag's heart cradled bloodily in his paws. He snarls. Clouds of fleas, gnats, lice, mosquitos explode from foul-smelling holes in the forest floor like a sudden pestilence. Wells clog with bewildered beasts fallen they know not where. Storms rumble and winds whistle. Flames lap at an eagle's nest. And from high in the sky, a frightened hump-backed tortoise falls.

The fox lies stretched out across the cave mouth, as though to define certain boundaries, or invent them, gnawing, ears perked, at the stag's heart. Inside, the fabler squats in the dirt, his hump resting against the cave wall, gazing morosely at the dying lion, a much sorrier sight than he'd anticipated. "It stinks in here," he says. The lion snorts sourly, cocks one rheumy eye above his paw. "Nothing's so perfect," he grumbles, "that it's not subject to some pisant's criticism." In the old days he'd have simply stepped on him, popped the runt like a blister. Now he's not even sure he sees him. "Misfortune stinks, crookback. Dying stinks. If you don't like it, why do you wallow in it?"

"That's not why I'm here." He stares out past the fox at the dusky forest, which seems to have brightened slightly, as seen from within this dreary cave. An illusion, like hope itself. It's darkening by the second out there. "How is it you've taken up with this miserable blot on creation?"

"Expediency."

"I expected more from you."

"Our expectations are often deceived."

He accepts this continuous mockery though it pains him. Somewhere just below the hump, in fact. What is he doing here in this shithole, taking this kind of abuse? And from an old friend once honored above all others—even his shabby new alliance with the fox is a kind of taunt, a way of rubbing the fabler's nose in his most craven cynicism, just when he needed something nobler than that. Courage, in a word. Proud example. "I've been condemned."

The fox seems to snicker at this. The lion too would appear to have a grin on his face. The floor of the cave is rough and damp, reassuring in its rude discomfort, but somewhere water is dripping, echoing cavernously as though there might be a leak in the remote recesses of his own skull. He shudders as if to shake himself out of here, but he knows he can never leave again. They'll have to come and kill him in this place. Mangy and decrepit as it's become. Sometimes in the past he has managed to stay away from his forest for days on end, imagining himself a man like any other, yet even then these creatures had a way of haunting his consciousness, lingering just beneath it like stars behind the light of the sun, visible only from the bottom of a well. That well he's always dumping them down as a cushion against his own clumsiness. His own attraction to abysses. "Which flap," the lion rumbles wheezily, "were you wagging this time?"

He shrugs his hump. "Sin against Apollo." This time the fox does snicker, standing to scratch a flea behind his ear, or pretending to. "Go have a fit and tumble in a hole," the vicious schemer once said, all too prophetically. His fate now, by decree, he the fabler become his own goat. "I told them the truth, they called it sacrilege."

"Same old story," sighed the lion.

"Same old story."

"Natures never change. You're a meddlesome foul-mouthed stiff-necked exhibitionist. You remind me of that story of yours about the wild ass and the tame ass."

"Well, but the real moral of that one was—"

"The real moral was they were *both* asses, just the same. What did you think you'd gain by taunting fools?"

"I don't know. A laugh or two?" What does he have left, if not the truth? It has shaped, shaped by his misshapen body, his entire life. One thing about being a monster, it puts you in touch with the cosmos, biggest humpback of all. "I wanted to make the truth so transparent even these pig-headed provincials could see it, that's all." He liked to think of it as a kind of remembering, as though all men were animals in some way, or had been.

"Yes, and turtles want to fly, too," the old king rumbles. "There's only one truth, my friend. If you've forgotten what it is, come a little closer and let me give you a few pointed reminders." A mere reflex. The old fellow hasn't eaten the garbage he's lying in. He laps his jowls with a tongue so dry it sounds like the spreading of sand on stone.

Anyway, it's . . . "Impossible. There's a barrier . . . ." At least there *was* . . . . Has it somehow been breached?

"If there's a moral to be had, fabler, it can be done . . . ."

He'd always thought of that distance between them as ontological and absolute, but now—he stirs uncomfortably. He's rarely come this deep before. The fox seems to have let one, his own commentary on the truth no doubt. He bats the air irritably, his hump scraping the wall behind: "Filthy bastard!"

"He does that from time to time just to let me know he's still here," the lion grumbles drowsily. "You get used to it. Familiarity, as they say . . . ."

Not they. He. The rich man and the tanner. Or better yet: the fox and the lion, almost forgot that one. Yet now, these words, too: only an echo . . . . He realizes he hasn't told many fables on the evanescence of truth, brain-rot as the universal achievement. The old lion snorts ruefully. He seems to be drifting off. The hunchback trembles. They'll be here soon.

He got away from them once, but they'll find him. Even from inside the cave, he can hear the turbulence out at the edge. He squeezes shut his eyes. Sometimes it feels almost like a dream. As though he might still be back on Samos, living with that fatheaded philosopher and his lascivious slave-fucking wife, the one who liked to say that even her arse had eyes. Any minute, he thinks, I might wake up to a beating or a bath . . . .

The tortoise, tumbling through the air, wags his arms frantically. If he just works at this hard enough, he knows, he can do it, persistence has paid off before, he's famous for it. In order to try to free his mind from extraneous matters, such as the rising panic which is threatening to freeze him up entirely and stop his wings, as they should perhaps now be called, from functioning at all, he tries to concentrate on the splendid view he has from up here of the forest, a view few of its inhabitants have been privileged to enjoy, and one he himself will probably forego in the future, even if he does manage to get the hang of this flying thing on this one occasion. Like he told Zeus, meaning no offense, though unfortunately that's how it was taken, there's no place like home. If you don't get there too fast. But his effort to concentrate is frustrated somewhat by the way the forest keeps looping around him, appearing over his head one moment, beneath his tail the next: probably this has something to do with his flying problem.

Why did he want to get up here in the first place? A question he might well ponder, since the second place, rushing up at him like the moral to a foreshortened fable, is all but imponderable. He always tries to judge every situation from its outcome, not its beginning, though each, as he knows, flapping wildly, contains the other, ambition being both goal and goad. But what *was* that ambition? Was it aesthetic? Philosophical? The pursuit of some sort of absolute worldview (already slipping away from him, he notes, as the forest loops by again, losing now in structural clarity what it is rapidly gaining in detail)? A moral imperative? The spirit of rivalry? A rebellion against boundaries? The desire for travel? Who knows? Why anything? Why is the pig's belly bare or the magpie bald? Why does the crab have its eyes behind? Why does the lizard nod its head or the dying swan sing? Who gives a bloody shit? Should *he* be singing? Why are turtles dumb? Why are their heads flat and their shells hard? But not hard enough? Why has that goddamn eagle left him up here—flap! flap! flap!—*all alone?*

When Aesop opens his eyes, he finds himself lying under a tree in a green, peaceful field, where all kinds of flowers bloom amid the green grass and where a little stream wanders among the neighboring trees. The most savage thing in sight is a grazing cow. A gentle zephyr blows and the leaves of the trees around about are stirred and exhale a sweet and soothing breath: he draws in a deep lungful, as a great relief sweeps over him. What a terrible dream I was having, he thinks. Those shits were going to kill me! He still feels vaguely troubled (it seemed so *real!*), but the stream is whispering, the cicadas are humming from the branches, the song of birds of many kinds and many haunts can be heard, the nightingale prolongs her plaintive song, the branches murmur musically in a sympathetic refrain, on the slenderest branch of a pine tree the stirring of the breeze mocks the blackbird's call, and mingling with it all in harmony, Echo, the mother of mimesis, utters her answering cries, all of it resolving into a kind of rhythmic tinkle, reassuring in its simplicity like the drip of rainwater after a shower. Better a servant in safety, he reminds himself, than a master in danger, though at first this comes out, better a savory never than born a masker in a manger. Which doesn't make much sense. Is it some kind of oracle? And why is that cow standing there with her teats in the fire and plucked crows in her antlers with meat in their beaks? The trees' breath, he now notices, is not as sweet as he'd thought at first, and what the stream is whispering (how is it he fell asleep out here in this open field with his breeches off?) seems to be some suggestion about staying in line or alive, or playing the—

"What? *What—?!*" He starts up in alarm, opens his eyes a second time. Ah, it is the fox, that treacherous foul-mouth, whispering something in his ear about flaying the lion and wearing his hide as a disguise. "Don't wait until danger is at hand!" He turns his head away. He must have dozed off. But it seemed so *real!* "Fuck these useless shows of strength, humpback! Remember the fable of the hunting dog! Use your wits!"

Perhaps a *third* time, he thinks, straining to pop his eyes wider open. He uses his fingers to press his lids apart. But they *are* apart. Is he dreaming that he's pressing his fingers to his lids? Alas . . . "It's been tried," he mumbles, trying his voice out.

"Only by asses. The morals of those stories are stay out of the wind and keep your mouth shut."

Would it work? Not likely. He can already hear his pursuers. "We were told to get the one in the lionskin," they'd be saying. "Why am I even listening to a double-crossing liar like you?"

"Because we understand each other. I wouldn't even be here without you, I know that, even if the others don't. You think I'd want to shit you now? Anyway, it's impossible. Think about it."

"He'd betray himself if he could figure out how to do it and profit by it at the same time," the lion growls from inside his paws. "Get back to your post, stinkbreath, before I decide to tear that red tail off at the root and sweep out this stinking boghouse with it!" He watches the miserable beggar slink, smirking no doubt (can't see a damned thing), back to the cave mouth. The hunchback stands to piss against the wall, at least that's what it sounds like. "And don't be fooled, fabler. Wit will *not* get the better of strength. Ever. That's just a fairytale for weaklings. Helps them die easier."

"But I can't outrun them and I can't eat them," the dwarf whines from the other side of his hump as he splashes against the wall. "What am I going to *do?*"

"What you can. There's an inscription here . . . ." The old lion knows, in the end, he is going to have to abide by it himself. If puffed-up toads and flying turtles are ridiculous, humble lions are worse. He shakes his mane. If he could just lift his jaws up off the floor. ". . . At the oracle . . . ."

"I've seen it." The hunchback is wiping that monstrous engine of his on his shirt. "But I don't know who I am and I don't know where to start."

"You know more than you know," the lion rumbles solemnly, and the fox snarls: "There he is!"

"What—?! *Who?*" squeaks the fabler, shrinking back against the wall he's just fouled.

"It's for me," says the lion, rearing his head up at last. It sways a bit like an old drunk's, but he holds it up there. This is not going to be easy, he thinks. But had he ever supposed it would be? "My herald, as you might say. My advice to you is to take a long walk."

"But—!"

"*GET OUT!*" he roars, and the hunchback, in panic, goes lurching out on all fours, nipped mischievously in the tail by the fox as he scrambles past. "Now come here, slyboots, I want to show you something. We're going to let you play the hero."

A plaintive ascendant whine silences the unruly forest. Flappings, snortings, rustlings, scurryings cease. The black-hooded magpie, death's acknowledged messenger, lowers his gaping beak and from his perch above the cave mouth shrieks: "*The king is dying! The king is dying!* Scrawk! *Long live the king!*" A kind of communal gasp sweeps through the forest like a sudden brief gust of wind, then dies away. The magpie hacks raucously as though trying to spit. "*Miserable morsels—harck!* tweet!—*mortals who, like leaves, at one moment—whawk!—flame with life and at another weakly*—prreet! *caw!—perish down the drain of Eternity in the mighty whirl of dust, the hour of*—wheep!—*equal portions has* arrived!" A furtive scrabbling and fluttering ripples now through the forest like gathering applause, from the outside in, rushing toward the center as though beaters were assaulting the periphery. Though only the magpie is visible (even the fox has disappeared), the area around the cave mouth seems suddenly congested, aquiver with terror and anticipation. And appetite. "*Cree! Cree! Creatures of a day, be quiet and have patience, not even the gods fright—purrr*-wheet!—*fight against the child within us! We go our—WARRCKK!—ways in the same honor already for*—caw! caw!—*forfeit!*" The magpie's long bright tail drops like a falling axe. Is it over? Is the tyrant already dead? Heads peek out from behind foliage. Insects hover nervously. Monkeys swing closer, swing back again. A snake uncoils from a limb. A boar in the underbrush snorts and paws the ground. A crab sallies forth, eyes to the rear. "*Either death is a state of nothingness and utter*—squawk!—*or better never to have been born!*" the oracular magpie cries, and parrots, cats, crickets, and hermaphroditic hyenas scream their assent. The entire twilit forest is alive with beasts surging furtively toward the dying lion's cave. "*Must not all things be swallowed up in*—shreek!—*a single night?* Just SO! Crrrr-*AWKK!*" As though in fear of being left behind, the animals at this signal burst from their hiding places and rush, squealing and bawling, toward the cave mouth—but just as suddenly pull up short. The old king stands there in the fading light, muscles rippling, fiery mane blowing in the breeze, eyes feverish with fury. With fierce deliberation, he steps forward, his teeth bared. Has this been a trap? "*Only one!*" shrieks the magpie. Ah. But a lion . . .

We found the fabulist at last in the Temple of the Muses, clearly deranged, howling about "death in the forest" and "the revenge of dungbeetles," and bounding around arse-high with his nose to the stone floor like a toad looking for water. After having abused us earlier, while still in prison, with filthy tales about the rape of widows and children ("A man put it in me with a long sinewy red thing that ran in and out," he'd leered:

had he been trying to seduce us with these simpering obscenities?) as well as racist slurs, insults against our fathers, and seditious threats to revenge himself upon us, even after he was dead, this grotesque little Egyptian, or Babylonian, was now, in one of our own temples, berating us with sacrilege, shrieking something truly offensive about "God with shit in his eye!" It was almost, we thought, as though he'd come here to our city *seeking* to die.

He was not easy to catch or, once caught, to subdue. As we chased him about the temple, wrestling with him, losing him, catching him again, he kept making brutish noises, now squawking, now roaring, now barking or bleating or braying, as though he were all these beasts at once, or thought himself to be, and at times we did feel somewhat like Menelaus grappling with the inconstant and malodorous Proteus. His stunted limbs were too rubbery to hold, his pot too sleek—finally we caught him by the ears (his Achilles' heel, as it were) and, twisting them, extracted from him a more human howl.

As we dragged him toward his site of execution, his madness took on a subtler, yet no less bizarre form. He grew suddenly serene, almost flaccid in our many-handed grip, and commenced to lecture us on the evils we were presumably bringing upon ourselves with this action. "Not much time will be gained, O Delphians," he proclaimed shrilly, as his pointed head bounced along on the uneven ground, "in return for the evil name which you will get from the detractors of the city, who will say that you killed Aesop, a wise man; for it will be said of me, that I never did any wrong, never gave any ill advice to any man; but that I labored all my life long to excite to virtue those who frequented me." Such pomposities, emerging reedily from that twisted liver-lipped mouth with its scattered teeth, under the squashed-up nose and squinty eyes, neither of which ever seemed to be looking at the same thing at the same time, struck us as so ludicrous we were all driven to fits of convulsive laughter, and nearly lost our grip on him again. "Fancy such a warty little thing as you making such a big noise!" we hooted.

"I prophesy to you who are my murderers, that immediately after my departure punishment far heavier than that you have inflicted on me will surely await you!" he squealed then, and we reminded him, laughing, that braggarts are easily silenced, as he was about to discover. "People who brag to those who know them must expect to be laughed at, gypsie, evil tricks don't fool honest men! Such play-acting has cost many a man his life, you will not be the first or last to perish of it!" We hauled the droll little monster up to the edge of the cliff and prepared to heave him over. Some of us had his arms, some his horny feet. "Destiny is not to be interfered with, melonhead—if you had any real wisdom you'd know that! A man should courageously face whatever is going to happen to him and not try to be clever, for he will—ha ha!—not escape it!"

"Wait!" he begged, gigantic tears rolling down the bumps of his temples and off his earflaps. He seemed prepared to recant at last and, though it wouldn't save his life, right his wrongs against us before he died. We set him on his bandy legs and stepped back, blocking any possible escape. He cocked his head impudently to one side. "Let me tell you a story," he said. Ye gods, the little freak was incorrigible. It has been wisely observed, natures remain just as they first appear. When you do a bad man a service, some sage has said, all you can hope for is that he will not add injury to ingratitude, but even this hope was to prove in vain. "There was this old farmer," he piped, "who had never seen the city and decided to hitch up the donkeys and go see it before he died. But a storm came up and they got lost among the cliffs. 'Oh God, what have I done to die like this,' he wept (and here *he* wept mockingly), 'in the company of these miserable jackasses?'" We rushed at him, enraged at such impiety, but he stopped us again with a wild bewitching screech, lurching forward as though stabbed from behind, and we fell back, momentarily startled. "A man once fell in love with his own daughter," he wailed as though in great pain, rolling his lopsided eyes, and pointing at all of us—what?! what was he saying? "So he shipped his old lady off to the country and forced himself on his daughter. She said, as I say to you, men of Delphi: 'This is an unholy thing you are doing! I would rather have submitted to a hundred good men than be fucked by you!'" We flung ourselves at this loathsome obscenity, but before we could reach him, he hurled himself, cackling derisively, off the cliff, flapping his stunted little arms as though the fool thought he might fall up instead of down.

He has just, with what dignity remains, his knees weak and threatening to buckle, stepped forth from the cave mouth to confront his erstwhile citizenry, when something whistles past his ear and explodes—*SPLAT!*—beside him, startling him just enough to tip him over. What an irony, he muses, shrugging tortoise shell out of his ear, nearly got him before he could even get started. As it is, his jaw is back on the ground again, his paws trapped under his belly. His rear legs seemed to have held, but he is not sure what overall impression this position makes. Perhaps they will think he is crouching, preparing to spring. More likely not.

Though he cannot see them, they are all out there, he knows, all the rejected, the trod-upon, the bitten and the stung, the ridiculed, the overladen, all of God's spittle, lusting now for this compensatory kill. The great equalizer that makes their own poor lives and death less odious. Let them come. He will have one last glorious fray, one final sinking of tooth and claw into palpitating flesh and gut, a great screaming music of rage and terror, before he dies. If he can just get his feet under him again. How was it he used to do that? He can feel his rump begin to sway, can hear them start to shift and mumble in the clearing down below. His aide-de-camp has slipped out of sight, of course. He has instructed the fox in how to kill him quickly when the time comes, when he's too weak to fight on. He doesn't want to die slowly, or ignobly. Or seem to. He has appealed to the fox's own ambition: let the opposition cut itself up, and then, when he gets the nod, move in as the decisive and heroic liberator. The wily bastard actually seemed moved: perhaps there's hope for him yet.

The sullen hesitant hush is shattered suddenly by another long shrieking whine from the intransigent magpie. "*He who hesitates*—SCRAWKK! —*flourish only for an omen*—hrreet!—*MOMENT!*"

And, just as his rump tips and smacks the ground, they are on him: wolves, boars, apes, moles, toads, dancing camels, plucked daws, serpents, spiders, snails, incestuous cocks and shamming cats, hares, asses, bats, bears, swarms of tongueless gnats, fleas, flies and murderous wasps, bears, beavers, doves, martins, lice and dungbeetles, mice and weasels, owls, crabs, and goats, hedgehogs and ticks, kites, frogs, peacocks and locusts, all the fabled denizens of the forest, all intent on electing him into the great democracy of the dead. A boar wounds him with a blow from its flashing tusks as he sprawls there, paws high, a bull gores him in the belly, a mosquito stings his nose, a cowardly ass kicks him in the forehead.

But even as they convene upon his body, something stirs in the enfeebled lion, something like joy or pride or even love. The rage of. His battered head rears and roars, his pierced muscles flex, his blunted teeth and claws find flesh to rend, bones to crush. The air is thick suddenly with blood and feathers and smashed carapaces, shrieks and howls, mighty thrashings about. He even, for a splendid moment, feels young again, that renowned warrior of old, king of the beasts. He no longer knows which animals he's embracing in this final exaltation—one eye is gone, the other clouded, an ear is clogged with bees, his hide's in tatters—but it doesn't matter. It is life itself he is clutching bloodily to his breast in this, his last delicious moment on earth, and it's the most fun he's had since he sneezed a cat.

But then, through the flurry of beaks and antlers and the blood in his eye, he sees the fox skulking toward him, head ducked, an insolent smirk on his skinny face. "No, wait!" he roars. "*Not yet!*" But he should have known better, take pity on such a creature, you get what you deserve. And what he gets is, too soon, oh much too soon, the treacherous villain at his throat. "You *fool!*" he gasps, while he's still voice left. "I can't help it," snickers the miserable wretch, nuzzling in. "It's just my—hee hee! —nature. . . ." With a final swipe of his paw (he's being invaded from below, he knows, a seeding of teeth in his plowed-up nether parts as though to found a city there, but it's ceased to matter), he slashes the fox open from heart to groin, then hugs him close, locking his jaws around his nape, their organs mingling like scrambled morals. "It's all shit anyway," he seems to hear the devil grunt as his spine snaps—one final treachery! He feels then as though he's falling, and he only wishes, hanging on as the light dies and the earth spins, that his friend the fabler were here to whisper in his ear, the one without the bees in it, one last word, not so much of wisdom, as of communion. Just so . . . What? What? "*SKWWAARRRK!*" replies the magpie, as the forest extinguishes itself around him.

MARC CHÉNETIER

. . . . . .

Ideas of Order at Delphi
(though at first this comes out, "disorderly ideas fell")

"Trop de preuves fatigue la vérité."—Georges Braque

"How does one cut an axe-handle with an axe?"—John Yau, "Chinese Villanelle"

"¡Ratón maldito!
que no se alimentaba de otra cosa
que de roerle siempre verso y prosa.
. . .
"¡Qué disgracia la mía!
(El literato exclama): Ya estoy harto
de escribir para gente roedora . . . ."

—Tomás de Iriarte, "El erudito y el ratón," Fábulas Literarias

All of the following happened, in this precise order. It is "true."

(1) *Spring 1985*: "Do I feel up to writing an essay on Robert Coover's work for a collection including an unpublished piece" by this author, whose work I relish and admire? I am asked by the editor of this volume.

I do not, never did, but am willing to give it another try, I answer.

(2) *15 September 1985*: A text arrives, this morning, in the mail. It is signed by Robert Coover. It is entitled "Aesop's Forest."

(3) *Later the same day*: I read it. I love it.

(4) *16 November 1985*. 10 A.M.: It is a warm and lovely, crisp autumn day. A friend is in town. We go for a walk. End up following the Left Bank of the Seine in the sun, chatting. The Pont-Neuf looms ahead, on our right. Christo has had it wrapped up in tarps. The bridge is teeming with Parisians who had never taken a minute to look at it up close before. They sound their memory to try and remember what it looks like when bare.

Many "bouquinistes" have opened their boxes over the parapets. Our stroll slows down as we sample the stacks of second-hand books. The third box contains an old, yellowed, and dog-eared volume on top of one pile. It is entitled *Aesop's Fables*.

(5) *Same day.* 11 A.M.: A long line of people meanders from the door of the Grand-Palais, waiting to enter the exhibition we wanted to see. We turn back, head for galleries, walk into one: engravings, black and white, lovely. After La Fontaine.

(6) *Later.* Back to work. In the afternoon mail, a set of proofs to be corrected. Enclosed, courtesy of the publisher, is a sheet of yellow bristol divided into two columns: to the left, the curlicues and chinese hats of "signs" accompanied by their "meanings"; to the right, vertically set is a short text, full of typos, covered with circles and slashes and triple lines and more chinese hats, immigrants from the left column, a text that runs parallel to the "marginal corrections." It tells of a goatherd that breaks one of his goats' horns and is afraid to tell of his act. "Please do not tell the master, cried the lad—You silly boy, the goat replied, the horn will speak though I be silent." This, I am told at the bottom of the card, is excerpted "From Aesop's Fables."

All of this really happened. Is it "true"?

What is the historical truth of such a sequence, is there—outside of this essay—historical coherence in this string of "coincidences"? What is the nature of this succession of moments when I felt transformed into Eleanor Norton[1] or made over into the protagonist of a new book by the title of *Origin of the Cooverists*, the freakish offspring of the adulterous copulations of Ralph Himebaugh and Mrs. Oedipa Maas?[2] I was doomed, from day one, from the moment I was extended this invitation to fiction making, raw, teleological, catching, contagious. "This, then, was his problem: beginning. And having begun: avoiding resolutions. Thus there were worse jokes his blood might have played on him. Its message might have read: All beginnings imply an apocalypse."[3]

I Coover and Myth

I

"Aesop's Forest" is the story of "a time when all the comforting old covenants are dissolving." And indeed, "covenant" may be allowed to stand unobtrusively in the midst of a paradigm that includes Kant's "regulative ideas" and Jeremy Bentham's "necessary fictions," the cohort of myths and abstract constructs with which men and women organize their world and recreate its coherence as their perceptions of it change under the influence of periodic epistemological dislocations. As Nietzsche used to put it, "fear bids us know," and the perennial longing for order commands more or less conscious discursive assemblages capable of accounting for a modicum of "meaning." Always read "fabrication" or "engineering" under "making" in "making sense."

We are born readers, one and all, however illiterate, decipherers who demand that the text of our existence in the world cohere around a set of provisionally trustworthy metaphors. We call them "relation," "movement," "space," "time," "God," "history": they are the "as ifs," the stories, the fables that we use to translate the rough data of our senses into the shapely curves of our desires, the instruments of our reassurance, the buffers of our anxieties and anguishes. They help us know. They provide —weave—the garments with which to cover our existential nakedness. They constitute what meager handles we may give ourselves on what we then call "the real." Meaning is an activity and creation is story. "Only we have created the world that concerns man," says Nietzsche in *The Gay Science*, and Valéry adds: "In the beginning was the Joke. And indeed all stories deepen into fables. Everything invariably begins with tales. Genesis, the exposition of the System of the World: birth in a cabbage."[4] Genesis. Genealogy. Etymology, too: turn to Latin and *fabula* will tell you of "conversation," "narrative," "tale." Turn to Greek and *myth* delivers "speech" and "tale" again. Earlier roots will suggest "to remind," "thought," and even—as it should—"to desire ardently."[5] We crave meaning and crave for it. We bid the world talk to (with) us. The world keeps mum. We make it speak, out of our "lust for motive."[6] "Humanity is compulsively driven towards creating pattern and meaning . . . because it fears more than anything else the alternative." Whence myth, the constellated structure of thought and ideal that results as social usage is added to pure matter. "Human history converts reality into speech, and it alone rules the life and death of mythical language." Because, should the world adamantly refuse to deliver, others, always, will make it speak for us: "The organizers of society—the politicians, chiefs, bureaucrats—will go ahead and rebuild the thing from time to time . . . ."[7] Indeed, as Blake had it, in times past, "I must build my own system or be enslaved by another man's."

There, of course, is the rub, and the self-confessed storyteller's legitimate preoccupation and responsibility. Because even though archaic usage indicates that "fable" and "form" used to stand as opposed as "shape" and "content" in rhetoric, it is indeed gainsaid by the reality of operations: myth and fable both preclude such dichotomy; their shaping power conveys meaning ipso facto: it *is* their shaping power that creates meaning. There is a poem by Mei-mei Berssenbrugge ("Farolita") in which the narrator makes the pattern of a set of clothes out of thin translucent paper only to realize that the pattern constitutes the clothes themselves. The French call such a pattern *un patron* (a "boss," you understand, not "a customer"), a term that goes a long way toward suggesting its matrical power and authority. Myths and fables organize meaning, but they also gel it, they arrange between the world and the self a sumptuously embroidered screen of sortileges that is hard to remove at will (*fascinum*), a screen that clings too tightly to what it is supposed to reveal and takes its place, making it unbareable and thus bearable. Mythification, as Coover's prologue to his "Exemplary Fictions" suggests,[8] is, *in proprio tempore*, mystification, a chain of choices and inventions, something like a structure forever after prearranged, a narrative pall from under which it becomes highly strenuous to escape. The "bogus myth-makers"[9] may be ourselves or our neighbors, or our institutional or spiritual leaders: debunking is in both cases in order, an indispensable step on the way to the sane ecology of mind we call freedom. Myth, to make a critical and philosophical long story[10] short, is so useful it is too useful, addictively protective, snug and comfy to the very last minutes of its inadequacy or dangerousness, similar in that to the old car you will not turn in for a new one for fear you'd have to walk in the intervening period. One would always rather crash than switch.

"We can destroy only as creators," however (Nietzsche), and whoever would fight the myth-making compulsion must be fully aware that the constructs of reason on which he would rely are not devoid of a germane fictional nature: cause and effect, relation and similarity, chrono- and other -logies may be the "regulative ideas" or "necessary fictions" others talked about, they are not for all that devoid, in their necessity, of fictionalist hunger. Whence the debate to which Coover alludes[11] between existentialist Karl Jaspers and existentialist Rudolph Bultmann. For the latter, unmythical thought can be pitted against myth: one may hope to "demythologize" the New Testament and interpret it in the categories of one's own philosophy; for the former, only myth has enough power to fight off myths that are perceived as discardable. This *might* potentially be the ultimate watershed usable by such as insist on an otherwise laborious distinction between modernist and "postmodernist" aesthetics.[12] More certainly, this is where the distinction proposed by Frank Kermode in *The Sense of an Ending* can come in handy: "Myth operates within the diagrams of ritual, which presupposes total and adequate explanations of things as they are and were; it is a sequence of radically unchangeable gestures. Fictions are for finding things out, and they change as the needs of sense-making change. Myths are the agents of stability, fictions the agents of change. Myths call for absolute, fictions for conditional assent."[13] To put things in a nutshell, the degree of consciousness involved is that around which everything revolves: a myth lived as myth is incontrovertible; a myth lived as fiction provides insight into and leverage upon the structure of mythological thought. The difference is not, however, in degree, but ontological. It is that which exists between the transitive beliefs and practice of the high priest and that, intransitive, of a Wallace Stevens. Giving shape to the real in the former case is a matter of instrumentality, a pathway to transcendence; in the second it is rather a self-conscious and critical use of constructs aimed at scraping clean the slate of received ideas. With new mythological propositions one foregrounds the potential *variety* and necessity of ordering structures but does not question their relation to the real. Fictional manipulations, on the other hand, aim at evidencing the nature of that structuring and thereby "the arbitrary commitment to design"[14] which it presupposes, the willingness, one might say, permanently to weave segments of the "New Webster" of "things as they are" into "new webs" of meaning, new "ideas of order"; they therefore—without denying the necessity of the process—introduce a chance for liberation and usher in a wide-ranging set of possibilities for renewal, defensive distance, and dynamic critical acumen.

2

Fiction, to a certain extent, is that by which our mythological heritage can be shown not necessarily to be forever "the same old story," that by which its recurring, redundant, insistent, and even obsessional bases can permanently be made into "another new" one, by which the acquired and the known can be turned into a "process of discovery." If, as Thomas Kuhn has shown in *The Structure of Scientific Revolution*—an idea pushed to extremes by Feyerabend's *Against Method*—rereadings, or, in the second version, propagandistic peddling, of an unchanged real afford new insights into the world of *physis*,[15] the recuperation, retreading, and recycling of nonscientific fictions have for a longer time been known to be the motor of literary evolution. Genre history demonstrates, if need be, the heuristic powers of formal approaches and the generative potential of the skew. Generic manipulations can indeed principally be seen as a means of staying literary entropy, of keeping "exhaustion" at bay; but the revisiting of ancient or merely existing material *on its own formal terms* is, in Robert Coover's work, underpinned by a greater ambition, one that could provisionally be defined as a desire to demonstrate in fiction the possibilities of poetic knowledge.

"Coover's predilection for subjects and vehicles which turn out to be already structured like a narration"[16] can be traced to the beginning of his literary production. Even though *Origin of the Brunists* was published before *Pricksongs and Descants*, the latter contains stories previously written. In both cases, however, and in spite of the former's "normal" form Coover gave it to satisfy the critical expectations of the readers of a first novel (after the method previously adopted by such modernist painters as Braque, Matisse, and Picasso, who went unabashedly figurative to gain acceptance), the same strategy is implemented, in more or less visible ways: in the novel the basis for religious mythmaking is pitted against would-be objective reportorial readings of events shown to be underpinned by the similar necessity of giving some order to random events;[17] in the stories, literary borrowings, and conventions, intertextual winks form the backdrop against which the voice of the fictioneer is sounded. The given may be different, the ironical patterns woven around the notions of history, narrative, and order, essentially, are not. They merely become more visible in the stories because the latter make formally explicit the isomorphism of the fiction and of the fiction-producing mechanisms.[18] They demonstrate the superior incisiveness of a fictional exploitation of existing structures over mere mythological overhauling or replacement, reveal the operations responsible for the very birth of the fictional constructs they exploit by burrowing insistently into the cracks, the gaps, the nooks and crannies varnished over by the imposed linearity of conventional narration. True works of art, whatever else they may do, insistently tell about their inception. The cubistic composition of the fragmented stories of *Pricksongs and Descants* favors speculation on the notion of angles, while other stories demonstrate the heuristic and creative potential of the cuckoo-like occupation of borrowed structures. Borrowing and burrowing go hand in hand in Robert Coover's work, whether his texts are predicated on the workings of overarching, general metaphors generating teleological readings of the real, thus enhancing the artificial cause-and-effect concatenations that humanity favors in its quest for meaning at all cost, or whether they make a special inquiry into the potential nature and consequences of a reformulation of a number of favored and stabilized fictions. Given the fundamental vision of a random universe whose only readings must be organized by fictions, and given also the fascination with the medium of film as it is exemplified and illustrated in Coover's early ("The Sentient Lens") and later work (*Charlie in the House of Rue, After Lazarus*, "The Phantom of the Movie Palace"),[19] one might be tempted to suggest that fixed narratives acquire in his mind the artificial status of arrested images in "the seventh art," an art defined by—precisely—"cinematic" qualities that preclude the suspension of a native and founding instability. Dynamizing the intertext that founds or solidifies our fictional deciphering of the world we live in becomes something equivalent to the partial rotation thanks to which prismatic kaleidoscopes reorganize the unchanging elements presented to the perception of its fixed objective. Perhaps because one of our dominant fictions has forever consisted in naturalizing the objectivity of our perceptions and measuring all other registering devices in terms of their closeness to or distortion of "natural" perception, Coover's strategy at all times, although in an admirable variety of manners, consists in demonstrating the illusory stability, the essential inadequacy and incompleteness of our fictional optics, its founding plasticity and lack of resilience under the creative assaults of imagination and desire.

3

Two series of digressive reminders, one nonliterary, the other literary, may serve here to illustrate the necessity and reality of such temptations. There is in effect a certain way in which one can never really be *about* Robert Coover; such an "aboutness" his own work entirely precludes. Coover's fictions defeat attempts to comment upon or clarify them, or else allow them only under penalty of pleonasm and psittacine reiteration. Aesop was a stutterer and so are we doomed to be, as growing piles of redundant commentaries and wooden critical language accumulate. One feels rather inclined to talk *to* Robert Coover than *about* him. But, lo, even *that* device of direct apostrophe has been used by him: "The universe for you, Maestro, was opening up . . . ."[20] Still, if one has understood at all what his work is about, the invitation is clearly to try and write things otherwise. Echo, "muse" of metafiction and criticism as well as "of mimesis," forgive me! I shall here introduce Aesop thanks to fictions come from elsewhere.

The first series stages metaphorical examples respectively lifted, for purposes of convenience, from the worlds of science, photography, and the movies. Reading Mandelbrod's explanations of the revolutionary conceptual and physical invention he is responsible for, the so-called fractal objects, looking at his computer-made images and meditating the connection between the two, one is compelled to draw a number of relevant inferences. Fractal objects are mathematically engineered constructs that could at times be described either as the creations of a Zeno gone wild or as quantum theory made graphic. Their ability to reconstruct images of this world on the basis of sheer mathematical manipulation foregrounds the presence of the abstract fictions that underpin not only our vision of the real but possibly its very nature, questioning, at any rate, our ability to describe it, by opening staggering avenues of perspectival choice. What matters for our concern here is that the mode of production of fractal objects is entirely predicated not on the immediate perception of reproduced objects but on a system of lures that send to the machine not elements of the real as it should be reproduced but coded information that has no reality, no resemblance to reality, devised to reconstitute a prodigiously "life-like" image only at the very moment when the information interferes with the constitutionally warped apparatus of reception/production. That creative alliance of warps and counter-warps may stand metaphorically for the processes at work, possibly in our own sensory life, but certainly in our intellectual life (and in the writings of Robert Coover): where myths and fictions meet desire and variously determined, programmed decoding abilities, the image acquires a status in which discrepancies from the real become the only access to and the ultimate test of its truth, understood as its necessity.

Consider now the photographic work of David Hockney, if he will consent to being dragged in: its goals could be roughly summed up as the desire to create a pure, living space where ordinarily there were only images of arrested actions. By reversing perspective within the individual shots, by multiplying the angles and juxtaposing proliferating views, Hockney manages to offer visions of the real that are simultaneously same and different; his work invites the eye to travel among and between the elements that compose it in an attempt to reconstitute an object whose reality is, *proprio sensu*, nowhere, but that colonizes attention, focuses it on the possibilities and modes of reconstitution. In the simultaneous multiplication of approaches to which the eye is submitted, there occurs something that is quite close to what happens in Coover's work, something that, if one is to believe Georges Poulet, may well be what happens to the "trajectory" of any book, but made explicit, dramatized: "Starting from one consciousness, it tends toward another consciousness and is never frozen onto the place of its fall: the form." In the case of Hockney as well as in that of Coover, however, it is the form itself that tells of the process which constantly underlies an identical itinerary. Far from being considered as the unburnt remnants of the process, the form in question cannot be considered as mere fallout as it insistently and dynamically spells out the fact of the incontrovertible in-between-ness of proposed images. In Hockney's case the eye is invited to connect moments of representation and some fixed, ideal, *nonexistent* vision of the object and, making that connection, one is invited to speculate on the fictions that regulate our representational moves. In Coover's case the encounter with a recognizable corpus invites manifest comparisons between text and reading expectations, interrogation of the motives underlying choices, meditation on the change of existential perspective offered by the possibility of such tinkering, reflection on the germane ties linking the fictional tinkerer with other sorts of "fixers": "There are all those that *fix* things, he continued. Bandits, thinkers, ministers of propaganda, dreamers, prophets, lovers, priests. Atrocious 'bricoleurs,' all."[21]

Let us finally turn to the work of Peter Greenaway. And particularly to *The Draughtsman's Contract*, a film that only he, Alain Resnais, or Robert Coover himself could have conceived. It is all patterns, the disruption of patterns and the reconstitution of patterns, the same explosion-cum-reconstruction process that one may read in *Providence* or *Pricksongs and Descants*. Emphatically, in that film, aim[22] is taken: the draughtsman's cross-threaded viewfinder cuts into the real, fragmenting it, decomposing and recomposing the disposition of figure and ground, butchering space, creating it. Phantasms of the retina displace whatever coherence was ensured by sequential memory, compel culture and imagination freely to associate on the canvas cut out of real scenes in which perspectival choices make for narration. Each viewer—each spectator in fact, as the viewfinder squares up the screen itself, superposing the creative process to that of reception—is invited to dispose all that is perceived according to his or her own inclinations. On the white (?) plane of the mind the succession of views takes the place of narrative. How fitting that Greenaway should confine to literature what contemporary fiction most often desires to expel: "I never thought the cinema was made to convey ideas, which is the function of literature . . ."! One perceives echoes of Coover's voice here: "In all the stories structure is at least a part of the plot, that is what you call the 'mythos' of the story—. . . structure and the irony of structure is part of the way it moves"[23]; or echoes of another voice: "I want literature to make paintings or play music for me; for the rest, I've got a phone . . ." (Conrad Detrez). It has been said of Greenaway that, since he could not have an exhibit of his paintings accepted anywhere, he put them into his films and that the latter also provided a home for the writings he could not get published. To a certain extent, mutatis mutandis, Coover could be accused of the same and feel quite happy about it.

With Greenaway's film as with Coover's writing, the layering and permanent conversion of meanings makes for structure and significance at the same time the eye is guided by a preestablished, solid scenario all parts of which, in both cases, can be numbered (numbed?). Meaning never lies in the twelve drawings of the film any more than in the, say, fifteen fragments of a Coover story, but underneath the texture of their hinges. Between the probable fiction proposed by a dramatized, mathematical, logical sequence and the possible fictions that emerge from underneath the visible order of an emphasized series, somewhere between the dictated sense of the adopted structure and the proliferating set of readings proposed by the vacillations and shiverings of associative, suggestive "écarts," lie skeins of threateningly new and meaningful combinations. "Threatening," for "the name of the game," in *The Draughtsman's Contract* as well as in "The Panel Game" or "The Elevator," is indeed . . . "La Mort."

Coover's narratives transform us in curious ways, ways that demonstrate how the tactical choices to which we resort in order to read and measure the real eventually compel us to invent that real, more or less consciously, to assume or delegate responsibility for the versions of it we choose to live out, ways that consist in proving experimentally that what we had always taken for natural, unconstructed reality is indeed merely the designation and fabrication of a set of fictional productive relations, relations capable of turning the tables upon our preconceptions. What they do can perhaps best be illustrated by one of Greenaway's powerfully pregnant literary vignettes; our favorite fictions are the tool in the following story and what we call the real is the fly:

An entomologist wanted to prove a certain fly could move at forty-five miles an hour; he devised a stick at the end of which a particular bait was then placed and, leaning out of a train moving at the said speed, caught a number of these insects; numerous verifications were undertaken; in the end a new race of flies was born: these could fly at fifty-two miles an hour on a distance of eight and a half miles and had developed enough of a memory to remember there were more trains on Saturdays. . . .

Greenaway's confessed desire is to write "A New 1001 Tales." Others also turn to the old ones for novelty, and Coover's destabilization of myths and fictions by fiction is not an isolated enterprise. One knows of John Barth's mythological manipulations. But one can also turn to our second set of references, literary coordinates of an identical paradigm, and become aware of Michel Tournier's several revisitings of myth, of his forays into the fictional underpinnings ("The King of Alders") of the "ideological" nature of *The Ogre*, of the story of the Magi in *Gaspard, Melchior & Balthazar*, where the famed trio falls apart as mythical trio both under the irruption of Taor, prince of Mangalore, the fourth participant who doesn't make it to Bethlehem in time to enter the legendary picture, and because of an investigation of the possibly mundane rather than spiritual motives that may have provoked the peregrinations of these kings. An endeavor similar to Coover's can also be found in Tournier's *Le Coq de Bruyère*, a collection of "tales and narratives" featuring the wife of Santa Claus (but it *is* her husband we see nursing the child Jesus), the Adam family, Tom Thumb as hippie, and other explicit or disguised tales of initiation. Among these, "Robinson Crusoe," a tale whose character was already central to the novel *Vendredi ou les Limbes du Pacifique*, in which Defoe's relation undergoes a type of broad eroticization that Coover could recognize for its capacity to reframe and reinterpret a narrative gone paralytic. The ideological move of Tournier's fiction is far from being as radical as Coover's, whose literary ventriloquism more often than not illustrates a conscious, brilliant, and courageous skeptical and anarchic stand; the irony of Tournier's utilization of preconstructed structures may have different heuristic purposes but its metaphysical implications are nonetheless eminently displayed: the unbearable nakedness of a world which fictions might have fled is placed as key before the opening of the volume under the guise of three lines of Lanza del Vasto's:

Au fond de chaque chose, un poisson nage.
Poisson de peur que tu n'en sortes nu,
Je te jetterai mon manteau d'images.[24]

Much the same type of preoccupation is illustrated by Pierrette Fleutiaux's revisiting of Perrault's tales in *Métamorphoses de la Reine*.[25] The brief and rare preface of a writer as reluctant to justify herself in theoretical terms as Coover is inclined to, within or without his fiction, nonetheless talks to us in terms one might ascribe him, telling us of "tales that have so early penetrated our consciousness that they constitute just as much of a real as the Real, with even, sometimes, a greater charge of reality,"[26] as well as of a double movement of fascination and rejection that triggers the writing impulse: "Perhaps it is because of that double movement of welcome and rejection that something moved in me where all had been petrified before, and that the desire to write returned. And then, nearly at the same time, the desire to re-write, to remake" (p. 11). Fleutiaux's "queen" is no more dead than Coover's own ("The Dead Queen"), and she even contributes to the general revivification of the dead fictions that gave her birth. The ogre's wife is but one of her avatars, among which Little Red Pants, who meets Bluebeard; all speculations on the bad mother's relation to Cinderella are cut short by the latter's being revisited as a male Cinderello ("Cendron"). Ashes to ashes. . . . The constructive, creative fight that pits these fictions against their revision feeds on discrepancies and explorations that do not claim the same type of coherence as the original texts, to the extent that a series of footnotes are deemed necessary to accommodate various readings of the possibilities thus let loose.

Much the same manipulation of fairy tales for much the same ends (liberation of the imagination; permission given to erotic phantasms, for heuristic purposes, to enter the sacred field from which they had been discursively expelled; erosion of the credibility of inherited and prestructured narratives) could also be found in a number of previous European writers of the modernist period, among which the Czech surrealist Vitezslav Nezval, whose *Valerie A Tyden Divu* (Valerie or The Week of Wonders, 1935)—where the young innocent heroine and most of the literary personnel have jumped straight out of folk and fairy tales and into, for one, the hands of an old lecher, for the others, a world of generalized concupiscence—may only be ironically subtitled a "black" or "gothic" novel at the cost of a brutal and comic hijacking of time-honored stories. Nezval's ironic and ambiguous quotations operate according to the same logics as that of our experience, indirectly described in his text as necessarily caught between "real" existence and cultural existence.

The wide and common use of such textual mercenaries, illustrated by these few literary samples, could tend to banalize Coover's enterprise, to relativize his importance by suggesting that he is just one other merely entertaining manipulator of tales already told. Such, however, is not the case, for reasons that will be gone into below and that have to do with the particular and specific effects this practice has on Coover's writing. When *Public Burning* came out, *Newsweek*'s reviewer called it "genuinely shocking: grossly funny, relentless in its determination to *go too far*," and Norman Podhoretz, commenting upon it in the *Saturday Review*, called the book "a cowardly lie." Taking my cue from W. C. Fields, I will thus later suggest that "anyone that can be simultaneously detested by *Newsweek* and Norman Podhoretz can't be all bad."

II Aesop's Forest

1

"When a critic says of a work, 'Aha! Clearly, this derives from X,' it's an almost sure bet that the writer hasn't read X. Without exception."[27]

May I suggest that when this critic says of Coover's work, "Aha! Clearly, parts of it derive from reading the Spanish fabulists," he stands a much fairer chance of being close to the truth? As good a chance, at any rate, as when suggesting he may have read Cervantes, if he suggests that Samaniego is not a complete stranger to Robert Coover. Samaniego's "Milkmaid," utilized for the centerpiece of "The Sentient Lens," can indeed be found in his 1781 *Fábulas Morales*, even though he, in turn, may well have lifted it either from Bonaventure des Périers's "Comparaison des Alquemistes à la bonne femme qui portoit un potée de lait au marché" (in *Les Contes ou les Nouvelles récréations et joyeux devis*), from La Fontaine's "La Laitière et le Pot au Lait," or, further back, from an allusion to the story in Rabelais's *Pantagruel*. And Coover's knowledge of Spanish literature is real enough for us to deduce from his interest in this fabulist that he may also have been guided in his literary use of the fable by the early "metafictional" or "metapoetic" use of the fable made by Samaniego's contemporary Tomás de Iriarte in his *Fábulas Literarias* of 1782. Incidentally, the latter actually contains a fable, "El Mono y el Titeretero" (The Monkey and the Magic Lantern), organized around an idea—the illusive power of discourse as it plays upon expectations—that had already inspired Cervantes's interlude "El retablo de las maravillas" (The Wonder Show) and that can be seen as just as sophisticated a speculation as Coover's—albeit differently oriented toward social satire—on the operational convergence of the creative imagination and fictional constructs.

What matters here is that Coover should thus turn to material, legends in their own time, that has not only been used before but also reused with spectacular frequency, and furthermore that he should, on the one hand, reshuffle the material in question and, on the other, stage the inventor in the midst of his inventions.

The elements of the tale can be found in a variety of sources. Aesop's own "Leo et Vulpes" (*Fables*, 91, 137) was allusively used by Horace (*Epist.*, I, v, 73) and by Philibert Hegemon in the ninth fable in *La Colombière* (1583) before it was used again, in its entirety, by La Fontaine in "Le Lion malade et le Renard," the last lines of which are an exact translation of the passage in Horace; elements of the same tale can be found in the earlier fable ("Le Lion devenu Vieux"), which La Fontaine adapted from C. Julius Phaeder's "Leo Senex, Aper, Taurus et Asinus." Such connections may well have been relayed in the present case by readings in the Spanish eighteenth-century fabulists. Samaniego's fascination for the French culture (half due to his Basque origins and half to his admiration for the Encyclopédistes), Iriarte's tempestuous relationship with him, probably suffice to justify the possibility of such a channel.

Aesop's existence itself may well be a mere fictional construct, due to the fact that his dubious biography may have been reconstructed to satisfy the Greek requirement, according to which all genres should have an inventor. The tradition that traces the stuttering hunchback fabulist to a Phrygian slave some time in the sixth century B.C. is stable enough, however, for Poislé-Desgranges to write a book in 1685 entitled *La Bosse d'Esope* (Aesop's Hump) and for Coover to be able to allude in the text to his physical deformity, to the suggestive fact that he should have been nearly deprived of language, to the characters surrounding his life (Xanus / Xantus / Zenas, Ennus, and others), to his being condemned for having sinned against Apollo in Delphi and thrown over a cliff in punishment.

What is equally clear is that Coover, in this text, relinquishes or transforms the founding moralizing purpose of the fable, retaining only an Iriartian goal of literarily oriented commentary, and concentrates, all things being equal, on the second aspect that made the fable so dear to the heart of medieval clerics: that which indulged their taste for the interpretation of things according to their "segnifiance spirituelle" and made them relish contemporary rewritings of Aesop in the vulgar tongue, seen as a genre in their own right and affectionately renamed "Isopets" (Little Aesops). His attitude simultaneously echoes and denies the judgment of such as Iriarte who held that originality precluded the use of ancient "intertextual" material[28] and demonstrates the fallacious nature of contemporary fears; the Abbé de Reyrac, preceding Barth's reminders of the exhaustibility of all genres, is known to have, around that same time, bewailed the impossibility of going on with the fable in the wake of its greatest practitioner: "Malheur à qui vient après lui! / La Fontaine a tout dit: que reste-t-il à dire?" Edmé Boursault had begun to suggest an answer to that question as early as the turn of the eighteenth century by making the father of fables a character in his plays (*Les Fables d'Esope, ou Esope à la Ville* [1690]; *Esope à la Cour* [1701]), a rather comically pathetic and Cooverian character at that, inasmuch as Aesop, in these works, cuts the figure of a waif who will tell fables at the drop of a hat, in and out of season, just as Jesus in Pier Paolo Pasolini's film "The Gospel according to Matthew" appears as a vainglorious, foolish, and easily triggered parabola-making machine.[29]

Prime among the "fabulators" of our time, among those whose technique, Robert Scholes wrote, "is to take motifs of folk literature and explode them into motivations and revelations, as the energy might be released from a packed atomic structure," Robert Coover, a seasoned practitioner of the reexamination of tales, myths, stories, and fictions of all kinds, could not long stay the temptation to use in his writing the founding father of the genre. If the fable is indeed nothing but "a metaphor or sustained allegory" (St. Marc Girardin), one easily understands how irresistible it may have proved to be for someone dedicated to "the intransigent penetration of metaphor."

2

"Aesop's Forest" stages the simultaneous demise of the fabulist and of his principal mainstay, the cornerstone, the kingpin of his metaphorical system: the lion. It is a tale of disaggregation. It is a speculation on the relations of fiction to the real. It is a carnivalesque debunking of the mental powers that hold our existential fictions together. It is a new and quasi-clinical summary of Coover's principal themes and techniques.

"Death is everywhere in Aesop's dark forest." Not only because the old lion is dying and because Aesop, if caught, having been condemned, will be executed, but because the tale heralds the advent of the death of a certain set of meanings. "The calamity that awaits him" is a calamity that awaits all creatures whose idea of order has so far been regulated by his suggestions. Not that "political power as such has [ever] held the fabler's fancy," but the fabler's job is constantly to attempt to draw morals from elusive and shifting situations, to decipher or cipher, to convert things and events into meanings, to construct myths and fictions in other words, thanks to the reduction of all attitudes on an identical fictional plane governed by a given set of moralities. These moralities even retain some power over *this* text inasmuch as the dead wood of their formulation strews it and affords minimal structure when the narrative hesitates to take any given direction, to the point where it actually provides the entire texture of paragraphs (the final paragraph of section 5 for example), spilled forth in a stuttering way that recalls both the infirmity of their enunciator and the technique of "The Panel Game": "once bitten and all that, no, seeing is believing . . . Sour grapes?" The fabler, faced with the collapse of an order he has vicariously engineered thanks to the organizing metaphor of power that depends on the presence of the lion at the top of the suggested hierarchy, is forced to recognize in the crumbling of the "old peaceful carnage" the dwindling of his structuring powers. The oxymoron of "peaceful carnage" is strong enough a comment on the nature of such regulative visions: any chosen fiction hacks out of a host of alternative ones an order ensuring stability. This "peaceful carnage" is the violent organization of the world along such lines as will not allow the beasts to realize that they may really "have butcher's work to do." As long as a given fiction can satisfy people's desire for a clear idea of order, its author becomes "the source of all their truths." But should epistemological dislocations occur and replacement become ineluctable, the fox may engineer a takeover and act as Aesop once did (its "grin . . . is his, the fabler's own"), only because "it is truth itself that is changing"; the lion dies largely because Aesop has been condemned and because, as the text has it, "we take *everything* with us when we go."

Faced with the collapse of his order, then, Aesop may possibly gain some inkling of the real nature of myth. As structures are going down, the chaotic nature of the world reveals itself, forces its artificial organizer into some realization of its random nature and of the fictional fight that perpetually attempts to reorganize it. To that extent may his "terror" be the "same thing" as "wisdom," a sort of Nietzschean awareness that indeed his endeavors have only been a mild and provisional but at bottom equally "mad violent effort to link the unlinkable, cross impossible abysses." When the beasts of the forest take the hint that indeed "boundaries are breaking down" and consort together in "unnatural" ways, in a fashion that brings to mind Gary Larson's defamiliarizing mode or French cartoonist Reiser's hilariously anarchic view of Noah's ark collectively gone ape, they do so because some order is being banished which ascribed positions, expectations, and duties. Reality is infinitely more cruel, in its chaotic violence, than buffer fictions of all kinds see it as their duty to indicate. "Fairytale[s are] for weaklings. Helps them die easier," says the dying king, a realpolitik individual who entertains no illusions on the ordering nature of power relations.

If approximate spoonerisms entertain with the unconscious the same relationship as puns and witticisms according to Freud, there may be no remark in the text more telling than the aphorism Aesop accidentally coins as he reaches for the closest comforting piece of wisdom available: "Better a servant in safety, he reminds himself, than a master in danger, though at first this comes out, better a savory never than born a masker in a manger." The fabulist thinks this "doesn't make much sense," wonders whether this might not be "some kind of oracle," as befits an inhabitant of the city that harbors the world's omphalos. No wonder he will be taken as one who insults Apollo: his disastrously incompetent awareness of oracular meanings too far removed from his pet views more than qualifies him for eradication. He may not be responsible for missing the allusion to the manger, being a B.C. creature, but he could at least have meditated the promising existential gratuitousness of a "savory never" and the indicting overtones of "masker" for a man of his particular mythological calling.

Eventually, whether he was guilty or not of an actual offense, Aesop's vocation *was* sinning against Apollo, a god that regulated order along different lines and relished metamorphoses over and against Aesop's artificial but stable moral constructs. Establishing the laurel as sacred plant tells enough about the institutionalization of change and the fetishization of desire, as Daphne is my witness. "The Ovidian stories all concern transformation; now that is not a startlingly new subject—after all, fairy tales, animal fables, and the like, deal with it—but I suddenly realized that the basic, constant struggle for all of us is against metamorphosis, against giving in to the inevitability of process. Encountering in Ovid the same agon that underlay my own writing was liberating; I realized that what I was already doing was not only possible but essential."[30] Aesop cannot really bear that, inasmuch as *his* transformations, a founding gesture for his particular worldview, are a-dynamic and irreversible. The text, taking advantage of his growing incapacity to control the framing fiction, hastens to reconvert what he once had translated: "Stupidity, fear, deceit, carnality, treason break out in the forest like scabies. . . . Suicidal hares and frogs hurl themselves out of their element, elephants eat their own testicles, worms blind themselves so as not to see the approaching catastrophe."

As, according to the same logics, "the fabler becomes his own goat"—as he will later on, off the rock of Phaedriades or Hyampea, turn into a turtle in a desperate and ultimate fictional move that redeems what tenuous grip "realism" might have acquired over the narrative—he becomes fair game for those who always took his "truth" for "sacrilege" because their allegiance was to another mental map. The Delphians who pursue Aesop may not adhere to his vision of the world but they are nonetheless internally regulated by another that is similarly fictitious in nature; they don't use the proverbs and moralities Aesop is fond of, but they *quote* nevertheless, to strengthen their official position: "Like Menelaus grappling with the inconstant and malodorous Proteus . . .", "It has been wisely observed . . .", "some sage has said . . ." punctuate the manhunters' own discourse. They are in the grasp of identical claws, but they do not know it. Mythologies have it out, and a variety of "common sense" may be the ultimate disease the old lion is ailing from. Perhaps because "we ridicule in others what we most despise in ourselves," those who live from fictions (and who more than guardians of temples?) give a particularly vicious caricature of their prisoner.

The first philosopher who owned Aesop—or so the story goes—had bought him along with a host of other slaves out of which he only kept a grammarian, a songster, and the budding fabler. Possibly because Aesop is neither the knower of words nor the poet in that trio, "he'd always thought of th[e] distance between [his creatures and himself] as ontological and absolute." Surprised that the "barrier" should have come down in the text he finds himself in ("Anyway, it's . . . 'Impossible. There's a barrier . . .' At least there *was*. . . . Has it somehow been breached?"), Aesop is in fact submitted to a treatment comparable in many ways to that of Henry Waugh in *The Universal Baseball Association*. His demiurgic function accomplished, he gets swallowed up into the world he has created and reappears in the sequel of the narrative he has invented, a sequel that goes on after his own demise. As in "You are language and you shall return to language," or in "He who has ruled by language, will perish and end up in language." The turtle we see flapping about in the early part of the text, after having been dropped by the eagle (a carrier of authority seals and princely baskets in the Delphic tradition), turns out to be none other than the fabler himself, if we are to believe the similarity of the desperate gestures of survival they both make. When an eagle had dropped the public ring onto the breast of a slave, Aesop had been required to interpret the sign toward the slave's emancipation. Now, as turtle-Aesop splashes by the ear of the dying king, all authority rests with the creatures. The superposition is complete (a "communion" indeed) when the lion, in the moment of dying, identically "feels then as though he's falling."

In this strategic distancing/implication of all "fiction-makers" in Coover's work (the remark goes for the "Fallguy" and the "leper" as well as for Waugh, Nixon, and Aesop) lies the characteristic that marks this writer's distinction and affirms his belief in the superiority of dynamic fictionalizing over arrested mythological conceptions. Had he listened to the grammarian and the poet, too, Aesop would have known as well that language always has the last word and that for all the possibility that exists of building stories within stories, putting them in new language always makes them a series of stories *plus one*. Fiction, in that measure, could be presented as the logical reverse of Zeno's equally "fabulous" paradox of the turtle and the hare: divide separating distances in halves and, given a headstart, the turtle will never be caught up with; multiply similarities by two or by themselves and, given that the story that tells of them comes last, it will always be new.

III On Squaring, Metafiction, and Writing
The Square-shooter as Poet

If poetry is the dance of the mind among words, Robert Coover can only be described as a square dancer. But, if his systematic reflexiveness has been the butt of many a critical piece accusing him of being, in a rather sterile way, a mere stager of processes, one wishes his detractors had had the decency to pay some attention to the exuberant pyrotechnics of his language and to compare its ebullience and pleasure-provoking zest to the dullness of our general critical discourse.

There of course always exists a risk that the systematic "squaring" that Robert Coover has chosen as the foundation of his art should become merely formulaic and thereby repetitious. Less gifted writers than he have indeed fallen into that metafictional trap, realizing too late that the adventure of an *écriture* could not be constrained by principled obedience to the sententious foregrounding of one's own smug refusal of narrative naïveté. They thereby relinquished, out of strictly theoretical principles, the exhilarating powers of the storytelling drive.

Coover, I suggest, very seldom falls into this trap, because he always gathers enough narrative momentum, always makes us wallow enough in opulent textures to make us take his allegorically theoretical asides in stride. To be sure, Coover "squares" whatever he touches: "history" gets "squared" in *The Public Burning* inasmuch as a historical event is exploited in terms of the forces that constitute the very notion of history and dramatizes their work within the culture, the media, the individual minds; myth gets "squared" in *Origin of the Brunists* and *The Universal Baseball Association* to the extent that we are made to witness the birth and efficiency of myths while all the time being dramatically kept aware of the psychic needs and social constraints that allow or make compulsory their rise. The fable, the fairy tale, the folk tale get "squared" inasmuch as we are simultaneously offered subjects that are lifted from a known corpus, in a sort of general and shameless generic contraband—a smuggler's biblos indeed—and exposed to the mechanisms, delights, and lessons that could originally and respectively be, first, recognized, nourished and helped along by the reader, second, enjoyed because of our incontrovertible taste for "stories" of all kinds, and third, drawn from situations that made one reflect, and that can now be respectively admired for the perfection of their handling, indulged in because of their added value (aesthetic, erotic, metafictional, or other), drawn, finally, on an altogether different plane from that on which the original piece operated.

Even desire and carnival get "squared," and that may well be the one feature that can account for the specificity of Coover's style and contribution. I have elsewhere tried to suggest[31] how Coover "carnivalizes" his writing even as he uses carnivalesque situations as his subject matter (*The Public Burning, A Political Fable,* available excerpts from "Lucky Pierre" and "A Night at the Movies"), and stressed the fact that desire, an indispensable acolyte in any sort of literary creation, is staged for what it is on the scene of Coover's own writing ("The

Sentient Lens," *Hair O' the Chine, Spanking the Maid).*

"Squaring" indeed, unlike a certain rainbow, may not be quite "enuf" and, were it not for Coover's views *as his writing illustrates them,* for his enthralling experiments with language, his exploration of limits—minimal in the case of his most Beckettian prose, as in *Pricksongs* or *After Lazarus;* maximal in his various toyings with dramatic excess and linguistic saturation, as in his overtly "erotic" and "political" pieces—and for his general fleshing up of revisited structures, the bare bones of the idea would soon enough poke through the cloth in an ungainly way and return the text to the skeletons of discourse it precisely tries to make it escape at all times.

By the same token, should his vision of an explosive, uncontrolled, and random universe, his suspicion of "rational" language, merely suggest a routine downbeat and commiserating tragic view of our condition, there were little new under our literary and philosophical sun.

But the name of Coover's game is emphatically energy. The uncommon courage and honesty of an existential vision that could lead many to seek a hasty comfort in the retreat to the familiar structures of pious liberal stands, wherein to await ineluctable but unassumed further developments (thus Kant whom Nietzsche berated for having been great enough to saw through the bars of his cage with his *Critique of Pure Reason* and having ignominiously "crept back in" with his *Critique of Practical Reason),* place him, on the contrary, on the offensive. Thus is a most "un-American" set of views (antiteleological, intransitive, defiant of the ready-made, anarchic) made operational by an emphatically American voice and buoyancy (tall-tale fluency, exuberant imagination, carnivalesque disregard for manners, open taunting of dogmas).

Just as subconscious desires and libidinous energy play an important part in the patterning of experience—a factor which reinforces Beckett's contention, shared by Coover, that fiction represents a fundamental desire for self-perception[32]—they play a crucial part in the formation of language that Coover would be loathe to overlook: "'Rational' language holds a precarious grip on our life and our unconscious channelling of our desires and fantasies into stereotyped patterns. Let its hold slip, and a wild energy is unleashed: words, names, associate freely and whirl faster and faster. Against the cold rationality of the many forms of order, power, censorship, another language begins to flow, carrying with it all that has been repressed and forgotten."[33] In other words, Coover does not only challenge the forms of our most favored fictions inasmuch as they have to be made apparent to relinquish their oppressive message of order, he also challenges the clichés and impoverished uses of a language, the lid-like, blinding influence of deadened, routine, fixed discourse, challenges the repressive forces that make someone like William Gass exclaim that one of the things society does to poor people is to cut out their tongue (*On Being Blue*). Seen in that light, and for never being so directly, all genuine poetic utterances are made eminently political insofar as they respectively displace the problem and identify the true nature of power. Over and against the victimization of Donald, in "The Square Shooter and the Saint," at the hands of the "coined," Coover proposes an explosive, virtuoso, labile, and endlessly proliferating language apt to forbid the gelification of speech perfectly—if ironically—qualified as "groovy," a language in expansion, liable to bring one to new verges of poetic discovery.

Energy, then, energy and fun; the whole gamut of fun, *starting* with the potentially most sophomoric kind ("I enjoy the fun of stirring things up, breaking the rules, punching holes in the structures so as to see through to the mysteries—even if only to rediscover what it was you liked about society when it was still of a piece."[34] "In everything I write there'll be this need to stick holes in overinflated worldviews and let the hot air out"[35]); *continuing* with more subversive views of the dionysian and the carnivalesque and the necessity to regenerate through "rebarbarization" (Schklovsky) ("Whatever form [the politicians, chiefs, whatever] set up is necessarily entropic: eventually it runs down and is unable to propel itself past a certain point. When it does that, it becomes necessary to do everything that has been taboo; wear women's clothes, kill the sacred animal and eat it, screw your mother, etc. A big blast reduces everything to rubble; then something new is built. Primitive societies, wiser than we, actually set aside a time to do this on a cyclical basis"[36]); *culminating* with the proposition that the comic is the indispensable key in which the potentially depressing nature of a free, limitless, expansive, and incomprehensible universe should be read: "I tend to think of tragedy as a kind of adolescent response to the universe—the higher truth is a comic response. . . . There *is* a kind of humor extremity which is even more mature than the tragic response."[37] Asked about the "humor" of his darkest creations, John Hawkes could, I think, put it not very differently.

There is therefore no reason to disassociate Coover's philosophical views on fiction and myth from his similar refusal of dogmatic images and discourses. Such refusals, accompanied by a creativity that demonstrates its renovative powers all the more forcefully by operating on previously exploited materials, clearly qualify as poetical; they afford the most persuasive explanation of the reasons for which Coover, in an apparent paradox, holds the American literary tradition in such high esteem: the mainstream for him, in effect, is that which links all artists willing to define themselves—in an admirable formula—as "the rebel, the iconoclast, the transformer."[38]

On the day when he received the Nobel Prize for Literature in 1960, "St-John Perse" said: "Poète est celui-là qui rompt pour nous l'accoutumance."[39] For all his having been ambassador to Washington, Alexis Léger may not have been aware, as a Frenchman, of the specific American literary overtones of such notions as "cutting loose," "breaking away," and "lighting out." But who will keep us, as we walk the last few steps of this informal and conversational stroll with Robert Coover, during which the virtues of "avoiding resolutions" and destroying the mental ruts and set grooves of discourse have been extolled, from overhearing this midwestern "prose" writer, this consistent "public burner" of stale untenable fictions and unacceptable myths, this literary Huck Finn berated for moral/literary choices that will ultimately prove right, defiantly exclaim, as he considers freeing us from mental slavery: "All right, then, I'll be a poet."

Notes

1 Robert Coover, *Origin of the Brunists* (New York: G. P. Putnam's Sons, 1966).

2 Thomas Pynchon, *The Crying of Lot 49* (Philadelphia: J. B. Lippincott Company, 1966).

3 Robert Coover, *In Bed One Night* (Providence: Burning Deck, 1983), p. 41.

4 In *Autres Rhumbs* (Paris: Gallimard, 1927), p. 235; my translation.

5 "*Lith:* mausti," *Webster's Third New International Dictionary,* p. 1497.

6 *In Bed One Night*, p. 42.

7 These quotations are from R. Grant Nutter and Robert K. Johnston's "Playing at Life: Robert Coover and His Fiction," *Christian Century,* 16 May 1979, pp. 549–53; from Barthes's *Mythologies* (Paris: Le Seuil, 1957); and from "Interview with Woolf" in Geoffrey Woolf, "An American Epic," *New Times,* 19 August 1977, p. 54.

8 In *Pricksongs and Descants* (New York: E. P. Dutton, Inc., 1969).

9 Coover, *News of the American Place Theatre* 5, no. 1 (November 1972), p. 2.

10 So many "scholarly" articles on Robert Coover's work have been published that I have chosen to make this as unscholarly as possible. One would rather be off track than redundant.

11 In Frank Gado's *First Person* (Schenectady, N.Y.: Union College Press, 1973).

12 It would, of course, clash with the distinction that can be established between *modern* and *postmodern* (circa 1807?), but jugglers of doubtful tags can be counted on to point out that Reason, like Art, is just another metaphor.

13 Frank Kermode, *The Sense of an Ending* (New York: Oxford University Press, 1966), p. 39.

14 As Coover puts it in the Gado interview; see *First Person.*

15 For Coover's awareness of this dimension of the problem, see C. W. E. Bigsby and H. Ziegler's interview in *The Radical Imagination and the Liberal Tradition* (London: Junction Books, 1982), in which repeated attempts at making Coover own up to liberalism are met with variations on such remarks as: "The history of [rational] discourse was like a kind of history of changing fashions, a swing from possibility to possibility, often accompanied at first by eurekas of discovery and ringing manifestos, but then a moving on when each possibility in turn revealed its own inevitable limitations" (p. 81).

16 Frank W. Shelton, "Humor and Balance in Coover's *The Universal Baseball Association, Inc.,*" *Critique* 17 (1) (1975): 78–90.

17 I have recently found a coincidence that might go some way toward accounting for the ambiguous image of Miller in *Origin of the Brunists:* a William Miller, American sectarian leader (1782–1849), was the author of a book entitled *Evidence from Scripture and History of the Second Coming of Christ about the year 1843*, published in 1836. His followers prepared for the second coming of Christ in 1843–1844 by neglecting worldly affairs, donning robes and . . . waiting on hilltops! I am more than ready to grant that Miller is common enough a name on American soil and that the whole thing might indeed be a mere coincidence; shall I in turn be granted extenuating circumstances for my temptation?

18 See my "Clio doesn't live here any more" in *Delta* (Montpellier, France), no. 8.

19 Robert Coover, *A Night at the Movies* (New York: Linden Press/Simon & Schuster, Inc., 1987).

20 In *Pricksongs and Descants.*

21 Pascal Quignard, *Carus* (Paris: Gallimard, 1979), p. 280; my translation.

22 Michael Davidson, in "More is Up" (*The Landing of Rochambeau),* suggests that aims are jails of the mind, as goals are gaols: "I will reach my goal / I already understand the padlock."

23 *Trema* (Paris), no. 1 (1976), p. 281.

24 "At the bottom of every thing, there swims a fish. / Fish, for fear you should come out naked, / I shall throw you my coat of images."

25 Paris: Gallimard, 1984.

26 Compare Coover's memories in *Trema* 1, p. 278: "The way we really start into the world is seeing the world as a series of stories. . . . I know that I was writing stories when I was six or seven and still writing them when I was ten and twelve; they were baseball stories and fairy tale stories, just like I'm writing now."

27 In Gado, *First Person.*

28 See his "La parietaria y el tomillo," in which the humbler plant thus placates the ivy's superb vanity: "Querida: chico soy, pero crezco / sin ayuda de nadie. Yo sí te compadizco; / pues por más que presumas, ni medio palmo puedes / medrar si no te arrimas a una de esas paredes."

29 And none of us, of course, is innocent of Walt Disney's iconographic domesticizing of the fauna in order to channel the blandest, tamest, paltriest, most sentimentally comforting, and most reliable moral and ideological tenets.

30 Gado, *First Person.*

31 "Robert Coover's Wondershow," *Amerikastudien* 29, no. 1 (1984): 75–85.

32 I am indebted for that remark to Prudence Rowntree's work on *Pricksongs and Descants* at the University of East Anglia.

33 In Gado, *First Person.*

34 Woolf interview.

35 In C. W. E. Bigsby and H. Ziegler, *Radical Imagination.*

36 Gado, *First Person.*

37 Ibid.

38 "On Reading 300 Novels," *New York Times Book Review,* 18 March 1984.

39 "He is a poet, who breaks away from addictive routine for us all."

GUY DAVENPORT

......

The Jules Verne Steam Balloon

King of Prussia I in D major K 575

Summer morning, awake a tick before the clock's ring, the work of birdcharm and circadian wheels, Hugo Tvemunding, assistant classics master and gym instructor at NFS Grundtvig, Troop Commander of Spejderkorps 235, and doctoral candidate in theology, sat bolt upright in bed to yawn and stretch. The Great Walrus, said Mariana beside him, her eyes still closed, is on the loose, grumping all rivals away from his rocks. His walruser is reared up like a gander trying to see over the hedge, but first we must say our prayers. Hugo recited the prayer to the creator of being that he'd said every morning since he was a very little boy, a prayer composed by his pastor father. Amen, said Mariana. Franklin has slept through it all. Have not, said Franklin. Amen, too. Tickle me, and I'll bite. My rocks, said Hugo. Franklin for all his contribution to the dialogue is still asleep. Long hairy feet on the floor, said Mariana, who wore a shirt of Hugo's for a nightgown, square pinktoed feet on the floor, shapely girl's feet on the floor, plop, slap, and gracefully silent. Who lost a Band-Aid in the bed? Your T-shirt fits Franklin like a potato sack on a weasel.

Hollyhocks

Hugo's run before breakfast was along a macadam road through pinewoods with an undergrowth of fern and laurel. He freed himself with every stride of the residue of dreams, of warm lethargies that had nested in his muscles, of anxieties that had made trash in his mind. He spoke to rabbits hopping across the road, to a cheeky fox doing a little dance in a clearing. The light was silver, early, cold. He had dreamed of his mother standing beside hollyhocks and coleus. Idiotically, he had said, *They're dead, aren't they?* She'd said, with her usual placid composure, *Why no, dear, they're not dead.* And indeed nothing could have been more alive than these dream hollyhocks and coleus, so crisply beautiful in the accurate light of the dream. And his mother's kindly ghost was like a blessing. She wore her apron, as for housework, and her voice was as sweet as springwater. White latticework of the backporch door behind her. A perfectly temperate summer day. *Why no, dear, they're not dead at all.*

Cabin with Skylight

Stables once, Hugo's room was designed and appointed by a drawing master who, having made it into a Danish Modern oblong of continuous space with a skylight, left to take a position elsewhere. Bed and worktable under the skylight, bookcases, chairs beyond, toward the kitchen area, which had a small barn window over the sink and cabinets. On the walls were a large photograph of Bourdelle's *Herakles the Archer,* a Mondriaan of the severest geometric period, a Paul Klee angel grinning about some sacred mischief, a photograph of Brancusi's *Torso d'un jeune homme,* and three paintings by Hugo: Mariana naked, slouched reading in a chair, a still life of meadow flowers in a coffee mug, and a large painting that had once been of the bicycle rider, repainted with Tom Agernkop as model.

Garden

The colors in the dream where his mother stood placidly in her coverall, print cotton polka-dot gloves, and straw hat were those of photographs in *The Country Garden* and *House and Family*: early greens, soft browns, reticent blues in sharp silvery focus.

Water

This is Franklin the Rabbit Who Invented Electricity, Hugo said to Rutger, Kim, Asgar, Tom, and Anders in the showers. We've run six kilometers, Franklin said. Oof! These wolfcub mystery knots you did my laces in, Hugo, won't untie. *Hugo!* Knowing eyes found laughing eyes. Let me, Rutger said, kneeling. Franklin, looking hard at Kim and Anders under a shower together, soaping each other, wiggled his fingers at his ears and ruckled like a dove. They like each other, Skipper, Hugo said.

Wheat

He wasn't out to set himself up through signs and wonders, Hugo said to his Sunday School class. He was not concerned about who he was. That showed in everything he did. And from moment to moment he was the people he suffered with, whom he could cure or comfort or free. Most of these are people estranged from themselves by pain or deformity. People who are out of their minds are no good to anybody else, and Yeshua's idea of man was that he was first of all someone who could help another.

Eyes Blue with Fate

A nipper, Mariana sighed, locked herself in the laundryroom and no amount of cajoling and instructions about the catch did anything but make her howl the louder, so I had to climb onto the roof and jimmy open a window the size of a handkerchief and plead with the little demon to listen while I showed her how to let herself out, and another nipper stuck modeling clay up his nose and turned blue, and another had hiccups for an hour, and another was passing around color photos of her big brother doing it with his girl on the sunroom floor, and another barfed on the vocabulary cards. So I've had it, and want love, understanding, and sourcream pineapple pancakes for supper. She was holding an ice cube to Franklin's knee, which was skinned bloody. His silkflop thatch had leaf-trash and twigs in it. A smutch of mud saddled his nose. The seat of his pants were piped with clay. They had all converged at the bus stop, Franklin from the soccer field, Mariana off the bus, and Hugo from class, going home. While Mariana set up a field hospital to deal with Franklin, Hugo, out of his jeans, exiguous briefs taxed by a randy flex, said that he would provide love, Franklin understanding, and Mariana sourcream pineapple pancakes. Iodine, Mariana ordered, and fill the sink with hot soapy water, skin Franklin of his pants and underpants and put the one in the other. The two in the other, Franklin said. Hugo is hanging out like the donkeys at the zoo. Better still, Mariana said, strip the lout and stand him in the sink, soap him up, and pour panfuls of water over his head. Family life is wonderfully exciting, Hugo said, lifting Franklin into the sink. You know Pascal? he asked. I know Pascal, Hugo said. He is the light of Arne Sigurjonsson's life, as everybody from the kitchen staff to the headmaster knows. He, said Franklin around the washcloth, lost one of his shoes. So I told him to throw the other away. What good is one shoe?

They tease him real pitiful about Hr. Sigurjonsson, so we beat up Otto with the weasel eyes. He was picking on Pascal. I heard him. I didn't know, Hugo said, that you were friends with Pascal. I am now, Franklin said. After we beat up Otto. Well yes, Hugo said, let's hear about that. I booted him in the butt, Franklin said, hard. He called Pascal a name, and Pascal just took it. I was behind them both, you see, and here was Otto's butt for the kicking. That's when he tried to pin me, and I did my knee there. I'm not listening, Mariana said, I'm not hearing a word of this. So, said Franklin, Pascal got in it then. He pushed Otto on a shoulder while hooking his ankle: laid him flat. Then we both jumped on him. Hr. Sigurjonsson showed Pascal how to defend himself.

Yeshua in the Wheat

Goose grass, said Hugo, found with knotweed in hard ground poor soil cinder paths. Old meadows are thick with it, an archaic wheat from which the horseriding plunderers made bread and foddered their shaggy shetlands. It came to Eleusis, Joseph Gaertner thought, by way of India. That's why he named it *Eleusine indica.* Crabgrass and crowfoot are of the same family. The florets are ashlared thick along the spikes, see? And there's no awn. Grass, Franklin said, is just grass. Here, said Mariana, is where we get Hugo's handsome blond crosseyed stare. Meaning I hear it but I don't believe it. The pathfinders never get it, only us, and the occasional Grundtvigger. Franklin calm and unheeding. What Mariana says is what Mariana says. It has nothing to do with him until she starts shouting. Emmer of the prophets embedded in the clay of Ugaritic pots under the botanist's microscope is like implicit information in a text. It came along, like Franklin underfoot, of itself. Now I'm grass, Franklin said.

Acorn in Its Cup

To get to the bus stop where Mariana with shining eyes and bright smile arrived at afternoon's end, Hugo damp from his second gym class, his book bag charged with Latin and Greek exercises to correct, had but to cross the soccer field and amble along two blocks of guardedly prosperous houses with colorful gardens behind low front walls. If he let the class go ten minutes early and skipped a shower, he had time to walk to the bus stop by way of the meadow beyond the wood where he could sit under a favorite oak, elbows on knees, and have a rich moment of calm and anticipation. The river shone at the other side of the meadow, if the light was right. Here passages of the thesis on Yeshua took form and texture, the day disclosed patterns, abrasions healed, letters were opened and read.

Papa's hollyhocks. Papa's reading, the lectures and concerts he had been to. A note on a Hebrew word.

Aakjaer Minor had begun a cataleptic syndrome that was as yet more comic than serious. He hugged people and wouldn't, or couldn't, let go. In the locker room he'd seen Golo Hansen embarrassed and helpless in Alexander Aakjaer's grasp. I don't want to hurt him, Golo had wailed to Hugo. He grabs people like this, his eyes go blank, and he won't turn loose. Hugo had said, quit trying to pull him loose. Just stand cool. He got me the other day, Asgar said, and two people couldn't pry him off. It's mental. He doesn't know what you're talking about when it's over. Hugo had studied the unfocused eyes, the sweaty back of the neck, cold wrists, locked knees and elbows. Gently he'd guided Golo out of Alexander's gripping arms, hoisted the suddenly slack Alexander onto his shoulders, and carried him to the infirmary where he said to Nurse that Aakjaer Minor had had a dizzy spell in gym and only needed to lie still for awhile. Nurse nevertheless stuck a thermometer in Alexander's mouth and took his pulse, seeing nothing interesting in either.

Jonas

The pompion or million creeps upon the ground if nothing be by it whereon it may take hold and climb with very great ribbed rough and prickly branches whereon are set large rough leaves cut in on the edges with deep gashes and dented besides, with many claspers also, which wind about everything they meet. The flowers are great and large, hollow and yellow, divided at the brim into five parts, at the bottom of which grows the fruit sometimes of the bigness of a man's body and oftentimes less, in some ribbed or bunched, in others plain and either long or round, green or yellow. The seed is great flat and white, lying in the middle of the watery pulp. The root is of the bigness of a man's thumb, dispersed underground with many small fibers. They are boiled in fair water and salt, or in powdered beef broth, sometimes in milk, and so eaten, or else buttered. The seed, as well as of cowcumbers and melons, are cooling, and serve for emulsions in the like manner as almond milks, for those troubled with the stone.

Blue Pup Tent

In the ferns beyond birches. Hugo slowed, running in place, and hollered *ho!* Whoever you are, he sang in stentorian *buffo*, I come in peace. Silence. Brilliant early morning northern light. *Ho!* from the pup tent. I'll go away, Hugo said, if you want me to. This is school property. Grundtviggers are you? Tvemunding here, having a run before breakfast. A head, bare shoulders, an ironic sleepy grin. Anders. Out of the tent on knuckles and toes, mother naked. Morning, he said.

Through the birches, behind Anders, Quark on a silver wolf loping.

Kim and I, Anders said. Kim looked out, blond hair over his eyes. He crawled out monkey-nimble. A hug from Anders.

River

The divesture of Franklin in the meadow by the river. Mariana flourished a toy trumpet. The grasses, Hugo said, go from Tolland Man's gruel of flaxseed and goosegrass to Roman porridge, which was linseed roasted with barley and coriander pounded in a mortar, salted, boiled, and served in a bowl to Horace dining with Virgil. Columella fancied it, and Pliny mentions the toothsomeness of rustic Tuscan porridge on a winter morning. Meadow with goats to gaze at as he ate. Like us, said Mariana, pleating and folding Franklin's togs. There were iron age grape pips at Donja Dolina. Bet they ate frogs, too, Mariana said, and green lizards. People upstream in a boat, Franklin said. Voices carry over water. Master Sigurjonsson and Pascal without a stitch. Ho, said Mariana. Pascal I mean, Franklin said, climbing Hugo to stand on his shoulders. Hr. Ess has on a cap, wristwatch, and little triangle underpants like Hugo's. Swim out, Hugo said, and climb aboard.

Old Mirrors Flecked and Tarnished

On a long walk that took him near the Nordkalksten seawall and warehouses, Hugo had seen the bicycle rider hefting his bike up the stone steps, swinging onto it in the road. Their eyes met, with no recognition in the rider's, though he was already a day student at NFS Grundtvig but not yet someone Hugo had tried to be friendly toward. His jeans were unzipped, the pod of his dingy briefs pouching through. His eyes had been dead, as when he had last seen them in the police morgue.

Asters and Zinnias

Papa in a folding hammock chair by his hollyhocks, straw boater over his eyes. Hugo's theology, he said, is of course his need to undo me. Not by cracking my head on a dusty road in Greece, but as an intelligent child takes its toys apart to see what makes them go. Ridiculous, but there you are. Papa, Hugo said, I know what makes you go. And the machinery is too fine for my fingers. I hope I'm something like. Peas in a pod, Mariana said, if you know what to look for. You have the same sense of house, of space, of time. You eat alike. I didn't know how to take a walk until Hugo annexed me. Or how a room can be the whole world. It's awful, Franklin said, but it's fun. Tell me, Pastor Tvemunding said from under his hat, holding out an arm to invite Franklin over. Franklin came, got hugged, and climbed astride. Papa, Hugo said, keeps his hat over his eyes so as not to look at Franklin snake naked. How modern I'm willing to be, Papa said, is, I see, still a matter for doubt. Notice everything, Franklin said. Know where everything comes from, a hundred years back.

Anemone

Matter, the physicists seem to be saying, was not stuff before creation: critical tensions in nothingness, the universal vacuum, became so energetic that they exploded. Critical tensions? Papa asked. Force, said Hugo. The only thing the physicists can reach back to is a great force present in all matter and space. Well then, Papa said, scattering leaves with his stick, there's God. As they see Him. If, Hugo said, man in God's image was Adam, God in man's image was Yeshua. If matter was not stuff before creation, then God can be a pattern of energy rather than an oxygen breather and processor of carbohydrates. That we are in His image then means that He is and we are, animations of the same energy system. Except, perhaps, His anima occupies the whole sea of neutrinos that is boundless but limited, and we each occupy bodies only, energy systems that are bounded but limitless, exchanging love and conversation, procreating both bodies and minds. God's procreation is continuous, ours occasional. Yeshua is an occasional aspect of a continuity.

Breakfast

Franklin. Hair carrot and brass. Irises seagreen, pupils hyacinth. Pathfinder brogans, collapsed socks. Lots of practical irony and cautious reticence, the hippety-hop who invented electricity. Love me some geography, he says to the mush bowl, because a map is a jigsaw puzzle. What I like is where the driblet islands make a trail at the south poke of things, left behind, all on a drift to the west. And to the north, crumbly islands. Love islands. Show him the inland island in France, bounded by four rivers. Plains islands bounded by mountains. A country, then, he opines, is a lot of people pretending they're an island, because they all speak the same language. Well, sometimes. Or because they have a common interest, like the Swiss. There is no place without time, no time without place. So, says Franklin, knuckling his nose, you can't say where without saying when. The Mediterranean when it had seals in it. Holland before tulips. Everything wanders, he says. Land, people, animals, trees.

Out from Joppa

Two ways, Hugo said, and Papa cocked his head to listen. Like John, as in eleven Matthaeus, neither eating nor drinking, and the opinion of the public is that you are owned and operated by a devil, or like Yeshua, eating and drinking, and the people say here's a glutton and a drunkard, the friend of tax collectors and sinners. And, Papa said, that's yet another logion where the sign of Jonas is the pivot. The vine is to be judged by its gourd.

Dove

By wholeness of being.

Fig

Neutrino here, Hugo said, our Franklin, is as yet all luck. Whenever the angel rings the silver run in a sound of trumpets, he thrusts his sickle in, the wheat topples in a golden rush, the chaff dances in the air, and the harvest song is the only one his red tongue knows morning, noon and night. Whereas those of us who shave and pay taxes always seem to get in line at the post office behind an oriental trying to mail a live chicken to Sri Lanka. Look at MacTaggart the English master. He loses his car habitually in the parking lot. That his disciples in Transcendental Meditation and Buddhist raising of the consciousness are all feeble-minded hankerers who will clot around any mountebank he does not notice. He walks across flowerbeds puffing the beauties of nature to one of his morons. He was the only one of the faculty the bicycle rider esteemed and thought a bright teacher. To blow like a dead leaf in the wind, irresponsible, irresponsive. Which beautiful teaching, Mariana said, laid the bicycle rider out on the slab at the police morgue.

Monkeys and Parrots

If, Mariana read to Franklin lying on the carpet and rolling a soccer ball inchmeal from crotch to chin, the forest were darker it did not seem to be more silent. They could hear a kind of buzzing in the treetops, a vague noise coming from the branches. Looking upwards, the three men could see indistinctly something like a great platform stretched out some forty meters above the ground. There must be at that height a tremendous entanglement of branches without any cranny through which the daylight could pierce. A thatched roof would not have been more lightproof. This explained the darkness which prevailed beneath the trees. Where they had camped that night the nature of the ground had changed greatly. No more intermingled branches or brambles, no more of those thorns which had kept them from leaving the footpath. A scanty grass, like a prairie which neither rain nor spring ever watered. The trees, at intervals from seven to ten meters, resembled pillars supporting some colossal edifice, and their branches must cover an area of several thousand hectares. There were masses of African sycamores whose trunks were formed of a number of stems firmly united toward the ground, bob bobs. Baobabs, Hugo said from his desk, a majestic great graygreen tree that huddles its trunks like celery. Bob bobs, read Mariana, recognizable by the gourdlike shape of their bole, with a circumference of seven to ten meters and surmounted by an enormous mass of hanging branches. There were silk cotton trees with their trunks opening into a series of hollows big enough for a man to hide in. Mahogany trees with trunks a meter and a half in diameter from which might have been excavated dug-out canoes from five to seven meters long. Ho, Hugo said, Zuntz on the centurion with Jules Verne from across the room has filled me with lovingkindness, especially as Monsieur Verne's expositor has had her hand inside her knickers from the beginning of the chapter. Can I help it if I'm a sweet person? she said. When, Franklin said, twirling the soccer ball on his chin, I get to my peter, it jumps. See? Chin to peter, peter to chin. Phenomenal! Hugo said. I'll bet if you went to the baker's, by way of the kiosk for an evening paper, you might find a half dozen strawberry-jam cakes with custard topping that we can have with coffee, which I'll make, as Mariana is not going to be able to see straight after our expression, or expressions, of mutual esteem.

Blue Summer Sky

Hugo under his oak at the meadow's edge saw the oval shadow of the hot-air balloon sliding toward him before he looked up and saw the balloon itself, a gaudy upsidedown pear shape the oiled silk of which was zoned in bands: the equitorial one was a rusty persimmon, a Mongol color, and around it were the figures of the zodiac copied from the mosaic floor of Bet Alpha Synagogue in Byzantine Israel, archaic but supple of line. The band above was bells and pomegranates in orange and blue, the one below was egg-and-dart Hellenistic. The basket was of wicker and belonged to the protomachine age, for a propeller that seemed to be made of four cricket bats was turned by a fanbelt connected to a brass cylinder leaking steam vapor. There was a wooden rudder, and levers at the taffrail. Three ten-year-old boys were the crew, as happy as grigs at their work bringing the balloon down right in front of Hugo, who stood and gaped, at a loss to account for anything he was seeing. The boys were dressed in nautical Scandinavian togs, with long scarves around their necks, as if the air from which they'd descended was very cold. One boy manipulated a lever that seemed to bring the balloon down, another braked the propeller, which stopped spinning and rolled to a lazy halt. Puffs of vapor smoked from the cylinder. The boys' bright grins were for the joy of surprising Hugo, for the joy of being aeronauts in a balloon on a fine summer day, and for the joy of being messengers, which they said they were, talking all at once. Who in the name of God are you? Hugo asked. Where have you come from? My name is Tumble, and my friends are Quark and Buckeye. Where we come from we're not to say, and we're messengers. Bringing a message, Quark said helpfully. The coordinates are right, Buckeye said, consulting a length of paper between two rollers. Oak tree, meadow, island, Denmark. Hugo Tvemunding by way of worldly name. Shapes alphabet into words about the Company. *Yeryüzü kendi kendine bir toprak*. Buckeye! Tumble said sweetly, you're off band: that's Turkish. Sorry, said Buckeye, I was about to blush anyway, this part of the printout about shepherd to the young, a good son, and superb lover in both flesh and spirit, *tam avidus quam taurus* in a different hand in the margin, the dispatcher I suppose. *Nesuprantamas disonansas tarp,* oops! sor-ree. Anyway, you're the right soul. Yes, said Tumble, and here's the message. Road auspicious. Though young, act like a man. Be steadfast, patient, and silent.

Why? Hugo asked. About what?

That, smiled Quark, we are not free to say.

Boundary

There is only one sense: touch. The sun, by way of caroming off a mellow brick wall with lonely afternoon light on it, firm plump pair of breasts with delectable nipples, a page of Homer, touches the eyes. Eating is touch carried to the utmost. Vibrant air touches the ear. Smell is so many particles from aromatic things. The world is a mush of matter rather than the separateness we ascribe to things. Franklin in his Wolf Cub cricket cap, blue shirt with yellow kerchief, little blue pants, tall ribbed socks, and red sneakers listened to Hugo in Eagle Scout khakis with solemn attention. Boys named Abel and Bruno had got out of him, moments before the powwow, that he has no father, that his sister Mariana is the bedmate of Scoutmaster Tvemunding, that he has only been camping with Hugo and Mariana, that he is poor, that Hugo makes love to Mariana lots and lots, and that his uniform is so new it has little squares of paper in all the pockets with an Inspector's number, to accompany complaint of manufacturing defect. As to other questions, Franklin had offered to bloody Bruno's nose for him. Knots, naming of tent parts and tools, cards with animal tracks, cards with flowers and weeds, and here was Scoutmaster Tvemunding, who taught Latin, Greek, and gym at NFS Grundtvig and Sunday School at Treenigheden, talking about everything being touch. Eugenius, he said, front and forward. Theodor, front and forward. Face each other, tall and straight, shoulders back. Theodor, cup your hands. Eugenius is going to give you something, out of his wild imagination, and you are going to feel it, in your wild imagination, and describe it, how it feels. A frog! Eugenius said. Well, said Theodor, I had a frog in my hands just the other day, and a snake, and a hedgehog, so I'm not up a creek. A frog looks damp but is dry, looks flabby but is hard. It twitches, trying to jump away, but can be still, probably because it's scared. I'd be scared. It's cool. Its throat pulses.

Zum Ziele Führt Dich Diese Bahn

Theodor, Hugo said, didn't know the dative of accommodation from a rat's ass and has been stricken with amnesia in the matter of ablative absolutes, Frits and Asgar bloodied each other in a fight back of the gym, nasty little beasts, the stupidly inconsiderate grounds trolls ran a power mower just outside the windows for half of Greek, and around three Ulrich gave me a frantic signal in gym to come quick. Golo and Abel were, for reasons best known to themselves, having a little conviviality outside study hall, where they were supposed to be, playing push and pull with each other's pizzles while gazing into each other's big soulful eyes I suppose, fine by me and nobody could care less though they have rooms and showers and woods and meadows in which to welcome puberty until they're crosseyed and gasping for breath, but why waste the ten minutes before study hall, and then Aakjaer Minor, who grabs people and goes cataleptic, happens along and pins them both. Ulrich was the first to notice this predicament, and knowing that McTaggart had study hall and would be stomping along crabwise at any moment, and would bore everybody for days with the psychology of it all, had the diplomatic genius to push all three into the broom closet and sprint for the gym. We nipped back. McTaggart was bleating about combining study with transcendental meditation, so we could craftily open the broom closet and walk the interlocked three down the hall, one walking backward and zipping himself up, the other sideways, and both carrying the clinging Aakjaer with my and Ulrich's help, God laughing at us all fit to kill. We disentangled the mass in my office. Abel, who had not managed to get his britches up with his arms pinned to his sides, stood there in pretty outrage. What in hell does it mean? he begged of me.

Mariana, listening with wide eyes, had deshoed and unsocksed Hugo as he talked in the chair where he had flopped and sagged, tugged his trousers off, and was unbuttoning his shirt when a banging on the door announced Franklin in full Cub Scout rig. O Lord, Hugo sighed, I was forgetting that tonight's the little bastards in yellow and blue, with beanies. Hi, said Franklin. Things look real interesting. Hugo, Mariana said, has had a trying day, and has taken a full ten minutes to get over it.

Zweck

In pipestem trews snug of cleft, flat Dutch cap, thickwove jersey, Norfolk jacket, hobnailed brogues, and Finnish scarf with an archaic pattern of reindeer and runes worked into its weave, Tumble climbed from the basket of the steam balloon, bounced from his jump, and cued Quark and Buckeye, poised with flute and glockenspiel, to give him a tune. *Master Erastus,* he sang, stomping with seesawing shoulders and chiming smile, *Equuleus quagga!* Likes, said Quark in recitative over the catch, clover bluegrass dill, spring onions oats and hay. Kin to, said Buckeye, lowering his flute, Eohippus Five Toes, silver wolves, red deer on Rum, dandelions, and Ertha when she's broody. Maybe, said Quark, depressing the declinator, which seeped vapor, but the mykla puts them in with asses burros zebras and horses of the good old Hwang Ho Valley, don't it? Yuss, said Tumble, but Buckeye means chord. Spartan spadgers, springbokker, leapers and runners. So hold fast, wait long, and don't speak. No, not to anybody.

Archaic Torso of Apollo

Even though we can never see the head that sang, with its deer's eyes staring at infinity, we have the strong torso from whose animal grace we can imagine the hot summer clarity of its gaze. If the gone head is still not there, in light, why then does the proud chest disturb your looking, or the sweet shift of the hips, slight as a smile, that takes our eyes down the cunning body, to its cluster of seeds? Otherwise this stone would stand senseless under the polished slope of its shoulders, without its wild balance, and would not be as rich with light as the sky with stars. The world sees you, too. You must change your life.

An Event Also Happens Where It Is Known

Out past the warehouses and quays on Nordkalksten is a seawall of gray stone. A catwalk at its base, a bicycle path along the top, with iron rail. Harbor, river, barges. Here one could see old men fishing, sailors sleeping off a terrible drunk, and sunbathers spread against the slant of the wall. Boys in dingy bargain-basement briefs, boys impudently naked.

Under

We distinguish this seventh stratum by stringers of the stone which readily melts in fire of the second order. Beneath this is another ashy rock, light in weight and five foot thick. Next comes a lighter stratum the color of ash and a foot thick. Beneath this lies the eleventh stratum, dark and like the seventh, two foot through. Below the last is a twelfth stratum, soft and of a whitish color, two foot thick. The weight of this sits on the thirteenth stratum, ashy and a foot thick, whose weight in turn is supported by a fourteenth stratum of black color. There follows this another black stratum half a foot thick, which is again followed by a sixteenth stratum still blacker in color, whose thickness is also the same. Beneath this, and last of all, lies the cupriferous stratum, black colored and schistose, in which there sometimes glitter scales of gold-colored pyrites in very thin sheets, which, as I have said elsewhere, often take the forms of various living things.

Hollyhocks Along a Garden Wall

I'm wonderfully delighted, Pastor Tvemunding said to Mariana, that you and Hugo are friends. He has always been a friendly boy. He used to toddle off behind the postman, and grieve that he could not stay longer than to hand over the mail and exchange comments on the weather. He made friends with the girl who delivered butter and eggs. He fell in love with all his schoolmates. He is indeed, Mariana said, a very loving person. His loving nature, Pastor Tvemunding said, causes him grief from time to time. You know about the student whom he calls the Bicycle Rider?

Who's dead, Mariana said. I know what you mean. He hurt Hugo.

Because, Pastor Tvemunding said, Hugo had never really before, I believe, encountered evil face to face. He doesn't want to admit that evil cannot be dealt with. He cannot believe that there are wholly selfish people drowned in themselves, beyond the reach of love and understanding. That there are people who, impotent to create, destroy. That there are people whose self-loathing is so deep they know nothing of generosity and invariably do the mean thing even when they might as easily do the generous one. The young man was on drugs, and had been for years, but I'm not one to blame drugs for human evil: the evil is there before the drugs, which are part of the meanness and not its cause.

All this theological work, which will not take him into the ministry, began with a remark I made years ago, that God will remain inscrutable and uncertain forever, but that Jesus—Hugo's Yeshua, for the Aramaic name is of the essence for him—had an intuitive idea of God that put goodness in our hands. He is light, of which we are free to partake, or be in darkness. We can be transparent to our fellow man, or opaque.

Buckeye

Possum ate a lightning bug and now he shines inside.

Red and Yellow Zinnias

I want to be up-to-date, Pastor Tvemunding said at tea, reaching over to wipe whipped cream from the corners of Franklin's mouth with his napkin. There's Hugo's room, and the guest room which is so jolly with the apple tree at the window. Mariana and I, Hugo said, will sleep together, and I'll rig out my old scout cot for Franklin. But, said the pastor, there's the guest room for him. Oh no, Hugo said, travelers should stay together.

Meadow with Goldflowers and Poppies

Buckeye in a Portuguese sailor's shirt, abrupt white denim pants, beret and espadrilles climbed backward down the rope ladder of the balloon, singing *onward under over through!* Quark tossed the anchor onto the meadow. The balloon tilted in its drift, exhaled vapor from its cylinders, bounced and swayed as Tumble pumped the declinators. Quark swung himself over the wicker taffrail with a deft scissor kick and landed springing. Tumble closed valves, cinched a line, made an entry in a ledger and vaulted out, rolling forward in a somersault. Ho! said Buckeye, Hi! said Quark, Hup! said Tumble. *For adoration beyond match,* sang Tumble pulling his sailor's middy over his blond rick of windscrumpled hair, *the scholar bulfinch aims to catch. The soft flute's ivory touch,* sang Quark sopranino, his gray American sweatshirt halfway over his head. *And, careless on the hazel spray,* Buckeye sang as he snatched off his Portuguese sailor's blouse, *the daring redbreast keeps at bay the damsel's greedy clutch.* Shoeless, sockless, Tumble backed out of his sailor's pants singing, *While Israel sits beneath his fig. With coral root and amber spring,* Quark sang with trills and a cadenza as he wriggled off his Sears Roebuck blue jeans. *The weaned adventurer sports,* tossing his short white pants into the gondola of the balloon. Tumble, pretending to blush, thumbed down his drawers, Quark and Buckeye pindling briefs, and the three in their pinkbrown slender ribby nakedness sang in chiming

Mozartian harmony, *Where to the palm the jasmin cleaves for adoration mongst the leaves the gale his peace reports. Now labor,* they sang, making a triangle of arms on one another's shoulders, *his reward receives, for adoration counts his sheaves, to peace, her bounteous prince. The nectarine his strong tint imbibes, and apples of ten thousand tribes, and quick peculiar quince.*

Trollflöjten

Ringtailed kinkajous trotting on the logging road, bouncing and siffling, squeaking and hopping, in pairs and trios, alone and quartets. Yellow parrots above them, monkeys and kingfishers. Franklin's world, Mariana said. Years ago he was a rat in the Pied Piper festival, he and scads of littles in brown and gray rat suits with rope tails, creeping along behind the Piper playing Mozart. I remember a rat who lost his way and had to be carried by a woman and restored to the pack. Wasn't me, Franklin said. I crept good.

Golden Samphire

Buckeye in the meadow, where the balloon was tethered. Tumble and Quark were leapfrogging by the river. He held out his hand for a meadowlark to fly to him and stand on his palm. She spoke to him. He answered in quail. Silly! she said. Do I look like a quail hen? He spoke goat. She laughed. Frog. Giggle.

Auriga. Betelgeuse. Barnard's Star.

In spite of their intangibility, neutrinos enjoy a status unmatched by any other known particle, for they are actually the most common objects in the universe, outnumbering electrons by a thousand million to one. In fact, the universe is really a sea of neutrinos, punctuated only rarely by impurities such as atoms. It is even possible that neutrinos collectively outweigh the stars, and therefore dominate the gravity of the cosmos.

Right the Second Time

Tom'll be here in a bit, Hugo said to Mariana nose to nose. I think I can walk, Mariana said, though my brains are all gone, so much jelly they are.

There's somebody. It was Franklin. O wow, he said, looking squiggle-eyed and pretending to barf. Who, said Mariana, pulled his piddler till his eyes rolled back in his head the whole week we were at Papa Tvemunding's, while we had to make do with teen-age smooching? You said Augustus would spoil me, Franklin said solemnly. I like Augustus. I imagine so, Hugo said. Nasty little spy. Papa with a dry cough to introduce the subject, which amused him tremendously, said that Franklin confided in him that we were not making love, but only kissing a lot and whispering, before we went to sleep. I guess, he'd opined, you wouldn't like them to, but he didn't tell us that Papa had laughed and said that love was a joyful and good thing, and that young people were very close to God when they made love. Franklin being Franklin, next got Papa to say a good word for rabbity nosed boys jacking off, in moderation, naturally. It's nature, Franklin said. To be thought of as fun. That was the afternoon the rascal so coolly shed his pants and stomped around upstairs whacking away. Afternoons, and once a morning and twice in the afternoon, Franklin explained, was because Augustus said I was to, but at night was because you said I was to, if I wanted. So I did. I suppose, Mariana said to the skylight, if a third party had assured him of the naturalness of the kinship between boys and monkeys, Franklin would have had no time to eat, sleep, or have all those long talks with Papa Tvemunding. Who, said Hugo, spoiled him rotten. I promised to write him a letter, Franklin said. I will, too. Tom's here, Mariana said. Hugo, who had pulled on long sweatpants and a singlet and was howling for coffee, set the painting of the Bicycle Rider on the easel. He had whited out the lazily handsome blond face and its dead blue eyes. The right arm, on the fist of which the head had leaned, was also overpainted. Dark background's going, too, Hugo mused: it wants to be white. Mariana, her breasts loose under a rich blue pullover, was zipping herself into tight coral shorts when big Tom, tossing his floppy hair out of his eyes, shifted from foot to foot. He crossed his hands on his behind, touching a lampshade with an elbow. He then cupped them over his crotch, seeing instantly that, expand or contract, he was equally awkward. He tried sliding his fingers into his pockets, hitting the lampshade again, and settled for knuckling his nose and scratching a convenient itch on his thigh. Shown the painting, he stared at it. That, Hugo said, was that dopey kid who was a day student, the one who floated around on lysergic acid and managed the ultimate in trendy distance by killing himself with an overdose of God knows what. I tried getting his head out of his ass. I failed. No, Mariana said, he failed you.

Anyway, Hugo said, I'm going to repaint. Tom hates coffee, Mariana said brightly. Every time he's been here, he has suffered and squirmed. Beer, milk, fizz water, which? Beer, Tom said, his voice rasping at his own audacity. Head turned slightly, so that you're looking at me out of the side of your eyes. Right elbow on the chair arm. Everything else the same, except that your body is harder and better muscled than the Rider's, so I have all sorts of changes to make. Take off your pants. This sloshed Tom's beer. Leave your briefs on. They're nicely stinted and stressed.

The balloon, Hugo could see through the skylight, was just outside. He had learned on a walk with Mariana that she could not see Buckeye, Quark, and Tumble. They had come and stood gravely interested around while they sat under the oak, Mariana's head in Hugo's lap.

Burnt sienna, Hugo said, raw sienna, titanium white. Franklin made a great show of finding the tubes and laying them on the little table that served as a palette.

Buckeye was on the skylight, peering in. Short khaki pants, grey white and ochre striped soccer jersey, and not till he came into the room, through the door, in less time than the blinking of an eye, could you see his dinky blue cap.

Calabash! he said to Hugo, straked gourd pumpkin vine!

If I had some paper and a pencil and an envelope and a stamp, Franklin said, I could write Augustus. And, Mariana said, if you could spell and write so that anybody but God could read it. Put in your letter, Hugo said, that while we visited I saw what I needed to see. Say that the casting out of demons is the hub on which everything else turns. He'll know what I mean. The self is the demon. Demon out, daimon in.

O wow! Franklin said. Start spelling. Hugo painted, Tom with only his good nature to see him through his ordeal, took courage from the fact that it was his beauty that got him into this, and thought of seducing Franklin without breaking Lemuel's heart, share him perhaps, and Mariana, and even Hugo, and the green-eyed sailor with the silver eyelashes, humped pectorals, and a sleepy friendly smile. Mariana spelled, Franklin wrote and erased and wrote again. Hugo painted.

Tumble was at the skylight, Quark looking over his shoulder. Why do you keep looking up? Mariana asked idly. The light, Hugo said. It's what I paint by.

Buckeye was inspecting Tom, closely, and with doggish curiosity. His eyes met Hugo's. Under all's a fire so fine it is and isn't in and out of time, a pulse of is, a pulse of isn't. But, Buckeye said with a shrug of his boney shoulders and a crinkle of dimples in his smile, that isn't worth knowing, is it? Over all's the nothing that's something because of the curving tides of the is and isn't. No matter, that, either. He stood behind Tom and put his hands around his neck and rested his chin in Tom's hair. Quark read Franklin's letter. Tumble sniffed Mariana. What matters, Buckeye said, is that there are so many who don't know their right hand from their left.

JOSEPH C. SCHÖPP

......

"Perfect Landscape with Pastoral Figures": Guy Davenport's Danish Eclogue à la Fourier

Guy Davenport, though undoubtedly one of "the very few truly original, truly autonomous voices now audible in American letters," is nevertheless a literary figure widely ignored by readers and critics alike.[1] "Neither militantly committed to the new nor assimilable to an 'old guard,'"[2] the author of three remarkable collections of stories and an impressive selection of forty literary essays[3] "goes underadvertized"[4] and is, apart from a few highly favorable reviews, almost entirely left out of the critical discussion. A professor of English at the University of Kentucky with a profound knowledge of classical languages and a genuine interest in archeology and ancient cultures, Davenport regards his writings—translations, poems, fictions, essays—chiefly as "extensions of the classroom," as "objective, useful, instructive" lessons.[5]

Davenport, the lecturer, seems to have learned these lessons, as he intimates in an autobiographical essay with the telling title "Finding," in the fields of his native South Carolina where he with his family used to hunt for Indian arrowheads on Sunday afternoons after an appallingly tedious morning in Sunday school. These field trips, he contends, taught him how to see; these outings trained his eyes and shaped his sensibility "with surer and finer hand than any classroom" (*GoI*, p. 367). Here objects for their own sake began for him to matter and things lying practically "at one's doorstep" (*GoI*, p. 131) rather than in a far-off exotic distance gained importance. As he observed them with a keen and "astute eye,"[6] they gradually disclosed surprisingly new patterns that were unlike any "things with nearby models" (*GoI*, p. 366). Like Henry David Thoreau, another Indian arrowhead collector, passionate naturalist, and true American "forager"—an expression Davenport uses time and again to characterize his own work as a writer—he learned to "forage" the allegedly familiar places of the neighborhood and to come up with new reports of what he had found. He taught himself to explore the ordinary world only to encounter the extraordinary. He searched "surfaces for all the details" (*GoI*, p. 367) and—mirabile dictu—discovered what lay hidden beneath them. The physical sight supplied him with unexpected imaginative insights.

Davenport began as a Pound scholar and, from the very beginning, seems to have appropriated, if not assimilated, Pound's rigorous aesthetic standards, his clarity of mind, heart, eye, and ear—qualities which, in his Harvard dissertation, he discusses as poetic key concepts.[7] The master's aesthetic of "the natural object," which for him was "always the *adequate* symbol," his avoidance of any "superfluous word," "which does not reveal something," his lifelong insistence on the clear-cut "Image,"[8] quite obviously reenforced Davenport's early field-trip lessons and his "connoisseur's sense of things for their own sake" (*GoI*, p. 367). On a predominantly postmodernist scene, characterized by labyrinthine ruminations and apocalyptic forebodings of an utterly impotent language, Davenport's advocacy of the powerful word sounds strangely out of place. Like Hugh Kenner in his study *A Homemade World*, which is dedicated to Davenport, he treasures the great American modernist poets Pound and Williams, Stevens and Olson, Moore and Zukofsky, "austere and astringent" writers determined to eschew ornamentation and embellishment and value the word "both in itself and in its power to denote."[9] The great men and women of the modernist generation of 1914 are Davenport's chief models whose poetics he is anxious to propound in his literary essays and to imitate, if not emulate, in his fiction. Thus one may indeed regard him as "a lateborn Modernist" and read his work as "a hymn of praise to Modernism and an attempt to practice its aesthetics."[10]

"The Jules Verne Steam Balloon" is a highly allusive and, at times, even elusive text. In the light of Davenport's own critical and poetic oeuvre I shall try to unfold the text's "*involucra* which when opened disclose the theme of foraging in various senses" (*GoI*, p. 379).

The most striking feature of the text is its fragmentariness. Broken up into little segments of varying length, style, and even content, it initially presents itself, as do many of Davenport's fictions, as a mosaic of sundry bits and pieces. It resembles a pictorial collage, a juxtaposition of seemingly meaningless objets d'art and trivial objets trouvés which the cunning craftsman assembles, thoroughly convinced that the "most beautiful order of the world is still a random gathering of things insignificant in themselves" (*T*, p. 110). For Davenport, who spent his childhood collecting and building things, drawing, reading, and playing (*GoI*, p. 366), writing is, first of all, a playful assemblage, a passionate act of design and arrangement, and a page resembles "essentially a texture of images" (*GoI*, p. 374). With his "Shakerish concern for the *built*" (*GoI*, p. 384), as he repeatedly characterizes his writing, he assembles and arranges his texts, spliced together with quotations and "built out of discrete pieces of imagery" (*GoI*, p. 315). Not unlike the great architectonic structures of his modernist models, Davenport's fictions are spatially designed and may be read as one reads anthologies. His repeated references to flowers, plants, and crops—hollyhocks, wheat, asters and zinnias, anemones, figs, goldflowers and poppies, golden samphire—which serve as titles to some of the miniature chapters, underscore the anthological character of the text. Together with oaks and acorns, seeds and weeds, stones, meadows, gardens, and rivers they delineate the poetic space within which the text unfolds its story. In order to organize his material spatially, Davenport abandons the principles of narrative consistency and chronological order. As a result, the text presents itself as an assemblage and has to be perceived and received accordingly, that is, simultaneously rather than successively. Like Pound searching for that "intellectual and emotional complex in an instant of time . . . which gives that sense of sudden liberation, that freedom from time and space limits,"[11] Davenport's concern is to manufacture an equally pregnant moment, "a moment which surpasses our usual perception of time and space."[12]

The text's spatial form is in perfect harmony with its message. Within his poetic space Davenport makes all times converge, and past, present, and future are fused in one "comprehensive view."[13] Amidst the pastoral ambience of flowers, shrubs, and trees Virgil's hot and glistening Mediterranean sun commingles with a cold and "accurate" "northern light," Sicily intermingles with Denmark, and a truly timeless event, the pregnant moment of artistic creation surpassing "our usual perception of time and space," is enacted.

Davenport treasures his findings and knits them into highly intricate allusive webs. The figures in his carpets enter into complex amalgams that conflate elements of heterogeneous origin, of past and present, here and there into a composite whole. Thus Davenport, the *poeta doctus* and classical scholar, wont to work with dictionaries and encyclopedias, asks for an equally disposed *lector doctus*, for whom handbooks are no burden and the tracing out of allusions and detecting unexpected configurations under the *textum* of a text is a delightful passion. As Pavel

Tchelitchew hides his figures in the branches of trees, Davenport, who counts the Russian painter among his favorite artists, likes to complicate his structures. Like the daedalian artists, whose maze-making propensity he admires, he conceals image within image and literally invites the reader to follow on his "forage," which proves to be an infinite process of hide-and-seek, an endless *cache-cache*.

Thus Jules Verne, like Davenport a writer who mistrusts the "made-up material" (*GoI*, p. 383) and bases his exercises of the imagination largely on verifiable facts and scientific data, is chosen as a title figure to represent the author's own aesthetic program. As the author of *Cinques Semaines en ballon*, in which three men in a balloon traverse central Africa, till then a true heart of darkness, Davenport triggers further associations. The three Vernian aeronauts on their *voyage extraordinaire*, determined to explore darkness and bring new things to light, evoke the three light-bearing pages of Mozart's *Magic Flute* (Trollflöjten) who also descend upon the stage in a balloon. Mozart's musical harmonies give rise to other kinds of a New Harmony as expressed in the writings of Charles Fourier, the early nineteenth-century French visionary of a new social and amorous world, who must also be counted among Davenport's favorite thinkers, as the numerous references demonstrate. Fourier's emphasis upon education may, in turn, have inspired Davenport to introduce another educator of the time, N. F. S. (Nikolai Frederik Severin) Grundtvig, the founder of the Danish folk high school system, in which young people of every class were to be encouraged to educate themselves and each other. And in the learned reader's mind, Grundtvig sparks yet another name, that of his great antagonist Søren Kierkegaard, whose life, in some respects, parallels that of Davenport's protagonist Hugo Tvemunding: like Kierkegaard an unsystematic thinker, heterodox theologian, artist-philosopher, and ardent admirer of Mozart in whose music, as the philosopher argued and Hugo would approvingly nod, "the idea repose[d] with transparent clearness in definite form."[14]

The alert reader is prepared for such allusions and ready to unravel the strands, hoping that eventually "in the *textum* a thread would become vivid, or a portion of the design would become clear and lead . . . on into the rest" (*GoI*, p. 382). Since the search, however, often turns out to be ambiguous and the direction only hinted at, the interpretations, at times, are liable to go astray, if the associations are taken too far. The highly elliptical character of the texts, which infold and withhold rather than unfold, lends itself to all kinds of misreadings, and the allusiveness, which asks for the lacunae to be filled, sparks "in the reader a personal chain of delightful, tangential thoughts"[15] that, if not checked and balanced by the more explicit portions of each individual text, remain mere surmisings.

To do full justice to the ellipses of the text under discussion some speculative thoughts must fill the gaps. At the same time, however, the text provides sufficiently clear clues and is explicit enough in its design and the usage of dominant motifs to make possible the necessary clearings into the *forêt des symboles* and lay bare those threads that will then lead "on into the rest," a rewarding attempt, promising a number of unexpected findings and surprising insights.

The field of action as delineated by the text is of the utmost simplicity. Displaced from the island of ancient Sicily, where Theocritus and Virgil used to stage their pastoral poems, "to the north, crumbly islands" of modern Denmark—"love islands" Davenport hastens to add—the text constitutes its poetic space, a setting replete and resonant with sundry associations that make it a symbol of "the whole world." The Greco-Roman idyll, a simple poetic form (*eidyllion*) celebrating the simple country life of shepherds and lovers, enabled the ancient poet to introduce detailed descriptions of natural objects, since it provided the adequate setting for an unspoiled life in the midst of nature, and above all constituted the appropriate ambience for all kinds of imaginative and artistic activities. Davenport, the modern pastoral poet, author of *Eclogues* and "philosophical landscapist" (*GoI*, p. 123), combines all three characteristics of the ancient eclogue and weaves them into a texture all his own, a Nordic idyll, so to speak, in which, amidst the modern world of randomness and loss of direction, suddenly "the coordinates are right" and a "perfect landscape with pastoral figures" (*E*, p. 232) is enacted.

From the very outset, the "summer morning," "birdcharm," and "circadian [*sic*] wheels"—a portmanteau word that seems to allude both to the pastoral world of Arcadia and its cicadas—evoke a truly idyllic atmosphere, further enhanced by the manifold local flowers, trees, and prickly and obdurate weeds. "Oak tree, meadow, island" are as homemade as the spiky weeds and rusty colors of the ancient poems (*E*, p. 208). Goose grass, knotweed, crabgrass, crowfoot, pompions, and melons creeping upon the hard ground generate a simple, almost archaic rusticity. But what is at least as important as the simplicity of things is the way Davenport describes them. Following Pound and the other modernist poets whose style he praises as "limpid, sharp, clear, and simple" (*GoI*, p. 143), Davenport favors descriptions that are equally precise, lucid, and of almost archaic naïveté. Like William Carlos Williams, he hammers out a poetics of the pure and unadulterated word, "treated with acid to remove the smudges, washed, dried, and placed right side up on a clean surface."[16] In order to strip his objects of their customary modes of perception and their conventional pathetic fallacies, he avails himself of an unmistakably objectivist diction. The descriptions often read as if lifted straight out of a dictionary whose whole virtue, Davenport is anxious to point out, lies "in the precision with which it defines words" (*GoI*, p. 341). They remind one of definitions as used by Samuel Johnson, a lexicographer after Davenport's heart, "impatient with 'noble wild prospects,' "[17] simple and blunt, "imagistic rather than schematic," and of a somewhat "homely" poetic quality (*GoI*, pp. 341f.) They, in short, provide some of the stuff of which the homely world of this Danish idyll is made.

However, there is another aspect inherent in Davenport's descriptive passages. As a poet-forager "trying to find God's complete plan of the universe" (*GoI*, p. 379) in an oak leaf, an acorn cup, a gourd, or a simple grain of wheat, he is never satisfied with mere descriptions. Like Marianne Moore, one of his poetic models, he may be characterized as a "literalist of the imagination" who utilizes encyclopedic entries not for what they are but for what they are able to achieve; that is, he uses them as sparks of a long imaginative process. Encyclopedias are blind, unless poets use them for their own poetic purposes; the encyclopedic mind is positivistic and purely literal, unless the letter is transformed by the imagination. Thus the lengthy description of the goose grass is not primarily interesting in itself and grass is not "just grass," as Franklin seems to assume at first. For Davenport, the poet, "the spiral inside the crabgrass seed, the source of life" (*GoI*, p. 67) sparks a whole chain of associations. The grass blends into "an archaic wheat from which the horseriding plunderers made bread and foddered their shaggy shetlands. It came to Eleusis, Joseph Gaertner thought, by way of India. That's why he named it *Eleusine indica*." And all of a sudden, the simple weed under the poet's microscope begins to unfold and, like a text, release its "implicit information." The grass, "a uniform hieroglyphic" (*GoI*, p. 73), is gradually deciphered and discloses its multiform, protean meaning. Probing into the past, Davenport comes up with all kinds of surprising constellations. Suddenly, "Yeshua in the wheat," Christ's epiphany in the holy host, seems to shine forth; "*bummo*," the divine force of the Dogo myth, becomes apparent "in the crabgrass seed" (*DVB*, p. 84); the "pattern of energy . . . present in all matter and space" begins to manifest itself. It is through the poet's learning and imagination that the merely literal is energized and the dead letter of an encyclopedic entry is brought to life. Davenport removes layer after layer of verbal smudge until, "last of all," he seems to have reached the deepest "cupriferous stratum, black colored and schistose, in which there sometimes glitter scales of gold-colored pyrites in very thin sheets, which . . . often take the forms of various living things." Dead matter suddenly becomes alive; the black and schistose stone begins to sparkle like gold in the poet's mind.

A perfect setting indeed for what the text unfolds. Hugo Tvemunding, assistant classics master, gym instructor, and doctoral candidate in theology, together with Mariana, also a teacher, and her brother Franklin form a triad of "pastoral figures" in total harmony with the surrounding space. "Kissing a lot" and "smooching," hugging and grabbing each other, they live a natural life, only led by their inmost desires. According to the ancient Roman maxim *ut sit mens sana in corpore sano*, they harmoniously cultivate and develop body and mind and are, in Davenport's own words, "superb lover[s] in both flesh and spirit."

So are the boys, Virgil's pastoral *pueri formosi*, "impudently naked," athletic, and unashamed to scratch their testicles and fondle their scrota. To welcome puberty, they play "push and pull with each other's pizzles while gazing into each other's big soulful eyes." Howling, bleating, ruckling like doves, and crawling "monkey-nimble," they undoubtedly enjoy and celebrate "the animality of their bodies" (*GoI*, p. 381). Arms interjoined and locked around each other's shoulders, they spontaneously form natural ensembles that radically differ from the forced, false, and merely functional bourgeois associations with their prudish moral codes. The Danish idyll, as enacted here, is quite obviously a modern version of the old Sicilian pastoral which blends into a Fourieristic *nouveau monde amoureux*, "free of the restrictions and evasions of 'civilization'" (*GoI*, p. 381). Fourier, "who thought civilization a mistake" (*GoI*, p. 76), envisioned a world that was to be formed by natural "composites" linked with love and involving soul and senses alike.[18] Not forced familyism, a mere "reproductive not a social unit," but the "true family," "an enormous gathering of people, like a primitive tribe" (*GoI*, p. 77), was Fourier's ideal of a new harmony, and his *nouveau monde* is, as Davenport points out,

> a world divided up into beehives of communities, each of which is a family of human beings and animals. All work is done by everybody,

> an hour at a time. The days are rhythmic and contain a little of everything good. All sexual predelections are arranged for and honored for their diversity. Ceremonial honors are given to those whose passionate nature encompasses the widest range. All are friend and servant to all. Children learn every skill by age ten, yet the dominant note of the community is play. (*GoI*, p. 76)

There are, however, a few discordant notes to be heard in this realm of harmony. Not all are friend and servant to all; not all is playful and good on this pleasure island of love. Two figures—McTaggart, a Kierkegaardian seducer, "hankerer" and "mountebank," irresponsible and irresponsive, and an advocate of "Transcendental Meditation and Buddhist raising of the consciousness," and the bicycle rider, his feeble-minded follower and final victim whose eyes are "flecked and tarnished"—disturb the social harmony. Both represent the "wholly selfish" kind of people, estranged from and "drowned in themselves, beyond the reach of love and understanding . . . who, impotent to create, destroy." Hugo, a responsible and responsive "immanentist," as compared to the two "transcendental" escapists, through his useful and instructive teaching tried to get the dopey kid's "head out of his ass," but failed. The boy continued to float "around on lysergic acid and managed the ultimate in trendy distance" so that he practically doomed himself to die in total isolation. His "lysergic" dreams, as it were, loosened and eventually destroyed his "energic" human potentials. This northern idyllic Arcady, where Pan's soft flute may be heard resounding through the woods, is once more affected by death and suffering. But as in Virgil's eclogues, where the death of Daphnis is transfigured through art, suffering and death are deprived of their factuality and the dissonant notes are resolved in a harmonious work of art.[19] In Fourier's words, the "discord" presupposes the "accord" and the "deviant," "of crucial importance in Harmony,"[20] has to be reintegrated into the social community. A harmony, composed (*composé*) and combined (*combiné*), is always superior to a mere natural order. Only through art, composed and combined in a new harmony, the chaos of life is transformed and transcended.

It is this process of aesthetic transformation that "The Jules Verne Steam Balloon" enacts. Hugo Tvemunding, the artist-philosopher, in the course of the story awakens from chaos to consciousness, from slumber to a true artistic life. Thus his run before breakfast functions foremost as a symbolic action through which the protagonist frees himself "with every stride of the residue of dreams, of warm lethargies that had nested in his muscles, of anxieties that had made trash in his mind." And the painting of the dopey, deviant bicycle rider, which Hugo tries to complete, shows the artist's struggle with his work. The dead boy who had failed Hugo in his life also fails him, at least initially, in his art, because the artist is obviously more concerned with himself and "out to set himself up through signs and wonders" than with his own work. Impatient to wait for the right moment to come, he seems to adhere to "the current vulgar opinion that [art] is self-expression" rather than "inspiration, possession, vision" (*GoI*, p. 211). Anxious to make it right the first time, he produces a painting that seems a mere reflection of his own inner disposition. The "lazily handsome blond face and its dead blue eyes" against a dark and somber background is a narrowly mimetic, almost photographic rendering and strangely incongruous with the artist's avant-garde ambitions, his Danish Modern studio decorated with reproductions of Bourdelle, Mondriaan, Klee, and Brancusi, Davenport's own aesthetic models "of the generation of 1914" (*GoI*, p. 107) who, without exception, revolted against the naturalistic mode of their time and disciplined themselves to see, as it were, with "prehistoric eyes," stripping their objects of any "fictive ornament" (*GoI*, p. 128) and reducing them to their essential forms of "rhombs and trapezia and rectangles," of "*cylinder, sphere, cone*" (*T*, pp. 29, 41).

Only the second time, when "the light [is] right" and the whole idyllic setting seems conducive to the act of creation, when Hugo can "sit under a favorite oak, elbows on knees, and have a rich moment of calm and anticipation," when his heterodox Kierkegaardian thesis on Yeshua, the divine light, "of which we are free to partake" takes "form and texture," do his personal abrasions begin to heal and can his work take its final shape and bring forth its hidden harmonies. The *demon* of selfishness has to be cast out before the *daimon*, that grand presence "moving from the source of being" (*T*, p. 251), can get hold of the artist. Both "the accurate light" outside and a strong, almost Shakerish belief in the inner light conspire to generate the true work of art. For it is the light, as Hugo rightly observes at the end, that the artist paints by.

The three boys, equipped with flute and glockenspiel and descending in a steam balloon, are Davenport's harbingers of light and personify the creative spirit. "Soon the dawn will bring us light, and the golden sun will rise," they sing in *The Magic Flute*, and the literal quotation from the German libretto—*zum Ziele führt dich diese Bahn*—emphasizes the role

Mozart and his music play in this text. Music that, both in an archaic and a Kierkegaardian sense, represents "words of power" and "is both a spirit and a summoner of spirit" (*GoI*, p. 275)[21] also seems to have summoned Davenport's text. Otherwise, the unmotivated reference to Mozart's King of Prussia String Quartet in D Major K 575 with which the text begins would be entirely meaningless. Mozart's musical harmonies lead directly to Charles Fourier, for whom opera was an important "*pathway [diese Bahn]* to social harmony,"[22] and back again to Jules Verne, the title figure, whose steam balloon, "an appropriate metaphor for the imaginative spirit,"[23] directed the three aeronauts desirous to reach their destination (*zum Ziele*). To Hugo, the artist, the balloon likewise promises the completion of his project. How intricately Davenport weaves his texture, he demonstrates with the recurrent balloon-forms, pear-shaped and gourdlike, which emerge from the text and dominate its structure, as if the gourd, "the sign of Jonas," through which God gave his prophet protection, were indeed "the pivot." The whole text, it seems, turns around this one geometric figure, which on a more metaphoric level stands for artistic perfection, as Cézanne, whose ambition it was "to paint one perfect landscape with pastoral figures" (*E*, p. 232), chose the spheric form to grasp the essence of nature (*T*, p. 41).

As does Davenport's entire oeuvre, this text turns out to be both highly allusive and, as a corollary, elusive. Its references often take unexpected turns and form sudden kaleidoscopic configurations. Everything indeed seems to wander and change, since "change alone is unchanging" (*GoI*, p. 89). The writing resembles the schistose stones, those metamorphic crystalline rocks, which "often take the forms of various living things" and to which the text, self-referential as it is, explicitly alludes. It sparkles and sparks ever new associations that, because of their ambiguous and protean character, the reader "must search forever, never finding" (*DVB*, p. 96). As a *mosaïque de citations*, a "texture of images" (*GoI*, p. 374), Davenport's texts are truly absorptions and transformations of other texts[24] and, therefore, qualify as typical postmodern intertexts whose information is implicit rather than explicit. It is *between* the texts, in the interstices, that the reader's imagination is activated without ever reaching a conclusive meaning. Davenport's writing, as all so-called intersticed prose, "bids us pause upon each of a series of discrete configurations, which have a detached relation to the overall context."[25] In this sense, he is a true "daedalian artist" who sees his task in concealing rather than revealing, in implicating and infolding rather than explicating and unfolding a definite meaning. "We beholders are involved in an *explicatio*; we unfold to read" (*GoI*, p. 51).

The textual *involucra*, fragmentary and opaque at first, eventually unfold their coherence and gain a clarity through the recurrent motifs and analogies that the text employs as unifying devices and signposts for the reader. Through these devices it gradually takes shape and leads the reader, if he is only patient enough, to the "rich moment of calm and anticipation" when relations begin to cohere and the allusions, all of a sudden, come together. "The Jules Verne Steam Balloon," not unlike Davenport's essays and other fictions, can therefore be justly regarded as a writer's and reader's *voyage extraordinaire*. Through the unusual foray into various cultures, writer and reader retrieve all kinds of forgotten things, rescue some of "history's hostages,"[26] and discover surprising relations hitherto unknown. Davenport, in and through his fiction, tries to redress what *The Book of Jonah* discerns as one of the great malaises of civilization, a diagnosis with which both this text and its biblical counterpart come to an end, "that there are so many who don't know their right hand from their left." What matters most for Davenport, the teacher of objective, useful, instructive lessons, is that we learn to find "the way we shape and use the world, indeed the way we *see* the world" (*GoI*, p. 4). Its shape cannot be seen on a conventional map, but on one that extends its coordinates into various directions and sundry cultures. The imagination has indeed its own unique geography.

Notes

1 George Steiner, "Rare Bird," *New Yorker*, 30 November 1981, p. 196.

2 Marc Chénetier, "Charting Contemporary American Fiction: A View from Abroad," *New Literary History* 16 (1985): 662.

3 Davenport's four major works, to which I refer, are abbreviated as follows: *T*: *Tatlin!: Six Stories* (New York: Scribner's, 1974); *DVB: Da Vinci's Bicycle: Ten Stories* (Baltimore: Johns Hopkins University Press, 1979); *E*: *Eclogues: Eight Stories* (San Francisco: North Point Press, 1981); *GoI*: *The Geography of the Imagination: Forty Essays* (San Francisco: North Point Press, 1981). All page references are identified in parentheses after each citation.

4 John Gardner, *On Moral Fiction* (New York: Basic Books, 1978), p. 93.

5 Cf. Davenport's self-characterization as a writer in *Contemporary Authors*, vols. 33–36 (Detroit: Gale, 1973), p. 232.

6 Hugh Kenner, "A Geographer of the Imagination," *Harper's*, August 1981, p. 66.

7 *Cities on Hills: A Study of I–XXX of Ezra Pound's Cantos* (Ann Arbor: UMI Research Press, 1983), pp. 75–79.

8 "A Few Don'ts by an Imagiste," *Poetry* 1 (1913): 200–201.

9 *A Homemade World: The American Modernist Writers* (New York: William Morrow, 1975), pp. xvi–xvii.

10 Alan Williamson, "A Lateborn Modernist," *Shenandoah* 26 (1975): 87.

11 "A Few Don'ts by an Imagiste," p. 200.

12 Roger Shattuck, *The Banquet Years: The Origins of the Avant Garde in France—1885 to World War I* (New York: Vintage, 1968), p. 345.

13 Joseph Frank, "Spatial Form in Modern Literature," *The Widening Gyre: Crisis and Mastery in Modern Literature* (New Brunswick: Rutgers University Press, 1963), p. 59.

14 Søren Kierkegaard, *Either/Or I*, trans. D. F. and Lillian M. Swenson (Princeton: Princeton University Press, 1971), p. 52.

15 Fred Goellner-Cortwright, "Guy Davenport's *Eclogues*," *Chicago Review* 33, no.2 (1982): 150.

16 William Carlos Williams as quoted in Kenner, *A Homemade World*, p. xvi.

17 Ibid., p. 93.

18 Cf. M. C. Spencer, *Charles Fourier* (Boston: Twayne, 1981), p. 180. Fourier's significance for Davenport is also discussed by Bruce Bawer, "The Stories of Guy Davenport: Fiction à la Fourier," *The New Criterion* 3, no. 4 (1984): 8–14.

19 Cf. Erwin Panofsky, "*Et in Arcadia Ego*: Poussin and the Elegiac Tradition," *Meaning in the Visual Arts: Papers in and on Art History* (Garden City, N.Y.: Doubleday Anchor, 1955), pp. 300ff.

20 Spencer, *Charles Fourier*, p. 88.

21 Cf. Kierkegaard, *Either/Or I*, p. 106, where he remarks on Mozart's Don Juan that "the music does not represent him as a person or as an individual, but only as Power."

22 *Théorie de l'unité universelle* as quoted by Spencer, *Charles Fourier*, p. 81.

23 Robert A. Morace, "Invention in Guy Davenport's *Da Vinci's Bicycle*," *Critique* 22, no.3 (1981): 85.

24 Julia Kristeva, *Sémeiotiké: Recherches pour une sémanalyse* (Paris, 1969), p. 146: "tout texte se construit comme mosaïque de citations, tout texte est absorption et transformation d'un autre texte. A la place de la notion d'intersubjectivité s'installe celle d'*intertextualité*, et le langage poétique se lit, au moins, comme *double*."

25 Edward Marcotte, "Intersticed Prose," *Chicago Review* 26, no.4 (1975): 35.

26 Morace, "Invention in Guy Davenport's *Da Vinci's Bicycle*," p. 79.

SUSAN SONTAG

......

Description (of a Description)

One day recently at eleven o'clock in the morning a delaying phrase. Memorabilia are things worth remembering, not things remembered. You can forget everything and then it all comes back. Better a scrupulous inexactitude. I give the time (eleven, morning) but not the village (New England?). Sketch, if you please, a genre picture. Tavern, church. Cowbells, churchbells. My insomnia, my bad dreams: it was already late for me. I had left my pretty, low-ceilinged room, a casing for neurasthenic privacy, and was already on the street, near the post office from where I'd mailed you so many abject letters. Under a tangerine winter sun and shredded clouds. On my way.

a man suddenly collapsed right in front of me scissoring my splendid ribbon of footwork. Someone unknown to me: mesomorph in a blue suit. There were few people on the street, and I just happened to be there —walking, stalling behind him. He lay by the curb, his right cheek on the icy pavement. Spoiling the genre picture: thatched roofs, an inch of snow on the road.

as if struck by lightning which will convey the idea that it was sudden (nothing had prepared me for this drama) and the cause was not evident. No one brained him with a tomahawk. There was no pistol shot. I had nothing to do with his calamity.

and all the women in the vicinity screamed aloud; it was hardly a common sight to see someone respectably dressed keel over The respectable stay vertical. The extravagance of village weather, the staidness of village manners. But because this is not a modern story, people were not indifferent. Switzerland, or the nineteenth century? Women were surprised, appalled, frightened. Who? The hunchbacked girl at the newspaper stand wearing a farmer's black leather cap with snapped-up flaps that come down over the ears, for instance. Others? Others, too. Not only women, of course. But no one did anything. My reaction was different.

I myself raised him to his feet the heavy body he had not fainted actually perhaps he had just yielded to the call of the ground. I grappled with his weight in my arms, I felt his body expanding. He was much older than myself, time had fallen in on him. Not a predator but someone in the process of perishing. His life-size gravitational pull, his death-size inertness. I remember his spasmodic breathing.

and attended to him I brushed off his coat and set his glasses back on his narrow intelligent gray face thus I brought him back from the brink. He was hatless and I dusted off the crown of his head. An act of intimacy. From him I heard a queer mumble of noises

until he had recovered his speech—for it was not until he could talk that I knew he was well enough to go on. He began to talk. He told me his name was Ralph, and that he had been let out of prison three weeks ago; that his wife had left him; that he had many enemies. I let his words chew into my heart. You can imagine . . . if you care to. As he talked, his face darkened, stained with dread. He must have wanted from me a little animal reciprocity.

during this time not a muscle on my face moved but there was perspiration on my forehead, hands, I'm sure perhaps I raised my circumflexed eyebrows It may sound vainglorious to speak thus I remained stoical. Deadpan

and I felt nothing, neither fear nor sympathy, at least so I said to myself at the time I hate vulnerable people I refuse to let others make a convenience of me I am not a warming pan for disabled souls. Others will coo and claw and caress. I will be more consistent I have rinsed out the influence of pity

but I did what needed doing listening to him, brushing him off, asking him if he wanted to be taken to a doctor (no) or helped to a taxi (no, thanks). His muddy smile, his puffy eyes. He wobbled down the street, after wishing me a good day. Perhaps it was a colossal misunderstanding. Was he merely drunk? I was ready to do more if he needed me, his laconic benefactor. I could have covered him with language like a blanket. My old feeling that the whole world is in need of my protection We are living in terrible times

and went coolly on my way. Some intercostal pain at the effort. A sense of having been effective, tranquil, smooth—not too much but not too little. Should I have obeyed an irregular impulse? No. I shall not be ashamed of this moment.

Suppose someone had told me the day before as people so often do telling you things, treating time as if it were a meal being ordered; a film to be previewed I listen carefully

that tomorrow at eleven o'clock in the morning like an appointment Am I so predictable? True, every day at fixed hours I paint and sketch outdoors. But, at said eleven o'clock, I could have been on my way to a funeral, a puppy at my heels. I could have been on my way to the railroad station, the start of my skiing holiday. I could have been buying a newspaper across the street

a man would fall down beside me in this fashion—not in front of me, actually. Without warning. The same tableau. But behind the school rather than near the post office, perhaps. Someone with rotting teeth, a cracked thumbnail. Hyperdrama

I would have suffered every kind of anticipatory torment wondering whether I would be adequate to the occasion wondering what he had (a disease? a grief?) it would have made me calculating. Following on a fearful lack of sleep I would have dressed for the occasion, overdressed (kid gloves, a silk pocket handkerchief), I would have been moist, sweaty. And I would have been even farther from my old innocence and tranquility. Is it true that we were happy once?

and at the decisive moment there are incisions in eternity according to the laws of fascination, time does seem to stop time is suspended in tableaux Reduced to a state of hypersensitivity.

instead of helping the man would perhaps have done what he did. Fall down. Then there would have been two of us, prone by the curb. As if struck by lightning. Requiring to aid us a third person, just passing by . . .

For in the meantime the time between the notification and the event . . . but who could have predicted such an event? No one. No one, that is, unless one believes there are people with the gift of prophecy, except the person who was to fell the man. . . . How exciting it all is, actually.

all possible drives would have had time to imagine the experience drives? And to be prepared. Forewarned, I could have brought smelling salts, a wheelbarrow.

and to comment on it.—Telling me how I ought to feel. I could have avoided that street at eleven o'clock. But why should I? There is much to be said for a moment of certainty. One disorder leads to another. I was in a fragile mood. You are leaving me. You are calm, very polite; I, though, am involved in the bad behavior of despair . . . weeping, pleading, lying, insulting. I sleep very little these days, I have much to learn. How to fight, how to make unkind gestures, how to parody oneself. My discomfort, my evangelistic fervor. Everything must be accepted. I discover who I have become.

What then are our experiences? That which befalls us, that for which we are not prepared. My campaign of enlightened selfishness: sometimes I manage to snatch composure from my insignificant terrors. Every event has a little label on it. Which says: And to think that this, too, is within the realm of the possible.

Much more there is always more we are always trying to prepare ourselves How to face the others without fear and weakness

that which we put into them than I knew you did not love me and could never make me happy but I could not relinquish my love for you my idyllic self

that which they already contain! No reason to react at all one could just keep on walking but I wanted to show I was strong and competent. No big time gestures. Out of lack of pride I behaved with pride I know I made many mistakes with you

Or must we go so far as to say that Being with you is like living with a bomb that keeps on ticking. I am always starting up, straining to hear a change in the sound, that slight hesitation, the dip in the rhythm before the wretched thing goes off

in themselves the experiences, if one can call them that, or the sense of loss. Tick tock. Perhaps it won't go off. I can get used to moving slowly.

they contain nothing? There is nothing now. I am not pining away. But one can forget everything and then it all comes back, enhanced with fantasies of violence.

To experience is to invent?—My watchful solitariness. An urban Robinson Crusoe, I have told this story many times.

RICHARD HOWARD

……

A Description of "Description (of a Description)"

By this text and even by its title (and by ours, if we would acknowledge what hers intends), we are faced with a process Sontag has invoked before, particularly in her fictions (novels, tales, fables, allegories, emblems, screenplays) but not only there, for her essays and meditations frequently engage with it, almost as a method, particularly when the argument profits, as she conducts it, from being not ongoing but circular; it is a process so frequent—if not popular—in modernity that we are prepared to find it wherever there might loom or lurk a resistance to narrative thrust, to linear time, to a merely mimetic scription.

This process has no name in English critical discourse, though its most celebrated instance occurs in our most celebrated drama, and though we recognize its existence throughout our literature—indeed we recognize its existence as an essential device of representation, and perhaps of culture itself. The French (whose name for it we must borrow, as we have borrowed *novel* or *nocturne, enjambement* or *paysage moralisé*) call it "putting (*x*) *en abyme*," an old expression from heraldry, whereby in the center of the shield is set another tiny shield, its replica in every respect, except for its diminution. We recognize it as the Quaker Oats effect, of course, or to catch up my reference to *Hamlet,* as the play within a play, the story inlaid within the story and, being thus compressed, adjuvant to the nature of the environing enterprise. But useful as such a figure may be (we recall how eagerly Gide would hail the device in his notes for *The Counterfeiters*), it bewilders as well, perhaps as much as it enlightens, by its suggestion of infinite regress. The word comes from the Greek *abyssos,* "bottomless." Bewilderments already abound: we commit a contradiction in terms when we speak of *the bottom of the abyss,* and a pleonasm when we speak of a *bottomless* one. Perhaps that is why Sontag, in a text of only four pages, finds it so prone to her purposes, among which

—inveterately—is the mirroring of writing by itself, so that her title invokes the geometrical sense: the tracing or traversing of a course, as the *description* of an arc or a circle; and of course the ingenious parallel to *deconstruction*—the de-scription of a description, the conversion of (any possible) function to WRITING.

Look first at her prose, as it takes the page. Many short paragraphs, the longest ten lines, each appended (what we may call an *adscript*) to a fragment given in italics. We recall examples of this not from fiction, of course, but from the literature of exegesis, most recently in Barthes's *S/Z*. It has been apparent to several writers of Sontag's generation—to Barthelme, to Gass, to Davenport—that there were figurations and contraptions which a new, or a renewed, fiction would find *generative* in Barthes's criticism, for just as the genre of such works as *Camera Lucida* or *A Lover's Discourse* is uncertain, so the fictions that have found a resource there make less of a claim to be fiction in the "story" sense, and more of one in the "poetic" sense, which is to say, a *made thing*, for in that sense a fiction and a poem are one.

There is no identification of the italicized text, much fenestrated so that each of its fragments—what Barthes would call a *lexeme*—is given the proprietary and instigating status of a *scriptural* utterance. Indeed, there is no identification of a great deal in the piece. We do not know even the sex of the speaker(s), and we are warned early on that the more elided, the more *comes back*. And many things are elided—it is almost as if Sontag had determined that she could set our narrative processes working without the usual bait, without the determinations which so much of modern fiction has appeared distressed by: where? who? when? But to keep to my observation, initially, of the way the piece *looks*, we notice that there is no paragraph *without* an italic *inscription*; apparently there must be something to get the commentary going in each case; the commentary or *midrash* cannot break away from its incitement, though it can argue with it, question its authority, wonder about its rightness. There has been something that has come first, that goes before, and Sontag's text manages to dramatize this response to predecession by the italic/roman script alternation, though neither the instigating text (the *prescription*?) nor what will become the extraordinarily personal gloss (the *subscription*?) is accounted for, is *ascribed* to a particular speaker. Let us search for some clues. No, clues are what we have—let us consider them.

The initial italic phrase offers us a triple temporal shoehorn, and though for all its detail we still have no certainty what year, what season, what century is intended, we recognize in the formality and the elaboration of the three elements that the italic phrase may be earlier in time than the comment, has perhaps an *old-time* flavor—with which the commentary immediately takes issue. If the person writing the commentary is to be perceived as the same person who *has written* the italic phrase (does this not appear to be the case? Certainly a kind of responsibility is being taken: "I give the time but not the village"), then a certain self-criticism is being made. Here we are on familiar grounds in Sontag's fiction, all of whose protagonists are—as this one, too, will be—self-doubters to the point of pain and debilitation. Yet the final italic phrase (skipping four pages ahead), disturbingly gnomic, sounds like something we remember, something we recognize: that notion of experience as invention, of truth as acknowledged lie—where have we heard that before? Where *will* we have heard that before, as it turns out? Certainly the commentary, here at the last, enters in the most forceful manner possible. We are given an identification, we are given a literary allusion, and we are given a powerful sign-off, a devastating coda that sends us circling helplessly into the abyss of exegesis and narrativity alike, compelled like the Ancient Mariner to repeat a "story," obsessively to suffer a fate, endlessly inscribed, even within *someone else's* expression. If the "I" of the commentary wishes to be known, to make himself/herself known, he/she latches onto the grand if familiar myth of Crusoe, invoking another set of recessions (Defoe over Selkirk, the novel over autobiography, revision over scripture —"an *urban* Robinson Crusoe"—a further impetus into the past) in order to do so. Only in the last phrases do the italic phraseology and the roman commentary overlap, indeed coincide. Between the testy beginning —are we in the nineteenth century? is it a New England village? is it Switzerland? Can there be thatched huts and a film preview in the same world of discourse?—and this mini-maelstrom of an ending, there are extraordinary divergences to be reconciled or at least acknowledged, room must be allowed for discrepancies of the most wildly confessional order, and a sense rehearsed that *any* experience—evidence, happening, continuum—will permit, if not compel, the author of the commentary to question once again his/her failures, obsessions, a dolorous stoicism.

The division in experience suffered by the author of the commentary takes on a decisive tinge not accommodated by the italic text, though the "I" there proposes the dilemma too: would the subject have done this rather commonplace humane thing, have responded to another's distress, had it been foretold? Can we rely upon ourselves, beyond the spontaneous (and irresponsible) fact, to project an hypothesis of selfhood that will account for and anticipate how we may (must) react to any and every occasion? It is one of Sontag's constant preoccupations, this location and vocation of the self. And I find it capital that the expansive speaker here, the author of the commentary (if that is what it is), chooses precisely this moment of uncertainty and hysterical supposition—if forewarned, would that speaker not have done just what the "victim" has done: fall down and become another prone, felled, resourceless being?—chooses, indeed, precisely this moment of indetermination to dilate upon that other world of experience not even hinted at by the italic text. The world of "you."

It is just the knowledge or the foreknowledge of response—the conviction that, under a given circumstance, this is what the self would do—which brings to the surface of the discourse what separates the experience of the italic text from the experience of the commentator. And suddenly there is a kind of solution of continuity, there ceases to be the rather snappish, resentful querying of the italic text, as if the commentator had been reading a translation not entirely trustworthy ("*For in the meantime . . . all possible drives would have had time to imagine . . .*" "Drives? Forewarned, I could have. . . . But why should I?"). And instead, the commentary ventures at last on its own submersion in the destructive element. Precisely the recognition that one fallibility makes us all free, or at least fallible, releases the commentator to that *self*-recognition which is decisive: "I discover who I have become," i.e., I suffer, therefore I am.

Between that inception which appears so querulous in its dealings with detail, so quizzical about the premonitions of a pathos to come ("mailed you so many abject letters"), and that decisive close which commits the speaker to a fetishized anamnesis, the glorification of what is sometimes called repetition-compulsion, Sontag's text proceeds by a device, or is it a division? which has become, over the years, her way of walking, her *enjambement*, precisely. If her structural metaphor is the figure *en abyme*, the principle of infinite regress, her metaphor of surface is the aphorism: a wisdom broken, a suspension between poetry which is always recurrence and prose which is always singularity. It will not surprise us that some of her most celebrated essays have been undertaken in this guise, or wise: fragmentation as voracity, break and enter, divide and conquer. And ever since *The Benefactor*, even her means of fictive characterization has been *this* means, epigram or aphorism; concision is her antidote to what Hegel calls *the prose of the world*, her saving grace in a medium that is damned for its mendacity. Barthes and Canetti are latter-day masters of the elliptical and the oblique, the aphoristic consciousness, and it is they, of course, whom Sontag eagerly salutes, along with Cioran and Pavese; not to mention, in its wilder ranges, Cage and Artaud . . . . The very international savor of these contemporary virtuosi of broken wisdom is one of Sontag's strongholds. Of all American writers of her generation, she is readiest to hurry after strange gods, aware that they may very well be the ones to shore up the holiness that has so continuously leaked out of the home-ground divinities (Emerson, so astutely hailed by Nietzsche, says little to her, or is not honored for saying it). As for the apothegmatic penchant, take "my love for you my idyllic self"—this is concision indeed, the reduction to seven words of an entire theory of ethical consciousness. What good is a theory, Sontag might say, that cannot be thus reduced? The awareness of being wounded, of flagrant pain ("to snatch composure from my insignificant terrors"), enables her stoicism, her widened awareness, what she calls, at the very end, "my watchful solitariness."

Momentarily it has seemed that I fail to separate Sontag from her speaker, her characterized commentator on that italic meditation which leaves us with the query "*To experience is to invent*?" I think my lapses into such an identification (who can doubt that it is Sontag who turns on herself and asks "is it true that we were happy once?") are warranted by the nature of the enterprise itself. Any text by Sontag, discursive or fictive, mistrusts a high mimetic surface, and she will go to strange lengths to puncture our ease in the narrative carapace, our security. The strangest length, as I have been surmising, is the explosion of narrative altogether (*Death Kit*, with its Dantesque allusions, is the largest instance), the recognition that in any story, any incident, any acknowledged *event* ("that which befalls us, that for which we are not prepared") is the likelihood and even the necessity for self-discovery, for self-recognition.

I think, our clues thus brooded upon, our devices grilled, we can now revert to the grander sort of identification: The description that Sontag has de-scribed, has pursued into its interstices, where she can lodge her own remarkable evidence of a wisdom shattered and thereby glinting, is a text by Friedrich Nietzsche, the merest anecdote from *Daybreak* (1881). I suggested, all unfairly by my reference to an untrustworthy translation, that of course we might recognize the tonality of "Must we go so far as to say that / in themselves / [our experiences] *contain nothing*? / *To experience is to invent?*" It is the tonality—questioning, subversive, liberating—of the early Nietzsche, before even *Zarathustra*, before *The Genealogy of Morals*, and Sontag has found within it—dividing it up into the lexemes that will enfranchise her own lacerations, her own liberations—the detonating mechanism, the trigger, the release that the modern writer readily finds in the work of the predecessor, the forebear, recalling that to find, *invenire*, is to come upon, is to invent.

A constant application to Nietzsche has been Sontag's resource from the beginning. I recall, some twenty years back, getting a glimpse of her notes for a series of lectures "Beyond Personality," and on one three-by-five card being startled to see the scrawl: "*NIETZSCHE—my hero!*" It has been ever thus. And so this text becomes, beyond its sorties into storyland and confessioncountry, a prepossessing *homage* to the enabling genius of the place. It is a kind of tribute by *collage*, a discovery of what there is to say, of what has to be said, by the force of juxtaposition, broken sentence against broken *sagesse*, past *versus* present, and otherness exacerbated into selfhood. I suggested, starting out, that Sontag may enjoy compelling us to respond to her plot without the usual linear inducements. For them she has substituted other temptations, other powers, and it is precisely the reversals and paradoxes of the Nietzschean resonance ("*What then are our experiences? / Much more / that which we put into them than / that which we already contain*") that let her get in her own licks, that allow her to discover or invent her *native strain*, in any sense that phrase will bear. Promptest exponent of the "modern" resonance, Sontag has always scrutinized the masters for what would make them "her" masters. She is the most generous of our critics because she has discovered that the excellence and the ingenuity of art is precisely what will empower her to an autonomous rage of actions. Admiration is her analytic device, Penelope's web which she will pluck apart by night (in the darkness of critical texts) so that she may weave it again by day (in the dazzle of fictions and fables like *Description [of a Description]*). I daresay there is no more poignant self-explorer ("I am always starting up, straining to hear a change in the sound") among her contemporaries than this resolutely errant venturer into the acknowledged mysteries of mastery.

What is remembered and what is forgotten are—Sontag is here to remind us—one and the same. It is the faith of our modernity: we remember what we wish to remember, what we regard as important (Freud); and yet we truly remember only what we did not know we remembered, what our senses bring back to us involuntarily from the abyss of the past by a kind of art, a reconstruction of that lost paradise that is the only paradise we do know (Proust). This is Sontag's pursuit, what I call her errantry. In the present text she proceeds by the *use* of memory (citation, much fragmented, of an unobtrusive Nietzsche text) to the use *by* memory of deeper incitations, what Wallace Stevens calls "ghostlier demarcations," a willingness to submit or surrender mere conscious process which engages the reality of what I call *scription*, that writing without purposive prefix which is the secret of our texts, our fabrications ("one can forget everything and then it all comes back"). How prescient she is when she (necessarily) concludes: "I have told this story many times"—it is the "one story only" that all her fictions and all her discursive forays tell, and will continue to tell, not always so diagrammatically as here through the baffle of the Nietzschean web, but always with the same passionate capacity for recognition, for admiration—for wonder and awe.

CHAPTERS FROM NOVELS

WALTER ABISH

......

Is this really you?

I

At present wouldn't it be correct to assess everything as having reached a standstill, with the awkward, yet pragmatically incisive term "normality" as an appropriate designation for the prevailing condition? If indeed there exists some reason for alarm at the now indisputable evidence that up to one-third of all the pine forests are turning yellow as a result of industrial poisoning and the accompanying disappearance of wildlife (not to overlook the justifiable concern over the degree of pollution in those fabled, shimmering rivers that wind their way across the country, their names: Rhein, Main, Weser, Aller, Mosel, Isar, Tauber, rich in historical association, evoking an elegiacal longing for the remote past), this alarm is for the time being still kept in check. It is muted if not actually suppressed. After all, no one wishes to undermine the very fabric of the society, for the postwar reconstruction of cities such as Selten, now almost entirely rebuilt, has been far too arduous an undertaking, too costly in every respect for anyone to permit or encourage the present, let us call it mild unease, to overwhelm what is for the participants of Germany's miraculous rebirth a well-deserved reward.

It is spring or summer! Love, exquisite in all its details, passionate love is in the offing. It flutters carefree, lightly in the breeze. It is a season in which on the faces, even plain or rugged faces, can be read the declarations of fealty, the fervent expectations of boundless love. One can say that everything oscillates—an inner emotional upheaval—with the sheer abundance of love. What else? *What else?* One cannot deny the beautifully serene countryside—the result of centuries of dedicated and painstaking toil. Plowed fields bounded by low stone walls, here and there a cluster of trees, a brook, a narrow paved road, a small group of buildings with red gabled roofs, a barn or two, a cobblestoned courtyard, livestock. A stallion in a pasture. Ah, stability! At dawn or dusk, what the eye can see resembles pictures from a distant childhood—*Ein Land der Märchen!* Is this really Germany? A kind of preciseness of detail prevails that is in sharp contrast to the almost warm and casually unstudied appearance of everything in Italy and even in neighboring Austria. Here, however, everything has been worked so thoroughly. One could maintain that there appears to be a striving for an almost unattainable agreement. But, perhaps it is only imagined. With the sun shining there is a matchless sense of expectation. Is it any wonder that for the time being any discussion of the dying 120-year-old firs is left to the more presciently outspoken groups on the far left? There are more pressing matters to be seen to for the less politically concerned. Things, after all, are not as bad as some Germanophobes would like them to appear. For the most part, what is on view shows a complete lack of neglect. Why, even the narrow, most out-of-the-way bridges receive a requisite biannual inspection and if repairs are in order they are done on the spot, without delay. Nothing is postponed! well, hardly anything. One more year has elapsed peacefully. The political uncertainties, the sporadic but steadily declining terrorist actions now seem to lack a former zest and conviction, the dying fish floating belly up in the Rhein, the declining steel production in the Ruhr valley, even the shiny brand-new Pershings poised to strike within minutes at the heart, the palpitating heart of the U.S.S.R. will not impair the societal stability, just as half-a-million (give or take a hundred thousand) from all walks of life, who marched, colorful banners aloft, in favor of nuclear disarmament and to sustain the peace, will not undermine it. Spring or summer! People everywhere are making final plans for their vacations. Everywhere people are mentally wrestling with the virtually unlimited choices of pleasure at their disposal. This time, is it to be Greece, or Yugoslavia, or North Africa?

Is there any reason, one may well ask, why people should not be utterly convinced that the trains of the Federal Republic will continue to run on schedule and that in the unlikely event of an accident—a collision or even a derailment—every available form of assistance will be rushed to the scene. After all, why not? And doesn't everyone also have a perfect right to expect that with the advanced wine-growing techniques the full-bodied Rhein wines and the somewhat lighter Moselle wines will match if not be an improvement on last year's vintage? In the city, that is to say in Selten, everyday one can see people quietly, meditatively withdrawn, sitting in the former palatial garden, absorbing the sweetness of life: willfully embracing what is in essence a kind of perfection as the copper dome-shaped roof of the Baroque palace retains the sunset's deep red glow moments after the sun is no longer visible, and the large variety of birds agitatedly hopping from branch to branch in the shaped trees and concealed in the clipped hedges, as if to accentuate the transition from afternoon to evening, suddenly, frantically inspired burst into song—their combined mad twitter and chirping leaving one with the impression that this almost artificial sounding din could only be manufactured by some ludicrous musical device, perhaps a hand-cranked contrivance, such as the one devised by the Swiss painter Klee? to imitate a *Vogelgesang* . . . as yet another edenic day, tranquil, uneventful, seamlessly slips into darkness, without there being the slightest apprehension that on the following day anything might occur to disturb the present tranquility, the present enduring state of peace! *Ein innerlicher Frieden!* Despite the dissension, despite the occasional 120-year-old fir, after an explosive crack, another victim of the acid rain, toppling over though its fall is cushioned by the younger trees, the country has settled itself—is there any reason why it shouldn't?—into its well deserved prosperity. It is a general well-being to which the generation of Adenauer's *Wirtschaftswunder,* the true pioneers of this present peace—though argumentatively some might consider it a stalemate—had with determined single-mindedness contributed their energies, their ingenuity, their talent, their imagination and passion. Granted that prosperity, in and of itself, may not be what matters most—as the philosopher Brumhold so ardently maintained in his writings—it does enable a society as diverse and historically complex as this one to attain an enviable economic and political stability. Not that there aren't any divisions or that all the past sores have been desensitized. Someone, even a visitor from abroad with an eye for such details, can locate them without great effort. But to what end? What purpose is served by endlessly unearthing the signs of an earlier disaster: in trying to read the labored handscratched markings that constitute a primitive calendar (but what year?) on some moist stone wall in a deep cellar that happily, once again, serves a more peaceful purpose: the storage of Rhein wines. One can quite easily live a pleasant life here without being weighed down by the funereal experiences of the past. If not for the occasional (actually all-too-frequent) deleterious magazine articles, the TV programs and the increasingly sanctimonious war movies that now demonstrate the new self-perception, the now acknowledged *Menschlichkeit,* a more open-minded evaluation of good and evil by combining entertainment with a peacetime propaganda, the latest form of denazification, so that everyone can once again take a certain pride in the bearing as well as the not negligible achievements of "our boys" . . . there's hardly reason any longer to let this thoroughly unsettling business of the past trouble one's mind. For god's sake, can't you understand, it's over. OVER. For those under twenty (what bliss!) there are no memories whatever of mounds of rubble, *Trümmer,* or rubble trains, *Trümmer-Züge,* or rubble women, *Trümmer-Frauen,* as the women who cleared the rubble with kerchiefs to protect their hair were called, no *Schwarzmarkt,* and history, *die Geschichte,* does not even inspire forgetfulness. Granted that their grandparents may have compliantly hung out flags and buntings to celebrate the occasion of Hitler's triumphant, albeit brief, visit to Selten. Who knows? By now everything has become attractively blurred. What is left is the history of the movie screen and the overly virtuous TV documentaries that like unctuous sermons are designed to press home a certain point—a moral issue! There is still, it should be said, a vague yearning for that turning point in the late forties in which everyone under occupation became more resourceful and consequently less asocial, less alienated . . . for freedom was in the air. Naturally, if one happens to have an eye for blemishes, the reminder of an unprecedented destruction, a virtual evisceration of a nation, can be located as easily as the somewhat scratched old 78 recording of Hitler's shrilly intemperate speech on the occasion of his visit to Selten. Ah, Selten! More or less his standard speech. What to foreigners verged on the obscene at the time was, by and large, greeted by the people of Selten—admittedly not by all—as reassuring and inspiring if not actually lofty. After all, one has to consider that Hitler, despite his dubious Austrian ancestry, appealed to their *Volksbewusstsein.* The shrillness, the sharp gesticulations, the threats he mouthed, constituted for the *Kleinbürger* as well as the workers and farmers a reassuring nomenclature of the everyday life—*die Alltäglichkeit.* To refer to the visit today is to invite subterfuges that parody the Hollywood version of history. That is why history is so unbalancing! But, let the dead bury the dead! The sense of renewal, the unflagging energy, the almost single-minded determination that enabled this society to literally yank itself out of the vast moonscape of *Trümmer* that at one time had been cities, is not yet depleted. For those under twenty, the present facades of the reconstructed buildings do not convey anything remarkable. Why should they? The past is a mournful flickering newsreel or Hollywood. The past lies embedded in their parents' or grandparents' reticence. For those under twenty it is more or less the way things have always been. It is not even a question of choice. For them, the present, the "now" is an impediment not a bridge to the past. One must accept that one is born into a certain period, be it the sixties, the seventies, the eighties, and pell-mell one comes into possession of a language—it is really as simple as that. Signs fall into place. *Hubschrauberlandeplatz,* Heliport, *Mittelstreckenrakete,* medium-range missile, *Höhepunkt,* pinnacle. And words fall into place: *Grundverfassung,* basic state, *Alltäglichkeit,* everyday life, *Nichtmehrdasein,* no-longer-being-there, *zweideutig,* ambiguous. As simple as that! *Du du, ja ja, ne ne, nun ja, doch, aber. . . .* From childhood gibberish to a clear assertion of the self. *Ich spreche Deutsch!* One comes to share the language with the street cleaner, the tram conductor, the manufacturer of spark plugs, the tobacconist, the headwaiter, as readily as one does with the 3rd-year student of philology. But why take the trouble to establish the etymology of certain words? Does it really concern us how or when the word "weekend" or "supermarkt" originated? What matters is the location of the "supermarkt." As for the foreign workers, they readily adapt. Not that they seek to shed their foreignness. That would be an unrewarding task. But, in time German becomes their second language—*ihre zweite Sprache!* For some of their children born in the Federal Republic it may even be considered their *Muttersprache. Ja. Natürlich. Ich spreche Deutsch!* Of course, how else to communicate the most rudimentary needs? Moreover, it is quite possible to speak and write an accomplished German without any knowledge of the works of Hölderlin or Nietzsche or even Brumhold. On their first lesson the foreigners learn to say: *Ja* and *Nein* and *Danke* as well as *links* and *rechts.* All too obligingly they commit themselves to *Ja* and *Nein* and *Danke*, even when the *Ja* or *Nein* or *Danke* is entirely inappropriate. They also rapidly pick up words for too much and for too little: *zu viel* and *zu wenig.* Everything, all of life, is encapsulated in these words. Everything!

Even the survivors (another one of those historically loaded terms), the people who have retained almost against their will a historical fixation, a compulsion perhaps to view the present only in terms of the past cannot, even when they try, completely reject the sweetness of life that now, like an offering, a balm to soothe their ruffled feelings, lies at their feet. All they need is to allow the unalloyed bitterness to recede, to fade. Breathe deeply and depending on one's distance from the Ruhr valley one can still inhale the sweetly scented air of the Schwarzwald. Divisions have always existed. Do they not resemble the divisions elsewhere? Are they not always the divisions between wealth and poverty, German and non-German, north and south, patrician and plebeian, workers and the managerial class, left and right? Of course, the magazine articles that focus with such relentless passion on the divisions of the past are not merely diversionary attempts to obfuscate all present divisions: if anything, their primary function is to codify the past and demystify it. A touch of the past! Reach out and in a flash you too will be able to respond, feeling a slight involuntary tingling sensation, part abnegation, part elation, part sheer revulsion.

For an isolated few, on setting foot in Germany, everything, the names of streets, the names of cities, denotes as does the language, *die deutsche Sprache*, an earlier indisputably vile and murderous intent that has never, to their satisfaction, been appropriately decried. For these few (many?) every German house door, every paving stone, every street light, every narrow passageway, to this day preserves a trace of that at one time violently enforced "solution" that—among other things—entailed the herding of "selected" people to collection points conveniently located near the railroads, and then their being transported across Germany and Austria sometimes as far as Poland to even larger staging areas—while along the way, here and there, from partially open windows or from the fields a furtive perhaps merely inquisitive photographer was able to obtain a snapshot. The railroad tracks, the railroad barriers, the railroad platforms remain icons of a now long past *Totentanz*. But isn't it almost meaningless to enter a discussion of what was or wasn't known at any given period of time: 1942, '43 or '44? After all, it is most unlikely that every single train in Germany was made to unload its passengers at Kauffering or Asbach or Zwidau or Lichtenburg or Fallersleben or Bad Warmbrunn or Charlottengrube or Königshütte or Sachsenhausen or Ravensbrück or Flossenbürg. There you go! A long list of place-names that merely signify dozens of stations in a vast network of terminals.

It is spring or summer! The shadows cast by the Residenz at sunset lengthen, enfolding the gravel paths, the benches, the glistening nymph at the center of the fountain. At this hour it is quiet here. Why not come here, whoever you are, and see if the Baroque splendor of the Residenz will not diminish your discontent . . . *tant mieux*. Foreign words? *Warum denn nicht?* Yes, the German language absorbs foreign words without any self-consciousness. *O.K. Sure. You bet. Ladida. Take it easy. Hotdog. Sock it to me, baby.* Granted that they are guest words, words that can easily fall out of favor in a few years. The foreign, especially the American, no longer produces the erstwhile frisson of pleasure, for by now, everything, but everything, is readily attainable. Why, even the jet fighters landing and taking off from the nearby airbase need not even be American for the German airforce flies the identical planes—and with just as much confidence.

2 How to resolve certain delicate questions of identity

Only now, almost forty years after the war, have the chronicles of Selten dating from the year 1930 to 1950 been published in three hefty volumes to join the long row of earlier volumes presently in the city archive. Well, these things take time! Just the research alone! So much pertinent material was destroyed or missing. As was to be expected, hardly anyone in Selten aside from the Mayor and the city council was completely satisfied with the results. The conservative newspaper *Der Überblick* found the chronicles spotty, uneven, written with an eye to the coming elections, whereas the two liberal papers heatedly maintained that the accounts had been willfully distorted and now what was required were three volumes of corrections to rectify the more glaring errors and omissions. Still, as the Mayor was heard to say, it was high time. They had to be brought out. A certain clearing of the air was called for. Now, on to more pressing needs! Selten!

What lies beyond dispute is the new Selten! *Das neue Selten!*

The tour buses from all over park in the new parking area across from the recently reconstructed Residenz, the jewel of Selten, and the disembarking visitors—for reasons that are difficult to determine—mainly elderly women, are given the rapid tour of the palace, *Eins, zwei, drei, Eins, zwei, drei,* the gardens and then, like so many compliant sheep led to a large restaurant on the Fasanenstrasse. Less then two hours after their arrival they are, once again, on their way, their scenic trip doubtlessly including the Trübendorf chapel with its marvelous altarpiece by Riemenschneider. There happens to be a far more attractive outdoor restaurant close by the chapel, but it is by no means large enough to accommodate one bus load after another of white-haired elderly ladies from the provinces. What do these women—these war widows, what else can they be?—make of this new vision of Germany? Everything is somewhat familiar and yet, at the same time, elusively foreign.

A number of the tour buses head in a westerly direction towards France, following Route 108 to the Schwarzwald, quite possibly—it cannot be ruled out—passing Altneu, though it is doubtful that any of the middle-aged guides would take the trouble to mention the philosopher Brumhold whose cabin, which he built as a young man, still stands on one of the tall hills of Altneu. But then, one can never really tell. Brumhold had constructed the cabin in the late twenties, moving in by 1930 or '31. It is questionable if the passengers, by now already inundated with historical details, have the slightest interest in Brumhold in spite of the fact that to this day Brumhold is universally accepted as one of the most significant German thinkers of the 20th century.

Like so much else, Altneu has changed. The population has increased to at least 700. Yet the changes are imperceptible—they take place gradually. Another house, another street, another barn. . . . Brumhold who preferred the isolation of his cabin in Altneu to the comfortable two-story house with garden in nearby Würtenburg failed to register, so preoccupied was he with his philosophical inquiries, the disturbing societal changes of the thirties as long as the landscape he was able to observe from the window of his study did not alter drastically. He preferred not to acknowledge the tractors and subsequently the harvesters and other farm equipment, the accoutrements of a technological age about which he had written critically if not disparagingly. He remained absorbed by his texts. He even spurned invitations to teach at the University of Berlin. He was not rejecting Berlin or its power, per se, he was rejecting its pernicious metropolitan influence. Its shine. He kept watching the landscape he knew so intimately go through the seasonal cycle—winter to spring to summer to fall—deriving his strengths, his philosophical convictions, and in part his identity from the serene valley he could see unobstructed from his cabin . . . though in 1944 he scrupulously avoided reading a moral disintegration into the stream of refugees, mainly women and children with their few belongings, then the orderly retreating soldiers and, such are the imperatives of war, at the tail-end, to everyone's disconcern, the long lines of concentration camp inmates in their all-too-recognizable striped uniforms being herded deeper and deeper into

Germany so as not to fall into enemy hands. The ones that collapsed by the side of the road were shot. However, by 1944, given the extreme eccentricities of that period, Brumhold, one of the professors considered most expendable by the department of philosophy—did it not occur to the government that in effect the entire department had become redundant?—was sent to fill sandbags and dig trenches somewhere along the Rhein, that fabled river, the Rhein. To what degree Brumhold, the author of *Das Denken: Ja oder Nein,* and, *Der Begriff des In-der-Welt-Seins,* helped stiffen the defenses is a moot point. What is certain is that Brumhold throughout his ordeal did not for a single moment relinquish his philosophical question of Being at a time when Being was being assaulted in every shape and form.

From the top story of the Stahl-Eins building, a twenty-story building three kilometers north of Selten, the building sheathed in mirrored glass presenting a kind of startling optical illusion in the country-like setting, one has an unimpaired view of the Schwarzwald on a clear day, and with a pair of powerful binoculars it is even possible—or so some claim—to see Brumhold's cabin. Really it's just another cabin. Some prefer to call it a chalet. The Stahl-Eins skyscraper—anything over ten stories is considered a skyscraper—has been reproduced on a number of travel posters printed and issued by the Selten Department of Commerce. Now, another building planned for the heart of Selten is vying for equal attention. The architects also intend to utilize mirrored glass despite the articles critical of mirrored glass for buildings in the *Tagesblatt* in which was pointed out how each day countless birds failing to see the obstruction in their flightpaths crashed into the walls of the Stahl-Eins building and fell to the ground below, their heads bashed in. The only thing to be said in its favor was that it kept the window cleaners busy. The *Tagesblatt* had also printed letters from irate citizens who maintained that the contemplated building would effectively block the view of the river from the center of the city, create additional parking problems, and, furthermore, that its outrageous design would come to dominate if not actually undermine the adjacent historically rich inner city. All familiar complaints! The vituperativeness of some of the letters may be put down to the fact that five years earlier several investors, all allegedly Jews, Eastern Jews at that, men who had survived the death camps, with a substantial assistance from a number of Selten banks at a time when banks were over-eager to lend money, announced their plan to construct a "much needed" highrise office building near the inner city, only to plead bankruptcy a month before the actual construction was to get under way—hence, the term: *Wolkenkratzerjuden,* Skyscraper Jews. However, the present builders, as far as can be determined, are not Jews, though the same banks are involved. The label, *Wolkenkratzerjuden,* used rather loosely, lingers on. It is merely used as an example. The people of Selten, as far back as can be remembered, have always linked Jews to their profession—so that Jews in the carpet trade are referred to as *Teppichjuden,* and the ubiquitous Jewish owners of jewelry stores—there are two in Selten—are called *Juwelenjuden,* just as, in general, stores run by Jews are commonly referred to as *Judenläden.* The Jews, it must be remembered, go far back in the history of Selten. There are, of course, numerous references to them in the chronicles of Selten. There is, to this day, a Judengasse in the inner city, and no one would dream of changing its name—it would be like tampering with history. But, by and large, the philosemitism of the fifties has been replaced by a vast unconcealed indifference. Jews are no longer a topic of conversation. For god's sake hasn't the Federal Republic done more than its share . . . and, now we even buy their weapons. In all, Jews number less than three hundred; of these fewer than two dozen are former natives of Selten who have returned to live out the rest of their days in the city they used to love. A large proportion of the others, as the tatooed numbers on their forearms testify, are survivors of the camps, mainly from the east. They speak Yiddish, a language that is said to have originated in the 9th or 10th century among Jews in a region they called Loter—the area comprising the basin of the Moselle and the left bank of the Rhein, between Köln and Speyer . . . only a three hour's ride from Selten.

Anyhow, who will take the time to wade through the three-volume chronicles of the city?

The author of a recently published guidebook on Selten and its immediate environs waxes lyrical on the beauty of the rebuilt inner city and the abundance of churches, Romanesque, Gothic, Baroque, their combined bells pealing on the hour and half-hour. The churches like so much else have been restored with an extraordinary attention to detail and authenticity. Standing inside the Baroque Heimatdorfkirche, one is offered only a partial glimpse of its former glory, the bare white vaulted walls connecting segments that were not destroyed, are made to represent a suitable otherness, an absence into which the viewer if so inclined can insert, in his imagination, what had gone up in smoke on that fateful day in August 1944 when several 100-pounders landed on the church. There is also the Residenz on which three famous architects had lavished their care, construction beginning in 1730, so that the princely family having shed their armor and emerged from the heavily fortified castle on the hill could take possession of their new home by 1742 and in utter tranquility pace the splendid formal garden—presently a public park—refining and redefining their princely objectives. Everything is now open to the public except for the wing that is still under restoration. However, the spacious palatial waiting rooms, the ornate staircase, the reception rooms, the mirrored ballroom and the Pink room, the Red room, the Green room, the Blue room offer little in the way of information—they merely signify (how accurately is hard to determine) a former presence of aloof courtiers. In truth, it could be any palace! The art is downright bad, frescoes by local talent or second-rate Italians, the taste runs to gold and blue draperies and an assortment of uninspiring palace furniture on shaky legs. Discomfort, one is made to feel, was rigorously enforced. It was a home to many but no one felt at home. From Hulbach Square with the somewhat insipid-looking Prinz von Hulbach Meinecken-Dumpf on a rearing horse the Norbertstrasse as in the past still one of the main shopping streets leads somewhat circuitously to the rebuilt railroad station, a low and less heroic building than the one destroyed in 1944. Norbertstrasse is lined with small stores, their windows densely packed with every conceivable object a consumer might wish to purchase. There are sewing machines next to a window with sides of ham, sausages, pâté, and dangling limply from shiny metal hooks, freshly slaughtered geese and rabbits, and occupying the center, a boar's head is displayed around which, like so many offerings, are tiny pyramids of canned truffles, mushrooms, oysters, this in turn next to a window of video equipment, tape recorders, cameras, then a travel agency in the window of which two model 747 Lufthansa planes, suspended from the ceiling, seem to be flying over a panoramic view of North Africa's coastline. The next window contains kitchen appliances, the one next to it rolls of fabrics, then a pharmacy window crowded with antiquated medicinal milky white jars and containers dating back more than a hundred years. By and large, no attempt has been made to "decorate" these windows—their main function being to activate the viewer's brain, to remind! Yet, here and there, often on a deserted side street, one can stumble across a fashionable boutique, a jewelry store, an expensive florist, a store selling modern chrome furniture, but even these stores seem to avoid that innate Italian sense of drama and finesse. True, the windows are less crowded, but why this disinterest in *display?* Is it out of an inherent fear of misleading the customer?—a fear that his response or expectations might be overly conditioned by the artistry of the window dresser instead of a genuine response to the intrinsic merit of the object on display. Does this indicate a distinct approach to life? A Spenglerian distrust of the Renaissance for, according to Spengler, it was born of defiance and therefore lacked depth, width, and the sureness of creative instinct? What is Spengler saying? Spengler further claimed that the seductive ease and clarity of the Renaissance rests largely on evasion—the evasion of deeper reluctances by the aid of speciously simple rule. Was that what the storekeepers mistrusted—Renaissance evasions? A mistrust of the superficial albeit agreeable surfaces of everyday life?

Industry is virtually absent. No tall chimneys on the outskirts, nonetheless the small inoffensive city was not spared destruction. Late in the war it was bombed day and night with an unimaginable relentless zeal, almost a religious fervor, as if the gum-chewing aviators from Arkansas and Iowa and the bombardiers from Illinois and Oregon had actually striven to replicate the acts of savagery rendered with such grim accuracy by the 15th-century German painters. The British, on the side of caution, bombing only at night, while the Amis with a brazen disregard for losses showed up as regular as clockwork in their flying fortresses during the day. Why so much destruction on this insignificant town? Was it a personal punishment? Or was it possible that all cities and towns were being treated democratically more or less alike?

The visitor to the Residenz can locate in a vestibule to the right of the grand staircase a row of framed black and white photographs depicting Selten after its destruction, with the palace, or rather what was left of the palace, always at the center. No sign of life. Every imploded building seems to provide ample evidence of the aim on the part of the Allies to reduce accident as a factor in survival. Yet, somehow, people managed to survive. But it's all ages ago. It's only one aspect of a long history. By now no one is any longer able to recollect what dropped where. Of course, there are convenient metal plaques on many houses to provide the date of its initial construction, followed by the date of its deconstruction, and finally the date of its reconstruction. If anything, the plaques indicate an ever-present attention and respect for historical as well as architectural details. Regrettably the city was not spared the overzealous attention of the third-rate architects and builders who came into their own in the period of the *Wirtschaftswunder*. In the fifties one did not closely scrutinize the results. What mattered was that the rubble had been carted away. Hills were formed out of rubble, hills that now, forty years later look as if in some distant past Charlemagne may have stood on their grassy slopes to reconnoiter the landscape. That is how history is given shape. New bridges span the river. Initially nothing fancy, merely functional to permit the traffic to flow smoothly. It was a city coming back to life. Stores, restaurants, beerhalls reopening. The first Ford Taunus came off the assembly line in 1948, then suddenly as a sign of this revitalization a growing need for parking space. Soon the large tour buses began to arrive with their full load of tourists, then as now, predominantly women —waxen-faced, bony ladies with watery eyes and large clumsy hands that seemed to be in a perpetual search for a new occupation, something to unravel perhaps, as the women obediently listened to the stentorian voices of the stern guides, men in their late fifties, accustomed to obedience. And soon on display, like so many imported exotic plants, the large splendidly illustrated books on the Greek isles, Sicily, the south of France, Yugoslavia, the splendors of Munich. Visit colorful Germany! By now Selten has reestablished a firm grip on the day-to-day and no one any longer pays the slightest heed to the busloads of women in their shapeless dresses. They are accepted as an aberrant necessity. On weekends it is only thirty minutes by car to the countryside—the vine-covered hills, everything *almost* unchanged. One can visit medieval villages untouched by the war. People still speak the local dialect. One can sit back lazily in the tiny garden of one of the restaurants and drink several glasses of the excellent local white wine. One can, if so moved, follow with sensuous detachment the outlines of the hills and then, retaining a mental picture of the tenth-century church steeple and the upper section of the archway, the entrance to this tiny community, focus on a cloud or, being alerted by a faint hum, finally locate the origin of the familiar sound, a distant plane, without evincing—and why on earth should one?—the slightest apprehension that the plane might carry a number of those formidable 500-pounders earmarked (that is the nature of paranoia) for this very picturesque spot. In 1943, '44, and '45, life was less predictable. Still there was always a chance that the oncoming bomber was headed for a more rewarding target, or that it might sustain a direct hit from one of the antiaircraft guns, or all else failing, that the bombs it dropped would prove to be duds. There were so many factors to be taken into account. So many variables. Also one had to consider the not inconsequential effect of having all those foreign and in many instances far less developed languages: Russian, Armenian, Ukranian, Bulgarian, Yiddish, Turkish, Slovakian, Iranian, Dutch, Flemish, Arabic, French, Spanish, Portuguese, and English clamor for attention as they rubbed abrasively against each other in the air, on land, and at sea. Each language upholding or attempting to cling to certain historical or human values, certain definitions, certain distinctions that could not easily be translated into German, for at that particular stage in history, and not the first time either, the German language had become relentlessly obdurate, so imprisoned in its inflexible principles and dogmas, its reinterpreted Faustian dynamics, its evident need to eliminate what was not linguistically hard or triumphantly *siegesbewusst*. But in the main it was the Russian, the English, and the American—if indeed the American can be distinguished from the English—the three language groups that were penetrating the German linguistically dominated space, that were intruding into the German awareness, presenting, if only subliminally, a kind of choice. Not at all like so many of the other subjugated or even tenuously allied languages which, at best, presented a compliant or uneasy presence. Some of the languages, after all, were being forcefully changed and even—in one or two extreme cases—cataclysmically extinguished as if it had been decided that they, these foreign tongues, would no longer convey any fruitful tidings to the world. Ultimately, toward the end of the struggle the Russian, the English, the American, now joined by the eloquent French, surged forward not only with the fervent desire to dominate the German language but also having the means to do so. The question remained which of the four would take root, which would henceforth determine Germany's cultural and metaphysical direction? Which would be in a position to exercise the most influence? Which would prevail and make the German language into something slightly more responsive to present-day needs? Would it be the language of Dostoyevsky, Tolstoy, Isaak Babel, and General Zhukov, or the language of Henry Green, Evelyn Waugh, H. G. Wells, and Field Marshal Montgomery, or was it to be the language of Proust, Gide, Exupéry, and André Malraux, or Hemingway, Gertrude Stein, Salinger, and Patton? Once the still self-assured and forever self-deprecating English and worldly French had been eliminated, it was to be a head-on struggle between the new titans, the drinkers of *Kvas* and those who quaffed Coke and Bud by the case, ultimately between the balalaika and jazz . . . between Russian poignancy and Chicago riffs. Towards the close of the war American slang intruded into German airspace with ever greater frequency. Words, snatches of brief exchanges, *Okay, Hunky-dory, shake a leg, sh-i-i-t* . . . remained suspended, like the tiny puffs from the antiaircraft, white pockets of meaning, signifiers in quest of a new home. But the Germans below were still locked into the conceit of Europe as their domain, or was it doom? How could they possibly interpret the simple slogan: *Keep the show on the road,* or comprehend when they, in one way or another, came face to face with some of the B-17 and B-24 bombers and saw—this was not to be dismissed lightly—that for this great offensive, for this crusade, the Amis had named their planes: *El Rancho, Battle Wagon, Power House II, Riley & Crew, Snufly, M'Honey, Vertical Shaft, Dances Wild, Lucky Thirteen, The Ex-Virgin, Rosie's Riveters, St. Regie's Reply, Nelson King,* and *Shangri La.* By 1944 everyone was already concentrating on the denouement, the outcome, few, however, appreciating the degree to which the Russian and American languages were already assaulting the mind and the spirit of the Germans and that in that respect the Americans seemed to have a certain edge, because their language proved to be more accessible—it seemed to promise greater rewards, ineluctibly it led to *Hollywood* and *Time* and *Life* and *The Hit Parade* and *Chickery Chick chala chala, checkala romey in a bananika bollika wollika can't you see Chickery Chick is me* and *Coca-Cola* and *Joan Blondell* and *James Cagney* and *William Holden* and *James Stewart* and *Pontiac* and *Buick* and *boy oh boy, Rocky Road,* and *Ten in One* and *Spearmint gum* and on the *Armed Forces Network: Benny Goodman, Artie Shaw, Glenn Miller, Tommy Dorsey . . . Fats Waller, Ella Fitzgerald, Duke Ellington . . . In the mood. . . .*

Well, admittedly, forty years later the allure has gone. Quite a few Germans still speak English with an American accent, but they speak with less enthusiasm. They still listen to the AFN stations and watch the soaps on TV but without that previously uncritical desire to merge, to become one with the product. The Amerikanists at the universities have not relinquished America, and each year a fresh batch of dissertations on Whitman, Poe, and Hawthorne . . . as well as a number of papers on Pynchon and Gaddis and Gass are produced. But is there anyone who can still remember that initial excitement when on January 27, 1943, over Wilhelmshaven the laconic voice of a nineteen-year-old navigator flying in a B-17 let his words, *Charlie Baker One, can you hear me, over!* enter that yet hotly contested German linguistic space.

CHRISTOPHER BUTLER

......

Walter Abish and the Questioning of the Reader

The title How German Is It *calls attention to a preoccupation, in this case Germany. It's a highly charged issue. Most of us have responses to Germany as we do to so much else. In general, readers compliantly accept what they are offered. Their chief concern is, "how readable is the text". For the most part, novels about Germany, or those simply located in Germany, without having to raise the question of, 'How German is it?' resolve the unspoken question by explaining Germany. In one way or another, they explain Germany away and thereby provide satisfaction. I have avoided an explanation. I have introduced German signs to create and to authenticate a "German" novel.*[1]

One might imagine a collective of writers of innovative fiction getting together in their own Geneva and coming out with a communiqué that says:

> At some stage the readers (too few) of our sort of fiction have got to shape up to the world; and we really mean to the world, and not just to those marvelous theoretical implications of our own techniques of writing, which are so flattering to the critic. They thus have a great deal more work to do than they thought: of course they can't treat writers like us as authorities who will tell them what to think. To that extent Barthes is right to say that "a text is not a line of words releasing a single 'theological' meaning (the 'message' of the Author-God) but a multidimensional space,"[2] but his further argument that we are all mere unoriginal citers of past texts cannot be sustained. If it were we would stop writing. Even when the author attempts a disappearance into intertextuality, the arranger's hand remains as much his own as did that of Joyce.
>
> Nor can readers go looking in our work for soluble modernist

puzzles, in which the kindly writer has tried to provide a solution for as many of the interpretative problems that he at least could foresee. The critic for us can't be a Budgen or a Gilbert. Our world doesn't make sense in that kind of way, and nor do our texts. It is not presented like Joyce's Dublin, Musil's Vienna, or even Kafka's Prague: it is a collage, and often enough an absurdist or alienating one.

One might translate some of this imagined declaration into "academic" terms by arguing that postmodern innovative writers often present evidence that is fragmented or skewed by its play within the web of independent semiotic systems, and the reader has to work matters out from there. What their texts demand, in the first instance, is not so much criticism or interpretation as cooperation in putting them together. Whether the reader is able to share such a cooperative reading with anyone else is not a primary concern. Experimentalists like Abish are not, after all, academics who have to keep that kind of talk going. If his texts do not easily create any consensus as to their interpretative meaning, then they may well be accurate symptoms of a subjectivity, a relativism, and even a confusion in the "postmodern" zeitgeist, to which more attention still needs to be paid.

However, I wish to argue that books like *Minds Meet* and *How German Is It* show us how this disruptive relationship of the text to our assumed knowledge of the world can still have a moral effect over which we might be able to agree. For central to Abish's writing is, I think, the way in which he can convict us of harboring prejudices, which he seems positively to encourage us to hold. This is a dangerously Swiftean use of experimental technique, and it has very few parallels. Since Abish achieves his effects essentially through irony and humor, we may find a way into the problems his work raises by considering the joke. If we laugh at a joke about Poles, or Jews, or WASPS changing a lightbulb, in the very act of "getting the point" we momentarily share the (often aggressive) prejudice that powers it:

> How many WASPS does it take to change a light bulb?
> Two. One to mix the martinis while the other calls the repairman.

And the same goes for the metajoke, which can only work, like Abish's metafictions, once a genre is established:

> How many feminists does it take to change a light bulb?
> That's not funny.[3]

Walter Abish's attacks on what he calls the "familiar" world work in very much this way. As we enter the contemporary German world of his novel with Ulrich Hargenau, we are slyly asked what a (French) visitor would notice.

> Undoubtedly the cleanliness. The painstaking cleanliness. As well as the all-pervasive sense of order. A reassuring dependability. A punctuality. An almost obsessive punctuality. Then of course there is the new, striking architecture. Innovative? Hardly. Imaginative? Not really. But free of that former somber and authoritative massivity. A return to the experimentation of the Bauhaus? Regrettably no. Still, something must be said in favour of the wide expanse of glass on the buildings, the fifteen-, twenty-story buildings, the glass reflecting not only the sky but also acting as a mirror for the older historical sites, those clusters of carefully reconstructed buildings that are an attempt to replicate entire neighbourhoods obliterated in the last war.[4]

This use of discomforting detail to build up the world of the book, which itself, we notice, incorporates some artfully chosen mirrors of past history, is a central feature of the book. So too are the narrator's many questions; for example: "But why this curious predilection for black leather?" (*HGI*, p. 3), which is the twelfth such question in the first three pages. However much we may like to think we can resist Abish's obliging anatomy of cultural stereotypes, in the very act of recognizing them we are made their accomplices.

Abish is thus an insidiously didactic and even moralizing writer, and this sense of engagement underlies much of his experimental technique in writing. Despite the modish emphasis of some of his interpreters upon his subject's being language, I feel that his texts are about something, even if this "something" is made strange or unfamiliar in narratives that often center on the important themes of cultural relativity, of skepticism, and of our proneness to be comically misled by the language that reader and writer both have to use.

Abish thus occupies that middle position described by Alan Wilde (who sees many surfictionists, by contrast, as uninvolved in the world and lost in a self-reflexivity and play which have given up the effort to engage the world through language). For Wilde discerns in postmodernism a mode of "midfiction" that still seeks, even if indirectly and ironically, to be referential:

> Midfiction describes a narrative form that negotiates the oppositional extremes of realism and reflexivity (both their presuppositions and their technical procedures). Further, it seeks to reveal the extraordinariness of the ordinary, frequently and paradoxically by trafficking in limit situations—thereby subjecting to interrogation the very foundations of the writer's (and the reader's) beliefs. And finally, it invites us not *through* but *in* the relationships and actions of its characters—and by way of some strategic *écart* or swerve in its fabric—to perceive, obliquely and ironically, the moral perplexities of inhabiting a world that is itself, as "text," ontologically ironic, contingent, and problematic.[5]

I believe that Abish belongs in this central postmodernist tradition. His main concerns seem to me to be three: (1) an attack on the notion of the self wishing to order the world in its own interests, (2) the defamiliarization of the world that results once the incorporating self is dethroned, and (3) the uncertainties thus produced, in his characters and in the reader, by the sense of relativism and conflict of cultures that results from this new relation.

Abish sees the self as perpetually attempting to make the world familiar, comfortable, and conformable to its organizing desires. Thus in traditional fiction, "We read a text and world falls into place. Both Proust and Henry James provide psychologically valid explanations that enable the reader to maneuver in their world and grasp the emotional content of what is at stake."[6] We feel, and feel secure, through a narrator whose consciousness and growing control of his material allows the reader to stand in for him. Thus Marcel conquers the "otherness" of the Guermantes way, or Lambert Strether finally decodes others' deceptions and finds out what they mean for him. Indeed, such a narrator attempts to possess his world in quite a straightforward linguistic sense, for "All that is required to depict the 'familiar' is that the possessive pronoun, singular or personal, be introduced in a sentence or attached to a word: Our doorway, our neighbourhood, my grandeur, his view."[7]

Abish often uses the metaphor of the house and its furniture for this sense of "possession," which he then disrupts. Thus his aptly titled "This is not a film, this is a precise act of disbelief" begins: "This is a familiar world. It is a world crowded with familiar faces and events. Thanks to language the brain can digest, piece by piece, what has occurred and may yet occur. It is never at a loss for the word that signifies what is happening this instant. In Mrs Ite's brain the interior of the large house with a view of the garden and the lake are surfaces of the familiar."[8] And Michael Bontemps, who replicates landscapes in his films and has come to America "to make a film exploring American needs," and indeed to concentrate on the shopping mall as the "museum of need," also chooses "to arrange the furniture and thereby create a topography for his daily needs" as do two other characters: Frank Ol and Mrs Ite. But this topography is not allowed to last in the story.[9]

Abish clearly feels that trust in the language we use, as the one that "truly" articulates the world, is often misplaced. Indeed, it may lead to a moral failing, for "the 'self' persists in regarding the world as an extension of its very being and its vocabulary."[10] The result of this is that many of Abish's protagonists fail to meet the post-Kantian moral demand that they achieve insight into another's point of view (a demand that is essential to the liberal tradition of the novel). Much of his writing indeed consists in the comic demonstration of the fact that too much reliance on our own way of engaging in linguistic transactions with others may prove, in a world governed by the contingent and the absurd, to be deeply unreliable.

This is a theme of all his work, but it is perhaps most directly shown in his ironically entitled story "Minds Meet," which is full (among much else) of messages going wrong (astray, misinterpreted) and coming into contradiction. As modes of ordering reality they somehow comically and significantly fail to be agreed between sender and receiver. "Not infrequently the writer of notes will feel impelled to address a larger audience. He may, on his way home, stop at one of the public conveniences in the subway and write in capital letters above the urinal: Does the past leave any room for the future? The writer will have the satisfaction of knowing that many men will ponder this question as they stand with legs apart on the brink of an incertitude that nothing will relieve."[11] These failed messages disconcert Abish's characters, and the reader, because they are in ironic contrast to the apparent clarity and certainty displayed by the helpfully explanatory narrator, who goes on to anatomize, in the following sections of his story, being "taken aback" by the message, being "abased" by the message, being "abashed" while receiving it, and so on in alphabetical order. For paradoxically enough, the narrator of the text seems to look at the world in wide-eyed innocence, and yet also to be the master of reported anecdote. Thus, for example,

> Harry discovers Gwen in bed with Tobias and is taken aback. He says to himself, I am taken aback. His face more or less confirms this. Dubiously he inspects his face in the bathroom mirror. He is filled with a profound melancholy as well as distrust. How confusing, he thinks, Do I mistrust my melancholy, or am I melancholy because I am riddled with mistrust?
>
> Most men feel frustrated by the time they reach thirty because there are only so many ways of making love. While the lower part of the body is actively engaged during this act of passion the face questions the veracity of its own existence. In its distress it beams all kinds of signals to the other face. These signals are by no means reliable. One might say that the faces are immersed in the self. (*MM*, pp. 6f.)

Here the self, as the supposedly certain, single origin of the "message," or of introspection, or of its "own" lovemaking, experiences itself as divided. It is a decentered self like that proposed by much contemporary theory, subject to contradictory beliefs derived from habitual behavior and ideology. This pathetic division in consciousness is comically paralleled here, in a rather Beckettian manner, by that between the mind and body in making love. For the self may be stricken by doubt at the most embarrassing moments. Thus Harry is "abashed" while receiving his message, which is a surprisingly equivocal reply to the kind of order that is supposed to be pretty clear:

> Harry steps into a bank in Queens and points a pistol at the bank teller. Let's have all your dough, he says. Dough, mocks the teller. What do you think this is, a bakery. Next thing you'll be asking for bread. Harry blushes furiously. He is being mocked. He feels abashed. It is a familiar quandary, so he shoots the bank teller, and then hops on the first passing bus outside the bank. Killing is a stabilising factor in this society. But in no time Harry is again filled with a familiar panic, he doesn't know in which direction the bus is headed. (*MM*, p. 10)

What Abish does is to translate our distrust of language and our mishaps in trying to make it work for us into a fictional model of human relationships. Harry's bus is as ambivalent for him as the "dough" he fails to acquire. Frames of reference and language games get across one another and mixed up. Abish thus uses his writing to contest the "perception of the everyday predicated on an unquestioning affirmation of the function and role of the 'self' in society, as rigidly governed by the 'reality principle' and as subsumed by the logic of everyday existence as we are. What the innovative novel must disavow is a self centered world in which the 'self' continues to reign supreme."[12] By a highly inventive and sustained poetic fiction of anecdotes he shows us what the world would be like if. . . . For the characters in many of his stories variously and comically misunderstand messages and significant expressions, and even doubt their own introspective judgments. They are led into contradiction and absurdity by the differing interpretations that can be put on them. They adopt incompatible strategies of comprehension and so deconstruct their own intentions and situations. They also enact the reader's own uncertainty, as he or she attempts to interpret signs within the story, looking within the narrative for a consistency and coherence that simply is not there, because all the old reliable methods of realist narrative are (partially) allowed to break down, along with their communicative codes.

These themes remain central to Abish's work subsequent to "Messages," such as "Ardor/Awe/Atrocity," "How the comb gives a meaning to the hair," and "Crossing the Great Void," which develop them in a more complex and indirect manner. These texts are perhaps most significant for what they conceal, of situations and motivation. They are, Abish tells me, "energized by sexuality," which is a key to the "subversive" meanings that lie just below the surface. These teasingly repel and invite those neo-Freudian explanations preferred by so many critics. They are almost, but not quite, case studies—as Marcel Proust in "How the Comb . . ." goes rat hunting in the Hotel Marigny in Albuquerque, and "starved for Albertine" plans to have her "trampled to death by a horse in the fifth volume of the English edition" of his novel (*MM*, p. 150). But Albertine hotly contests her fate and dies when her single-engined plane explodes over the desert. A similar fate awaits the detested uncle of Zachary, the hero of "Crossing the Great Void" (in the collection *In the Future Perfect*). His car is blown up by his nephew, with him in it, on the Cross Bronx, perhaps because he is Zachary's mother's lover. This story, which is a family romance of sorts, also concerns Zachary's search for his Italian Fascist father, who disappeared behind enemy lines in the North African desert in 1941. Perhaps deliberately cut off from others by deafness, he has been obsessed since his school days by deserts: of which the "authoritative study" is *Crossing the Great Void* by one Major Klip D. Jars.

He is aided in his quest by his lover, Track, who has a map of the oasis Blitlu, in which his father disappeared, tattooed on her back.

> Your back?
>
> She had taken him by complete surprise. He was dumbfounded. He was also unprepared for what was to follow that evening at her place. He had no prior experience, no knowledge upon which he could base an appropriate response when hours later, at her house, she unbuttoned her blouse and began to take it off. With the lights off, it was too dark in her bedroom to see the map of Blitlu. In addition to your hearing aid you seem to need glasses, she said matter-of-factly. He was convinced that her remark was devoid of malice. It was not an accusation, but merely a statement of fact. (*IFP*, p. 105)

Once in North Africa, he passes a hotel doorman who curiously resembles an old photograph of his father; he then sets off for Blitlu where, he thinks, he may be able to find the batteries he needs for his hearing aid. The story concludes with a stripping away of the furniture of the familiar world:

> Now he is bound for the center of the desert, and every step he is taking is bringing him closer to the center, and every step he has taken in the past has led to him being there. Even before he was aware of the center's existence, he was traveling towards it. Everything he has encountered so far appears familiar, as if at some time in the past his mother must have described it to him as she spoke of his father in the Italian Expeditionary Forces crisscrossing the desert. Consequently he feels convinced that what lies ahead will also prove to be familiar. After all, the emptiness he expects to encounter at the center will be no different from the emptiness he might experience in the interior of his room after it had been denuded of all his possessions, stripped of all the things he had clung to with such persistence, such tenacity, such great effort, as if his life depended on it. (*IFP*, p. 113)

Such Kafkaesque allegorical quests are of course open to all sorts of interpretations, but to none that are certain, for the characters of stories like "Minds Meet," "Parting Shot," "Access," or "Crossing the Great Void" are comic rather as they are in Beckett or Pinter. We can see that what they think and do has absurd consequences and so are tempted to feel superior to them. But insofar as they cumulatively reveal to us the instability of all communication (in a way that my quotations only feebly exemplify), we do not manage to feel so superior. Within the illogical world presented by the text we cannot solve their problems for them, any more than we can those of Estragon and Vladimir. This impotence and anxiety is part of our sense of the metaphysically absurd, as originally conceived by writers like Kafka, Sartre, and Camus. But in a post-theological age in which all philosophies, including the existentialist, are suspect, this sense of alienation has become centered on the linguistically absurd. Where metaphysical props are taken away, only language, which as Wittgenstein so brilliantly demonstrated can bewitch our intelligence, remains. This is painfully funny, since it abandons traditional comedy, where the audience can usually grasp a rational solution to the cross-purposes of the plot and so feel superior to the dramatis personae. In a world like that presented by Abish there are no such solutions. (These considerations would apply equally well, I think, to much of the work of Apple, Barthelme, and Coover.)

The insecurities to which Abish subjects his characters are passed on to the reader by the defamiliarization of the world he presents. This is brought about not only by the estranging effects wrought by his perpetual asking of questions and his authorial commentary, but by his very mode of description. This can be deliberately simplified. A children's copybook style is presented, sometimes quite explicitly (as in the coloring book introduced in *How German Is It*, pp. 176ff.). We are invited to see it as unreliable or naive, and above all, as politically unaware or innocent.

The air in such passages is one of patient explanation, or of what Abish often calls in his subheadings "An Introduction" to the extraordinary:

> The number of cars on the F train is considered adequate. During the early morning rush hour at least eight people are crushed each day. This number is considered tolerable. The following day the next of kin can pick up the morning paper and on the front page compare the accomplishments of their loved one to the accomplishments of the other victims. It has become common practice for the newspapers to embellish these accomplishments. For a slight remuneration the victim can receive a one-day posthumous honorary membership in the Yale or Princeton eating clubs. . . . The people who disagree that the number of F cars on the train are adequate have been forced to go underground. They are said to exist as a movement.[13]

This example is chosen pretty well at random and may seem, in isolation, merely anecdotal, whereas it is Abish's skill at working observations like this into complex narratives that makes him such a distinguished writer. In this example and in many others that might be cited, such extraordinarily detached descriptions of bizarre situations are part of fictional worlds that are, to say the least, at a peculiar angle to our own, as for example in the story "Life Uniforms," where buildings collapse each day, and an electric company records this, noting their loss of electricity-consuming customers (*MM*, pp. 21ff.).

There is thus a defamiliarizing withdrawal and detachment in Abish's presentation, even when he deals with situations that would naturally prompt us to consider their real-life analogues, and that the reader might expect to be emotionally involving. In this he follows one of his most important predecessors, for as he points out: "Disfamiliarisation was Kafka's intuitive response to any situation that demanded his emotional attention."[14] His central characters are deprived of "depth," as in so much postmodern experimental writing. But unlike Handke, and like Barthelme, Abish combines this withdrawal with a sense of humor. This implies a peculiarly behavioristic description in his writing, a pretense that the bizarre behavior of others is beyond psychological or moral explanation, or simply doesn't need it. What is more, his characters' reflections on their predicaments often have a relevance to them that is, to say the least, oblique.

These considerations apply most strikingly to his descriptions of sex, as for example in his short story "Parting Shot," which depends on one of Abish's many triangular or quadrangular relationships. Here Gregory, a literary critic who is an expert on Maupassant, falls in love with a photograph of Irma and leaves his wife Maude. In section 14 of the story

> Without the slightest trepidation Maude enters the room in which two men are sitting on the couch with Irma. No one prevents her from walking to the window and looking at the West Side Drive, as she pretends not to notice that the two are quite openly caressing Irma's small white breasts, breasts that resemble her own breasts. In order not to see the men and Irma, she is compelled to partly close her eyes, or focus them elsewhere, on the wallpaper for instance. It is a pity about the wallpaper. The wallpaper destroys the room. It makes the room smaller and less attractive. Obviously Irma had little sense for colour or design. Maude would have suggested a bolder

> pattern. But Irma had an incredible body. Most men noticed her body. Irma, at their first encounter, had quite casually mentioned that her legs were her best feature. What an amazing thing to say, Maude had thought at the time. For some reason the two men were not touching Irma's legs. Perhaps, it occurred to Maude, they were saving Irma's legs for some other time. Perhaps they were satisfied to look at the legs while concentrating on other parts of Irma's anatomy. Who can say? Who can tell what is on the mind of a man who is caressing a woman. (*IFP*, pp. 38f.)

We are back in the world of "Minds Meet": these men have purposes that Maude cannot know, and Abish won't tell us. They are, after all, "sunk in the self," and their division of attention neatly parallels and subverts that which Abish exploited in the earlier story. But it is only the willingness of the author to include the irrelevant along with the "moving," to observe the scene in a nonvoyeuristic but not anaesthetized manner (for Maude has good reasons, as can be seen from other parts of the story, for noticing the details, and in particular the legs that she does), that can leave the matter wholly up for the judgment, rather than the participation, of the reader.

The unemotional manner of Irma's description is ipso facto defamiliarizing, even as it picks out familiar detail, and it is deeply expressive of Maude's alienation. It is "inappropriate" for Maude to be thinking about wallpaper, and a more conventional writer would leave the matter as a simple gesture of self-protection, the noticing of something irrelevant because one cannot "face the situation." Abish does allow for this, of course, as an essentially compassionate writer, but he does more. Since Maude is not developed in the narrative as a conventional character (this is virtually all we see of her), she seems to us to be divided or decentered in some more profound way. She observes sexual acts, with us, but she has to conclude that she simply doesn't know "what is on the mind of a man who is caressing a woman." We grasp and sympathize with this disassociation and division within her, because these men, as described by Abish, don't seem to have any emotional involvement either. Even within the most intimate of contexts, cross-purposes still abound.

Like Brecht, Abish thus denies us "the culinary theatre of the emotions" and refuses that kindly liberalizing commentary that would allow us to impose "our" values on the text, to hierarchize his descriptions with them and so make "familiar" moral judgments on a world arranged, as his is not, to obey our wishes.

Thus, as Jerome Klinkowitz remarks, with reference to *How German Is It*: "All hierarchical values are removed from Abish's perceptions, not so that we see the thing in itself (a *nouveau roman* attitude he satirizes through the philosopher Brumhold) but rather to emphasize the opaque nature of the sign. Once we humanize, Abish implies, we become subject to the same flawed rules of communication from which his characters suffer."[15]

This unreliability of the sign is exploited by Abish in many virtuosic ways, as we have already partly seen, but I wish to pursue here one of its most important effects, that of making us aware of the trickiness and indeed playfulness of our perception of signs as they function between different cultures, with reference to *How German Is It* and to his present work in progress, *House on Fire*. Abish warns us that in reading texts like these, the reader is invited to consider their mode of narration, rather than to make facile judgments on contemporary political history. For he doesn't simply rely on his own or the reader's cleverness in matching *histoire* and history, but on his or her awareness of a much more slippery common bond, that of language:

> Essentially, I am questioning how we see and write about something. Levi-Strauss, wherever he went in Brazil, embodied Western culture. How could he avoid that? He reduced everything to *signs* in order to comprehend it. At the same time his own cultural as well as personal history may distort the signs he uses by attaching a particular Western significance to them. Perhaps that is why I feel that the text I write lies between me and the experience.[16]

The underlying chain of events is thus meant to be much less important than the dislocated manner of their narration. And yet the accessibility of the book does partly depend on its running very close to a conventional narrative, concerning Ulrich Hargenau, who is the son of a soldier implicated in the plot against Hitler of 1944, and his brother Helmuth, a successful architect, in and of the "new Germany." Ulrich has helped to convict by his court testimony the Einzieh left-wing terrorist group, in which his wife Paula, now living in Geneva, was implicated. The activities of this group threaten the buildings Helmuth designs. A post office is blown up. When Ulrich returns to visit him in Brumholdstein, he meets Franz, a former servant of the Hargenaus now working as a waiter, who is also designing a building, this one a matchstick model of the Durst concentration camp, which was in fact on the site of the present Brumholdstein. This begins to open up another of Abish's themes, which is indeed the relationship of the new Germany to its past. Later in the novel one of its few dramatic events of obvious symbolic significance takes place: a street caves in, and a mass grave is discovered beneath the town.

Ulrich also becomes involved in a number of those interlocking sexual relationships we find in Abish's other stories: Egon, who lives in a house designed by Helmuth, is unfaithful to his wife Gisela and takes up with Rita Tropf-Umwert, a photographer. But Helmuth also seduces Rita.

In the final part of the novel we are by the sea with Ulrich, Egon, and Gisela, at Ganzlich near the East Frisian islands. While they are all there, Gottfried, the keeper of a bridge between the islands and the shore, and who has possibly been recruited by Paula's Einzieh group, shoots two policemen. His bridge is blown up. In the last scene of the book Ulrich visits a doctor for hypnotherapy, recounts his childhood, admits that he is a bastard and not a Hargenau, and under hypnosis begins to raise his hand in what may well be a Nazi salute. The novel ends with a final question: "Is it possible for anyone in Germany, nowadays, to raise his right hand, for whatever the cause, and not be flooded by the memory of a dream to end all dreams?" (*HGI*, p. 252).

It is the sections inset into this narrative, whose effect is primarily metafictional, that reinforce Abish's theme of the sign, and of the dreams, or hidden purposes, or suppressed past history, that might underlie it. These metafictional episodes include the memorial meeting for the recently dead philosopher Brumhold (very like Heidegger indeed), and Helmuth's speech on him (*HGI*, pp. 164ff., 169f.); the section on the coloring book *Das Neue Deutschland*, which is sent to Ulrich by Daphne (*HGI*, pp. 176ff.); and the section on the purposes of an antiterrorist film (*HGI*, pp. 243ff.).

All of these place the main line of the narrative in a very problematic light indeed. The novel slyly invites the cooperation of the reader, who lives after all in his own "familiar" ordered world, to assess an imagined German society, which only *seems* to be subject to an "all pervasive sense of order" (*HGI*, p. 2). This "order" is a characteristic that runs directly contrary to a narrative mode that thrives on the doubtful perspectives of internal mirroring and ironic self-qualification, and so threatens to lead us into self-deconstruction and contradiction. For example, Ulrich

Hargenau himself slyly resembles his author: he proves to be writing a book called *The Idea of Switzerland*: "where only a few years ago Nabokov lived, as much a prisoner of the past as I am a prisoner of the present" (*HGI*, p. 54), and this is indeed the title of this part of *How German Is It*. Ulrich's book is as concerned as Abish's own, it seems, to diagnose a culture through its products, and to contrast the idealized, stereotypical, and treacherous "idea" with the reality of the exemplar: "it's based on something I read about Paganini. Apparently Berlioz loved the idea of Paganini but was revolted by his music" (*HGI*, p. 52). This contrast of "idea" and "revulsion" may well lie at the heart of Abish's novel.

The lesson given by Ulrich's lover Anna Heller to her young pupils on the "familiar" (*HGI*, pp. 119ff.) also stands at an interesting remove from the main narrative and helps to expose its method: for the familiar here relates to the comfortable matching of cultural stereotype to external reality but also makes, we might think, a barrier: "We want to visit museums and monuments and ruins that we only know from reproductions in books. Having seen the photographs of what we have come to visit, we naturally know what to expect. So the ruins, the works of art, the foreign cities are not entirely unfamiliar" (*HGI*, p. 120). Nor indeed are the scenes Abish describes. And yet he almost literally digs below this level of response, in revealing the camp Durst hidden below the new German town of Brumholdstein; and so there is no little irony when Anna also explains that something her pupils often see, like the railway station of Durst, behind which lies the history of the camp it once supplied with prisoners, may become so terribly familiar that "we stop seeing it" (*HGI*, p. 120).

Abish's method in *How German Is It* is I think most clearly exposed in his chapter on Egon and Gisela, who are indeed "representatives" of his imagined new society of the postwar years. Their picture and the article on them in the magazine *Treue* depends on all sorts of illusions. Their stereotypical description (*HGI*, pp. 123ff.) conforms so well to an image of what the new Germany "must" be like that even as they project a way of life for the admiration of the readers of a magazine, they at the same time inspire distrust in the readers of Abish's novel, particularly if those readers are aware of the type of analysis to which Barthes has subjected this kind of material. This is because Egon and Gisela as described here are too perfect, too close to what "everyone" believes (informed as they so often are by nothing better than just such journalism, with its glamorized notions of the quotidian). Our image of Gisela and Egon thus derives from that "manuel scolaire" of *idées reçues* that Barthes ridicules.

It is most important to realize that such a mode of narration does not simply play with theory and make the narcissistic demand that we theorize in interpreting it. Instead, it exploits the relationship between stereotype and prejudice to disturb the reader. It goes beyond Barthes, because his theory is really a very comfortable one from the critic's point of view, insofar as it allows those who accept it to feel that they are somehow superior to the delusions encoded by "bourgeois" realistic texts, the popular media, and so on. Abish destroys any such complacency in the reader by ensnaring us in prejudice and stereotype from the start. After all, we know what "black leather," and "cleanliness," and "the innate German upper-middle class instinct to combine 'perfection' with the 'menacing'" (*HGI*, p. 127) really "mean" . . . or do we? Even if the text is parodic here, it entraps us as surely as the joke does.

These themes are beautifully orchestrated in our extract from Abish's latest novel, which begins once more with a question: "Is this really you?" The reader is put on the defensive in confronting a reborn and reconstructed "German" world, where trees die from industrial poisoning, under conditions ironically described as "normal." This serene countryside is the setting for "passionate love" and also "Ah stability!" It is a land populated by the "*Wirtschaftswunder*, the true pioneers of this present peace." We are once more in an imagined country, more "precise in detail" than Austria or Italy, where the trains run on time. For the reader of Abish's earlier work, this is indeed a "familiar world," but as treacherous to the reader's presuppositions as ever.

Abish likes societies where things seem to work but which have an underlying unease, and he likes the source of that unease to be a past history, and bygone ideologies that haunt the present (for the philosopher Brumhold soon makes a reappearance here). "But to what end? What purpose is served by endlessly unearthing the signs of an earlier disaster: in trying to read the labored handscratched markings that constitute a primitive calendar (but what year?) on some moist stone wall that happily, once again, serves a more peaceful purpose: the storage of Rhein wines." It is our answer to this question that will, presumably, justify the whole novel.

Abish's problem here is to find new topics for this type of political and yet playful analysis, for that is what it is in essence. His writing here has all the signs (a treacherous word, interpreted in poststructuralist manner) of aiming at a greater depth of suggestion as to what might underlie it.

This chapter sets the scene for an investigation, in which: "Signs fall into place. *Hubschrauberlandeplatz*, Heliport, *Mittelstreckenrakete*, medium-range missile, *Höhepunkt*, pinnacle. And words fall into place: *Grundverfassung*, basic state. *Alltäglichkeit*, everyday life, *Nichtmehrdasein*, no-longer-being-there, *zweideutig*, ambiguous."

These military features, which we might just fail to find on a map, and the all-embracing network of words, might be expected to come together at some point, but they are here subjected to that skepticism concerning their marriage that is a central theme of postmodernism. A common language, whether it be the English of this text or that of contemporary Germany, is inherently treacherous, even when, as we are told, it is shared by tram conductors and third-year students of philology. The latter may indeed be studying the present hospitality of German to "guest words" of American origin. But such divisions within language are echoed by and encode the social divisions of the past and of the present. Every door and paving stone may carry the "trace" (another theoretically loaded word) of "that at one time violently enforced 'solution.'" This sort of comment runs the risk for Abish of being too overt, but it is indeed the risk of this type of writing that it should willy-nilly become politically engaged.

So here we are in the town of Selten, which is pored over by elderly female tourists, observed by the far-from-touristic eye of Abish. They pass Altneu, the site of Brumhold's log cabin home, from which "in 1944 he scrupulously avoided reading a moral disintegration into the stream of refugees and . . . concentration camp inmates" who were passing by him. There is a further problem here, which arises not just from the painful potential of engagement with this part of history. Abish's writing scrupulously and ironically exploits a metalanguage, with its references to "signs," "traces," "reading," and so on. We are aware that this metalanguage is indeed at a remove from historical reality. Brumhold shouldn't have been doing nothing more than "reading" the events that were immediately present to him, even if he was a mere philosopher. But the text almost conspires with him, to keep the events of history at a distance from the author's story. It is once more the reader who is expected to outdo Brumhold and to "see through" this ironically distanced and metafictional language, to history, to make the critically much-disputed transition from language to reference.

This preliminary tour d'horizon can no more claim a disengagement from the presentation of the scene of politics than can Conrad's at the opening of *Nostromo*. At this point, of course, like the most naive reader of a realist text, we await the stirrings of plot. About this little can be said. Much is already in place: but as yet no Ulrich-like antihero. There is indeed the society of a revived Germany, with its business and its architecture of past and present, including the Stahl-Eins building and the Baroque Residenz of Selten, restored after a thorough Allied bombing aimed "to reduce accident as a factor in survival." But it is presented through Abish's metaphors, which after all may attempt to match universes of discourse to one another and find interesting ways of failing to do so. Thus he describes the Allied invasion after the war as a conflict or competition between languages: "In the main it was the Russian, the English, and the American—if indeed the American can be distinguished from the English—the three language groups that were penetrating the German linguistically dominated space, that were intruding into the German awareness, presenting, if only subliminally, a kind of choice." But the nature of this choice, as it might await a character in a novel, or us as readers, will have to await the publication of the full text. This will no doubt develop very significantly the problematic, based on cultural relativism and linguistic unreliability, of Abish's earlier work, and this is in itself sufficient promise.

This problematic seems to me to be of considerable importance, because experimental fictions like this are competing with others for mental space, and they are inherently more liberating than many others, because they leave us so many choices. They leave the finding of the truth up to us, having set the questions correctly, and thus confront the terrible simplifications of moral, sexual, and political doctrine, which are so powerfully transmitted by politicians and the media they control. We need, I think, to take Abish's fictions very seriously, given this type of contrast. It is one to which he himself points, with typical good humor and depth of ironic perception:

> SL: In a sense the production of the "Holocaust" is the right answer to the German problem.
> WA: It's the popular answer. The Walt Disney answer. It's the only answer possible. Walt Disney is our truth.
> SL: History returns not as a comedy or tragedy: a cartoon.
> WA: The Germans had Wagner to designate their space in the world. We have Walt Disney. Where is the grave of all this. In Hollywood?[17]

This "grave in Hollywood" may prove to be as sinister in its way as the one Abish led us to discover in Brumholdstein. His writing is an eloquent protest against its existence.

Notes

1 Walter Abish, interview with Sylvere Lotringer, *Semiotext(e)* 4, no. 2 (1982): 160f.

2 Roland Barthes, "The Death of the Author" in *Image Music Text*, ed. Stephen Heath (London, 1977), p. 146.

3 Ted Cohen, "Jokes" in Eva Shaper, ed., *Pleasure, Preference and Value* (Cambridge, 1983), pp. 120–37. The examples are cited from pp. 127f.

4 Walter Abish, *How German Is It* (New York, 1980), pp. 2f. Cited from here on as *HGI*, with references in the text.

5 Alan Wilde, "Strange Displacement of the Ordinary: Apple, Elkin, Barthelme, and the Problem of the Excluded Middle," in *Boundary* 2, no. 10, p. 192.

6 Walter Abish, "On Aspects of the Familiar World as Perceived in Everyday Life and Literature," a paper delivered at a conference on Innovation and Renovation, University of Wisconsin, Milwaukee, in 1981.

7 Ibid.

8 Walter Abish, *Minds Meet* (New York, 1975), p. 31.

9 Ibid. Cf. pp. 32, 33, 36, 41, and 66.

10 Abish, "On Aspects."

11 Abish, *Minds Meet*, p. 5. Subsequently cited in the text as *MM*.

12 Abish, "On Aspects."

13 Walter Abish, "Read Only Memory," *In the Future Perfect* (New York, 1977), p. 59f. Subsequently cited in the text as *IFP*.

14 Abish, "On Aspects."

15 Jerome Klinkowitz, *The Self Apparent Word* (Carbondale and Edwardsville, Ill., 1984), p. 131. Compare the description of Ulrich and Anna making love in *HGI*, ch. 29, pp. 172ff.

16 Abish, interview in *Semiotext(e)*, p. 162. I have written at greater length about these aspects of *HGI* in my "Scepticism and Experimental Fiction," *Essays in Criticism* 36, no. 1 (January 1986): 47–67.

17 Abish, interview in *Semiotext(e)*, pp. 174f.

WILLIAM H. GASS

......

The Sunday Drive

This was years ago . . . . Martha, the children, and I had driven into the country to collect weeds. At that time, Martha was in what I called her "pluck and pickle" phase, and she loved to gather great heaps of weeds each autumn to tie and hang head down in carefully sorted bunches in the basement. Placed in vases later, even the most unlikely plants displayed an intensely distilled yet vagrant beauty: dry pods like petals, petals like furled flags, the stiff twigs like an explosion of cracks in a wall. We would choose, when we could, one of those fine fall days when the sky is such a deep and cloudless blue it descends straight to earth like a curtain to the stage, and you can almost see the leaves beginning to turn, as if hastened by the light. We would take some baloney for the kids, some bread and cheese, and lunch among the leftovers, down old roads and unmowed berms, where life still went on randomly, out of the reach of sprays and scythes. The cheshire would crumble on the bread, as suddenly out of place as pollen in this world of the ripe expended seed. The cattails stood like daydream candy on a stick, and the fields were thick with brittle stems and cream and gray grasses resilient as wire. It was difficult, sometimes impossible, to make footway through them, and of course we wore long pants and sleeves to protect ourselves from burrs, insects, poison ivy, barbed wire, nervous bees.

With my parents, during the Depression, I had prowled the country roads, too, with a cardboard carton in the back seat of the car to collect apples dusty from the tractors, their ripeness ready to be restored with a wipe like objects found in an attic. We also carried paper sacks for walnuts in their tough green hulls, as well as for the hazelnuts we would pick up in convenient groves and abandoned patches of trespass grass which experience had identified as likely locations, and greed had staked out as rightly our property the instant those branches incautiously overhanging the fence brightened with fruit. My father was devoted to "the Sunday drive": late afternoon excursions to check on the progress of spring, the building of a road, the extent of flooding or wind damage, the color of the leaves across the state line in Pennsylvania; and so we knew the territory, and had driven cautiously down many a narrow, deeply rutted road past more than one neglected grove of russet pears or apple trees, by ditches which had disappeared beneath a flood of goldenrod, along lines of lark, blackbird, and swallow wires, beside fields whose fences were all broken and bent down in the embrace of bushes—flowered, fruitful, and blazing.

I had a passion for buckeyes which I would rub in my palms until they gleamed like bulbs—bulbs whose planting I could easily imagine would produce paneling for a men's club, mahogany sideboards and dining tables, stately chairs—and their smooth, almost oily glisten, often distracted my eye from its pursuit of more useful things, annoying my father who always suspected me, anyway, of goofing off. The truth is that the apples we gathered were knobby and wormy, the nuts terribly difficult to break into, frequently infested as well, causing me to wonder how the bugs had got there, when it was so hard for me, unless they had been born in the stems that nourished the meat.

My mother was mainly after elderberries which grew along the fences and in almost any unploughed place, the blackly purple heads like a beaded dress. Snipping off the bursting umbrella-shaped crowns, we laid them on newspapers—whatever was handy—always carefully because the juice stained. I called the stuff "Lady Macbeth's blood," my messed-up possessive slightly confusing the play's plot, but conveying the juice's indelible character nevertheless. Small for my age, I often felt engulfed by the thick tall weeds and grasses; their perfume was like a fog—in such a cloud of scents I could not see—everywhere insects were rustling and clicking and stridulating, and when I reached up to hack off the head of an elderberry, my face and neck would be brushed, as though there a bug crawled, while each hole in the ground beneath my feet was hidden in grass and leaves, where, in some, black water lay like a snake's mouth.

Wines, pies, jelly, would result from our labors: stripping the berries off, sifting out the stems, cooking and crushing and straining the fruit; although I remember I thought "fruit" far too fine a name for such a nuisance, and I claimed the berries were poisonous: the juice would eat away your mouth and turn your eyes black. The pies were infinitely seedy and discolored the tongue and teeth, the jelly was worse than grape, wholly generic, the jars went on and on across the shelves (and if we had to eat our way systematically through them, I knew we should never get to the cherry flavors or the apple butter) until even the little cheese glasses we had collected were filled, sealed with wax, and neatly though unnecessarily labeled.

In those days it was not enough for a product to be pleasant or nutritious, it had to be as useful as a jacknife in the hands of an Eagle Scout, consequently cheese spreads came in glasses equally excellent for breakfast juice, snack milk, homemade jellies, swallowing pills, and chasing whiskey. My favorite flavor was cheese ’n bacon, I believe. The glasses were sometimes striped or polkadotted, or decorated with red and white asterisks which stood out in front of the dark jelly like stars. What a universe, I thought, full of cranberry-clouded space and constellations designed to attract dimes.

In this part of the country autumn is the only season one can celebrate; and it is not simply that the land becomes violet and mauve and pink and gold, as if sunsets were its new cash crop and sprang freely from the earth; or because the trees turn, overcoming the eye with color and the soul with misgivings, the way we presume the weeds do; or that the pumpkins and gourds are gathered, potatoes forked into unrinsed heaps; or even because the densely enclosing stands of corn have been cut, unshuttering space along the roads like a sudden shout. These things count, of course, as does the limpid blue we're drenched by. This blue is what "azure" means to a French poet: a palpable infinity, something in front of which one puts a rapturous "O" and after which a point of exclamation. This time of year rain falls through a dry sky, while in the summer the wet air wets it, so the raindrops come down coated like pellets of moist dust. Flamboyance and poetry aside, it's how this season goes to its death that is finally entrancing, and one feels compelled to "get out in it," as if the season were a process one could enter and exit like a dance going on on a dance floor.

Provided the weather was fair, I planned to be impulsive and suggest an expedition. By keeping my counsel, and waiting until the last minute, I would avoid the anxious anticipations of the children, their possible disappointments, their inevitable nervous nagging. It had become more and more necessary, like a State in tumultuous times, to keep control, to prevent outbreaks of opposition and squeals of protest. Fortunately, one can count on the calendar to play every tune in its time—the roll with its prefigured holes has simply to come round—and the right weekend did, almost at once. Sunday rose to the eye as blue as a burnt knife. Sighting the sky as if I were going to shoot it, I determined the precise degree of its fidelity: the true blue of its ulterior blueness, the whiteness of its inner wind. My verdict, which I handed down to a sceptical courtroom, was that it would remain fine. So we packed the picnic basket; put a ground cloth and blanket in the trunk of the car; collected two pairs of kitchen shears and one pair of tough garden clippers, lots of paper sacks; and threw in at the last a can of insect repellent beginning to rust around its rims, somewhat as I was. In the glove compartment of the Dodge, Martha stuffed a little illustrated book of ferns and flowers, crudely colored, as if there were only four hues, each harsh; and then we coasted backward out of the drive until the car's engine caught, its starter being somewhat cantankerous. Carl cried out, "here we come, critters," and I got the gears engaged.

When I was a boy, my father never let me choose the moment or suggest the route, and I continue, like a Czar, to be opposed to foolish freedoms; although as Sunday sank through the third hour of the afternoon I knew a drive was becoming more and more unlikely. I was grateful for the lapse in his habits—happy for this reprieved, hence precious, time—but the week seemed somehow unended then, as if it had dried to a pale paste like an overlooked spill of milk. At least the drive managed to put period to a week of otherwise merely days.

I resented my father's princely habit. He couldn't just take the Chevy out by himself; he had to have his entourage; he had to drive more than the car; yet I grew used to his ambitions; I became resigned; whereas my kids mostly hated our little outings, despite the fact that they happened only rarely and there was nothing routine about them. They appeared to be arbitrary disruptions of their plans, and because they occurred so infrequently, the children never got used to them, and were never resigned. There is no justice in any of this.

Certain movements signaled the Sunday drive. It was never announced. It was never suggested. One was never asked. My aunt would begin to hunt for her coat, which took a long time. My mother would wonder whether she should take her purse. My father would fish out his car keys and jingle them. I would usually drag my ass. Then my father would say, "I'll back the car out." I could read an article in *Liberty* magazine (reading time: 11 minutes) while they made their preparations and still manage to meet the car when my father backed it from the garage as slowly as slime. Culp's snide spirit delights to tell me that my father was a creep in reverse. At any rate, *his* car was always in first-rate shape, unlike the Dodge, which was incompetent even as a lemon. It was, by Culp's characterization, only a lime.

Put in the car like teddies in the same carriage, we suffered, then, the same experiences, and so had something in common, as families are supposed to have; and we might have talked about them, these joint perceptions, like fans at the same game—of Mr. Wendell washing his car in freezing weather until the hood shone like glass, of the tools we saw fall into the river while they were repairing the bridge on Highway 95, of the inordinate number of custard yellow aspen leaves littering the road to Mineral Ridge, as if shortly before a king had passed or there had been somewhere near a wedding, or of the vicious contest we witnessed between competing kites—thereby, with our exchanges, forming a familial consciousness; but we generally didn't talk, and didn't join, and didn't form. Our hearts were as bare and beatless as the teddies; our thoughts were elsewhere than the highway. I daydreamed down the avenues. I had taps on my shoes. I danced down a thousand marble stairs. I sang a lot of lowdowns, soured my mouth with Lifesavers, and practiced my blues.

No one ever asked where we were going on our Sunday drive. There was nowhere we were going, of course, so my father moseyed. He wandered. Like flowing water, he was infinitely circumspect. He strolled us along the roads as if the woods and meadows alongside were windows full of fascinating goods. I came to learn that there was nothing in his life my father enjoyed more than making these seemingly fortuitous loops. Yet there was always a point which, when we passed it, determined our return, and put us on the downward slope of our *e*, as it sometimes was, or our *l*. We would arrive at the edge of a lake, or cross the campus of a small college, or crest a neighborly hill for a familiar view, and I would recognize these locations as the far end of our cast. Having caught the scene, he would then reel us in. I wonder now how he understood these quiet departures and unheralded returns, what led him to modulate his course, sometimes taking us so far afield we were threatened with the loss of the tonic. But I was frequently deceived; I did not have the local map in my head as he had; and we were often nearer the end of our one-hour odyssey than I thought. I didn't try to outfigure my father because he could sense when I was trying to anticipate our course, and then he would change it. For the most part, all of us were passive, peering through the windows of the car at gas stations and farm buildings, billboards and cows, the car appearing to roll along at the road's request.

At harvest time, however, we changed our characters like coats. It was the night of the red moon. We became predatory. We became primitive food-gatherers again. The bloody berry hunt was on.

As a child I was more than once reminded that God had rested on the seventh day. Well, it wasn't, I was sure, because He was tuckered out; and there was certainly a lot left to do—damn near everything, if you asked me—rather I thought God understood—he respected—the weariness and boredom which had already befallen his created creatures, and which he could see come over them, unaccountably, like a cloud on a clear day; one that floated, that is, through the earth, and whose shadows arrived everywhere from underneath; thus—as if decreed—there were Sundays in store for us, and Sunday drives, and a scavenger's eye out for the edible. Thirty years later—would it be?—Carl would sing hit songs in the back seat just as I had, only my father didn't shush me, simply drove on, his then uncrippled hands a part of the wheel. Almost like weights of a clock, they directed the driving.

To all ordinary eyes, the weeds in our yard are signs of our neglect, of our untended souls. Nearby, as though our turdy nature were a cause, vacant lots fill with weeds the way tin cans and wheel ruts flood with rain—with goldenrod and feverfew, plantain, pepper grass and fleabane. Rust, too, in the gutters and eaves, speaks our neglect, of our impoverishment of spirit. Peeling paint quite as well. Broken glass. There was a lot of that: cracks closed with masking tape, holes stuffed with old clothes, panes replaced with cardboard. From a bleeding pipe orange ooze would follow a crevice in a board and down the side of someone's heart. Neglect was necessary in those days. It was like a physical necessity, neglect was; it was a need. The farmer couldn't afford to care about the trees he couldn't spray; he could only feed his hogs the rotten nubs and wormy cores. And we were like his glut-loving, rude hogs too. Uninvited strays, we rooted even in the treetops. Not as useful as the wolves who weeded out the weak, we grabbed hard corn to grate into cakes, sidling down the stiffly military rows, cutting ourselves on the coarse leaves, stealing to keep our weaknesses alive. At least, as a kid, I felt that way about it. When another car would cloud the road while we were cutting or picking, I would grow hot with fear and shame. It would be the farmer himself coming to complain; it would be the sheriff with siren and six gun; worse, it would be someone who knew what we were up to, if they didn't know who we were.

Unlike the stealing of apples from neighborhood trees, or grapes from nearby arbors, a bunch of rhubarb or a hard brown pear: robberies which small boys are almost expected to commit (I certainly was no exception); this pilfering was organized, approved, overseen, and executed by adults, those sources of righteousness and rule. What would it lead to? Why not sneak pies from cooling ledges, scoop cream from morning milk, steal onions from their owners' gardens?

On the other hand, when Martha, the children, and I went out weeding later (though it's years ago now), our values were—well—compared to that earlier time—as upsidedown as the weeds would soon be, their green life draining off like blood from beef so their heads wouldn't droop, their spirit evaporating in our basement. We wanted, we believed, what no one wanted. We paid scant attention to fallen fruit, nuts, bearing vines; our eyes sought not the moist but the dry: froth that burst from the pod of the milkweed, berries hard as marbles, thorny stiff twigs which would savagely shadow our white walls, loose sheaves of spumy wheatweed we hoped would bring a few relaxing lines to those rooms so solemnized by their massive regimental decor I sometimes felt like a petitioner, for Martha had begun to collect, even then, the heavy majestic furniture she would come to resemble.

I call the stuff geegawdawful to tease her, but my hate for those massive Victorian wardrobes and settees, and the dark pools they make me wade through, is honest enough. Even when a little sunshine is allowed to pass her damn plum-colored drapes into the living room (or parlor, should I say?), the shadows simply sharpen themselves, as if to dare me to enter them. I don't dare. To enter them. And the mirror that's set back in that swollen oak sideboard of hers, behind columns pretending to a Palladian porch: it reflects only haze and dustlight, discolorations which graze upon discolorations like herds; and one's hands, since the glass is too low except rarely to register a face, if they were to reach for a teacup or one of the nested teaspoons, would appear to be floating on a steaming and desolate lake of the sort found in Caspar David Friedrich: a purple palm in a black cup.

Martha is quiet, and the roads are so calm and empty we almost motor—as it was once called—we almost motor along. When we reach the river road, the Wabash will begin to loop in and out of the eye, the turgid brown stream papered now with the sycamore's wide dry leaves. I slow down to my father's speed, to the days when thirty-five was still a brisk pace, but I sense in the kids some thrust in their limbs, some running alongside, and I realize, too, that Martha doesn't enjoy having cars come so swiftly up behind us and horn their way around. I used to watch the shadow of the Chevrolet accompany us in the other lane, my flat black head framed in an oblong window which the bodies of passing automobiles would blot out and wheel over. A pickup truck rushes up, then bleeps by, so I sort of slip us off the road down a gravel track that only tractors take, sometimes with their low wagons in tow, and bump a bit from rut to rut until we reach a steep bank where the water stands below us so still and thick the leaves have to tell us it's flowing. From the slope where I've cautiously parked the car in order to provide for a deadstick getaway, Carl has already picked up two stones and a short piece of branch and thrown them through the leaves into a water which rises sluggishly above the hit, a hole the leaves close; and his brother has had to be grabbed by the backside of his sweater as he staggers drunkenly along the bank. It seems to me I'm still pulling the key from the ignition when Martha calls out to Carl, "Kumm!" and drags his brother back into the car by the scruff. There is an uninteresting patch of scurfy-leafed French grass, some winter grape, a briar, a bit of thug bush, in my face. "Not here," Martha says, so I release the brake.

At least let Carl get *in* before we go.

Carl can try getting *in* as quick as he got *out*.

We stick these short words like tacks into one another.

I consider tossing Carl into the river where he'll make a plop like a mushroom made of mud and disappear, the leaves quilting over him: nightie night. The engine of the old Dodge coughs, catches, the car bucks briefly as the gears go in, but we're off. Martha frowns in lieu of a public statement. She's sore because I haven't had the battery replaced. Perhaps that's what's wrong: today the battery, yesterday the yard, tomorrow the gutters or the drains. Carl is testy because he'd counted on playing football with a friend, and had, in fact, his shoulder pads bra'd across his chest and had thrown himself like a model into a sexy pose when I snapped on my surprise like a morning light: hey, it's Sunday, I said; there's sunshine; the sumacs have set fire to the woods—smell the smoke? the weeds are high and crawling with nasty bugs—awhisper with them like gossip passed along a pew—how do you like that? yeah, the Sunday drive has arrived like an unexpected guest. Carl half suspects I'm punishing for his little play with the pads. So we try a better spot farther on—no luck—the children complaining because they want to see a muskrat, play ball, and catch fish—all at once. Martha argues with them as if they really expected to see or do anything of the sort. She denies even our most fanciful wishes as if they were complaints about her food, her love, her motherhood. How dare you dream without my permission: that's her attitude. We enjoy periods of being used to it.

"You don't want *that*," she likes to say, staring at the piece of pie we've chosen, while a white wad of Kleenex, no doubt the rejected wish itself, falls from her suddenly relaxed fist. "You can't want to chew such goo," she says, fishing a hunk of purple taffy from behind a cheek, wrapping it at once in tissue, flicking it out of existence with a swift wrist as if snapping something evil or ugly from her fingers. "You *don't*," she says to Carl with conviction, "you *don't* hate your brother; you *love* your brother," she says, lightly slapping the face he's made and gently shaking his shoulders. The kid is genuinely confused. He knows how he feels about his brother: he hates him; but mothers are mothers, and mother must be right. "We *all* love one another in this house, you hear me! *my god,* we sure do, it's *awful* how much. Her slaps are both admonitions and gestures of condolence. Brothers, after all, have been given by life many reasons for hating one another. Where, one wonders, are all those welcome causes for love?

"Don't slouch, dammit. Sit straight. Throw back your shoulders. You jumble your inner organs like apples in a sack when you sit like that. Breathe properly! In! Up! Escalate!" And her shoulders pull partly away from her body, the straps of her bra tighten, her breasts swell like inflating balloons. Perhaps that's where Carl got his notion of how to play with the pads. "You *adore* carrots—since a baby! don't you remember? you used to chew the spoon." The tines of the fork showing through the vegetable like a row of nails, a round is firmly thrust in the kid's pinched-open mouth. And to me she used to say, "you can't *like* doing that," in competing tones of scorn and incredulity, so that now my wishes no longer run downward in those directions.

Soon the wrangling is intense, Martha a-sea in a cut-rate storm, winds whistling across the soul's mouth, angry with the children because she's mad at me, the children willing to carry on the crabbing because neither of them wanted to come or cares what happens now. I could let the car careen into the river, leaping out at the last minute, of course—Carl has shown me how—geronimo!—momentum would carry the Dodge clear of the immediately muddy shore and drop it into the liquefied shit beyond. A splat would rise like a wild cry. Blessed momentum. I see our venerable vehicle upsidedown in the silt, sinking slowly out of sight, the wheels wobbling around as if all the shafts were broken: bye bye.

I can envision it so clearly because my mind's been trained by the movies.

Is that a fragment of white arm?

I wonder how many men and women, kids and dogs, go through life in a state of modest misery; how many are married to lazys and losers, to drunks and drudges and nags; how much communal coldness there is, how much extinguished hope. Perhaps I should form a party for the disappointed people.

If all had gone well (and all's well did not always go), the ceremonial conclusion to the Sunday drive (the only part of it I liked and looked forward to) would begin when my father pulled up to one of Daisy's Dairy Stores for a cone. He knew what I wanted and waited for, eager as an itch for its scratch, so he liked to worry me, to play and delay, as Culp would say, toy and enjoy. Sometimes he would find one in a spot I hadn't known about (he discovered them the way he discovered the road around Milton Dam, or routes through woods; the way he went up and down dells, found post-cardly pleasant points of view); for there were a great number of "outlets" (as it's the fashion now to call them) in our area (the Daisy Chain, everyone said, an expression of derision I didn't then understand); or he would drive determinedly by one of the stores to tease me—to tease and to please—only to turn toward another one suddenly, in a gravel of surprise. My father wandered—dillied, decoyed, and dallied—but he knew the roads as well as the Highway Patrol. The car would halt and, in the shudder of the stop, each of us would start searching for change; my aunt, if she was along, digging futilely in her big black purse, as polished as a shoe, and puffing, as though it were heavy work. She always begs to be allowed to pay. Okay. Just don't cackle on about it. But she pleads anyway. It's her treat, she insists. Finally one coin or other appears. If there isn't enough, that's all right, my mother says, I don't feel famished. My father swears.

At first I thought that Daisy was a girl, then a flower, finally a cow; but Daisy was only a name.

The cones came in countless flavors and the shape of the scoops were as conical as the cones. I liked the symmetry. They offered the tongue an uninterrupted lick along their sides and encouraged callow obscenities from the Junior High School kids. Daisy's remote management called the cones Dubble Darry Delites for short, or Daisy Dairy's Double-dip Delites, for long, and wrote the name, DeeDeeDeedeeDee, like a bird's song, and then stood it erect to resemble the cream on a cone: 

A list of the flavors, in appropriately colored chalks, was posted behind the counter. The *R* in Rainbow, I remember, was written in peach, the *o* in grape, the *w* in butter pecan. At a nickel apiece, they were one of life's great bargains.

My parents, and my aunt if she had decided to obnoxious us with her presence, remained in the car. I'd take the money in my hand and crack the door a sly anticipatory crack. My mother would invariably choose chocolate, but she always chose last, no matter what, and my aunt could never make up her mind. Oh, I don't know, she'd say, giggling a bit. I really shouldn't have any.

That's right. You've got fatter than a stick.

In our house my aunt made the fudge, the cocoa, the popcorn, the cutsie sugar cookies, the custards, and then she watched us eat whatever it was like a starving dog. After we had gone to bed, she would suck up what was left and hide the results in her hips. Oh well, it doesn't matter really. Butter pecan, I guess.

I want black walnut, my father said with a promptness that tried to pass itself off as decision.

After my father had declared his choice, my mother would sigh. She knew her preference would provoke complaint. I assume that's why she preferred it. Chocolate, I suppose.

Chocolate? What a surprise! Hollow Santas are made of chocolate, you know. Nigger soldiers, too. Chocolate. Why don't you take a chance, go crazy, pick something daring like strawberry or outrageous like vanilla?

I did once. I had a lime slush, remember? I didn't like it.

Lime slush isn't ice cream.

It's sherbet.

It isn't sherbet. It's just slush. Slush isn't sherbet.

It was too watery and too tart.

Well lime, for christ's sake.

Lime slush.

Slush is supposed to be watery. That's what slush is. It certainly isn't sherbet.

It wasn't a nice green. And there didn't seem to be that much of it.

I'd stand in front of the long white counter where the glass curved back over the tubs of ice cream and study the excavations. Strawberry always had a deep, redly streaked hole in it, a sign that it was popular, I supposed, but it was a flavor I scorned, at least the way Daisy's Dairies made it. It looked like wounded vanilla. Neopolitan was another kind I despised. Neopolitan was nuthin alongside the gayety of Rainbow. Neopolitan was like eating a flag. The chocolates and the fudges made the best quarries. The ice cream spade would cut great cliffs in chocolate, make Maine coasts, shape desolate shores. My mother knew nothing of the qualities of chocolate in the tub. I would imagine myself a counterboy, and I would dream of the designs I would cut in the ice creams as I packed pints or scooped for cones. Later I'd decide that my mother chose chocolate because it contained a narcotic. Riling my father was a secondary benefit.

Finally I'd be handed a clutch of cones and would carry them like a bouquet to the car. There I'd pass them carefully through the driver's window a bloom at a time. Rainbow, my father would say. What a surprise! Rainbow again. Well, I'd say cheerfully sometimes, when I get to the end there's a pot of gold. I've been there, and there's a chamber pot at the end of the rainbow, my father said, precociously showing a streak of Culp. My mother made a moue, protesting the reference. Everyone's mouth cooled. My father considered Rainbow nothing but a hash made of tub leavings; dinner's garbage reboiled for breakfast, he said it was. But I loved its accidental and chaotic benevolence. It was like having a noise melt in your mouth. Grape eased into pineapple, then bent itself about banana. A nut would turn up.

You're licking leftovers.

Rainbow was a letdown only when the scoop took up too much of the same flavor. What is a rainbow of one color? It is grape—my god!—it is lemon.

Later I could have compared Rainbow to the stock pot at the back of the stove; I could have extolled leftovers, stews and hashes; but the youthful mind is a barren plain: there is no range of reference.

Crows eat what nobody wants.

I want Rainbow.

Crows go for what's run over on the road.

Later I could have compared Rainbow to complicated batiks and tie-dyes, to color swirls, the northern lights. But then I could only confess to my wants. I often wanted to get my father's goat, and I could have compared my cone to the mixture of nations and races which composed our country. He'd have nannied at that all right.

You don't know what you want.

We would try another place farther on—no luck—so then I would veer away from the river, cross the main road and go up the ridge on the other side, passing people carrying dressed up babies out of a country church.

At this time of day, Martha wondered. The males made no remark. They had grown sullen. We sat in our silence as though in heavy coats. I watched for fragments of my children in the rear view mirror. Carl licked at a place where his nose had run. Carl's brother untied his shoe. Martha gave it up. My aunt pretended not to want, my mother was afraid to want, I didn't know my wants, and my father was sick of the lot of us. I should have remembered how hard it was to find a place to picnic on a trip, I thought, or a place to pee, a place to pick elderberries, or, as now, weeds. There would be poison ivy or fierce persistent bees, a stretch of soft yellow mud, a steep bank or some other kind of unpleasant footing, cow plop, brambles, burrs. It was easier to find a place to neck. I don't want any of that cattle crap carried back to the car, my father would warn as we got out. I would have begun to clash the shears—a sound which seemed to annoy everyone. Maybe I'd see a snake. My mother would encounter something which would cause her to break out. My aunt would harvest fruits which were inedible and nuts nobody wanted. Once home we'd agree it'd been fun.

I had at last got us lost down a half-grassy track which kept wandering in and out of a thin scrubby woods while following, I suppose, the path of least resistance, when we approached an artificial rise on which a spur of track had been mounted. Just over the hill ahead is heaven, I promised in the tones of a travelogue, but I couldn't raise a scoff. I proceeded slowly. These roads are not kind to large cars. Once gingerly over the track bed, we saw the barns—a line of them—and an abandoned barnyard: an overgrown fence, broken gate, high grass, of course weeds. We are like lambs who have found our way, I falsetto'd to no applause. White, with red shingled roofs, the barns are beautiful. Even Martha looks pleased. I know better than to believe in looks, but she does look pleased. Four doors open simultaneously and we pile out. I am, however, not parked on a slope.

I had a cousin Lois once. I may still have a cousin Lois for all I know. She was said to be my first love, but I learned very early that adults lie about every feeling, so I never put any faith in the claim. Growing up and covering up were secret synonyms with them. Anyway, Lois was visiting us from Iowa, and she went along on one of our elderberry expeditions. She was only ten and didn't have to pick walnuts any longer than she wanted to—one privilege of a guest: to have one's wants recognized—or wade through the high weeds to get at a few remote and knobby apple trees, or watch out for the occasional damn dog.

We found ourselves that trip in the middle of a rather marshy meadow where a long warped board, gray as sea wrack, had apparently floated ashore, somewhat as we had, so while the rest of us gathered and rescued and thieved—Lois set out a row of mud pies decorated with flowers and grass and circlets of burrs, red berries for the centers of some, a yellow blossom or two, or red leaves braced with mud to make a bow. Little alyssum-like flowers covered one, I remember, like a nosegay poking out of a bride's fist. In the middle of a pie that might have been a cow's paddy, it was large enough, I noticed with disgust a pale emaciated pink worm she had rolled the way you'd roll a broken rubber band around a finger to create a satisfying whorl to place within the heart of her design. I stomped on several of her pies with a foot so fierce it set the board to shivering. The result was I carried gobs of mud mixed with tiny fruits and seeds back to the car on my shoes, the little shit screaming as if I'd pushed her down in a puddle. It was difficult for my aunt and my parents to make out what was the matter.

Since Martha and the kids are happy clipping stalks and stems, I walk back to the rails for a better view of the barns. They appear to have been built of wood shingle, melancholy, and roofing tin. I could come upon them, from this vantage point, like Pizarro or Cortez upon the habitation of an ancient people. The barns are separated from the road by two isolated lines of track, by a drainage ditch which a crude little bridge skips, and by a clearing now crowded with vegetation: a tough looking patch of thistles and then a silver gray swatch of immeasurably delicate grass, and finally a lot of plants quite tall and imposing which I cannot identify. So the barns seem to rise out of a sea of fronds and pods and tiny leaves. There are three of them, steaming beam to beam like ships, each gable ridge a prow, although they vary slightly in size and certainly in design. To the west, the one struck last by the sun when it sets, is attended by three scaling gray silos. Wrapped in loops of fine wire, they rise beside it like the gigantic stumps of some prehistoric tree, and their shapes, as well as the patterns of the stains which have descended their sides, and the lines of the vines which have climbed them, delight the eye the way good monumental sculpture does, by the force of its immediate mass and the caress of its eventual texture. There they store all that darkness which a day like this has defeated, and retain it for release at another time.

The middle barn is appropriately crowned by a four-square, double-shuttered cupola which holds into the wind the cut-out metal figure of a circling hawk. It is a conceit I find in a farmer almost metaphysical. The eastern barn is slightly smaller, though more romantic, as if its lofts held whisps of nostalgia instead of the absent hay it has. Nearly circumscribed by a limping fence, the building's large upper loading door arrows abruptly into its own angular eave, while the barn's undeniably solid presence seems to be receding while I watch—into the past perhaps, into never-never land—as though there were, in its world, a vanishing point from which it might not choose or be able to return. Rimmed in red like tired eyes, the windows of all the buildings are watchful black voids. It's as though the holes themselves were looking out. They seem symmetrically placed in the barn with the hovering hawk, and in the one by the silos as well, but they are irregularly set in the smaller structure, which also lets its west wall lean out beyond the high hip of its roof to create a creature of singularly gawky beauty. All three face a large tract of bottom land which the Wabash regularly floods and thereby feeds fresh mud. Their tin roofs, in the shape of a Dutch girl's lacy cap, are what you see first, for they slope toward their own feet like local hills, and serve both as roof and wall for a while, their color a melted run of rust and pale blood the sun seems to have set in motion as though a clear stream were passing through the pigment.

Although at home, they are lost, alone, alive. They send a shiver through me.

I was humming hit tunes in the back seat and watching the roadside go by as dreamily as it was watching me when I heard from my father half an inarticulate outcry and my head was slammed into the watching window. Almost immediately all of me was jerked back as though Martha was yanking one of the kids from the edge of an embankment, only now I was to be thrown onto the pile of elderberries we had wrapped in funnels of newspaper or stuffed in grocery sacks. As I rebounded from the floor of the car I received, like the rapid rasp of a saw, a series of terrible sounds: of rending metals, shattering glass, pissing vapors, unstaged screams. Actually, hearing scarcely intervened. They were palpable things, these noises, there like the rear window, rear seat, scissors, bags of berries. Through that window, back on the highway we had so abruptly fled, I saw two automobiles still shuddering from the force of their collision. Gray white steam rose chaotically. Glass began to patter upon the roof of our Chevrolet where we were stopped upon the shoulder. Then, almost slowly, eight doors fell off or opened and people fell or otherwise came out of them, some hugging themselves and rolling over on the highway or down the bank beside it near where we were. A fragment of white arm appeared in the steam. I stared. Staring was all I was. How quickly —inexplicably—my peaceful window had been entered by this other. A woman asmear with blood stood up, fell softly down, stood slowly up again, wavering like a little flag. The car which had been in line behind us was new and shiny. I had noticed it because it had followed us awhile, unable to pass and impatient because of the traffic. The car which had struck it was a heap of rust, and now its weakened fenders and body panels were broken and scattered. Both hoods had risen in the air to allow the engines to rush at one another. One man had hopped away from the wreck on his unshattered leg and hugged a tree. Water appeared to be running down the leg of a lady who'd got no farther than the running board. The dust still rose in rivulets making the air seem to shake as if it were a pane of glass in the process, like the sky, of coming to pieces. My god, we've got to get out of here, my father said. Then I also smelled the gasoline. People began to come from other cars with coats and their own anguish. They appeared to be oblivious of the gasoline. I didn't utter a word—not one. What I saw entered me like a spear.

Finally my father got slowly out of the car as though drugged and went passively as a thistle to where a man with one shoe lay in the road, and when there he covered him with an old shawl we sometimes carried walnuts in by pulling the four corners together in a tramp's knot. Don't look, Billy, don't look, my mother said, sick in the front seat, and certainly not looking herself. I had both eyes out, as they say, on stems. I felt hot, yet I was without feeling, like a warm stone in a fire. Someone I couldn't see was sobbing. Two well-dressed men arrived, looked anxiously around and talked. One pointed up the road and shook his head. Suddenly a dolled-up little boy appeared running toward the wreck, and the man who'd been pointing howled no-o-o-o-o and rushed toward him arms spread, as though to scoop him up, the way I always feared a bull might run at me in a meadow. My father stood in the road by the figure he had covered and looked down and didn't do anything further except draw his foot away from a wet spot. I watched first the man up and then the man down until the police came in sirens like their Sunday best and eventually we were sent away. My mother said, good grief, Billy, look at you. She had a hankie still pressed to her mouth. It wasn't my bruise she meant. I was spotted with purple berry juice like someone with a disease you draw for a cartoon. We drove home slowly in a hush like held breath. We drove home without stopping for a cone. We reached home before my head began to hurt. By then I was ashamed to say anything, as if I had just thought it up. My father hung my mother's coat in the closet. They sat together on the sofa. We were silent all the way into supper, which my mother annoyed my father by not eating. She always prolonged pain when possible. She prolonged her death twenty years. In those days she had just begun to drink without appearing to do so, and had begun to seek excuses for her lack of appetite. This time she toughened my father's very temporary tenderness. My father did say in wonderment at one point: I don't know how I managed to get out of his way. My father was thinking about our near miss, my mother about the bloodshed. Being unharmed made my father hungry. What was wrong with the rest of us? When my bedtime came, they let me stay up to listen to the Hit Parade.

Well, I was right, the wind is white. There is a slight sliver of ice in it, the last hint of coolness in a dying drink. A calm elation has come over me, and the barns are the cause. I understand that much, although I am unable to explain why I am elated or why I am calm. Perhaps we aren't in the ordinary world any more and these are the barns of the three bears. I watch my wife and the children move about cutting and collecting. Carl is in a hurry as if someone else will get everywhere first. Martha is wearing, I notice, one of my old favorites—a grannie dress she's put on now because the dress is long and old and doesn't matter. I liked it because it hid her fat. But she knew that. In a moment I shall leave this little rise and look for a place to set out lunch. A piece of brie is melting on my tongue. What good has it done me to love olives? It would be wonderful if the rails were to tremble and hum and life come down them ahead of some train. The white shingles gleam in the sunlight, and the sky whistles its blue way everywhere, taking its tune to the deepest woods. "Red Sails in the Sunset"—wasn't that one of the songs? Wait now. I am staring at the trunk of a sycamore and imagining I am peering out the window of a plane. The trunk is a river beneath the shadow of the wing, and the scales are islands. This river is wider than the Wabash and has many banks and bars. No. I was considering the symbolic character of leaf color: that's where I was. Olio di Oliva. The sumacs soften, despite their intensity, and even the clear yellow of the mulberry leaves has a gray interior. Anyway, it's not a palette which would appeal to Mondrian. Only in a painting or a poem can you find true purity . . . perhaps in a little song, a little Elizabethan lyric, possibly by Ben Jonson. Never in a man or woman. The colors of the ice cream called Rainbow didn't really run together, even when you licked them; they didn't blend but jostled one another like people with packages in a crowd. Yes, "Red Sails" might have been the song. When the ice cream had melted in my mouth, then the butter pecan might drown in banana and peach become walnut. No one was some one then. As for the barns, as for them: the contrast between sky, roof, and wall, is pleasing indeed—pleasing—as if the lid of your eye were kissed—so is the difference between what is natural here, and what is man made: the wheatweed stem, the shingle, a puddle, the rope's end.

While the barns have been neglected, they were obviously in wonderful condition once, and the vandals have somehow avoided them—"spared" is, I think, the wrong word. My father took persnickety care of his car, and even when he could no longer drive it, and it stood in the garage, he kept it shined like a gun in its case. Our near miss was for him the car's close call as well. In the little bear's barn I'll discover later one rear window which has a triangular hole in it and out of that hole will hang the frayed end of an old rope. When I cut into our bread's crisp crust, tiny bits of it will fly about, and the softness of the sawing sound will be pleasing as a creek. I notice now that the silo'd barn has undoored openings, and that deep within the feed passage, near where I'll find an ancient tractor parked, dangles a single bare and burning bulb, lit as if to say, "I am alive," so maybe the fallen condition of the fences—the unmowed yard and rampant weeds—is relatively recent. After lunch, beside an outbuilding of indeterminate function, I'll encounter an old gas pump, its glass gone of course, the screw still up in the wire which once supported the bowl that held the fuel; and it will be dressed in rust like a fashionable statue of a pump, half a lifetime out of use. Another mark of man's presence here, the pump has become a work of art, but not one of man's making unless neglect is liberating. Water stagnates in a wheel rut and weeds fill the clearing. When I slice the bread little bits of being fly up whenever I make a cut.

Winter covered the Sunday drive with cold and snow, and there were no cones for a long time. There were quarrels about money and my aunt almost moved out, standing symbolically by the front door, holding her handbag as if it were her huff. They did the berries anyway, though some were squashed. They'll all be squashed soon enough, I said. Consequently, a row of jelly glasses got marched across the shelf. I imagine our Dodge sailing over the edge of the bank through an opportune opening between hawthorne and hackberry—hurrah!—and spilling its contents under the mud. The doors will come slowly open and moles emerge in search of their runnels. These barns have been abandoned, but they have been abandoned to beauty. They are no longer barns. They are themselves. A leftover light is burning. The barns . . . they have been left alone to breathe. I see I am standing three times in three times—mine, theirs, the weeds'—now. It is utterly awful and confusing and I don't mind. I am thinking about lunch and a mouthful of wine. Carl will not peel off the crusts of his baloney bread. Martha is waving, holding five feet of black mustard stalk above her head. I shall have the furniture carried out, heavy as it is, and the kids, light as they are. My life shall become barns. In one barn of me—the blessed barn—lonely as a rented room—I shall keep one light lit. Sometimes I know what I want, but I'm not on that account allowed to have it. DeeDeeDeedeeDee. In an earlier season of our association, on a day and in a place like this, Martha and I would have made love. Sheltered one another like awnings. My seed won't dry into anything a vase can celebrate. Our history is as leafless already as these trees will be, though one of them is wider than the Wabash. Still, all of this was years ago now; we are waging other wars; and now none of these conditions obtains.

TONY TANNER

. . . . . .

On Reading "Sunday Drive"

A picnic. As a topic, a topos, it is at once simple and inexhaustible. It is the festive gathering of teddy bears in a children's song: it is the incongruous group and equivocal, obscure occasion evoked in Manet's *Déjeuner sur l'herbe*. It is the mellow enigma of Titian's *La Fête champêtre*, which is surely one of the great generative "picnics" in Western art. It is William Gass's "Sunday Drive." Even a glance at—a thought about—Manet's (or Titian's) painting will suggest how many themes and ideas can converge in the picnic; how many ambiguities and contrasts, meetings and oppositions, boundaries and interfaces it can convene and contain. Labor and rest, contrivance and indolence, tending and neglect, conviviality and separation, harmony and discord, consummation and loss, permanence and transience, ripeness and rottenness, gratification and melancholy, sociability and loneliness, sexual abandon and decorous civility: in two words, nature and art—their mutual encroachments and exclusions, blendings and oppugnancies, consonances and dissonances. The naked and the clothed, the raw and the cooked (and fermented), the wild and the cultivated, the Dionysiac and the domestic; and—you don't have to look too hard to find them—joyous intimations of fertile renewal and fecund abundance, shadowed by more somber, autumnal premonitions of mutability, decline, and death: all this—it simply amounts to every aspect of life—may be found, touched on, alluded to, glanced at, provocatively foregrounded or dimly marginalized, in the resonant, modest occasion of the pastoral picnic. And so they may be in Gass's version of a suburban pastoral. He always puts everything in.

It is, of course, a specific version of pastoral. To be sure, the bears are there (if not the teddy bears, the Three Bears), or rather there are bears as barns (or barns metamorphosed into bears), as is a whole range of European art and literature in specific allusions or echoes and traces. But there is also a temporal, historical reference and location—the Depression years in America. Indeed, the complex sense of time, of times, is one of the marked characteristics of the piece. Apparently stable references to fixed points of historical, biographical time are merged with, unmoored by, the flowing extensions, digressions, regressions, projections, of memory, imagination, anticipation, meditation. Consider the deceptive ostension of the opening statement, repeated in the body of the text, and in the closing sentence—"This was years ago." What does "this" refer to: when was "years ago"? We expect what follows to amplify and clarify this proleptic statement, but when by the end we read "all of this was years ago now," we are scarcely more securely situated though we are certainly more richly informed. For "all this" has comprised many different times and time scales, and "now" (a notorious deictic) could refer to the time of writing (but then it should read "*is* years ago now"); the time of the Sunday drive (but which one?); or even our time of reading. The relationship between *this, was, ago, now* is an endlessly teasing one that cannot be disambiguated (such teasing can be found in Beckett of course) but that produces provocative uncertainties, duplicitous blurs, disorienting conflations, in our habitually more tidy, discrete, treatment of thens and nows. Gass, or the narrator as I should say, draws attention to what has been going on just before the end. "I see I am standing three times in three times—mine, theirs, the weeds'—now. It is utterly awful and confusing and I don't mind." *Theirs* refers to the barns, and he is referring to the conjunction, the copresence, of the distinctly finite time of the single human life, the more imponderable longevity of artifacts, and the eternal, cyclical time of nature's proliferating replacements. All there "now." And three more times. The time of the drive, the time of the remembered drive the narrator went on as a child, the time of his writing about all these times. Now. This pastoral confuses and introduces a sense of awe into our awareness of the ramifying complexities of our relationship to time(s). We shouldn't mind.

It *is* confusing, though humanly so. The narrator is remembering a Sunday drive he took with his family; he is also remembering an earlier drive (and drives) he was taken on by his family as a child. But he is also remembering remembering the earlier drive on the later one—all memories surrounded, linked and separated, fused and amplified in and by, the remembering, narrating now. Preoccupations, pleasures, regrets, nostalgias, recriminations, shocks, epiphanies, resolutions, all begin to merge in, emerge from, his writing and re-collecting. Like the Rainbow ice cream that gave him such delight as a child ("like having a noise melt in your mouth," a marvelous and not gratuitous simile), the result is an immensely pleasurable "accidental and chaotic benevolence." Like having the sights and sounds and feelings of multiple times melt in our minds. Pleasure is an important concern, as befits a meditation on what is intended as a pleasure excursion. There is a distinct, though subtly dispersed, sense of the tensions (dialectic) between authority and freedom, wayward impulse and firm control, relaxation and repression, wants and rules—more largely, between weeds and barns. Indeed, a whole politics of dominance and desire is intermittently sketched out and explored. The narrator, like his father, is a "Czar" only in metaphor, and his wife's instinct for the "regimental" manifests itself in oppressive furniture rather than military force, but problems of power gust around, and we are reminded that authoritarian regimes (monarchies, dictatorships, totalitarianism—they are all dimly present, remembered by occasional adjectives, revived in unexpected nouns) can take many forms and appear in various guises. Not least—certainly not least—the family. And as the picnic is often seen as, and intended to be, the family outing par excellence, an occasion when the disparate members of a family can re-experience and celebrate their familiality in a shared pleasure excursion (or excursion into pleasure), it is hardly suprising that the piece becomes, among other things, an excursion—"a drive"—into matters and problems related to and generated by desire and the family. And if the narrator's picnic is in some ways a disappointment and a failure, like the one organized by *his* father which he most notably remembers, it is because all pastorals are—in some ways—failed pastorals. Because death—literal or metaphoric, experienced or adumbrated, in large things or small (of the body, of the year)—is always there. *Et in Arcadia ego.*

A family on a picnic can, should, form "a familial consciousness," but as the narrator recalls about his earlier outings, "we generally didn't talk, and didn't join, and didn't form." As it was then, so it is/was "now." The family on a picnic reveals, discovers, enacts, its fissile properties, its centrifugal tendencies—its inherent disposition to scatter (like the wind-borne seeds). "Wandering"—errancy, divergence—tends to prevail over coherence and formation: disaggregation rather than aggregation, though of course the family—as families one way or another, through affection, dependency, or coercion, usually do after such temporary, "sabbatical," ventures into nature—comes home together. On the narrator's picnic (to distinguish it from his father's, though they constantly merge as the tenses shift and mix, forcing strange synchronicities, unmarked discontinuities, odd realignments) soon "the wrangling is intense," between fractious children, imperious mother, and silently resistant, oppositional, and withdrawn father-narrator. The inflexible, autocratic maternal imperatives and strictures of Martha—"'You don't want *that*. . . . you *love* your brother'"—tend to promote discord even as they seek to impose concord, as such orders and orderings often do. But clearly, if mutedly, the rifts in the family run deeper, particularly between the narrator and Martha, whose irritated, clipped exchanges—"We stick these short words like tacks into one another"—seem like the recurrent skirmishes of a larger, longer battle. Recurrent fantasies of driving the family into the "liquefied shit" of the river and jumping clear at the last moment—"bye bye," flickering dreams of annihilation and abandonment, suggest that this family is something of a time-bomb on a tolerably short fuse. Like all too many families, as one supposes. The last sentence opens up wider, even global, perspectives: "we are waging other wars." In this context *wars* might suggest that the intrafamilial war has moved onto another plane, escalated exponentially, in line with (or on the model of) the larger wars abroad—the Second World War, Korea, Vietnam (wars proliferate like weeds). To what extent this may serve to tie the piece into the larger intentions of *The Tunnel* it is, of course, impossible to say. But, as it is, it is an appropriate enough, or suggestive enough, point of termination. Memories of the soiled, spoiled picnics and pastorals of two generations can serve admirably well to suggest the seeds and growths of embryonic tendencies to violence and conflict, the smoldering, imperfectly suppressed rages of sadistic manipulation and dissatisfied desire, to be found in the microcosm, heterocosm of the family.

Let me comment on the interplay between desire and art—one of the many issues which, compressed and teeming, are growing, working, playing in the rich undergrowth and blossom of Gass's prose in this piece (which can affect a sensitive reader much as the "embrace of bushes" appears to the narrator in memory—"flowered, fruitful, and blazing"—though, like the "difficult" grasses he remembers, Gass's prose may, in unsuspected places, be as poison as ivy, as barbed as wire, as nervous as bees). I am thinking of the extraordinary passages concerning the ice-cream cones, and the barns. Near the end, after the part concerning the barns, the narrator writes: "Sometimes I know what I want, but I'm not on that account allowed to have it. DeeDeeDeedeeDee." The slight ambiguity of "on that account" (*precisely* because, or *merely* because) reminds us of the joyless prohibitions of the negating matriarch that Martha has become. (Once they would have made love, but now everything in the relationship is dry, like the weeds they collect to serve as house decorations. There is a Freudian dictum to the effect that where there is love, there is usually wetness. On some of their picnics—"it's years ago now"—the narrator recalls that "our eyes sought not the moist but the dry." So it is. So it has become.) The quintupled "Dee" refers of course to the cream cones at Daisy's Dairy Stores that were, for the narrator as a child, the climactic, often deferred, pleasure of those bygone Sunday drives. Gass's recreation of this primal scene of pleasure is masterly. But more than that, the narrator effectively reveals the difference between the relative simplicity of his childhood wants and satisfactions and the far greater complexity of their adult manifestations. The difference is, crucially, a matter of the relationship between desire and language. "At first I thought Daisy was a girl, then a flower, finally a cow; but Daisy was only a name." Daisy, the source and locus of pleasure. At first, it must have been another person, or at least something flowering, or lowing. But "Daisy" is only a signifier. The narrator knows that now. Thus we lose the world as we grow in language (in every sense). But it is not all loss. A bit later, remembering his ecstasy at the color and taste of the Rainbow cone, the narrator (now) adds a retrospective commentary. Four times he writes, "Later I could have compared (extolled) . . . ." and he gives the possible comparisons —stews, batiks, northern lights, mixture of nations, etc. But that is later. Now. "Then I could only confess my wants." The child has its wants, and its satisfactions, and very intense they are. But something is missing, or more accurately, not yet present (the addition might not be a completion, but a supererogatory supplement, an excess): "the youthful mind is a barren plain: there is no range of reference." Range of reference is the result of accumulated language in the head. "Could have" is an impossible tense—the past conditional, a time we can inhabit only in language.

But, living in language, there is no limit to the possible range of references. The barren plain of a youth's life is, among other things, the relative absence of any mental obstacle looming between the feeling and formulation of "wants." But the dense lexical vegetation of the adult mind (this adult, but really any), while it increases the range of reference to (theoretically) infinity, also serves to defer, divert, long-circuit, desire interminably. The enrichment also entails a loss. "You don't know what you want." The placing of these words in the text makes the source of their utterance or inscription undecidable—the narrator's father to him as a child? the narrator to himself? to us? No matter—uncertainly originated, it is a certain truth. Living in a Rainbow richness of language, the narrator can no longer reach simply out and take hold of the bouquet, the bloom of a five-Dee cone. But he can cup and relish the thought of that cone *as* a bouquet or a bloom, or whatever else he chooses to select from the infinite range of possible comparisons/flavors that are on offer in the great Dairy Store of language. And this the youth cannot do. He and she is limited to real cones with real cream in them. There is no point in attempting to adjudicate between the two states, the two Stores. In suggesting that Gass is—effectively—dramatizing something of the loss and gain involved in our inescapable linguicity in these refracted memories of childhood visits to an ice-cream parlor, I am not being frivolous nor, I hope, precious or fatuous. Gass unmistakably has a very gustatory sense of language—he really tastes his words and invites us to do, too. It is, of course, a very basic gratification, since we first begin to grow, sucking and being suckled. To the extent that the adult state seems to deflect or debar us from the site of actual gratifications, the chances (the dangers? the compensations?) are that the adult will solace him or herself on a cone of words. Daisy is only a name. But there is a pleasure of, and in, the name as well. It is a pleasure that, as Gass's prose continuously demonstrates, can be very considerable indeed—weeds, poison ivy, barbed wire, frigid wife, and all.

But they will tend to be lonely pleasures, as the narrator, desires denied, wants disallowed, indicates. Which brings me to the barns. "Just over the hill is heaven" says the narrator, trying to amuse the children. They are not amused, but just over the hill are the barns, and "the barns are beautiful." Even Martha looks pleased. Perhaps they offer a visual point of extrafamilial peace and rest. But note that the first sight (as remembered) of the barns triggers an apparently unrelated memory of what might have been a childhood love—Lois. However, what the narrator remembers about this episode is "stomping" fiercely on some rather disgusting mud pies that Lois had built and somewhat sickeningly decorated. First love—nauseating, embellished little constructs—revulsion, anger, violence: in little, it could be the pattern of a life. It is all that the barns are not. Or better, the other way around. The barns are like ships, like "good monumental sculpture" that gives the same sort of pleasure "by the force of its immediate mass and the caress of its eventual texture" (not for the first time a description of the aesthetic, kinaesthetic effect of something in the world offers, at the same time, a perfectly apt description of the effects to which Gass's prose aspires—and achieves). The barns remain, retain. They hold. Hold together, hold and "store" "whisps of nostalgia," a rich darkness that the present may defeat but cannot destroy. One barn has an "undeniably solid presence" that nevertheless seems to recede into "the past perhaps, into never-never land," as if it contained its own "vanishing point from which it might not choose or be able to return." A satisfying, solacing, solid presence that contains the principle and possibility of its own absence—in which the gaps and holes seem to be actively gazing voids. Wondrous, enduring artifacts, sailing in and on time, cargoed and freighted with the rich absences and occlusions of the past, memory, and imagination, these barns are not only like works of art for the narrator, they activate the creative, metamorphosing, dreaming faculties in him—effectively solicit and inspire, indeed create, the artist. The barns, as transcribed and *in the transcribing*, become the site and venue of somberly exuberant metaphysical and aesthetic speculation and epiphany.

But—"Although at home, they are lost, alone, alive." A way a lone a last a loved a long the . . . . yes, Joyce is present at this foregathering, and such an echo and evocation makes us realize that the narrator sees some of his own pathos in the barns, for he too is lost, alone, alive. Immediately another apparently unrelated memory follows. This is of the car crash he experienced and witnessed on that earlier picnic drive, or drives, which ended both in ice creams and, on this occasion, violence and destruction. DeeDeeDeedeeDee—and Death. The mercy and mortality of the pastoral. After the crash the narrator is covered with purple berry juice, stained indeed with his first horrified experience of the reality of death. This memory extends into a more general recollection of the decay and decline of his family—his mother's drinking, the spreading pain. Family outing—a fatal collision—family disintegration: it is another pattern of a life. It could be a continuation of the previous one—the love that generates hate, the family that shatters on violence and death. Once again, the narrator's memory swings round to the barns, for consolation. They are the cause of a "calm elation." They now seem to offer a point of exit—retreat—from the "ordinary world," where, indeed three barns can become three bears, and the mind can begin to play. The tenses go in all directions—I liked, I shall, I am, I was. Thoughts and things can run and jostle together—like licking the Rainbow. That, indeed, is life. But it is not art—at least not pure art, or an art of purity. Not Mondrian. "Only in a painting or a poem can you find true purity . . . . Never in a man or woman." The barns seem to stir and awaken a dream of, a longing for, some unattainable realm of purity, transcendence really, beyond the messy entanglements of our creatural condition. Certainly one of the things the narrator finds "pleasing" about the barns is "the difference between what is natural here, and what is man made." After the mixed pleasure of the Rainbow cream, and the more painfully mixed pleasure of love and family (hate and death), the only pure pleasure would seem to be in the artifact—the vacated, unused and useless, man-made structure. The uselessness is important—the barns have receded beyond utility. The narrator remembers his father's car, kept shining in the garage when he could no longer drive it. He remembers "an old gas pump" which "dressed in rust," has become "a work of art." Note that it was not of course conceived or constructed as one. Through "neglect" it has been liberated beyond function and become what some aestheticians would call an object of intransitive contemplation. And thus and thereby—art. Neglect and rust mark the narrator's own habitation, indeed, his life. It would seem he has some sympathy for these processes of letting things go, rot, stagnate, rust, fragment as the bread crumbles to bits as he cuts it. Certainly the barns have been liberated by being freed from tenants and purpose, by becoming, as it were, unbarned. "These barns have been abandoned, but they have been abandoned to beauty. They are no longer barns. They are themselves. . . . they have been left alone to breathe." This beautiful passage contains a whole implicit aesthetic, which would seem to be close to Gass's own—at least in part. There are ambiguous implications in it concerning the relationship of art to human community and intentionality. For if the barns are most beautiful when least being barns, wherefore should and shall they be built? We cannot rely on art based on the fortuitous felicities of neglect. The man made is always made for some kind of purpose, even if that purpose be just play. There is something potentially nonhuman in the abandoned beauty of the barns. And indeed, that seems to be a major attraction for the narrator. He imagines emptying his house, his life—of furniture, of children—and living alone in the cherished vacancy. "My life shall become barns. In one barn of me—the blessed barn—lonely as a rented room—I shall keep one light lit." It is a dream of a distanced, lonely vigil in a rich and hallowed vacancy, some precious purely illuminated space beyond the mess of family, the greater mess of war, beyond, perhaps, the rainbow multiplicity of the "ordinary world." It is one of the dreams of, and in, art. But it remains a dream—a barn dream. By the end—"we are waging other wars; and now none of these conditions obtains." It suggests a barn-less, as well as a love-less, world.

The narrator is not untouched by the world—insects rise and swarm about him, as they have done for other Gass narrators. He feels "the embrace of bushes"; weeds and grasses "engulf" him; bugs "brush" him. Such caresses and cradlings are not conventionally pleasant. They derive from the rank, the rotting, the rampant aspects of nature—there is a "perfume" of putrescence, and a somewhat perverse frisson of what may be called erotic entomology. And there are bees; "nervous" and "fierce persistent bees." What does not, no longer, embrace the narrator—what he no longer embraces—is the human world. He is as if more aware of, drawn to, the barns and the bees. In an essay entitled "Culture, Self, and Style" from his last book of essays entitled, characteristically one might say, *Habitations of the Word*, Gass writes as follows:

> It is simply not enough to live and to be honest—happy, to hump and holler, to reproduce. Bees achieve it, and they still sting and buzz. To seek the truth (which requires method), to endeavour to be just (which depends on process), to create and serve beauty (which is the formal object of style), these old "ha-has," like peace and freedom and respect for persons, are seldom aims or states of the world these days, but only words most likely found in Sunday schools, or adrift like booze on the breath of cheapjacks, preachers, politicians, teachers, popes; nevertheless, they can still be sweet on the right tongue, and name our ends and our most honorable dreams.

Gass stresses and marvelously demonstrates continually the supreme importance, value, responsibility, and creative reach and possibility of language. He seeks to so use it that it will have the force and caress of the mass and texture of the barns, the hum and sting of the bees. He wants us to taste the sweetness and pungency of words. For it is in that realm of the extra, the surplus, the supplement, the over-and-above which is the gratuitous buzzing of bees, the unusable loveliness of unused barns, and—for us—simply language, that we discover and create meaning and beauty. A truism, to be sure. But reading Gass is to re-experience the quite immeasurable significance and excitement of that truism. In "Sunday Drive" the narrator recalls and evokes the autumn in almost extravagantly rich and allusive prose. Then adds: "Flamboyance and poetry aside, it's how this season goes to its death that is finally entrancing, and one feels compelled to 'get out in it.'" Flamboyance and poetry aside, there is always—and only—the undeniable real world and the undeferable reality of death. It is precisely in the flamboyance and poetry—the whole "aside" of style and language finely used—that we find our fun, our dignity, our point. It is one of the great merits and energizing joys of Gass's writing that he constantly makes us realize that it is the "aside" that really matters. Matters, really, quite as much as, if not more than, the given world and its decline—no matter how often, and from what urges and urgings, we are compelled to "get out in it."

JOHN HAWKES

......

The Equestrienne

The days that followed came to the visitors like song birds to bits of varicolored glass in the sun. The crisp fall weather held. Their accommodations in the Old Gentleman's chateau followed exactly the discreet and orderly arrangements of their shipboard cabins, as if the Old Gentleman had somehow known in advance his ninth son's domestic dilemmas and had quite carefully placed the parents here, the sons there, the secretary here and the maids down there with the other domestics, thus assuring privacy and decency to all. There were feasts, there were toasts, one night they sat down to twenty geese, the next to whole coveys of pheasants in hunter's sauce, the next to a flock of roasted lambs. The pâtés, the sherbets, the dishes of glazed fruits outdid by far the dishes that the two French maids occasionally prepared to the cook's disapproval at Deauville Farms. The visitors were shown the countryside and entertained by chamber ensembles and by male singers whose basso voices might have belonged to Deauville heirs, and by female singers whose soprano voices were so pure and pleasing that they quite disguised their unmistakably erotic cast and gave virgin wings to their songs of insinuation and desire. The Irish matriarch and her mother-in-law did not know why they found the songs of the women singers so attractive, but so they did.

In the late mornings they all rode off to the hounds, except for the Irish matriarch and her mother-in-law, who followed the hunts in a light two-wheeled carriage. In the afternoons they strolled through the gardens, visited the chateaux of the Old Gentleman's nearest acquaintances. Darkness brought candlelight and celebrative meals and the inciting songs. Billy Boy was as good as gold; the Old Gentleman was kinder to Granny and tolerated Doc, and never again did he show to Uncle Jake his visage

From *Innocence in Extremis* (Providence: Burning Deck, 1985), pp. 36–46.

of inexplicable blame. Uncle Jake felt happier than he had ever been at Deauville Farms.

But the days of harmony and pleasure were further enhanced by certain occasions deemed by the Old Gentleman to be specially enjoyable to his assembly of delighted guests. The first took place before even a week had elapsed since their arrival.

One afternoon the bell in the Old Gentleman's private chapel began brightly ringing as for a wedding, and in the best of humors the Old Gentleman summoned everyone once more to the courtyard; with arms flung wide he herded them outdoors where they found awaiting them four rows of Empire chairs. The gilded frames and red plush cushions of the chairs shone in the agreeable light and contrasting as they did with the expanse of smooth and faintly purple, faintly pink cobblestones, moved everyone to exclamations of surprise and keen anticipation. The boys and their mother were seated in the front row.

Then the Old Gentleman gave a flourish with his right hand, curving the open and graceful old hand as might an impresario summoning an actor from his place of concealment in the wings. And in response to his flourish there came a tiny, sprightly clattering of hooves and through the gateway rode a young girl on a small and shapely dappled gray horse. Here was a sight to win them all and audibly they sighed and visibly they leaned forward. The girl, who was the youngest child of the Old Gentleman's eighth son, was the same age as Granny—fourteen—and though she had been shyly present in the chateau since this Deauville family reunion had commenced, she had from time to time caught Uncle Jake's attention when he had seen her firm young face in the candlelight, like a pale petal on a white china dish, or had spied her slipping gracefully into seclusion behind a mass of garrulous adults, still he had not been prepared for the vision she now presented to her already grateful audience. She looked like neither boy nor girl or like the best of both. She wore a trim black riding coat, a white stock, black boots and a black skirt that reached to her ankles. Best of all she wore a black silk hat which, befittingly small to suit her little head, nonetheless called to mind the larger and bolder silk hats generally worn by aristocratic men. Her dark brown hair was drawn tightly to her head and arranged in a short plait that barely touched the velvet collar of her coat. Around her silk hat, which was tilted becomingly forward, was tied a white silk ribbon that fluttered down the back of her neck and provided exactly the right touch of freedom and formlessness against the plait of hair. She was wearing gray gloves and riding side-saddle.

As for her horse, its size could not have been more appropriate to the size of its rider or its color and markings more complementary to her costume. The distance between the top of the girl's silk hat and the saddle, which was hidden beneath the skirts of the riding coat, was the same as from the saddle to the brightly varnished black hooves that were the size of teacups; when the breeze tossed up the gray silken tail in a filmy plume of abandon, the spread tail was a perfect counterpart to the horse's head and neck and rose to the height of the little creature's comely head. The gray mane was so long that it echoed the tail; the black colorations of the horse's legs were like tight stockings that mirrored the prim costume of the rider. The small gray horse looked like a hobbyhorse, its rider like a little man. Yet the horse was filled with the supplest life and no young girl could have sat upon its back more decorously than did the daughter of the Old Gentleman's eighth son. Together they were toy-like and so pretty that even the Old Gentleman in that moment watched his granddaughter with admiration and not the slightest sign of desire.

But the Old Gentleman had orchestrated the young girl's exhibition, for so it was to be, in such a way as to bring to absolute fruition the beauty of the young girl and her steed. He had gone so far as to choose the hour so that when the young girl stopped her horse in the center of the courtyard, as now she did, the sun was at such a distance above the westerly wall as to make fall across the cobblestones the largest and longest possible shadow of horse and rider. He had had the rows of chairs arranged at the eastern end of the courtyard so that his audience faced not only the girl and horse but, more important, the shadow that made them one and the same. He had even instructed his equestrienne to keep the head of her mount facing to the north throughout the performance so that she presented to her audience only her right side and never the left, and by so doing—since both her legs were positioned on the left side of the horse—created for her audience the illusion of a legless rider seated in perfect balance upon her horse. The fact that she appeared to have no legs was to the entire ensemble as was the white ribbon affixed to her hat: the incongruity without which the congruous whole could not have achieved such perfection.

There sat Uncle Jake leaning forward in the front row with his hands on his knees and his mouth open; there before him were the performers, quite motionless but for the fluttering ribbon and the mane and tail stirring in the breeze. With shame he thought of himself and his shaggy and dumpy pony back at Deauville Farms; with helpless ardor he beheld in the girl and her gray horse a vision of poise such as he thought would never again be his to savor.

The exhibition began. The miniature portrait came to life. The young girl did not move so much as a finger, as far as Uncle Jake could see, but her steed responded to her invisible command: it cocked its right front leg and then the left. And again. The reins were gently curving from the young girl's lowered hands to the silver bit; she was applying no tension to the reins. Now the horse moved sideways three paces, no more and no less, in Uncle Jake's direction, and then returned to its starting place and stopped. Then it took three paces forward and returned. And then the small full-bodied animal began to dance, as did the elongated shadow, and drummed with all four of its pretty hooves on the cobblestones in a medley of pure obedience to the girl it bore. It danced, it drummed, it turned, but never so far as to destroy the illusion of its impossibly legless rider, and all the while the girl disguised as a little man did not move but remained ever and easily vertical and did not vary in any way her pretty posture as the horse continued to captivate hosts and visitors alike in its dance.

Nearly everyone in that audience rode horseback. Most of them were fox hunters. Their lives depended on horses, whether or not they hallooed while hurtling over high fences, and whether or not they loved their massive mounts as much as they did their own children. Some of them secretly feared past injuries and those to come; a few had little aptitude for riding. Yet for all of them their mares and geldings and fillies and stallions were a matter of course like stones in a brook or birds in the boughs. Most of the horses they bred and rode were large, rugged, unruly, brutish beasts of great stamina. The horses raced and hunted, pulled their carriages, carried them ambling through sylvan woods and took them cantering great distances. But little more. So here in the Old Gentleman's courtyard the spectacle of the young equestrienne and her gray horse schooled only in dressage appealed directly to what they knew and to their own relationships to horse and stable yet gave them all a taste of equestrian refinement that stirred them to surprise and pleasure. They had never thought of horsemanship as an art, but here indeed in the dancing horse they could see full well the refinement of an artist's mind.

As they waited, hoping the finals would never come, the Irish matriarch, who for days had regretted that her past refusal to ride with her husband now prevented her from joining the Old Gentleman in the hunting field and consigned her instead to the two-wheeled carriage driven by her mother-in-law and from which she could see little of the old and brave patrician, suddenly found herself constrained to whisper behind her hand to Uncle Jake.

"Jake," she whispered, "mark my words, dear boy. That child is dangerous."

He was stunned. He envied the girl, he likened her to their youngest maid, he loved her, he wanted to become her and take her splendid place on the gray horse, even though he had no use for horses. Surely the girl who might have been his sister could not in any way be sinister, as his mother had said. He was confident that there was nothing sinister about her.

But the Irish matriarch, who was proud of her self-control, did not know why she had been so suddenly stung to spite by a young horsewoman as clearly innocent as her own second son. So quickly she added in a gentler voice: "But she is a beautiful little rider, Jake. You might try to ride as well as she does. It would please your father."

In his relief he smiled, leaned briefly toward the once more reassuring bulk of his mother, and returned to concentrating on the girl and the bobbing and swaying horse.

Then came the finale.

All at once and above the dainty clatter of the hooves, they heard the loud and charming tinkling of a music box. Heads turned, a new and livelier surprise possessed the audience, the fact that they could not discover the source of the music, which was the essence of artificiality, added greatly to the effect. Thanks to its quick and pretty strains that were suggestive of the tips of quills picking silver strings as fine as hair, the horse's dance attained its childlike crescendo while the rider allowed herself the faintest smile. The tempo of the music began to slow, with no distortion of its tinkling notes, and with it slowed the dance of the gray horse. The slower the music, the slower the dance; and just as the even longer spaces between the notes caused each note to stand increasingly alone as if it were to be the only one struck on the scale of poignancy, so the modulation of the horse toward motionlessness brought to a head the lovely aching quality of its movements. Then the music ceased, leaving behind its song in the silence, and the horse and rider grew so still that they might have been waxen figures in an equestrian museum. And then, with a slowness that brought everyone to the edge of his seat, the gray horse bowed. Out went its front legs, down came the head and neck and chest, lower and lower in the greatest possible contrast to the vertical line of the young girl, until the audience could no longer bear the nearly human tribute paid to it by the little horse and broke out in sustained and mellifluous applause. At once the animal returned to its proper stance, the girl laughed, and horse and rider backed out of the courtyard and disappeared through the gate.

As one the audience rose to its feet, still clapping. They exclaimed aloud to each other, while clapping, and smiles vied with smiles and no one had praise enough for the exhibition which had taught them all that artificiality not only enhances natural life but defines it. Footmen came with trays of sherry, and the sunlight deepened, the voicing of appreciation grew softer, more lyrical. The Irish matriarch looked about for the Old Gentleman while Uncle Jake stayed close to her side and thought of the girl in the long skirts and black silk hat.

Then the Old Gentleman appeared and as one the audience realized that though they had all seen him act the impresario and with his raised hand start the performance, still he had not taken one of the red plush chairs for himself, had not remained with them in the courtyard, had not been a passive witness to his granddaughter's exhibition. He was smiling broadly; he was perspiring; clearly he expected thanks. In all this the truth was evident: that not only had he himself orchestrated the day, but that it was he who had taught the girl dressage, and he who had from a little balcony conducted her performance and determined her every move, and he who had turned the handle of the music box. Never had the old patrician looked younger or more pleased with himself.

Weeks later, in the final days of their visit, when the Irish matriarch had learned well her lesson about the Old Gentleman and had suffered once more the full brunt of disillusionment, she remembered this afternoon of the dancing horse and thought, with a return of her terrible grimness, that even a lecherous man can be seduced into a state of the purest innocence.

CHRISTINE LANIEL

......

John Hawkes's Return to the Origin: A Genealogy of the Creative Process

"Anyway my father packed us all off to France. Mother, my three brothers —Billy Boy was just a baby—our maids—we had a lot of pretty young maids in those days—the entire lot of us. He wanted to have a reunion with his eight brothers and the Old Gentleman, which is what they called my grandfather." This is a very special moment in *Adventures in the Alaskan Skin Trade*, when Uncle Jake, just after experiencing the shock of his wife's death, allows his childhood memories to consciousness and relates his journey to France, as a boy, back in 1892.[1]

Yet this short quote can also be read as an epitome of *Innocence in Extremis*.[2] The protagonist of the novella is precisely a twelve-year-old boy named Uncle Jake, whose father, the ninth son of the illustrious French Deauville family, has settled in America as a horse breeder in a vast estate called Deauville Farms. The text of this short fiction starts with Uncle Jake's father deciding to take his family—composed of his wife (the Irish matriarch), their four sons (Granny, Uncle Jake, Doc, and Billy Boy), his favorite secretary, and the maids—across the Atlantic to visit the birthplace of the Deauville line in France where the patriarch (the Old Gentleman) still lives with his sons in a chateau near Chantilly.

The narrative structure of the novella is both simple and symmetrical since it is based on three tableaux, which are the three shows organized by the Old Gentleman to entertain his guests from America. Thus, *Innocence in Extremis*, although it was originally part of *Adventures in the Alaskan Skin Trade*, still forms an autonomous whole because of the forceful triadic structure that makes it self-contained.

The first of the three tableaux is the extract published herein, describing the equestrienne's performance on the dancing horse. The passage focuses on one of the most pervasive metaphors in Hawkes's works, which he analyzes as essential to his fiction writing when he refers to "horsemanship as an art," thus forestalling interpretation by anticipating it. As a consequence, the critic is thwarted in efforts to unveil supposedly hidden significations, which are obtrusively exposed by the writer himself.

Yet this tantalizing sense of frustration is inseparable from the alluring fascination created by Hawkes's writing. I have used this baffling effect as the starting point for my study in an attempt to show that the extract perfectly exemplifies the illusionism conveyed in his fiction, which can be defined as a strategy of seduction. Then, by situating the passage within the context of the novella as a whole, I have tried to demonstrate that the rhetoric of seduction must inevitably be reversed into derision, as an insidious vein of self-parody gradually penetrates the text. And finally, by following Uncle Jake through his several adventures in Alaska, I have suggested that Hawkes has probably reached a stage in the development of his fiction writing, when a return to the origin is inescapable, dictated by the very necessities of the circularity inherent in his writing.

The Strategies of Seduction

"The days that followed / came to the visitors / like song birds / to bits of varicolored glass / in the sun." The introductory sentence produces a mixed effect on the reader: the impression of harmony resting on the strong syntactic framework (comparative structure), on the distribution of words into symmetrical clusters (4, 4, 3, 5, 3), and on the alliterative rhythm, is questioned by the feeling of strangeness due to the semantic incongruity involved in the double association: "days" → "song birds" / "visitors" → "bits of varicolored glass." The images, connoting both music and light, call up the natural, organic fluidity of birds singing as well as the elusive flicker of glittering tinsel. The unusual connection is underlined by the paronymous play on the words "birds" / "bits," which reproduces an illusion of scintillation as though the slightly altered repetition of the same sounds made us feel the presence of the Other within the Same, the notion of a vacancy, of a lack, of an absence within the most consistent fabric.

We are compelled to experience the harmony of a perfect balance as well as the antagonism of the forces that constitute it, as though our expectations were both frustrated and fully satisfied.

An Impossible Desire

The dialectics of desire underlies the text, as shown by the development of the singing metaphor: "The visitors were shown the countryside and entertained by chamber ensembles and by male singers whose basso voices might have belonged to Deauville heirs, and by female singers whose soprano voices were so pure and pleasing that they quite disguised their unmistakably erotic cast and gave virgin wings to their songs of insinuation and desire." The use of the word *wings* operates a transformation through which the natural singing of birds is changed into the singing of human voices presented as deceptive ("disguised"), since they blend the eroticism of desire with the purity of virginity. Thus, the forcefulness of desire is negated even before being expressed. Negation again—and as such not devoid of ambiguity—in the description of the Old Gentleman observing his granddaughter: "even the Old Gentleman in that moment watched his granddaughter with admiration and not the slightest sign of desire."

As for Uncle Jake, he can only behold the performance of the equestrienne with "helpless ardor," the privative suffix denying any possibility of fulfillment. The equestrienne is inaccessible. She is defined by her very inaccessibility, in the same way as any aesthetically oriented desire can be sustained only through the absence of its object. Beyond natural desire aiming at mere satisfaction, this is an introduction to the realms of artifice and delusion: one of the most seductive elements in the performance of the equestrienne is precisely her side-saddle riding combined with the carefully worked out orientation of the whole scene "so that she presented to her audience only her right side and never the left, and by so doing—since both her legs were positioned on the left side of the horse—created for her audience the illusion of a legless rider seated in perfect balance upon her horse." And the illusion will be maintained throughout the performance, never destroyed by the movements of the dancing horse: "it danced, it drummed, it turned, but never so far as to destroy *the illusion of its impossibly legless rider*" (emphasis mine).

The object of desire can conquer its artistic quality only through the deceptiveness of its very impossibility. It is because she is inaccessible, distanced by loss or absence, that the Muse inspires the Poet, and if we were to give the equestrienne an (assumed) name—she has none in the novella—why not call her Beatrice?[3]

At the origin of creativity is a feeling of bereavement, a basic sense of deprivation, the notion of a yearning never allayed by mere satisfaction, so that the act of writing is equated with the "art of fasting."[4] This might account for the profusion of privative prefixes and suffixes scattered throughout Hawkes's texts, such as the two adjectival derivatives ending in *-less* ("legless," "helpless") which we have just mentioned. In the same way, negative structures are so insistently put forward that they have become a highly distinctive trait of his writing. The device has already been analyzed at length,[5] and a few examples taken from *Innocence in Extremis* will be enough to illustrate the point. This is a self-portrait by Uncle Jake's father: "In the summer of 1892 he considered himself nothing if not the head of the household" (p. 9), in which two negatives are used instead of a straightforward, affirmative turn of phrase. And, further on in the novella, on page 75: "The young equestrienne said nothing and made not a sound," the negative particle being emphasized by the refusal to use the auxiliary ("made not" instead of "did not make").

Hawkes's works are haunted by an absence, by the sense of an inner lack, of a fundamental vacancy, which his writing aims at defining or delineating.

Seduction as Delusion

Another metamorphosis of the singing metaphor will guide us on: the music that accompanies the dancing horse originates from a music box. The singing of birds, then the singing of human voices are changed into a string of thin, subtle, fragile, and totally artificial musical notes. The equestrienne and her mount have become pure appearance, pure signs, and this is precisely the reason why they are both seductive and innocent, as shown by the Irish matriarch's remark about the Old Gentleman: "even a lecherous man can be seduced into a state of the purest innocence." As is frequently the case in Hawkes's writing, several metatextual incursions underline the link between the artificiality of the scene and its artistic quality:[6] "here indeed in the dancing horse they could see full well the refinement of an artist's mind"—"no one had praise enough for the exhibition which had taught them all that artificiality not only enhances natural life but defines it."

The strategies of seduction meet with the strategies of illusion. And their ideal meeting place might well be the theater, in which signs are both enticing and delusive. The scene of the dancing horse has been orchestrated by the Old Gentleman as though for a stage performance. On his order, and for the comfort of the audience, four rows of Empire chairs[7] have been set up in the courtyard of the chateau. Their upholstery is red—a color that is far from being thematically innocent since it is associated earlier in the novella with the father's favorite secretary, "with her firm body, lewd mind and auburn hair, which was the source of Uncle Jake's later interest in women with red hair" (p. 8). Yet the obviously thematic[8] use of the red color is counteracted by the allusion to the gilt frames of the chairs, the genuineness of desire being denied, negated, and exposed as fallacious, in the same way as the authenticity of gold—asserted a few lines before through the set phrase "as good as gold"—is questioned by the use of the word "gilded," which ushers us into the realm of artifice by its connotations of sham and false colors.

Then we have the horse described as a "hobby horse," and its rider, who looks like an "actor." But why an actor, and not an actress? Because the equestrienne is dressed in such a way as to hide her identity: she looks like "neither boy nor girl or like the best of both," which adds to her enticement, as suggested by the use of the superlative. She is one of the many androgynous figures in Hawkes's texts,[9] and she is all the more seductive as she does not look like a woman but like a "little man," because the deceitfulness of her disguise designates her as an artifact. Her identity is as arbitrary as any artificial sign, so that, as Baudrillard would write, she can reach the ultimate of seduction by wielding her powers of delusion, thus inspiring a fascination that is more seductive than sexual.[10]

And, in order to exacerbate the deceptiveness of the whole scene, the Old Gentleman has had the rows of chairs arranged in such a way as to enable the audience to face "not only the girl and horse but, more important, the shadow that made them one and the same." The equestrienne and her mount matter less than the illusion they create by casting their shadows on the ground, an illusion that will be preserved throughout the performance: "And then the small full-bodied animal began to dance, as did the elongated shadow." The use of the comparative clause, introduced by *as*, is a device so frequent in the novella that the text seems to cast its own shadow or to reflect its own image as though in a mirror ("as it did" p. 7, "as was his wife" p. 8, "as they were" p. 12, "as he thought" p. 25, "as he was" p. 25, "as they did" p. 37 . . .). But the mirror is a preeminent symbol of seduction, and it is mentioned as such in the portrait of the equestrienne. Her description is scrupulously precise and symmetrical, as regards colors, as well as movements, distances, or dimensions: "the gray mane was so long that it echoed the tail, the black colorations of the horse's legs were like tight stockings that *mirrored* the prim costume of the rider" (emphasis mine). The portrait can be paralleled with Uncle Jake's description of the Old Gentleman's dwelling, presented in the first few pages of the book, as a well-proportioned chateau in harmonious correlation with the surrounding landscape: "The approach to his grandfather's chateau was through a wood so carefully tended that it resembled a park and through a village of small and colorful shops and houses as old as the Deauville chateau itself. Beyond the village, across a rolling expanse of green fields that looked as carefully tended as the nearly artificial forest, lay the chateau" (p. 19). The repeated use of the comparative form, which is systematic in the text, gives it an excessively—and purposefully—regular rhythm, even to the limits of meretricious sophistication.

Yes, the mirror is deceptive and Uncle Jake himself will be ensnared in its trap, since, while watching the equestrienne, he acknowledges her as a potential sister, or even, why not, a virtual duplicate of his own self: "he wanted to become her and take her splendid place on the gray horse." By identifying with her, he comes face to face with his own image, so that the refracted figure of the equestrienne seems to be absorbed and dissolved into its several reflections. This is the way of seduction, which implies the obliteration of reality and its transfiguration into pure appearance. Another passage from Baudrillard deserves quotation here: "Prismatic effect of seduction. A different space of refraction. Neither does it consist in mere appearance, nor in sheer absence, but in the eclipse of a presence. Its only strategy is: to be there / not to be there, thus creating a sort of scintillation, a kind of hypnotic device which focuses attention beyond any effect of sense or meaning."[11]

The equestrienne is there, without really being there, in a scintillation of presence/absence which calls to mind the elusive flicker of "varicolored glass in the sun": "she had been shyly present in the chateau," and Uncle Jake "had spied her slipping gracefully into seclusion behind a mass of garrulous adults."

The Equestrienne as Metaphor

By conjuring up the shimmering grace of the equestrienne and her dancing horse, Hawkes presents us with yet another analogue of poetic writing as an art of evanescence, which consists in trying to pin-point the very moment when presence becomes absence.

Metaphor implies a perversion of the referential function of language, a distortion through which words are made to imply something different from what they mean. Metaphor is an act of suggestion that consists in the substitution between two signifiers, the implicit signifier being virtually contained within the explicit one. According to Lacan, a metaphor can occur when one signifier substitutes for another in the chain of discourse, the implicit signifier being present from its (metonymic) connection with the rest of the chain.[12] Poetic writing is an oblique approach, since the missing words are only indirectly suggested by the explicit ones. It is a strategy of seduction, based on the elusive vibrations of the linguistic signs as they appear and disappear,[13] which calls to mind the delusive and enticing image of the equestrienne. Through the verbal prestidigitation of poetic language, words are concealed and yet more subtly revealed.

The poet is the one who uses words as they have never been used before, by warping and distorting their ordinary meanings. Poetic writing necessitates a violation of the common usage of words. I have already tried to show that metaphor involves the suspension, the amputation of some of the semantic components (or "semes") that constitute the signifier.[14] It implies that the main function of everyday language—which is to produce meaning—must be suspended, temporarily abolished, postponed in order to recreate new significations. Thus, by making her horse dance as slowly as possible, even to the extreme limit of motionlessness, the equestrienne reproduces the process of semantic suspension inherent in the creativity of metaphor, like the film of a fall or an explosion in slow motion, which is poetic because we are given enough time to feel the lack of something before its accomplishment.[15]

And the metaphor will be all the more compelling as the infringement of the laws of common usage will be violent, all the more forceful as the signifier introduced within the discourse will be semantically incongruous with the context. But the infringement will have to be controlled in order to achieve another improbable—and yet necessary—form of coherence. According to Manonni, the absolute metaphor is the one Vian has chosen when using the signifier "nenuphar" to designate a deadly disease because this unpredictable and semantically unaccountable word seems to be "tearing a hole" in the discourse, thus opening out disquieting perspectives.[16] In the same way, the equestrienne, whose almost monstrous shadow becomes one with the reflected image of her mount, can achieve her ultimate power only from her being legless: "The fact that she appeared to have no legs was to the entire ensemble as was the white ribbon affixed to her hat: the incongruity without which the congruous whole could not have achieved such perfection."

We are made to experience both frustration and supreme satisfaction, since the expected word is missing and yet is virtually present, enhanced by the strange, incongruous connections that implicitly suggest it. By establishing the curious relationship of the logically unrelated, by uniting the like with the unlike in sudden and unexpected juxtapositions, the poetic text produces a jarring effect, so that we are left with the notion of a fundamental vacancy, of a basic lack that is the very essence of aesthetic pleasure (maybe the "sense of rich desolation," which Hawkes describes as essential to the origin of his fiction writing[17]).

But the performance will reach a climax only when the bowing horse draws a figure so perfectly poised and yet so extremely tense that the sight of it becomes unbearable: "Out went its front legs, down came the head and neck and chest, lower and lower in the greatest possible contrast to the vertical line of the young girl, until the audience could no longer bear the nearly human tribute paid to it by the little horse. . . ."

"'Tis Opposites—entice—"[18] and the figure of the bowing horse illustrates the extreme tension of Hawkes's writing, the desperate attempt of the "stationary traveler" to reconcile opposite poles in the same way as the equestrienne and her mount are trying to reconcile movement and motionlessness: "so the modulation of the horse toward motionlessness brought to a head the lovely aching quality of its movements."

The equestrienne is an oxymoronic[19] figure, and as such not devoid of subversive potentialities that are hinted at through the subtle evocation of her image by the flickering light of a candle: "she had from time to time caught Uncle Jake's attention when he had seen her young face in the candlel*i*ght, l*i*ke a pale petal on a wh*i*te ch*i*na dish" (emphasis mine).

The reference to china, confirmed by the allusion to the horse's hooves said to be "the size of tea-cups," suggests a fragility that belies the rider's seemingly unquestionable mastery and self-confidence. The sentence seems to reverberate with the echoes of assonance—another distinctive trait of Hawkes's writing often enriched with alliterative patterns or even rhymes—on both sides of the two central words: "pale petal," whose juxtaposition involves an anagrammatical and paronymous variation. This play on words, which Hawkes often indulges in, is far from being innocuous since it leads to the wilful deterioration of language as the vehicle of meaning: the signifiers break away from the signifieds and become pure signs whose circulation on the surface of the text guides our reading. This play on words is a challenge, as Baudrillard puts it about Saussure's *Anagrammes*, that involves a form of "extermination of language, a minute and ritual de-construction of sense and value."[20] Such is the danger inherent in any enterprise resting on the precariousness of language, an enterprise as risky as Handke's *Ride across Lake Constance*, an adventure as "sinister" as Hawkes's equestrienne.

The paronymous play on words is amplified to become a pun on "sister"/"sinister"—since the strategy of seduction necessarily implies the reversibility of metaphor into pun that is its inverted figure—emphasizing the destructiveness of the whole process: "'That child is dangerous.'"

Why? Lacan, who is a master in the art of handling the rhetoric of pun and metaphor, might provide us with an answer: "It is his own destiny that man challenges through the derision of the signifier."[21]

Unrelenting Derision

Let us trace, through the novella as a whole, the metamorphoses of the equestrienne and her mount. The paragraph situated just after our extract presents her in a very different light when Uncle Jake, whose interest in riding seems to be renewed, catches a—necessarily elusive—glimpse of her following the hunt: "Occasionally he was rewarded by the briefest glimpse of the young equestrienne soaring as dangerously as the rest of them over some high obstacle of hedge or stone or rail, the white ribbon flashing from the black silk hat, her hunting whip cruelly punishing the flanks of a gigantic brown gelding that was one of the largest and most unruly brutes in the field" (p. 46).

Such malicious mistreatment of the brutish horse—dissimilar, indeed, to the subtle mastery of the equestrienne's performance—indicates that the art of riding might not be as innocent as it first seemed to be. So why has it suddenly become so alluring to Uncle Jake?

The Reversibility of Innocence

Uncle Jake's repeatedly asserted innocence is his most distinctive feature, which distinguishes him from his father's libertine tendencies. Yet, the very conspicuousness of his overemphasized innocence makes it suspect, as several elements carefully scattered throughout the text seem to imply.[22] This is, for example, the way Uncle Jake reacts when, after being introduced to the mysterious woman who is his grandfather's favorite, he finally comes face to face with the Old Gentleman:

> The old patrician reminded Uncle Jake not only of his father but, more dreadfully, of the mysterious woman. From the aged eyes and the translucent facial skin there shone forth the selfsame quality of youth that also distinguished the face of the mysterious woman. It was a quality of youth that scarred and made compelling the faces of the old patrician and the mysterious woman. It stirred the ripples of Uncle Jake's perceptions into a terrible turbulence: he now intuited that his grandfather and the mysterious woman were far more advanced in whatever it was that he most feared in his father, and Uncle Jake was so shocked at what he now knew unconsciously, as the Old Gentleman was happily and consciously intrigued by what he had seen in his grandsons, and especially in Uncle Jake—namely, an innocence that it had never occurred to him could exist in a male. (p. 26)

The description of the Old Gentleman's visage hinges on the duality of old age and youth, so that the character is presented, from the start, as oxymoronic. The portrait is completed by a typically oblique and convoluted sentence that underlines Uncle Jake's purity—thus differentiating him from his father's and grandfather's corruption—while pointing to the rare shrewdness of his intuitions. The sentence seems to be doubling back upon itself in order to suggest Uncle Jake's terror ("terrible," "feared") on the verge of embarking upon the paradoxical itinerary of his initiation into the masculine universe ("male" is the last word), which will confront him with the tumult of hidden and contradictory forces (oppositions: "knew" / "unconsciously" / "consciously") challenging his innocence (assonance: "turbulence"—"innocence").

And how will the Old Gentleman contrive his grandson's initiatory ordeals? Like "an old master," he will create three consecutive tableaux for his guests and, above all, for Uncle Jake whom he has singled out, perhaps because of the boy's unusual perceptiveness in sensing the strategies of seduction (which might also be the origin of his newly developed interest in horseback riding).

We are now familiar with the first of the three tableaux, the equestrienne's performance. The second scene involves the treading of the newly harvested grape by the village virgins in the nude, and the young equestrienne among them. Finally, in a last display, the Old Gentleman will stage the covering of his favorite brood mare by the best of his stallions.

The progression is obvious, from the delicacy of the small gray horse—as innocent as a child's toy—to the fury and "brute urges" of the rutting stallion. This does not escape the Irish matriarch's notice, who, after watching the treading of the grape by the nude girls, will refuse to attend the third performance and blame the Old Gentleman for corrupting Uncle Jake's innocence: "'Monsieur,' said the Irish matriarch, whose anger had been suddenly restored, 'you have corrupted my son'" (p. 66).

Is corruption under way and has Uncle Jake actually lost his innocence? In fact, the boy is never directly involved in the action, since he belongs to the audience, and further, stands aloof from the rest of the guests by never answering when spoken to. The theatricality of the three tableaux is unmistakable, so that the whole process of his seduction is nothing but fake and counterfeit: the barn in which the treading of the grape takes place is equated with an opera house (p. 52). As to the stable, which looks like the reflected image of the chateau itself (p. 70), and which will be used as a scenery for the third scene, it contains an arena around which are located box stalls closed off by curtains of red velvet, evoking the wings of a theater (p. 71).

Thus, the Old Gentleman is not aiming at the de facto corruption of Uncle Jake but at instructing him in the strategies of delusion. The old master's intention is not to corrupt, but to seduce, to deceive, to mystify, "to beguile his favorite grandson" (p. 60). He wants to grant Uncle Jake the privilege[23] of having access to the realm of artifice, which is also the way to aesthetic creativity. He wants the boy to be initiated into the deceptiveness of seduction, he wants him to experience the transfiguration of reality into sheer appearance through the deceit and treachery of artificial signs.

Will the Old Gentleman succeed? His striving after increasingly poignant effects inevitably leads to an escalation, the second scene being supposed to outshine the first performance, and the climax will be reached only during the final scene. Yet the audience does not seem to react accordingly: "This scene provided far more incongruity than they had yet been treated to, so that the voicing of their expectations might understandably have reached a new crescendo. But it did not. That which was most surprising kept them silent" (p. 71).

The growing magnificence of the tableaux orchestrated by the Old Gentleman changes into "resplendent decadence" (p. 30), as though the failure of his enterprise was predetermined by its very excessiveness: "The

Old Gentleman had reached the height of his orchestrative powers . . . . He had done his best and had failed, as he knew he must" (p. 81).

Even the old master himself cannot avoid being caught in the trap of his own deceit and treachery. His discourse cannot escape the subversive forces of its own seductiveness. His contorted, diverted rhetoric deteriorates even as it builds up and will necessarily be reversed into derision.

Self-parody

The Old Gentleman seems to be gradually losing his control over events, which will escalate into the accidental death of his best friend's son during the last hunting party described in the novella. In the same way, the text seems to turn upon itself in self-mimicry, as an insidiously burlesque vein penetrates it.

Let us consider the episode of Billy Boy's sudden outburst of anger, which can be analyzed as a *mise en abyme* of the novella as a whole. As soon as he meets his daughter-in-law, the Old Gentleman undertakes to seduce her by all the possible means. In order to achieve his purpose, the seducer contrives a stratagem: he will hold the baby who is dozing in her arms, using the unprecedented honor thus bestowed upon his youngest grandson as "a bridge between himself and the handsome mother" (p. 29).

Of course, the Irish matriarch will be lured into the trap set by the old dissembler: "Now if she had had her choice she would have exchanged without the slightest hesitation her forty-four-year-old husband for his seventy-six-year-old father" (p. 30).

But at the precise moment when the Old Gentleman seems to be reaching his aim, the baby awakes and starts screaming furiously, thus exposing the treachery of the seducer and emphasizing the fallacy of the whole scene while ridiculing the illustrious Deauville line: "Billy Boy . . . was making of himself a humiliating spectacle, an overpowering spectacle, small as he was, and hence making a mockery of his three brothers if not all members of the Deauville family in America" (p. 31).

The sudden and unexpected glimpse of Billy Boy's death forebodes the tragic ending of the novella while initiating a shift that will gradually entail the alteration of the text into burlesque self-parody.

According to Uncle Jake, the incident was "fated to occur" (p. 28), as though the performance of the seducer must necessarily be derided and debunked, by virtue of its own deceitfulness. Yet, Billy Boy has good reason to scream, for he is the victim to be offered as a sacrifice to the ominous dictates of seduction: "And on went Billy Boy, screaming precisely as if he knew why his mother had given him up and as if at eight months he could suddenly see himself at the age of thirty-two slumped over dead in the Stutz Bearcat" (p. 31).

During the performance of the equestrienne the burlesque element is extremely slight, only hinted at when Uncle Jake mentions his own riding on the back of a "shaggy and dumpy pony." In the second tableau the vein of self-parody becomes more insistent when the youngest American maid rushes down to join the village virgins and presents the audience with a grotesque caricature of the equestrienne's graceful frolics: "She vaulted into the middle treading trough and, by so doing, quite overshadowed the sweet antics of the young equestrienne" (p. 62).

The totally unexpected interference of the young maid, which the old patrician had not planned, seems to indicate that events are no longer totally under his control despite his minute and precise planning of the whole performance. Yet order still prevails, as shown by the perfect synchronization of the show, and by the tidy way the guests find their seats (p. 56) in accordance with the master's contrivance. As for Uncle Jake, he finds himself seated precisely between his father and his grandfather, as though he had replaced Billy Boy in the role of the victim to be offered "as the purest sacrifice to their gender" (p. 57).

The ominous allusion to the destructive powers of seduction, the discreet but inescapable deterioration of the old master's orderly composition, are progressively amplified in the text. Whereas the Old Gentleman had been invisible during the equestrienne's performance, he is present as a spectator during the treading of the grape, and he assumes an active role in the last show. His orchestrative powers seem to wear away in proportion to the degree of his interference with the action. The more insistent his presence becomes, the less efficient his organization turns out to be. The guests will take their seats for the last show "randomly, with unexpected confusion" (p. 72). Whereas the old patrician had not pronounced a single word to introduce the equestrienne, he makes a short speech (pp. 54–56) to announce the treading of the grape and launches into several bombastic comments on the different moments of the last scene (pp. 73–74, 76, 77, 79).

Yet his discourse whose tone reminds us of many a Hawkesian narrator (Cyril's pomposity, Papa's paternalism, Allert's mannerism) is not convincing, precisely because of its overemphasized persuasiveness. This is the way he describes his favorite brood mare:

> "Oh my dears, what could be worse than generations of poor breeding? But in this horse we have not a single defect. Quite the opposite. Symmetry, my dears, and balance," continued the old patrician . . . "symmetry and balance. For these she was created. For these she lives. Note well her head which is in direct proportion to the neck and is not too heavy nor too small; see the neck, which is long and muscular and flexible; look at her deep broad chest and well-sprung ribs, the loins that are short and strong, the hindquarters that are wide and symmetrical. Yes, my dears, note well the glorious muscles of these hindquarters that are so nicely rounded. Oh my dears," said the Old Gentleman. . . . (pp. 73–74)

The description echoes the portrait of the equestrienne by its scrupulous precision as regards the harmony of distances and colors. But what a difference! The hyperbolic style (interjections, rhetorical questions, pompous vocabulary, strict parallelism of the syntactic structures) emphasizes the explicit "symmetry" of the scene to such a point that the whole speech becomes a grotesque travesty of the young equestrienne's portrait. The Old Gentleman cannot escape the inevitable shift from seduction to derision.

In the same way, the inordinate size of the stable and its central arena ("around its white-washed walls were hung greater-than-life-sized portraits of illustrious mares and stallions done in oils"—"the box stalls twice the size of ordinary stalls," p. 71) makes them the appropriate scenery for a performance that necessarily drifts from virtuosity to pantomime. How far from the proud and graceful bearing of the equestrienne to the "clownish and princely" aspect (p. 78) of the stallion in his ungainly efforts to mount the mare! How far from the thin, subtle, and artificial notes of the music box to the bestial trumpeting of the stallion "that could not have been made by any musical instrument" (p. 75)! The mere satisfaction of natural desire inevitably coincides with the deterioration of the text, which deliberately sinks into self-parody. And the anticipation of death announced by the allusion to Billy Boy's tragic end is confirmed by the insistence on the oil paintings representing the mares and stallions, which are qualified as "dead horses" (p. 80).

A Death Challenge

The artist's enterprise of seduction must inevitably be reversed into derision in the same way as Hawkes's writing cannot function without initiating its own ironical debunking. The "morality of excess" (p. 55) that guides the artist in his work also guides Hawkes in his writing, as exemplified by the profusion of superlatives and comparatives in the novella and in all his fiction. But this very excessiveness entails a crescendo, an escalation into more and more incongruous associations, so that his texts are relentlessly undermined by their own grotesque redoubling.

The derision inherent in Hawkes's writing is a fatal process, so that the comic flavor of his work is close to the Shakespearean grotesque or the absurd of Beckett,[24] in which the human condition and man's destiny are at stake. For there is a loss of life in the novella: after the staging of the last show, everything seems to be going from bad to worse. The crisp autumn weather that had enhanced the equestrienne's performance changes into frost and freezing rain, "making of the landscape around the Old Gentleman's chateau a terrain of mud as hard as iron" (p. 81). The progressive encroachment of the cold that threatens to congeal everything around—an obsession to be traced in most of Hawkes's fiction[25]—corresponds to the slow penetration, the gradual impairment of the text by the deadly forces of derision. And what was bound to happen, finally occurs: the death of Bufont junior (from the French word "bouffon" = buffoon?) who breaks his neck by falling off his horse to the frozen ground. But at the moment when the accident takes place, Uncle Jake himself falls off his horse: the text insists on the simultaneousness of the two events (p. 81), thus pointing to a process of displacement through which the boy is made to experience a symbolic, "metonymic" death. So the Old Gentleman's failure will be reversed into brilliant success, since his grandson will go through the initiatory ordeal of annihilation: "For Uncle Jake there was only emptiness and silence and injured pride, there was nothing to do but wander empty corridors and empty rooms" (p. 83), which will lead the boy to the last stage of his itinerary: his encounter with the mysterious woman in her private library. Uncle Jake's sentimental education will at last be completed when the mysterious woman grants him the privilege of beholding the image contained within the locket which she always wears: "I was that girl. Your grandfather posed me in the garden for this portrait. He himself undraped me" (p. 90).

Thus, the boy will be seduced symbolically, as the Old Gentleman had wished him to be, since he will not possess the woman nor even keep the locket, but only contemplate an image. This metonymic seduction, which answers the metonymic death he has just experienced, turns his sentimental education into an aesthetic education. Uncle Jake's itinerary, calling to mind the initiation of so many Hawkesian protagonists, makes him familiar with the treacherous strategies of seduction so that he can grow into an artist himself, which his adventures in Alaska will prove him to be:

"But no matter the treachery of his innocence, and misguided masculinity; no matter his Alaskan history of ever-increasing brutal flights of fancy that finally broke Sissy's spirit and caused her death; and no matter that his entire life was my seduction and betrayal—all this aside, Uncle Jake was a storyteller."[26]

A Return to the Origin?

Uncle Jake has now achieved the status of "storyteller." But whose story is told in *Adventures in the Alaskan Skin Trade*, if not Uncle Jake's?

The whole book is an attempt to answer the question asked at the beginning of the text by his daughter, Sunny: "Dad? Where are you, Dad?" She tries to elucidate the enigma of her father's disappearance by reconstructing the several episodes of his life in Alaska through her dreams and childhood memories.

It is the feeling of bereavement, the sense of frustration caused by her father's absence, that stimulates Sunny's creativity, just as the main allure of Alaska to Uncle Jake was the presence / absence of the palm trees that, according to him, had flourished there: "Nothing pleased him so much as the notion of palm trees growing on the sites of present glaciers in a warm sun that has long since been displaced by rain, in all its endless varieties, and by wind and snow and darkness" (p. 15). The "missing palm trees" point to the impossible desire in which the text originates and emphasize the conflict of oxymoronic metaphors, while the very name of Sunny is mockingly set off as a pun against the polar scenery of the fiction.

Sunny's search for her lost father, and her lost childhood, induces her to reflect back on her life, as she tries to recapture impressions of the past or to recall unconscious memories. The retrospective and introspective movement that characterizes the book is illustrated by the frequent occurrence of the reflexive pronouns in the text: as an example, Uncle Jake's name is very often paired with the pronoun "himself," whose recurrence is so conspicuous that it points to John Hawkes's own return to the origin.

Autobiography?

The publication of *Adventures in the Alaskan Skin Trade* coincides with a reflexive process as Hawkes reverts to the sources of his imagination by attempting to recollect the personal memories of his past life in Alaska. Autobiography is obviously playing an unprecedented role in the book, all the more so as the reference to the Alaskan period of his childhood seems to be especially relevant to his fiction writing—a fact he readily acknowledges: "What I remember of Alaska is like what can be dug from the unconscious, and our five years up there helped to determine not explicitly but psychologically the future cast of my fiction."[27]

Let us consider a few of the most obviously autobiographical elements that permeate both *Innocence in Extremis* and *Adventures in the Alaskan Skin Trade* (without claiming to make an exhaustive study, which is not the point here). This is a passage from a recent interview in which Hawkes reviews his family background and retraces his Alaskan childhood:

> My father's Irish family was landed gentry. There were nine brothers, one of whom was my grandfather, and these nine brothers rode to the hounds. That, in one sense, accounts for the genesis of my interest in horses. My father was one of four brothers, all of whom were well off. If I think of my father (he was very tall), I think of him in a camel's-hair coat. . . .
>
> My mother wanted very much to play tennis; she wanted, most of all, to be a singer and play the piano. These things she gave up because, in the early '30s, after the Depression, my father went to Alaska in order to speculate. In 1935, my mother and I went with him to Alaska, when I was ten, and we stayed for five years while my father did all kinds of exploring on various bays, islands, cliffs, was reported lost, and was injured. There's a character called Uncle Ben, I think, in Arthur Miller's *Death of a Salesman*—my father's a little bit like that. My father was tall, good looking, adventuresome, and overly honest; he was taken advantage of all too often. He was also a great storyteller, and terrifically artistic.[28]

The family tree drafted by Hawkes is comparable with the genealogical structure described in his latest fiction:

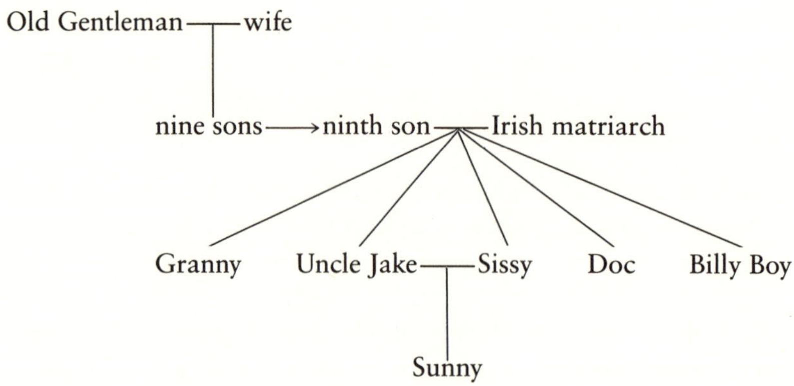

The overall similarity is evident, except for the names and the slight variation introduced by the supposedly French origin of the Deauville line, while Hawkes's Irish background is indirectly represented by the insistence on the matriarch's descent. There are several outstanding likenesses between the fictional characters as they appear in the texts and the members of the author's family as they are summoned in his memories: the grandfather's interest in hunting and riding—reminiscent of the Old Gentleman and his sons, the mother's taste for tennis and her passion for music—reminiscent of Sissy, the impressive father-figure, dressed in a camel's-hair coat, risking his life to satisfy his craving for adventure and a master in the art of storytelling—Uncle Jake, of course.

But beyond the individual personalities of the characters—whether real or fictitious—which we do not wish to discuss here, a fundamental question must be raised: that of the position occupied by each of them. In the genealogical structure Hawkes (called Jack) would hold the place of Sunny (whom her mother calls Jackie). This is a privileged position, as shown by the phrase "the important one," which is assigned to Sunny in *Adventures in the Alaskan Skin Trade* and which Hawkes appropriates in the autobiographical notes published in *Delta*.[29] So that the author openly implicates himself in his identification with Sunny who, in turn, identifies with her father, thus establishing the filiation of the names, Jack–Jackie–Jake:

"And was I not like my father—size and gender aside—I was his replica" (p. 41).

Yet, Sunny's father is not called Jake, but Uncle Jake, and he insists on keeping this nickname, irrespective of his daughter's reticence:

> My father was christened John Burne Deauville, but from his earliest boyhood was known as Jack, until, a few months prior to going to Alaska, he renicknamed himself Uncle Jake. . . .
>
> My father, then, was Uncle Jake. I was not allowed to call him Father. I was never allowed to call him Dad. Especially was I never allowed to call him Dad. (p. 22)

How can the shift from Jack to Uncle Jake be accounted for? There is the same distance from Jack to Jake as from Dad to Uncle: Jake sounds like Jack and yet it is slightly different; an uncle is almost—but not quite—a father. We are once more compelled to experience the jarring effect produced by the notion of a slight difference within identity, by the dialectics of the Same and the Other. By not allowing his daughter to call him Dad, Uncle Jake deprives Sunny of her rights, he refuses to satisfy her longing, which is only natural, for a father. Uncle Jake is, first and foremost, the absent father, the object of an impossible desire. He is as inaccessible as the equestrienne and his presence becomes all the more alluring, all the more obsessive as it is illusory.

The name "Uncle Jake" is a fallacy. It has no referential value. It is not only a nickname, but also a false nickname, referring to a purely metaphorical family relationship. The word "Uncle" substitutes for the word "Dad" by holding its place in the chain of discourse, the implicit word being present from its metonymic connection with the rest of the chain. Because the word "Dad" has been metaphorically abolished, it becomes virtual and all the more insistent as such.

The Genealogical Metaphor

The referential value of the family tree is challenged and revoked by the use of a fallacious element (the name "Uncle Jake"), which cripples the whole structure so that the prevailing role of autobiography in the latest development of Hawkes's fiction can only be interpreted as metaphorical.[30]

Let us briefly come back to *Innocence in Extremis* in order to analyze what can now be called the genealogical metaphor. The text of the novella is saturated with the compulsive repetition of the family name (used three times in the first page) while the significance of the lineage is strongly insisted upon by several direct or indirect references to the male Deauville line: "At twelve, Uncle Jake was unable to formulate what were in fact his feelings for the past and what was to become in later years his obsession with genealogy" (p. 24).

The protagonists of the novella are most often defined by the place they hold in the family structure: the equestrienne, for example, is mentioned as "the daughter of the Old Gentleman's eighth son." The text is based on a complex network of comparisons in which each member of the family occupies a position determined with the most scrupulous precision. The characters are always accurately situated in relation to each other, either in time, by their age and size, or in space, by their geographical position, whether it be in the boat taking them to France or in the chateau near Chantilly (p. 36).

The characters seem to obey the rules of a spatio-temporal game that dictates their circulation as though they had become mere elements in a vaster system overstepping their finite destinies. Writing is a circular process that consists in distributing elements of signification according to the inner necessities of a precise and specific game. The comparative structures whose profusion we have already mentioned are often combined with a reversal of the usual word order—the subject being displaced after the verb—so that the text seems not only to redouble but also to go back over itself in a reflexive movement "as did the elongated shadow" of the dancing horse during the equestrienne's performance. Another conspicuous device transmitting a markedly circular rhythm to the text is the repetition of the subject at the end of the clause. Here are a few examples taken from *Innocence in Extremis*: "They were large, his sons" (p. 7), "He has a broken neck, that man" (p. 84)—or from *Adventures in the Alaskan Skin Trade*: "It had a prow of iron, a salt-encrusted hull, our dark ship" (p. 39), "So they're hungry, all those baby seals" (p. 111), "They are sailors, these fur hunters" (p. 112).

A Circular Game

The circularity of Hawkes's writing illustrates his recent return to the origin, so that it is only logical that his latest fiction should hinge on the recurrence of the word *game*. Hawkes had already played on the several meanings of the word in his previous works, but in *Adventures in the Alaskan Skin Trade* the pun is amplified to such a point that it structures the whole text. This is the way Sunny presents her "ultra-artificial settlement, which guarantees sex twenty-four hours a day" (p. 26): "Everyone knows that the Alaska-Yukon Gamelands is not for fishing, hunting, or the innocent study of wildlife" (p. 25).

This circuitous understatement is the starting-point for the development of two metaphorical clusters: the metaphors of hunting introduced by the crucial choice of Uncle Jake's rifle, "one of those big-game rifles" (p. 62): bear-hunting, seal-hunting, deer-hunting; and the metaphors of playing: tennis, cards, billiards.

The interrelations between the two clusters are constantly put forward so that the metaphors modify and modulate each other in a deliberately polysemous enterprise: when Uncle Jake is about to shoot his first bear, he admits that he was perturbed "to find [his] expected act of slaughter turning into an amusing game" (p. 86). In the same way, the tennis match opposing Sissy and the red-haired woman—the same thematic use of the red color as in *Innocence in Extremis*—is described as a hunting party during which the loser is pitilessly executed by her adversary (p. 30), the event being premonitory, since Sissy will die when her heart suddenly stops beating as her companions were quietly playing cards, their favorite "game of hearts" (pp. 239–40)!

The permanent reversibility of metaphor into pun is obtrusively reinforced in the book by several typically Hawkesian metatextual incursions, such as the following question asked by Sunny: "Can such a dry chronology be loaded like Gamelands itself with sex? It can" (p. 94).

The pun encompasses the creative process itself, as though the metatextual commentary whose relevance in Hawkes's fiction has sometimes been questioned by the critics[31] proceeded from the very necessities of his writing, as though it were an integral part of the game.

The notion of game necessarily involves a double movement, as Deleuze puts it: "The player temporarily gives himself up to life and temporarily contemplates it from a distance. The artist places himself temporarily within his work and temporarily above his work; the child plays, leaves the game and then picks it up again."[32]

This statement has two consequences:

First, the notion of game implies a cyclic and recurrent process. Playing a game means producing a combination which, according to the necessities of a conventional rule defined beforehand and beyond any relation of cause and effect, will inevitably entail the production of another combination and send the game spiraling onward. It is a vertiginously escalating process that involves higher and higher stakes in an endless striving for ever-receding satisfaction.

Second, the game cannot function if the two moments inherent in its definition are not preserved: a time for action, then a time for contemplation that will initiate a return to action.

Uncle Jake is the very embodiment of the child-artist, both a player and a gambler, caught in the spiral of a deadly game in which he repeatedly stakes his own life as he accepts a series of increasingly excessive and dangerous challenges: "There was no more reason for Uncle Jake to leave in Rex Ainsworth's plane on an afternoon of scattered fog and steady drizzle than there was for his journey to Alaska in the first place—that precipitous nomadic northward venturing from which there was no turning back. No reason or just as much, since Uncle Jake had little or no belief in cause and effect, or did not admit to the effects he had caused, or did not perceive the causes that drove him on, or lived outside the ordinary orbit of cause and effect" (p. 66).

Hence the repetitiveness of his adventures, which, like the tableaux created by the Old Gentleman, are inevitably reproduced according to the inner necessities of the game. They are different and yet oddly similar episodes whose recurrence induces the whirling movement into which the protagonist is drawn.

The tooth-pulling scenes will provide us with a good illustration of the process: the situation, carefully announced by the assimilation between the block of ice detached from the glacier and a "sharply pointed tooth of ice extracted there" (p. 47) is repeated several times in the text (pp. 178–88, 222–29, 323–24), with variations. The first and the last scenes relate the initiation/seduction of Sissy and then Sunny by the dentist Doc Haines, while the central tableau presents Uncle Jake, who has become the master of the game by playing the dentist's role and who marvels at his own craft by exclaiming: "How's that for artistic achievement?" (p. 228). Another untimely incursion of the metatextual commentary? No, since the remark is generated by the reflexive movement inherent in the definition of the game, an indispensable stage to initiate the return to narration and send the text spiraling onward.

Recurrence and reflexivity seem to be characteristic features of *Adventures in the Alaskan Skin Trade*, which can also be applied to Hawkes's other works. For example, an overdramatized and grotesque model of the tooth-pulling scenes can be traced in *Virginie*,[33] where the same ordeal is inflicted on a horse (just as the covering of the mare was a burlesque duplication of the equestrienne's portrait).

Adventures in the Alaskan Skin Trade must be read as a genealogy (hence the relevance of the genealogical metaphor in the book). Like the notion of game, the concept of genealogy implies a double movement: "Genealogy means both value of the origin and origin of the values."[34] The concept involves a return to the origin but also a difference or a distance within the origin, an interpretation of the origin, action being inseparable from contemplation in the same way as criticism is inseparable from creation. Which can account for the insistence of the metatext in Hawkes's works justified by the inner necessities of a writing that can exhibit itself only as an ars poetica since it can progress only by producing its own criticism.

Hawkes's latest fiction is a reorchestration of the previous texts, integrating the polar and solar aspects of his works in a concentric motion, as well as a reinterpretation of these texts. Such a reading would require ample study, and I will give only two examples: first, Billy Boy's suicide, on page 321, is both illustrative and interpretative of *Travesty*. And then Sunny's fictional genealogy—beyond the obvious dramatization of the theme of incest—can be gathered from a double filiation that corresponds to her double identity: her name connects her with Sonny (*Second Skin*) and although seemingly feminine she feels masculine as well: "I am something of a man myself" (p. 24), so that she is another androgynous figure like Ariane in *Death, Sleep and the Traveler* (they share the same attraction to the wireless operator!) or like the equestrienne, who is herself reminiscent of Virginie because of the innocence that characterizes both of them.

The last characteristic of the game played by the child-artist is precisely its innocence: "Innocence is the game of existence."[35] One sentence from *Adventures in the Alaskan Skin Trade* deserves quotation here. It is the portrait of Suslota John, the old Indian who will help Uncle Jake to achieve the goal of his journey: the Lincoln totem pole, another—mythic and parodic—father-figure: "He had taken his pipe from his mouth and was watching Uncle Jake closely and smiling at him with a smile as sinister and innocent as a child's" (p. 372).

Of course the combination of the words *sinister* and *innocent* calls to mind the portrait of the equestrienne, and, at the end of this study, the child meets with the old Indian. The reflexive movement of return to the origin goes beyond the limits of the individual to involve a descent into the collective unconscious: the insistent dreams of the West, of the frontier, of primitive innocence. Yet the Indian is not to be trusted, no more than the child, and the rotten, decayed totem will crumble and break apart under Uncle Jake's horrified gaze: a symbolic and parodic debunking of the colossal Myth of Lost Innocence.

The discovery of the unreliability of the myth coincides with Sunny's discovery of her own father's unreliability when she faces the revelation of his suicide. But was not death the inescapable outcome of the fatal spiral into which he was drawn, had not death been his destination from the outset, as suggested by the obsessive repetition of the phrase "dead ahead" throughout the book?

Yet between the episode relating the disintegration of the totem pole and the revelation of Uncle Jake's suicide, Sunny discloses a very strange dream (section 53) in which her father is supposed to be buried alive according to the rites of the Sundown Indians. We are once more confronted with the reversibility of the text, since the myth of primitivism has not only a parodic function but also a metaphoric function.

The notion of ritual is strongly emphasized in *Adventures in the Alaskan Skin Trade*, through the reference to primitive societies able to exorcize sufferings, death, and treachery by dramatizing them and integrating them into a vast and innocent cycle. This corresponds to Hawkes's conception of his own creativity as a ritualistic enterprise involving an initiation to the deceptive forces of derision, so that his writing must inevitably contain its own parody and its own criticism, in order to achieve innocence . . . in extremis.

Notes

1 *Adventures in the Alaskan Skin Trade* (New York: Simon and Schuster, 1985), p. 244.

2 *Innocence in Extremis* (Providence: Burning Deck, 1985).

3 Cf. O. Manonni, *Clefs pour l'Imaginaire ou l'Autre Scène* (Paris: Seuil, 1969), p. 106. Manonni mentions the role of Beatrice's name as a signifier of the poet's creative urge, explaining that for Dante the desire to write is sustained by another desire, which he acknowledges without being able to analyze, but which he can refer to by an (assumed) name: Beatrice.

In the same way, the autobiographical origin of the equestrienne can be traced back. She is defined, by Hawkes himself, in relation to the metaphor of the horse and in terms of impossible desire: "My earliest recollections pertinent to writing fiction are of childhood and of lying awake wheezing in my nightly asthma attacks and listening to the thumping and snorting of the horses in the riding stable that adjoined our yard back there in Old Greenwich, Connecticut. . . . One afternoon, while squatting in a little plot of dusty ground beside the barn, I looked up at the sound of hooves and watched as a trim young girl trotted by on a large and handsome chestnut mare. She did not see me of course, where I squatted at the age of six or so in my humiliation, admiration, and envy. It was a very impossible love at first sight, and I think that my writing has always depended in one way or another on those first configurations of suffocation, faint stirrings of desire, and horses." *Delta* 22 (February 1986): 1–2.

4 See the epigraphic quote from "A Hunger Artist" by Kafka, in *The Passion Artist* (New York: Harper and Row, 1979). See also the epigraphic sentence by M. Leiris, quoted in *Travesty* (New York: New Directions, 1976).

5 Cf. P. Gault, *John Hawkes: La Parole Coupée* (Paris: Klincksieck, 1984), pp. 105–111. Cf. M. Chénetier, "John Hawkes Contre John Hawkes," *Delta* 22 (February 1986): 17–18.

6 Hawkes emphasizes artificiality as essential to his fiction writing: "it's just that I want whatever one creates out of words to be so clearly something made, so clearly an artifice, artificial." O'Donnell interview, *Review of Contemporary Fiction*, Fall 1983, p. 111.

7 The Empire chairs will be used by the audience during each of the three shows organized by the Old Gentleman. The link between repeated reference to these chairs and the creative process can be traced in an autobiographical remark by Hawkes, who evokes the beginnings of his writing career: "My wife and I lived in two rooms in Somerville, just beyond the edge of Cambridge, in a two-room apartment; I sat in a golden Empire chair and wrote on my lap." *Delta* 22, p. 4.

8 The thematic use of colors is also one of the characteristic features of Hawkes's writing. As an example, the text of *Innocence in Extremis* is obsessed with the red-gold association—a device J. Ricardou has traced in several "fictions" by Butor, Robbe-Grillet, Simon, as a means to question the referential anchorage of the text by putting forward an excessive, even aggressive structure: *Le Nouveau Roman* (Paris: Seuil, 1978), p. 83.

9 Jutta's child in *The Cannibal* (London: Chatto and Windus, 1968), Sunny in *Adventures in the Alaskan Skin Trade*, the statue of the hermaphrodite in *The Blood Oranges* (New York: New Directions, 1971), and so many others. Cf. Gault, *John Hawkes: La Parole Coupée*, pp. 230–32.

10 Cf. J. Baudrillard, *De la Séduction* (Paris: Galilée, 1979), whose reading has influenced my analysis of *Innocence in Extremis*. Baudrillard has devoted some very interesting pages (pp. 24–28) to the similarities between theatricality, transvestism, and the myth of androgyny in relation to the strategies of seduction.

11 Baudrillard, *De la Séduction*, p. 117 (translation mine).

12 J. Lacan, *Ecrits I* (Paris: Seuil, 1966), p. 265.

13 A passage from "Avant-dire au Traité du Verbe," by Mallarmé, *Oeuvres complètes* (Paris: Gallimard, 1945), p. 857, might illustrate the point:

"A quoi bon la merveille de transposer un fait de nature en sa presque disparition vibratoire selon le jeu de la parole, cependant, si ce n'est pour qu'en émane, sans la gêne d'un proche ou concret rappel, la notion pure?

"Je dis: une fleur ! et hors de l'oubli où ma voix relègue aucun contour, en tant que quelque chose d'autre que les calices sus, musicalement se lève, idée même et suave, l'absente de tous bouquets.

"Au contraire d'une fonction de numéraire facile et représentatif, comme le traite d'abord la foule, le Dire, avant tout rêve et chant, retrouve chez le poète, par nécessité constitutive d'un art consacré aux fictions, sa virtualité."

14 See my analysis of *Travesty* in *Review of Contemporary Fiction*, Fall 1983, p. 184.

15 Baudrillard, *De la Séduction*, p. 117.

16 Manonni, *Clefs pour l'Imaginaire ou l'Autre Scène*, pp. 101–102.

17 Hawkes, O'Donnell interview, *Review of Contemporary Fiction*, Fall 1983, p. 109.

18 Emily Dickinson, poem 355, *The Complete Poems of Emily Dickinson* (Boston: Little, Brown, 1960), pp. 168–69.

19 Cf. P. Gault, the oxymoron as "Central Trope in *The Passion Artist*," *Review of Contemporary Fiction*, Fall 1983, pp. 130–36.

20 Baudrillard, *De la Séduction*, p. 81.

21 Lacan, *Ecrits I*, p. 266 (translation mine).

22 Several elements in the novella point to the puzzling ambivalence of Uncle Jake's innocence. For example, p. 11: "Until then Uncle Jake's boyhood had been tranquil, secure, in a way sensual even though the maids refrained from making the slightest gesture to disturb the innocence of himself and the two brothers with whom he spent most of his time, no matter how erotically well-tuned they had become, those pretty maids, thanks to the father." Our attention is drawn by the conspicuous use of the word "sensual," and by the redoubling of the concessive structure which can be equated with a quasi-affirmative turn of phrase. Moreover, the emphatic superlative, "the slightest," whose usage is often equivocal in Hawkes's fiction, arouses suspicions that are confirmed by the reference to the relationships between the father and his maids. We are indirectly led to question if not the purity of Uncle Jake's intentions, at least the purity of his intuitions.

23 Uncle Jake is presented as "privileged" from the outset (p. 13). The adjective is also used several times to qualify the assembly of guests. Yet the word is not innocent in Hawkes's writing, since it refers to the driver in *Travesty*, who will explore the creative process even to its most extreme and paradoxical limits.

24 Cf. Jan Kott's analysis of the Shakespearean grotesque in *Shakespeare notre Contemporain* (Paris: Payot, 1978). The theatricality of the Hawkesian comic is particularly obvious in *Virginie* (London: Chatto and Windus, 1983), as exemplified by this short passage: "Now, and as never before, Monsieur Malmort was himself a comic actor, a poor twisted creature who dragged himself across a stage devoted to displaying naked women bathed in the rich colors of slowly revolving lights" (p. 79).

25 A superb illustration of this characteristic obsession in Hawkes's fiction can be found in *Adventures in the Alaskan Skin Trade*, pp. 251–55.

26 Ibid., p. 92.

27 *Delta* 22, p. 2.

28 O'Donnell interview, *Review of Contemporary Fiction*, Fall 1983, p. 107.

29 *Delta* 22, p. 2.

30 Hawkes has already warned us against any purely referential interpretation of the autobiographical element in his fiction: "I've always resented what we could call biographical poetry . . . and I'm not interested in writing as it becomes personal." O'Donnell interview, *Review of Contemporary Fiction*, Fall 1983, pp. 110–11.

31 Cf. Chénetier, "John Hawkes Contre John Hawkes," *Delta* 22, pp. 31–45.

32 G. Deleuze, *Nietzsche et la Philosophie* (Paris: Presses Universitaires de France, 1967), p. 28 (translation mine).

33 *Virginie*, p. 66.

34 Deleuze, *Nietzsche et la Philosophie*, p. 2 (translation mine).

35 Ibid., p. 27 (translation mine).

JOSEPH MCELROY

......

Choor Monster of the Long White Mountain

That sounds good, somewhere. Close as the next room (if you happened to be downstairs). Soft, loud, high, low; not without end, but still continuing. Song, yet then again like argument talked—not to you, or anyway not you alone. Space between it and you. Soft, loud, like music you would overhear when you were growing up.

But that's it. It *is* that music. Or was it the person playing you "heard"? Was that the feeling? Heard but not seen! A sound of Experience itself. Weigh it, store it; luckily in *your* "life" you can be dumb about it. Her privacy inseparable from the noise of the instrument: piano *or* violin; some days both. The musician's secure devotion. Practice, yet not to make perfect. Scale-like up-and-down workouts on violin that were more like real music when the in-between notes got crazily played. Early experience of somebody else's, yes, thought earned. Or could it have been some teenage, fairly early experience for you of pausing: pausing to Look Back! But why back, when what you were hearing was your mother's concentration right now? But where was it going?

This was you going too. Does that mean "growing"? Or that you doubled *her* going? Who could you report such claptrap to? Is it monstrous that to this day you have not thought much about her going? Fact was, she went, dead or alive.

Decades later, an event now in the apparently near future may get away from you. Two persons stand upon a metal plate: alloy to the best of your knowledge unique among late-century alloys in being natural; occurring in a natural state, and mined, not made in the lab. But upon this plate two persons stand waiting to be elsewhere. And behind them, more twos wait.

Wait: what *was* this Choor? she asked, with a passing affection in her and even in her word *was* that let you feel you might plead ignorance (here when you were headed out the door) or chance the intimacy of denying her the answer. I never heard about any Choor, she said, humorously but it bothered you but didn't surprise you because the stories your grandmother Margaret had been telling up until not so long ago were for you, not for this daughter of hers who was your mother ("independent as hell," your father said as if admiring, but you didn't quite understand). Choor *what*, did you say? she said. *What* Choor? she persisted, it has a funny sound, are you sure it's right?

She meant to bother you, but you were the one who had dropped the mention: so on your way out of the house you stopped and you told her what maybe she wanted to know—your large, soft-oiled first baseman's mitt enfolding a slightly reddened and browned American League hardball there beyond where your thumb and fingers reached that would always let the long mitt do its own finding of a ball coming at you high overhead or vacuum a low throw out of the dirt—a mitt with powers of trustworthiness beyond even the warlike leverage of your friend Sam's black rubber fins at the lake, which were fun, but cheating—but magical.

You told her only what you knew.

Margaret made up Choor, you thought. This Princess got sent away on a mission or something by her father, who was King of Choor. Margaret didn't tell them like stories much anymore except once in a while referring to some Indian or mountain or agriculture or cure as if she was one of the *listeners* nowadays. Choor had a long white mountain, white in the summer too and just as white after some of the white broke off up into the sky and became one of the giant birds that grew there though they grew a good deal darker when they flew away. The Princess flew away on a giant bird on this mission and where she went to was really Out West where Indians lived, but they weren't all Navajos. What mission? his mother asked. To explore the New World, he seemed to remember, see if they had any monsters. What did the bird look like? his mother asked, chicken-in-the-car-and-the-car-won't-go, she added, sort of between the two of them. Hey that's "CHICAGO," he said; no, her bird looked more like a big duck but the size of a house. Margaret's stories eventually got to be more like what you would have seen if you'd been there, you know what I mean? They had cures for everything.

Such as?

Well, tobacco ash makes your teeth white.

How 'bout tobacco *smoke*, Jimmy? (But his *father* was the one who got mad when Sam's father told him the boys rubbed lemon juice on their first two fingers to clean off the stain.) But this Choor, she said, it was just some place to be from? was that it?

Well, soon as the Princess left, things changed, he said.

Oh, shrugged his questioner (his mother, the daughter of Margaret) sounding like now she didn't need to know anything more, and to *Go* on, Jimmy, *scat*.

And he did, sailing like a broad jumper off the porch, not hearing the screen door (is this true?) clap shut until he hit the sidewalk at the end of their walk—but today without that calm shout from his mother from inside to not let the DOOR slam.

Meanwhile, decades later in the near future two persons stand upon a metal plate waiting to be elsewhere. And sure enough, behind them more twos wait their turn to step onto the plate and be transferred from sight. What becomes of these people? The plate is a type of transformer plate and the occasion is not a 25th-century movie in a theater in the 1940's where you know a dozen guys and girls plus your friend Sam and your brother Brad is there in the dark somewhere with a real girlfriend. No, the people on the plate are bound for a frontier colony out in Earth-Moon space; and while it feels like home it is uniquely economy-oriented in that, unknown as yet to these pioneers, they wind up on arrival one person, not the original two. But what does that feel like? Is this Experience again? What happens to their clothes?

This is a future where you have been, and not by dream, Jim Mayn, because you don't do dreams; and not by vehicle or through the aether to the best of your knowledge. Which you heard of only long after it had been found to be not there. (Is that a trend?) And how did *you* get to the colony? In your same body? Maybe you didn't stand on the plate. Were you simultaneously reincarnate?

But not dreaming, not dreaming.

A curve felt through your nature cuts distance brain-like and seeks in you to have been there first and retroactive to have guarded you through absence or secreted your viral memory from itself for a generation during which the future went ahead, homogened, homosomed, heading these willing pioneers for the hills of, after all near-space, but getting there each pair as one person.

Which would make for richly human letters frequency'd back home, you can imagine, reluctant journeyman. But it didn't make hard news you might readily share, cast as you could feel from that future like a shadow, whatever half-known way you got there to begin with; and while you're not listening for more, maybe it is listening for you, for it seems to be there, and who was There First is like what Came First (the Indians or their Great Spirit that sets in motion our own stake in it).

But if Two Pioneers into One comprises one beginning ongoing, here is already another: a room, a city room, a mid-room of a railroad flat: and on the chipped walls big blood-red/blood-black working drawings on brown supermarket bags opened out, cut up, masking-taped together. And you are listening to an elder meteorologist with a broken yet rebroken and lengthened face expound too fast (then too slow, ignoring you, Mayn) —that these represent another weather that may arise from convergence of atmosphere with some coastlines that of late actually have seemed disturbed, have varied suddenly like subtle fronts.

And while the world doesn't interfere now with this elder maverick's work, he does have a few correspondents left. One is a native American adolescent, New Mexico Pueblo Indian, y'know, who calls the hermit-meteorologist "great-uncle" and mails him bright chalk pictures (they're in the other room) of sunsets and faces and mesa-based Apollo rockets like individual ears of corn; the second correspondent is an established inmate of a penitentiary, and he sends—God!—tips of some telepathic iceberg, y'know, reflecting what he found in *his* mail: *write* a lot of letters, you *get* a lot, the Hermit observes: oh this fellow's much exercised about the high cost of opera tickets (that popular art!) and the current claims of women yet their "will" (!) to give themselves up for their men; but more to the point, letters re: precipitation of New Weather in new self-supporting communities. In return for all these letters, the Hermit's afraid he's sent back only a postcard now and then (like the one you got, you bet, brief-scrawled so it looked like a sketch: COME AHEAD—[naming this afternoon]).

The Hermit, like a discoverer in this bare room chock-a-block with his concepts and his weather: it was there to be found. (That epithet "Hermit-Inventor" adhering like a given name he has lived up to—did you actually hear it given this man? There's some hum he makes you resist around him of catastrophe. With it comes calm as sharp as a second voice, female far away in some next room of this dilapidated "railroad," babbling soft and old and dearly.) He has pivoted one coastline so it runs cross-country, you'd swear. He has replicated another so it comes on like crabbed waves across the continent. Mountain range, you suggested (to say something). What do you know about a mountain? the man demands.

Is some time-defying coincidence afoot here? Hermit-weathermeninventors-of-New-York talked their way into and out of fond histories your grandmother told you portions of; your mother did not tell stories. Were those hermit-inventors all one hermit, as you were one boy? "Great-uncle" to an Indian? It hardly rings a bell; coincidence anyway is against your religion. Jim Mayn will settle for just *this* oldtimer, tall and irritable, who can't afford an unlisted number to cope with these screwballs and probably foreign powers who call up (he guesses you're O.K.), and so is phoneless, hence more concentrated on what's here: snowflake-fringe coasts and diagraphs of pressureless voids that look like meteorite showers of infinitesimal equation on the wall of this Greenwich Village railroad flat—these could make their clouds of fingerprint considerably more than New Weather (as you clock these curious clouds—their curves of whorls blowing down to smaller and smaller whorls)—no, not just coasts of a weather but, up there on the walls across vertical piece after piece of brown paper, *mountains* seemingly as well (for *your* money) or just any old graph contour of some expert's risk-benefit analysis yet coming right at you or your brain anyhow (friendly dried-out polyp of a still two-gun arsenal, leftrightleftright) receiving obstacles of turbulence that your guy's differential equations for the evolution of the atmosphere and doubtless half a dozen other things at same time and/or unseen isn't going to help you with (and if you're this recycled man some woman called you warmly you have to admit the other day look around at the accelerated evolution of practically everything including these . . . what? you feel the word move your throat and mouth, the word "angels," where'd it come from?) and hell anyway this elder maverick New York Hermit-Meteorologist says forget it if you're not up to them, the equations, he as for him never got *family* relation straight, left it to the women—second something twice removed—"Great-uncle to an Indian?" you ask—"Oh my gosh who knows what the boy meant by that? Second cousin I would have guessed, if my uncle or was it great-uncle *was* his grandfather. Leave that to all our kinship hunters in the field," your host mutters . . . "—where'd you say you're from? Jersey?" People underrate the grandeur of New Jersey, he laughs the very laugh you heard in his postcard replying to your humble inquiry. Pretty much over your head, you had inquired if radioactive mists might breed atmospheric "sports"—freak fronts, stacked weather—say, like a tree with no trunk, you half-see, half-hear (but did not say in your letter), or a mountain you can't see.

Word of this man's bulletins launched from a local radio station near Cape May had come to you—the Coast Guard had complained—then elsewhere he was fired by an offshore pirate television station because, according to (he laughs) his prison correspondent, the hermit has powers of warning communicable in a bee-line to others—so no need for wire service, radio, or TV. (Wait—the *powers* communicable? or the *warning*?) But "the grandeur of New Jersey"? For a second the old tales wander back—all of them and for just one second.

The old geezer's not after publicity. Unless it could get him the funds to hire the plane and the infra-scan gear and a human or two on the ground to prove his guess. Oh you're willing to believe weather and coastline connect: this is no hare-lipped hype for the news-margin traders—you could name one who will send and, yes, buy photo-illustrated rumor linking a mountain of mineral matter with an intelligence strategy undermining what might have been one of the more interesting socialisms in South America: whereas the hermit's meteorology finds only a relation between unprecedented atmospherics and the behavior of little stretches of coast that may alter infinitesimally overnight: work he's done that's solid and odd: but hardly your staple all-points conspiracy theory like what the South American (Connecticut-resident) owner of newspaper chain you James Mayn currently work for asked you to look into: that has a Chicago industrialist's estranged son thousands of miles south arranging President Kennedy's Texassassination to impress a Chilean woman he is pursuing while he's studying magic music-stories with which Araucanian Indian *brujas* in the South demoralized their Spanish conquerors, but at same time north of there near the port of Valdivia helping rebuild after an earthquake: and the woman? she's a member of far Left MIR (*M* for Movement) but soon to flip her coign to equally anti-liberal Rightist revolutionary hive; *nor* is this New York maverick weather-discoverer's coastline/atmospheric-pressure correlation any suspense-loaded Doom ding-a-ling in all probability, certainly not mystery'd like family closet within closet complete with (remember the Edison light bulb that goes on and off with the) door, so let's make it last and leave the madness, folly, deaths, and their relevant skeletons back in there—for this isobar-tailed atmosphere freak in a railroad flat in New York's legendary Greenwich Village is coming up with science that resonates. And while you don't grasp all he's saying, if he has found a New Weather of enclosed voids that like "strangers" do not draw outside pressures inward, the old guy's right to call it "weather-possibly-without-a-cause" and at the same time relate it to "outlandish parallel phenomena" he describes as infinitesimal breaks in fanatic coastline indentations directly beneath the weather in question

—breaks that are not supposed to be there—"where" both weather and coastline turn out to be expressible in these (he calls 'em) "erratic shape equashuns"—"regular monsters, 'fya look close, like each surprised by the other, sky, land, sky."

Oh, some middle room of a Greenwich Village "railroad" and someplace along the hall, you passed the room with that babbling lady voice—a mother as old as she sounds far from children, who her hermit-companion says tells him to "go tell it—tell your message." The weather diagrams polygonally strengthened here and there by the appearance of the supermarket bag's bottom look like coastlines, but also vertical layeroids rising one upon another: the rock of history, not the history you don't believe in but some history of rocks you do.

O.K., this meteorological speculation plus this broken and rebroken face hosting you is another beginning less necessary than equal, more equal than prior—work of an out-of-work savant, unfrocked more than unemployed, who beams his suspicion through you as if you, James Mayn, have sensationalized him, made him a household word. He didn't know your name when you announced it, did he? He of course knows all these other things you don't, the fact and math—even the grandeur of New Jersey, O.K., but not who you are, except your job.

His face is changing on you again, fabulous geezer—O.K. Cut . . . cut, please.

For in still another beginning, a man and a woman—had once been married—but they didn't know each other necessarily—because it had not been to each other they'd been married. Which is an O.K. opening for a friendship. Or Open Marriage (OM), as we once said in sanction of some liberty to fuck our freedom. But they've not really met yet, and on this new beginning we now leave them, you see, it takes so long for people to meet. Others have to meet first.

No order, that; but you're in Florida, not all these other places: like Choor, the homeland of Margaret's Princess; a railroad flat in New York; a metal plate to turn pioneers to a transmissible frequency; marriage OMing into friendship; these other other situations. (There are no situations, there's only people. You missed your chance to tell the Hermit Meteorologist about the visits you would swear you paid to a future where pairs of people get transmitted from Earth elsewhere only to arrive as *one* person. A technological economy, literally breathtaking.) You have just come in out of Florida where the night will smell of unused daylight and, come to think of it, of used daylight, too. Which might just be the

Fountain of Youth Vaca de Léon. You have happened into a roadhouse in Cocoa near the Space Center, and here is where you are. Give the order. Is *that* an order? It's only for drinks. They're waiting. That's all you do, you're the one that says the words, let others carry them out.

A home passes overhead in orbit, 'least you saw it launched this A.M., an empty household fully equipped, built-in cabinets, now it's over the Andes, downtown Won Ton, Tunis, you wouldn't know, and sure to come by again in ninety minutes, no need to duck.

You know what you have to do. Think of those waiting. Nothing to it: it isn't as if this is even a *mock* killing-at-a-distance—nor that you have to be one whole person to give this order at a protracted time when you are letting a divorced whim bring you down here to Florida looking for a once encountered Chilean only to find one of the best women you can remember.

"Shoot, kid," came the father-type voice (meaning, "Speak") far away in time but close inside the void.

But you, you don't have to do the shooting. You just give the order.

Just? (For somebody hammering away at somebody else in a self-help workshop has just shown us that the word "just" often is minimizing our own self's felt needs, as in "I just called up to tell you.")

Yes, that's what you do. You do just. They take it from there. Standing up. Against a wall. In a revolutionary courtyard or an appropriated playground. But you don't know *what* shooting: because maybe we have here a trial run, with blanks. Trial run to gain experience. Or give the squad waiting to take their best shot the real thing of hearing the blankety-blank gust of the weapons' waiting life. And as for the terminal others waiting opposite, assembled in one timeless scheme all together or coming up in another time one by one to face the squad, the trial run gives them the complementary experience of, say, passing out at the explosion the shock of which we'll hazard they'd have been condemned to run the risk of not quite hearing (whether they went-to-the-bathroom then and there or not) if the blasts had not been blanks—which "Victim then fills in" as blanks are to be filled in, with indifference, hope, rage, self, the blindfold smell of self's waste, or say some tortured failure of heart (for who would go through that fake execution again? don't ask), or (to reverse the words and economize) *heart failure* (for risk's a factor and there's such a thing as torture that goes too far) while on the other hand (human nature being what it is) failure of heart threatens to widdle and resolve itself into mere you know temporarily decreased cardiac silhouette or arhythm; or, after all, temporarily decreased cardiac silhouette may be but *terminal* arhythm.

Dry run or wet, give the order. It's waiting to come into existence in order to be executed. A mound of sanitary landfill waits to be a layer a quantity of vegetable, animal, mineral-kindred (not controlled-toxic, though literally mind-boggling) landfill, and some of those waiting are to be under the layer, and some not. So give the order. You have to anyway. Don't distract yourself with memories of the future and a metal plate with persons standing on it, two at a time, two to the zero power it comes to you. Save your breath. Think instead of those waiting here; be considerate, you have to bring the order to the point of execution. So give the order. Give it your best shot. Yet hold it.

Oh sure, talk about the weather while we don't know enough about it anymore unless we wire Venus for un analogue much less consult weather's novel rethinker in his disintegrating apartment furnished faintly with a sound of a cheerful old female talking aimlessly: or unless we hold to those ancient cumulus towers given us by the very Great Spirit who'd never incarnate vast self even in sign, even in spiral idea much less stiff hat and short braids. But before getting into the weather, first give the order. That's what *you* do. Take the power that's fucking yours. The mayor's spiel has gone on long enough. Don't look back down the short circus of the century to a bomb or some such which once upon a biggish bang was set off in a territory named New 'merica by desert marksmen, who knew better or worse after the blast to confirm that their preliminary risk-yield analysis had shown that the blast just might kindle the atmosphere (its enthusiasm?), evacuate our oxygen, take our breath away right down even to what we'd saved. But like the vacant furnished household swung round overhead tonight every ninety minutes, that one-time risk will stay where it is and take care of itself while you give the order.

Yet hold it, you know—hold the mayo; no, hold the mayor, no, hold the mushroom, hold the landfill, hold the lettuce (but don't get *caught* holding the lettuce), hold the bacon it's on the way home come to think of it for Mom had her first day on the job having broken the firing squad sex barrier—hold it, we said: but tell where we are, say we're in a roadhouse late on a Florida evening and have approached the bar.

A young woman's at our elbow while the micro-seconds that won't settle into each other fall out of you into a noise umbrella like the *we* that you are and that you join.

But hold it, weren't we a team, a squad? weren't we about to do the necessary with the weapons at our disposal in the real field of a revolutionary system? Go on, don't screw around, say it, say we're one place or another. Go on, they're waiting.

But somewhere else you see folk standing on a metal plate in fact of an alloy unique among late-century alloys in origin. Somewhere else—forget the chain of fire sphering the planet (call it Earth), forget that orbiting household (it'll be there), forget that stand-up firing squad routine did you think you were some young Chilean lieutenant?—no, forget all that, for people are standing on a metal plate you recall at a site called Locus T.

And they're waiting for what better than what could happen.

Which they would embrace but it embraces them and raises them to its power to rid them of their twoness—elsewhere, not here in Fla—where the night smells of sugar percentage in the ketchup field.

And the couples waiting at Locus T—married? lovers? comrades? —seem cool and content, made of titanium, say, and about to be alloyed with a corrosion-resistant future. And only you know something, and you're carrying it on you. It must be communicable, herd-wise; what is it? A number of those here seem not to find you dangerous. Hell, we all show traces of this 'n that.

You were in future: that's why you're slow to execute. A shadow of the future? Hell no! You've no less than come back from the future. You have a power. Naturally don't want to overuse or underuse it.

But here you are to give the order. Your teeth press your lower lip, or is that the floor, it's so rough.

Give the order, give it through the gap. The gap? This vacant space between the arms. Left arm, right arm. The order can't be executed if it isn't heard (it says here). So execute, man, execute. You've been well coached, you have desire. Where's the inspirational coach who said, "My guys like to hit and be hit"? The football coach in New Jersey, which if it had a decent mountain could have been a great state (had the coastline, the weather, the soil, the horses, had the good position north and south), New Jersey where you were a boy and where some storybook truth about (was it?) a hermitage invented of New York—we don't ever get that right—not to be confused with the defrocked meteorologist whose wall diagrams you interview—not to be confused much less alloyed with some geezer arising in your monster-and-Choor-Princess-and-Navajo-Prince discussions in the late Thirties and early Forties with your Grandmother Margaret down the street, but that was not on the football field where the coach should by now be laid to rest in the end zone staring up with all his heart at one stump of a goal post timber impaled above him in the sod of state soil where the confined but still-functioning beep-bleep of his athlete soul picks up year-round the cleat-beats of his own executed plays thundering downfield, the football coach who wears a baseball cap to practice, to skull sessions, who hardly feels his tongue say *execute* when he takes his field general to task during drill for an intersectional clash (for we've graduated into America now, and the coach has been turned by sheer frequency of voice into many coaches). And where's the general in the field or behind the scenes—a rebel of the Junta (so goes the report), a revolutionary, but against what?—where's the general who'll say, "Execute them," much less "Have them shot" or "Off them" (like your economical syndicate voice), when just plain "Take them away" will do the trick? Or (in fewer words compounding the economy of removing-without-replacing) "Remove them." Or, to effect this liquidation, he may confine himself to a look, a look intent and/or blank, the look his lieutenant sensed well and truly like the light clamp on the butt the first-base coach gave the rookie after a clothesline single who stood on the bag and now takes a healthy lead off first, his arms hanging from his shoulders.

But can the future know all that was meant by such orders and communications? That is, if you, this Jim Mayn, have really come from there. Or are still partly there or will be there. There *is* no future, it's sentiment about what might have been. What say we make a package and see the future gets it. Why, then the future does exist. Yet wait: it *has* gotten it, and inside is the history meant for the future, but the package is so flat it can't be opened, it can only be "read" or reconstituted. History is cover, but the cover story is increasingly worthwhile. But the package is being opened after all by its unknown receivers.

Are they the two by two waiting for what is to happen to them at Locus T?, standing to begin with on a four-cornered metal plate of an alloy mined not lab-concocted, found in its pure impurity in a mountain of America, discovered and extracted and used As Is. No: call them a bad dream, though you don't do dreams; and forget this business about your having shuttled back from that future where the people are waiting on that transformer plate.

They don't know what they're getting into.

It's as well a legendary package about an Inventor of New York giving a secret sendoff to a regal young woman, only to receive her on her return almost a year later, all told by a steady grandmother who seemed to make up so much it threatened to be true; maybe it's throwaway advice from a mother to go away where you belong (now you saw her, then you didn't)

—some fleshly difference between advice and prediction which is the filling between them, block that kick the crowd goes on and on except for a recognizable father who doesn't say anything but watches him chase around the cold football field. Maybe it's a fifth of sour mash; maybe it's one compressed person for the agony of two—some loot for the future so they know.

But he don't know. A guy somewhere near the gap we were speaking about just said loudly that he don't know.

But that's not you, you're a guy who knows, who knows an onus from a behoof. Yet wait: give the order. See yourself warp along some curve of inkling that in this Florida roadhouse, or Void Between, you can know a thing or two right here worth knowing, send it or not to that future where people by twos are waiting to be transformed into one. No, that's jumping the gun. Transfed to frequency then to be transmitted from Locus T elsewhere. And when the frequency reaches that other place, the two transmissible as one have become one and we shall have no right to miss one or the other. Two into one. An economy the future holds like word that is carried but not known in so many words. Is there divorce there? After this two-into-one technology?

Forget there: you're here, facing a gap between arms, this gap awaiting your order. Your stomach warps and you hang fire, you don't need to be accounted for by some group you're being interrogated by that sounds outside you.

Where you coming from? Is this just another life-crisis in face of which you know you do your work? But you're not down here on assignment, you said. And not on vacation, so what is it?, though here is this subtle young person whose heart swims toward your body.

What's going down? It isn't new love, this powerful drift. And it's not mid-life consciousness infection sluicing you in/out of the Untapped Reservoir of voices you figure all belong to (those that honestly don't dream, those that honestly do). And it's no more Chile than violence: because your job is nuts and bolts—fundamentals—not slow-blowing a bloody cover so that in five years the truth of who gave who the business can come out covered by the healing objectivity of time's clarity wherein is the only safety upshot column by column into a morning news of riveting investigative reporting to be read in order not to think about what happened last night. And if the Argentine owner of a string of papers you work for has a brother who fakes his death by plane on a foreign continent, where it leads is probably not worth even dreaming about; nor are you any more into tracing several underlings named, say, Contreras, several with same first name too, some in receipt of political asylum in Texas but some spirited to a reputedly apolitical mountain and put into it like value one day to become minable veins; nor if you can help it are you into fielding blind volts of hardball played by proprietors of a stadium where you don't tell the spectators from the game.

Where you coming from? A metal plate ahead where people stood Indian file, butt to gut (or are they being held up?) waiting to be reformed into frequency and at once transited elsewhere—where when you wake up there's one of you. Two become one: did the Hermit-Meteorologist have an equation for this little monster? Two *times* almost collide! Is that a new one? And again, unreportable! The miss slides one between the other. New front-like shapes in the coast-cum-upper-void weather diagrams of an elder maverick fired for speculating about new weather as well as reading his mail on camera on an off-the-Jersey-coast non-commercial pirate TV station. Meanwhile, you saw Locus T like never before. Why's it recede, then? In *this* void, to call up the future is to *re*call it. (Like division of automobiles ordered to have their mildly poisonous air-conditioners reconditioned?)

But no. Say what is so true that it recedes. Grasp it; it recedes. Grasp what? That that scene at Locus T was not future; it was a now, only one, mind you: the gathered point with one person in position right behind another person. They two are about to go. Isn't it sad? But didn't we toy with this for decades? Here it is, and not an experiment where hazard yield waits unknown.

The place is a station not a lab, though an all-white operator runs the trans-frequency send-off as if the controlled element were research, and after the send-off of each two the inspection of the transparent elevator-car-like bubble where they stood and its Locus alloy-plate might seem like tracing the still unknown. But unknown traces *you*, you can be either a jerk or a monster, your last choice, you have a moment to decide. The weight of your very own body is falling all the time. It's your neck, look about you.

Bubble indeed! A million templates of electro-magnetism jointed continuously to make an ovaline so clear that with the help of a base-plate made of a unique innovative alloy mined in its natural state, it throngs two waiting bodies with non-visible radiance, it brings out the cells in all their glaring boundaries like graphed skin.

Till the instant when the million templates at what used to be the touch of a button collapse into one idea.

No experiment here, for this was no imaginary future; it was present. At least for you, who have not much in the way of imagination (you tell the girl beside you). But its vividness got so overdrawn on its own bearable present that you couldn't stand what was happening to others, two by two and you were about to speak when you were cast out of that future (you won't tell her any of this—*yet*, anyway) like a shadow though were you ever sufficiently dangerous and wasn't your exit then also because you made up again an earlier time, well 1973? Where now you are for a while. While now those future scenes at Locus T are vivid—they live —because they've been seen before (for it's, from Florida 1973, a future you've lived in, but as well because the scene at Locus T aligns itself with the arms and legs of that memory of two becoming one elsewhere in time—at a time when two becoming one did not mean this that is before one now in what can already be remembered as having once been foreseen as future. Seen, though, now with awful life because that memory helps the rememberer see that the T of Locus T isn't just TRANSFER—the dissolving of a person or persons here in order to be reconstituted elsewhere in order not to have to slog from here to there through spaces as a running displacement of volume—but T means another change. It is a clean economy so clean who would notice it? So awful, yes, that if one can find the right past to call up, why then this clear economy transpiring at Locus T makes one's notice recede (T for TRANSFER, T for TRANSFORM, *t* for *future*). You're not a dreamer; you're at best a trace.

When you told her you lacked imagination, she said she thought you were instead a recycled man. But then she said to forget she'd said it.

Two become one. This gets unbearable. You're hard-headed, plodding; real as need be, but you're invaded lately. Two become one. It might be three, it might be more. Four become one if you make a good enough plate to stand on. Two-become-one seems, here in the future-become-present, to mean people made congruent to fit an aim that's beyond them yet with which they are in tune and which if viewed wrongly and with alarm recedes, as this flawed witness unable to bear what he has seen would be bent simply (as if he'd had an attack of superfluous gravitation like a head cold) off toward Locus S, Locus G, or N, or P; Locus L.

The spoken L lets off L_1, L_2, L_3, L_4, L_5, from marked memory; and you who kept subjects and faces target-distinct from one another so as to never seem to know what you figured you did not, can't tell how you know (but you do) that those Ls with the numerals aren't *lunar* and aren't *locus*, yet how you knew locus with all these letters escapes you (but into the friendly void). No. L_1, L_2, L_3, L_4, L_5 are points in Earth-Moon space, quite comfortable space, yes, that's it—libration points. What is *libration*? Libration *points*—that's all you know and plenty more than a man like you needs to know, which is in turn a reassuring conclusion that, as soon as you divest yourself of it, feeds back in its recession some new stuff coming at you obstacle-like, the fact that *at* these libration points you can stay put because the pull of Earth and Moon balance out with another force you were not maybe to know. And around these libration points are gravity valleys; for every school kid knows that gravitation makes valleys in space as well as mountains, vales as well as hills—and wells, too, which is not to say Earth's the bottom of the bucket, just the bottom of *a* bucket, or of the well of somewhat made-up gravitation like the Moon's, but far greater: you forgot, you forget, for you've really been there—whereas this girl at your elbow (your bicep) in this infra-redneck roadhouse in Cocoa near the Space Center is sure to know, though she has not come from the future (though in turn will have been told by someone at school and/or college that she is the future): but as for you you don't feel like the future, you feel like your future's angling past, but this isn't what you know to be the truth, that some future to come is what you've come from, and you're not persuading yourself of this, you know it's true and you don't want to know.

Can't speak of it. You have to give a simple order.

Through this present gap which is an opportunity. (Team's fidgeting, squad's waiting, squad's right.)

If worse goes to worse you can make a package without knowing all that's inside it.

Which represents a further economy. Hey, while we've got us here, say we make two or more *places* one, so we know where we are, even if in theory we sacrifice a few powers of people, there's a limit to S.R. (standing room) when you feel you owe it to them to bring them out of frequency back into body. You saw what was happening, that the twosomes out of earshot on the metal plate waiting to be emigrated to libration-point space settlements necessitating unusual economies had not been told just how light they would travel, and you knew the (so to speak) theoretical "joke" was on them though in the interest of human survival, and they really did know, somewhere in those beings of themselves that had invited mountains to come to them bearing natural alloys that made them invisible to people living in their vicinity.

Yet the basic economy was borne by those who left as two and arrived as one. So what were *you* to do? Warn others it could happen to them?

Give the order, give it through the vacant, noisy space between two arms.

A left arm and a right arm, of course. ("Shoot, kid," an old voice says in you.)

ROBERT WALSH

......

"A Wind Rose": *Joseph McElroy's* Women and Men

for Richard Howard

Every bit of us at every moment is part and parcel of a wider self, it quivers along various radii like the wind rose on a compass, and the actual in it is continuously one with possibilities not yet in our present sight.—William James

I should like to have it emphasized that the symphony begins where the love affair leaves off.—Gustav Mahler

"As you remember . . . " could well be the first words of Joseph McElroy's six novels: a phrase to ready us as a generous and assured spirit begins his characteristically detailed exposition, fills the gaps in our sentimental education, and helps us recognize what we may not even know we know.

Passionate attendance to the full particulars of our daily lives and the plural worlds we inhabit; love (and imagination) bridging loss, separation, loneliness, and estrangement—these have been McElroy's interests for the past twenty years as he has explored and elaborated the ways in which we are thrown back on our unsuspected resources in the face of functional breakdowns in everyday life. "I didn't realize when I finally got down to writing novels . . . ," McElroy told the critic Tom LeClair in 1978, "that my books would be about disintegration and reintegration, would be psycho-philosophical mystery stories about the self putting itself back together again."[1] From David Brooke's late father in *A Smuggler's Bible* and the kidnapped boy in *Hind's Kidnap* to the suicide of *Ancient History*'s Mailer stand-in, Cartwright's stolen film in *Lookout Cartridge*, and the very body and memory of *Plus*'s Imp, who or what is missing becomes the core around which McElroy's stories turn. It is loss that prompts the "psycho-philosophical" investigations his characters undertake.

McElroy's long-awaited, monumental *Women and Men* (1987) carries the moral and physical weight of half a dozen major works of fiction; it is surely one of the most ambitious books in world literature. An extension and rewriting of McElroy's earlier novels, and a nearly complete assortment of his themes and subjects recycled and transfigured, *Women and Men* properly belongs to the genre he has called the "heart-gripping mystery-thriller."[2] Again we have a virtuosic fiction focused on what is missing—here an epic-poem time capsule of the past century of American life which circles oneirically around the mysteries of several generative absent figures: a late-nineteenth-century Navajo prince and his child; a Chilean diva's Pinochet-imprisoned father; Joy, from whom the male protagonist, "journeyman-journalist" James Mayn, is divorced in the 1970s; and, most important, Mayn's mother Sarah, presumed drowned in the 1940s. "A great field of process not confined to one narrative drama"[3] bursts forth from buried kernels of complex, unresolved emotion—mourning, postdivorce fears, the thrills of new loves and friendships, the joys and sorrows of the growth of children—and from an intuition, as in *Lookout Cartridge,* that "Knowing is Not-Knowing," from a sense of "being caught between what is known too well and what is known too little . . . being caught between wanting to be free, independent, and wanting to be secure, protective."[4] After the stripped-to-the-bone style of his last book, *Plus,* McElroy spoke of *Women and Men* as "my reentry, my coming back to the world and attempting to understand relations between men and women, women and men, in a way that will answer more honestly and fully questions which I only groped at before."[5]

McElroy's panoramic fiction often proceeds by indirection: it is sometimes difficult, or beside the point, to distinguish figure from ground, and we must piece information together as though it were overheard from a swarming next room. *Women and Men* produces its most powerful effects by accretion, too; it is so vast and fragmented that it may not be immediately apparent that McElroy is addressing "the most important thing in my life . . . the possibilities . . . for men and women living together."[6] Nevertheless, in much the same way that *A Smuggler's Bible* can be seen to build piecemeal toward David Brooke's triumphant imaginative participation in his father's life and death, McElroy's latest work can be read, at its most basic levels, as Mayn's coming to terms with his divorce (and his changing relationships to women in general) and as his mother's trial in absentia for having abandoned her husband and children. It is his attempt to understand her remoteness and emotional opacity and to account for her strange life and death.

McElroy's protagonists have all followed "personal leads" in their attempts to regain who or what they have lost. Mayn's oblique quest takes him from New York to Cape Kennedy and the American Southwest and back to Manhattan and the New Jersey town of his boyhood. In the course of his travels this "journeyman" decodes messages concealed in the thickets of his public and private lives; with new knowledge comes a recovery that is both reclamation and healing. In McElroy, such cures of the soul are invariably the product of imaginative reconstructions of memory that yield deepened experience: his characters retrieve the people they have longed for, as well as the substances of the unconscious, of dreams, and of their own histories.

McElroy has a keen appreciation of how individuals are buoyed and swim in fluid realms of relations, of how we are constituted (and constitute our selves) within many social worlds; he has shown us in fictional form "this reaching out to other lives through widening rings of relation."[7] However finely meshed the layers of coincidence and synchronicity, contrivance plays only a minor role; recognizing those networks of interconnectedness that make up what William James called our "wider selves," McElroy has devised a comprehensive new realism. The strength and direction of the diverse forces impinging on his characters could easily be charted on a diagram like the wind rose (mentioned by James in same epigraph above), which is the emblem of *Women and Men*.

James Mayn's wider self includes both his intimate apprehensions of a future self and paths of experience he shares with the female protagonist of the novel, Grace Kimball, a radical feminist workshop leader who lives in the same New York apartment building. Mayn and Kimball, for all their differences, are described as simultaneous reincarnations of the same personality, and the novel takes shape as a kind of double concerto for two soloists and chamber players.

From the beginning, commentators have emphasized the science in McElroy's novels as a means of enlarging the worlds of his characters by providing them with unusual new models with which to make sense of their lives. But it has become more obvious with each successive book that his project has been to put his characters and readers *into* life with every means at his disposal. Science is less conspicuous in *Women and Men* than in McElroy's previous novels. Instead, we find economic theory; Native American legends—and other nineteenth-century historical materials—provided by Mayn's grandmother; calculatedly outrageous views on everything from masturbation and group sex to enemas and "clean breaks" with the past, offered by Grace Kimball; and incisive, quasi-scientific imaginings from a trio of eccentric pivotal characters—an earnest teenage boy, a very funny serious-crackpot prison inmate, and "the Hermit-Inventor of New York." "Simultaneous reincarnation," "the periodic cluster," "obstacle geometry," "the dread modulus," "people-matter," "the colloidal unconscious," and "dual-screen consciousness" —one can imagine these notions (and even the Hermit's specialized theories about a new weather) entering the language and popular culture in the manner of Heller's "Catch-22" or Irving's "Undertoad." All fulfill the crucial function of science in McElroy's earlier work: to "beckon us out of ourselves."[8]

McElroy's attempt to expand our awareness—to exercise all our intellectual and emotional muscle groups—has left him with several difficulties. First, though widely praised, his novels—lyrical, late-Romantic, and often comic attempts to deal with the anguish of loss and other violation —have acquired a reputation for being abstract, intellectual, or cold. Asked by LeClair about this misperception, McElroy replied: "When I first started writing, I saw myself being divided between a cornball and an iceberg. . . . There is a cerebral, analytic, even sometimes manipulative strain in my work, but I see this as subordinate to the emotional, the impulsive and uprushing. I see the books as emotional, almost too much so."[9]

Microscopically scrutinized thoughts and feelings slip by and wend their way back—or suddenly jump out at us—in McElroy's work. The mercurial moods of each twisting sentence and the musical unpredictability of larger units of narrative are perhaps the signal marks of his prose, but he runs the risk of undercutting the emotional power of the narrative—even that of the individual sentence—with delaying tactics and ornate digressions worthy of Sterne, Diderot, or Kundera, and with his quiet, consistently skewed humor. (In *Women and Men* there are dialects and joking asides and boys glimpsed out in the middle of the night in their pajama bottoms. The rhapsodic "Breathers" sections offer pointed punning, in the main, and a lot of it, but McElroy can't resist a few terrible puns, such as "There are more things than are dreamt of in your whore ratio!")

On first acquaintance, some readers react with daunted impatience to the proliferating variation or to the plenum of incident and unanticipated detail in McElroy's winding and rewinding passages. Yet most of the enormous body of his work is in familiar, accessible, settled forms, particularly the previously published short chapters of *Women and Men* scattered among its enormous, unconstrained Breathers and its middle-range episodes of certain 1970s events. ("Choor Monster of the Long White Mountain," part of which is published here, is taken from an early chapter's 1970s narrative, which introduces several characters and prominent tropes. Because the style of this excerpt shares equally qualities of both the short chapters, which function as perches or resting places, and the necessarily longwinded, exhaustive Breathers—and because its puzzles are those of opening moves—it serves as an excellent introduction to the novel.)

Second, McElroy makes demands upon our energies and time warranted only by the largest and longest forms of art. His imagination stretches like rigorous poetry toward more complete incorporation of burgeoning detail and, at the same time, toward greater abstraction, in order to enhance the familiar and formulate the inchoate. And he clearly recognizes the implicit dangers of his ambitions for a utopian memory and attentiveness:

> There is in the sentences and in the information a vast amount of overload to give the reader a sense of teetering on the edge of not understanding. At the same time, he is tantalized by the sense that the information is all here if he just knew how to understand it. . . . The overload of information is partly an act of giving. . . . The obsessive attention which the writer seems to pay to the world is not paranoid or defensive primarily but appetitive, an attempt to say here the world is, to be loved and to be received.[10]

The criticisms leveled against McElroy's work have been made of modernist literature from Henry James and Proust to Gass and Ashbery in our own day (i.e., carping about the dense, all-over quality of language, willfulness, disorientation or apparent aimlessness, sheer variety of formal invention, shifting tone, and mixed dictions). His work requires no more stamina than Joyce, Broch, Musil, Pynchon, Brodkey, or Lezama Lima (to name only a few), and it is as emotionally satisfying as the richest pages by any of these writers.

Finally, although many long sections in McElroy have the deceptive look and feel of fanciful, even wild, improvisation, the novels themselves stand squarely within an aesthetic of reflective art. As Susan Sontag wrote in 1964, "Great reflective art is not frigid. It can exalt the spectator, it can present images that appall, it can make him weep. But its emotional power is mediated. The pull toward emotional involvement is counterbalanced by elements in the work that promote distance, disinterestedness, impartiality. Emotional involvement is always, to a greater or lesser degree, postponed. . . . Reflective art . . . imposes a certain discipline on the audience—postponing easy gratification."[11] Along these lines, McElroy himself has written of his desire for "a poise of emphasis in which one is even more conscious of pattern than of the mass of life yet not through any lessening of that mass."[12] Like Manny Farber's schematic but fluid tondo still-lifes of movies and domestic scenes, McElroy's novels are dazzling mandalas-in-motion wheeling briskly along, but they invite (and withstand) close and leisurely rereadings and contemplation of their exquisite detail and grand designs: "I do at times rather grandiosely imagine a book as a human-made system that through elaborate, labyrinthine intricacy can bring us to a threshold of ravishment and wonder."[13] McElroy's aspiration suggests a definition of the complement to science in his work: dreams.

From the stuff of musical forms and the latest news—"almost song yet then again like argument talked"—McElroy's prose forges a convincing dream logic, overdetermined in its details but nonetheless free. *Women and Men* develops a set of complex, interacting metaphors ("wide load," "hearing the noise," "obstacle quest," "the void," "multiple dwelling," "articulated structure," "trace window," etc.) that constitute an entire poetic universe. Within the swirling, unstoppable, multiple-perspective free associations by the recording and reminding messenger angels of history in the wide-arching Breathers chapters, where the diva's tapeworm—real and figurative—burrows through large swaths of the narrative, stories and experiences circulate among the characters' lives and consciousness in echoes that can threaten or sustain. As in *Hind's Kidnap,* "the independent parts are . . . parts of systems which no doubt interpenetrate."[14] Strictly speaking, there are no margins or peripheries to McElroy's dream song: figures and objects are in focus throughout the entire field of this folded and unfolding universe, enabling us to accept what might otherwise strike us as a kind of loony mysticism. In *Women and Men* we find only the matter-of-fact mysticism that stems from placing ourselves in a unique state of readiness as for the profound surprises of our dreams.

After the fashion of the narrator of *Lookout Cartridge,* who prepares himself for a revelatory "lookout dream," the middle-aged James Mayn, asleep on the grass of his family cemetery plot toward the end of *Women and Men,* has what he believes to be the first dream of his life. Mayn's need to keep the facts of his life in separate files—his refusal to see himself as anything more than a nuts-and-bolts newsman and his unwillingness to acknowledge that he might be an agent of change or an actor, however minor, on a historical stage—will not allow such blending as dreams accomplish, for to dream is to disintegrate and reintegrate, to de- and recompose (exactly what Mayn is unable to do). And until Mayn has dreamed, he cannot know the full interweaving of experience and understand what has happened to him. In the final chapter of the novel—in a sense the retroactively realized death of the family, an ordeal of initiation into manhood, and an experience already unknowingly lived through and overcome—Mayn's understanding and acceptance of his own history and its long-gathered momentum, his coming to terms with the women in his life, yields his only authentic power: to love again and differently.

Dreams and Mayn's not dreaming are part of other equations in the novel as well. Dreams offer the origin of the important Indian "Trace Window" of the novel, for they are both windows on another world and traces of this one, traces of another world and windows on this. Because dreams have always been accepted as portents, not to dream and yet to need to know what will occur draws the Mayn character into a future where two people can become one, and then returns him to the present to report his discovery. As though every relation between a character and events granted access to any moment in that character's history, dreams tunnel through time like the tapeworm of the Breathers, connecting various levels of reality. And like dreams, the Breathers inhale the future and exhale the past (as D. H. Lawrence wrote of "the poetry of the immediate present"[15]), gathering and reshaping the previously unearthed narrative material (and then some) as though the mechanical voice of *A Smuggler's Bible* ("who was urging Davey to have more, to take more, to be more"[16]) had divided, multiplied, and become a plural voice evolving toward omniscience. The knowledge of and participation in relations among the characters expressed by these angels go far beyond the immediate evidence, and, like dream messages, make clear that the past is not yet finished, that it lives on in our present, and that experience is continuous in all its parts.

Opposed to the dream narratives of the Breathers is the built-in commentary of a superego critic-with-a-vengeance, an Interrogator in the tradition of Beckett, Pinget, and Sorrentino. Rooted in the circumstances of the diva's imprisoned father but, like the tapeworm, growing to mythic proportions and with access to the book's entire saga—from the birth of an unknown child to an inevitable love-death known only too well—the censor/inquisitor/torturer voice tries to pin down the fleeting testimony of the scrambling angels and resolve every ambiguity. This voice is identified to some extent with the compartmentalizing, skeptical turn of mind of James Mayn, as the angel voices are linked to the more "open" Grace Kimball, whose body-awareness workshop forms the nexus of the novel, which imitates its structure—"a rhythm of gatherings and dispersions."[17]

Women and Men is exemplary in its depiction of relations between the sexes, not least because there are no scapegoats in its fictional world. Encouraging ambiguity and the acting out of impulse and desire, Kimball has a touch of the charlatan about her; but with her acute powers of observation, her vitality, bravado, and willingness to risk confrontation, and her fearlessness about participating in the lives of others, she emerges as a sympathetic figure despite her cruel honesty and her anti-intellectual feminist cant about escaping the conditioning of the patriarchal past.

A less skillful novelist would force a synthesis of viewpoints; McElroy allows his characters and perspectives their independence. His aim—"defining a relation between a man and a woman that will be both ideal and possible"[18]—is accomplished late in the novel upon the reappearance of Barbara Jean (from the "Choor Monster" chapter). McElroy has said that *Women and Men* would be about "intuitions that may be possible between men and women if they live together and know each other."[19] The casual, teasingly affectionate, and very knowing conversations between Mayn and Barbara Jean, as they lavishly, gently probe each other and learn to love, fully demonstrate this ideal.

McElroy would agree with the American philosopher John J. McDermott, who writes in *Streams of Experience* that "despite the thickness and complexity, for good or ill, of our daily living . . . it is still possible for us to weave a continuous reflective thread throughout this maze of perceptions, affections and experiences."[20] McElroy directs his characters and narrative materials effortlessly—magically—in the exhilarating late chapters of *Women and Men;* his intricately braided story lines seem to hover like a lace of fireworks in the air around us.

Women and Men is quintessentially American in its democratic ideals, in its brisk language, in the rhythms of its intimate and vast spaces and the architecture of its time schemes, and in its pioneering spirit. Donald Barthelme once spoke of *Finnegans Wake* as inescapable, part of our landscape. *Women and Men*, too, is such a novel—as large as America, a lifetime's reading. While holding firm to his deepest sense of our complexities, McElroy has taken the necessary next step for us and begun to explore new worlds of relation between private and public realms, bringing closer to our day-to-day lives our contemporary history (the aftermath of the Chilean coup, radioactive waste, imprisonment, exile, the space program, the Bomb). His is necessary, moral fiction we may take courage from, in which plural consciousness engenders conscience. His original American eloquence humbles us, inspiring reverence for our world and for his work, no matter where we stand to watch it: far away, admiring the broadest strokes of his design; from a middle distance, engaged with the flow of heartrending, comical story; or up close, enraptured, mesmerized by the phenomenological miniature.

Notes

1 Tom LeClair and Larry McCaffery, eds., *Anything Can Happen: Interviews with Contemporary American Novelists* (Urbana: University of Illinois Press, 1983), p. 237.
2 Joseph McElroy, "Growing Up Embooked," *New York Times*, May 13, 1973.
3 Joseph McElroy, "Neural Neighborhoods and Other Concrete Abstracts," *Triquarterly* 34, p. 210.
4 LeClair, p. 241.
5 Ibid., p. 250.
6 Ibid., p. 251.
7 "Neural Neighborhoods," p. 203.
8 Ibid., p. 238.
9 Ibid., p. 250.
10 Ibid., pp. 249–50.
11 Susan Sontag, "Spiritual Style in the Films of Robert Bresson," in *Against Interpretation* (New York: Farrar, Straus & Giroux, 1966), p. 177.
12 "Neural Neighborhoods," p. 203.
13 LeClair, p. 244.
14 Ibid., p. 241.
15 D. H. Lawrence, "Poetry of the Present" (Introduction to the American Edition of New Poems [1918]), in *The Complete Poems of D. H. Lawrence* (New York: Viking Press, 1971), p. 182. I am indebted to Richard Howard for this reference and for many remarks during his Spring 1986 YMHA seminar on ante-modernism.
16 "Neural Neighborhoods," p. 239.
17 LeClair, p. 242.

18 Ibid., p. 250.
19 Ibid.
20 John J. McDermott, *Streams of Experience* (Amherst: University of Massachusetts Press, 1986).

POSTLECTURE

JOHN BARTH

......

The Limits of Imagination

My principal line of work is making up and setting down stories, not holding forth upon subjects of a philosophical character. But not long ago, the brochure of a lecture series sponsored by the College of Wooster, in Wooster, Ohio, so caught the eye of my imagination that I set aside a few Friday mornings to write this lecture on the limits of imagination. (The routine in my shop is to do fiction from Mondays through Thursdays, nonfiction on Fridays, and nothing serious on weekends. My work habits are as essentially middleclass as the genre of the novel itself.)

Three things about that brochure particularly interested me. First, the general subject was terrific: Limits and Constraints. Mr. McGeorge Bundy, the late President Kennedy's Special Assistant for National Security Affairs, was to speak on the limits of unlimited power, the scholarly syndicated columnist Garry Wills on the limits of national autonomy, others on the limits of culture, the limits of personhood, the limits of law. Well: I am a writer who has spent his professional life monkeying around with the limits of the ancient art of storytelling, setting the bar ever higher on my personal high jump at the risk of ending up with a mouthful of turf (and believe me, I have learned the taste of turf, though I shall never learn to enjoy it). I wished I could have heard every one of the lectures: The Limits of Dissent, The Limits of the Unknown—wow. It was easy to imagine lengthening the series: The Limits of Love; The Limits of Intimacy; The Limits of Any Human Being's Capacity to Understand Another Human Being. The subject of limits struck me as limitless.

The second thing that interested me was that *my name* was on the list of speakers. Indeed, in a long-ago telephone conversation I had agreed to lead off the series with a lecture on the limits of imagination, if I could imagine anything on that topic worth saying in public. Having thus tentatively committed myself, I had gone back to my novel in progress—my latest expedition to the limits of my own imagination—and more or less forgot about the subject of limits and constraints until that brochure arrived in the mail.

Whereupon—this was the third thing that arrested my attention—I found that for some unexplained reason my subject was advertised not as The Limits of Imagination, but The *Limitations* of Imagination.

Think about it: The Limitations of Imagination! I did think about it, and was hooked. Not how far can imagination go; not whether that human faculty has its bounds, and, if so, what those bounds might be and what might imaginably lie beyond them; but, as it were, the shortcomings, even the hazards, of the faculty itself. The limitations of imagination: irresistible.

Why was Imagination the only topic on the list thus singled out? I couldn't imagine—and here we go: first into the preliminary definitions and distinctions that every teacher/lecturer likes to test the public-address system with (if not every storyteller; storytellers prefer to begin with action and then interstitch the exposition as they go along); thence into a little cadenza on the inherent paradoxes of the subject; finally into a chorus or two of what I take to have been meant to be my real theme: The Limits of Imagination. Specifically—since I am a writer of fiction and not even an amateur philosopher—the limits of artistic, especially literary, imagination.

I found out when I got to Wooster that the *limitations* business in the brochure was a mere clerical inadvertence. Happy fault: It had prompted me to a lecture upon some home truths about the art I practice.

Let's tune the calliope with those preliminary definitions: the *limits* of imagination, as distinct from the *limitations* of imagination, as distinct from *limited* imagination, which we might as well throw in too.

In fact, I'll begin with that last one:

A limited imagination gets things wrong. From its mere deficiency, like limited intelligence or limited physical strength, it mucks things up. It fails to anticipate accurately and to come up with the really new or more effective idea. Never mind that even the most powerful imagination may not be literally unlimited; "limited imaginations," as we commonly use the term, have low SAT scores, so to speak, in that area—like those political imaginations which advised President Reagan some seasons ago to celebrate the fortieth anniversary of VE day by visiting the German military graveyard in Bitburg, where a number of SS troops are buried, and there declaring the murderers and their victims equal in death. That's limited imagination, among other things.

In the literary sphere, limited imagination is likely to be limited to the most conventional and obvious: a mere lack of originality in the material, the form, the treatment. In the case of potentially capable apprentice writers, this defect may come from overmuch information about or insufficient distance from their material: Why does the young woman on page 5 of the story drive up to her lover's Cape Cod beach house in an ice-blue Mazda rather than a mustard Mercedes or a gamboge Cadillac? Because she *did*, replies the limited imagination. You can bet that when the hero of Flannery O'Connor's first novel, *Wise Blood*, drives through that story in a "high, rat-colored car," it is not because—at least not *simply* because—some factual fellow did.

We are reminded of Henry James's habit of interrupting the teller of a potentially usable anecdote, lest he hear too much about the matter and thereby limit his imagination. We are reminded of several of Thomas Mann's early artist-protagonists, who at a certain point turn their backs upon capital-K Knowledge, or capital-W *Wissenschaft*, in order to liberate, to unlimit, their artistic imaginations. Typically, though, limited imagination is a defect of the individual, or the committee, not of the imaginative faculty as such. When William Makepeace Thackeray begins or ends a novel chapter with such words as "Words cannot describe the scene that followed" etc., we may legitimately imagine that perhaps Dickens's or Tolstoy's words *could* have described that scene, perhaps unforgettably. (A sly genius may even do so after declaring that it cannot be done. Dostoevsky, for example, says of Raskolnikov's terrible dream in chapter 5 of *Crime and Punishment* that such dreams "are so plausible, the details so subtle, so unexpected, so artistically in harmony with the whole picture, that the dreamer could not invent them for himself in his waking state, even if he were an artist like Pushkin or Turgenev." He then proceeds to give us Raskolnikov's dream in its unforgettable entirety.) Your problem, Mr. Thackeray, we may say to ourselves, may not be in the language, but in your limited imagination of its possibilities.

The *limitations* of imagination, on the other hand—assuming a high score on one's imaginary SAT in that area—strike me as likely to come from a contrary deficiency: an insufficient ballast of information and experience. As an undergraduate student writer in the late 1940s, too young to have served in World War II, I had the chutzpah to try to write a military combat story in a workshop that included several war veterans among my fellow apprentices. The class was presided over by a gentle former Marine Corps officer (currently an Edgar Allan Poe scholar) who had survived a number of amphibious landings in the Pacific Theater of Operations. In my story, I blush to remember, a young soldier, en route to hit the beach in an LCI or LST or whatever, is duly frightened by the sound of heavy-caliber machine gun bullets ricocheting off the bow ramp of his landing craft; that ramp will soon be lowered so that he and his comrades can storm ashore. The veterans in the classroom were patient with my naive poaching on their preserve; they granted that I had a pretty good imagination. But the former combat officer gently pointed out to me that heavy-caliber machine gun bullets did not as a rule ricochet off the bow ramps of landing craft; they came right through. Thirty-five years later, I still stand humbly corrected upon that datum. I hadn't imagined.

In writing workshops at every level, as well as in the larger workshop of the world, we see this variety of limitation all the time, with respect both to particular details and to the author's—or our neighbor's—general inability to "project" with authority his or her sensibility across gender, class, age, culture, whatever. And we understandably admire the opposite, for that ability, or its lack, affects our relations with one another as well as our relations with literature. A Russian critic praised Leo Tolstoy's story *Kohlstomer*, which is written from the point of view of a horse, by saying, "But Count Tolstoy, surely you must have *been* a horse, in some earlier incarnation." That's high praise. On the other hand, a woman critic recently took John Updike to task—unfairly, in my opinion—for having one of his female characters (in the novel *The Witches of Eastwick*) reflect that it takes a woman longer than it takes a man to begin to urinate, once she sets about it, her plumbing being more considerable. I forget whether the criticism was of that datum itself or of Updike's having the female character reflect upon that datum. In any case, the critic found the passage unconvincing; she compared it unfavorably with a passage in a novel by a woman of her literary acquaintance describing a *male* character's pleasure in urinating over the lee rail of a sailboat under way, instead of having to go below to the "head." *There*, she believed, was genuine transsexual literary imagination.

Let us leave this fascinating aspect of our subject: what I call in my Johns Hopkins writing seminars "the lower criticism" (though we take it seriously indeed; even writers of fantasy need to get their facts straight, and not put carburetors on fuel-injection engines). But we ought not to move on before remembering that the phrase *limitations of imagination* covers also, or shades off into, the more interesting subject of imagination's being a liability, at least a potential liability, as well as an asset.

The phenomenon is too general and familiar to warrant more than a mention. When a dog bites another dog, the bitten dog hurts but presumably does not worry—about rabies, for example. When my wife, on the other hand, was bitten last spring not on the other hand but on the right leg, by a farm dog whose rabies inoculation turned out to have expired, the bite itself caused far less pain in our house than our imaginations did. All of us have tasted this edge of imagination's two-edged sword, which so often enhances our fear of both the known and unknown. The fish in my fish tank in Baltimore are presumably unaware that they are alive and therefore that they are going to die. The tank's owner not only knows that he must die but knows also that he doesn't know when or how. I don't know which of us is better off. I think of Jorge Luis Borges's Czechoslovakian playwright (in the story called *The Secret Miracle*), arrested by the Gestapo and condemned to death for the crime of being Jewish; in his death cell, he reflects that reality very rarely conforms to our anticipation of it, and therefore—"armed with this weak magic," Borges says—he deliberately imagines in vivid detail the most gruesome and excruciating deaths, precisely so that they will not happen to him. The consequence, of course, is that he suffers scores of deaths before he undergoes his actual one.

On the less dramatic scale, we have all known persons whose comfortably successful, even quite enviable lives are rendered wretched—at least less than satisfying—by their implacable imagination of how things might have gone even better for them; *much* better, had they only made *that* move rather than this, chosen *that* partner, taken *that* road.

Good old imagination.

The last item in this parade of distinctions that probably go without saying is a touch slipperier and maybe a touch more technical, but it brings us closer to our real subject: It is the distinction between the limits of artistic imagination and the limitations of particular media—a not-uninteresting subset of the larger topic.

It cannot be doubted that every medium of art has its inherent limitations. The narrator of Samuel Beckett's novel *Molloy* says at one point, "It was raining. It was not raining." I cannot imagine that disorienting assertion effectively translated into film, any more than I can imagine filming the lyrics of *Oh, Susannah* ("Sun so hot I froze to death," etc.). On the other hand, we can't literally verbalize primary physical sensation; the medium of writing is strictly anaesthetic. Written literature may render indirectly any and all of the physical senses, but it is the only medium of art I can think of that deals directly with none of them—not even the visual, though its symbols are apprehended through the eyes (or through the fingers, if you're reading in Braille). Characteristically, there are no literal sights, sounds, smells, tastes, or feels in written literature: only their names. (I'm excluding from these generalizations certain modernist literary experiments with visual effects, and the anticipations of those experiments in earlier literature. I'm excluding also many children's books, with their three-dimensional pop-ups, their scratch-and-sniff effects, and, of course, their pictures. "What good is a book without pictures?" asks Lewis Carroll's avant-garde Alice.) The best verbal description of a chase is not likely to approach the impact of the literally kinetic depiction of one in a movie, or the well-directed enactment of one on the stage. On the other hand, neither film nor television nor theater nor opera nor ballet nor pantomime, for example, can render directly the universe inside our heads and under our skins: the nonphysical universe of mentation; the *registering* of sensation. That interior universe is at least as important in our human lives as the exterior physical universe is, and the written word, alone among artistic media, has immediate access to it. Literature cannot give us the sights, sounds, smells, tastes, and feels themselves, alas, but it can dwell at any length upon what things look, sound, smell, taste, and feel *like*, to the characters. And it can reflect, deliberate, decide, generalize, interpret, without anyone's necessarily moving or speaking aloud.

"Happy families are all alike . . . ." "The great shroud of the sea rolled on . . . ." "Once upon a time . . . ." We can't film or stage *those*, either.

No need, I suppose, to dwell further upon the strengths and limitations of the several media, though it is a subject I am perennially fascinated by: the sea itself, say, versus the English word s-e-a, or Homer's "wine-dark sea," or James Joyce's "snot-green, scrotum-tightening sea," or a briny passage from Hart Crane, or the ending of Melville's *Moby-Dick*, or any of those versus Debussy's tone-poem *La Mer*, or Hokusai's famous drawing called *The Wave*, or Gericault's painting *The Raft of the Méduse* and Winslow Homer's *Breezing Up*; or all of those versus a still-photograph seascape or some marine footage for a TV nature series. Each has qualities that the others cannot duplicate or in some instances even approach, whatever the artist's skill.

This is of course why some people become poets or novelists and others become photographers, composers, painters. It is also why most people enjoy the experience not only of love, say, but of love stories, love songs, love poems, love sculpture, and the rest. We humbly (perhaps gratefully) recognize not only that each medium of art has its assets and its limitations, but that our own experience does, too—as does for that matter our experience in experiencing experience, so to speak, and our experience in experiencing art, which is part of our experience of living. The story of Dido and Aeneas in Virgil's *Aeneid* is not likely to move a reader inexperienced in the ups and downs of love as deeply as it moves one who has him/herself painfully abandoned a lover, or who has been by one abandoned. It will move even more exquisitely a reader experienced in poetry as well as in love. Needless to say, the connection is coaxial: Our ability to experience life may be more or less limited by inexperience of art, as well as vice versa, since each tends to increase the wattage of the great illuminator of both—namely, the imagination.

To move from the consumer of art to its producer, and directly to our subject, let us suppose a strong, mature artistic imagination, soundly ballasted (but not swamped) by information and experience both of life and of the artist's particular medium; powered by high intelligence and energy; controlled and focused by artistic discipline and training to the point of mastery. Is anything beyond the reach of such imagination? Are there, in the history of the medium, effects it cannot hope to surpass? Are there subjects it cannot encompass, or should not even attempt?

Some knowledgeable people have certainly thought so. In our time, the great crux has been the Nazi genocide of European Jewry: an evil so appalling in its scale and nature that George Steiner and other critics have argued not only that art fails in the face of it, but that the unassimilable fact of it may negate the very values that make art meaningful, that give our art its cultural validation. The eloquent and frightening argument (much simplified here) is that in a civilization whose members can admire Rilke and Goethe while running Auschwitz, art is effectively rendered spurious—not just Holocaust novels and Holocaust television miniseries, mind, but *all* art. I'm sure that many of you are familiar with this troubling argument and its counterarguments, such as William Styron's defense of his novel *Sophie's Choice*. The well-warranted fuss over President Reagan's ceremonial visits to the Bitburg military cemetery and the Bergen-Belsen death camp refreshed lots of memories in this area and no doubt introduced many younger people to some of the darker corners of the subject. I hope so—and I'll come back to the matter later.

Turning to the positive side of the essentially negative topic of imagination's limits, we find that well before the Holocaust—in fact, through the whole history of Western literary criticism—knowledgeable people have been moved to say, of some particular passage or of some entire literary artifact, "Beyond this, art cannot go." The late dilettante Huntington Cairns (I use the term *dilettante* in its best sense: a person who delights in the exercise of a large and various personal culture in addition to his or her professional specialty, which in Cairns's case was the treasurership of the National Gallery of Art in Washington) was even moved to publish forty years ago an anthology as fat as it is ingenious, called *The Limits of Art* (Washington, D.C.: Bollingen Series XII): 1,400 pages of such selections in their original languages, followed by English versions when necessary, followed by some critic's declaration that this is it, man: a perfect 10 on the scale of literary possibility. The texts themselves in this remarkable anthology run from Homer and the Bible up to Marcel Proust and James Joyce; the critical superlatives come from as far back as Aristotle (praising Homer's metaphors) to as recent as the French critic Denis Saurat praising Paul Valéry in 1946 (the anthology, remember, was put together in 1948). Cairns's book is an ideal place to explore our subject.

Most of the superlatives, as you'd expect, are hedged, and not to our purpose. To say that no verbal picture of girlish bashfulness together with the daring of first love surpasses Walther von der Vogelweide's *Under der Linde* (as the German critic Kuno Franke declared in 1901) is not to propose a bound on the possibilities of either language itself or the imagination itself: It is a historical assertion at best, like the proposition that no building on Earth in 1939 was taller than the Empire State Building—only less subject to empirical verification. Amusingly, a declaration by Longinus that Homer's version of blinded Ajax's prayer for light in Book 17 of the *Iliad* is superhumanly majestic is followed by a declaration by Charles de Saint-Evremond that Longinus's praise of that passage in Homer is itself as fine a passage as anything in *that* literary category.

Et cetera. But here and there one finds what we're looking for: the knowledgeable critic who declares of a certain text not only that no one has ever done better than this, but that this *cannot be surpassed*—and that that is the case not because of the circumstance that we cannot nowadays write authentic late-Latin elegies, for example, or medieval French rondels, but because the author cited has achieved the very limits of linguistic imagination; because beyond this, art cannot go.

Does any critic really stick his neck out so far? Yes, indeed. Sometimes, of course, it's mere hyperbole: When Francis Thompson says of three lines in Edmund Spenser's *The Faerie Queene* that "the mournful sweetness of those lines is insurpassable," all he's really saying is "Wow, those are three really dynamite mournful sweet lines, those three." But when George Saintsbury says of certain passages in Shakespeare's *Tamburlaine* that they are "examples of the NE PLUS ULTRA of the poetic powers, not of the language but of language," or when T. S. Eliot says of the closing canto of Dante's *Paradiso* that it is "the highest point that poetry has reached or ever can reach," I believe them to have meant just what they said: not "This really knocks my socks off"; not "This is the best example of this sort of thing that I myself know of in all of literature"; but "Here is the absolute limit of artistic *possibility*, at least in the category specified. Beyond this, art cannot go."

What can we say of such assertions, other than "Well, you have our attention"? One thing we can say is that they involve us in the essential paradox I mentioned earlier. When we say that we cannot imagine poetry or language or even the creative imagination going farther than this, or dealing commensurately with that, are we describing real limits of the medium and/or of the imaginative faculty? Or are we merely demonstrating the limitations of our own imaginations, which the experience of a new masterpiece might disprove tomorrow, if such things were really measurable? (The title of one of Samuel Beckett's later and bleaker works, *Imagination Dead Imagine*, embodies this paradox.)

I suppose it's foolish to imagine that the imagination is literally unlimited. Whatever it is, like other qualities and aspects of mind, it is a function of the physical human brain; and while human brains, like other parts and systems of the human body, admit of a considerable range of capacity, that range is not infinite. Granted, athletic records are always being broken: What physical and disciplinary evolution it took in the sport of foot racing to achieve in 1954 the first officially recorded four-minute mile! But then, a mere quarter-century later, the record was shaved down to 3 minutes 48.8 seconds. Who would presume to say now that a three-and-a-half-minute mile is beyond human capacity? But who on the other hand would therefore presume the possibility of a *two*-minute mile? A two-*second* mile (I mean on this planet, run by somebody indisputably of our species)? No: A prodigy, a genius, may astonish us like Kafka's Hunger Artist with a performance so different in degree as to seem almost different in kind, but that difference will not be infinite. The average lobster caught commercially of the New England coast weighs about a pound and a quarter; the largest ever known to have been caught, there or anywhere, was a 44-pounder taken near Nova Scotia on February 11, 1977. It is not difficult to imagine that there is yet a larger lobster down there somewhere; maybe even one twice as large: an 88-pounder! But is there one the size of Nova Scotia itself? The fact is, we can *imagine* such a beast, as in a Japanese monster-movie or Edward Albee's play *Seascape*; but with fair confidence we may assert that there are inherent physical design-constraints upon the upper magnitude of lobsters.

With the creative imagination the case is more problematical, by reason of the now-familiar inherent paradox: The human imagination is limited only by the limitations of our human imaginations. And the parameters are softer in the area of art than in the areas of foot racing and lobsterology. We have no electronic stopwatch or objective calipers with which to verify that such-and-such a play or novel refutes Mr. Steiner's argument concerning art and the Holocaust. Indeed, the same Holocaust novel that proves to one critic that Steiner is mistaken may demonstrate to another that he is not.

And yet, even if I myself happen to agree with that second critic in some particular (hypothetical) case, I can nevertheless *imagine* the imagination doing what Mr. Steiner for example declares it cannot do. Here is a little thought experiment, the specific terms of which I invite you to exchange for others more to your liking:

There are certain literary-artistic images, most of us would agree, of such extraordinary imaginative power—one might say, of such mythic resonance—as to be larger than the works that contain them, or rather, that fail to contain them. They live on forcefully in our imaginations long after we've forgotten the details of the texts (or whatever) in which we first encountered them. Indeed, because it is characteristic of such transcendent images that they translate readily from one medium to another, we may be quite familiar with the image even though we're unfamiliar with its source.

The short list, in my shop, comprises just four such images: In literary-historical order, they are Odysseus, striving homeward from Troy across the wine-dark sea; Scheherazade, yarning through the night to save her neck; Don Quixote and Sancho Panza, chatting their way across the plains of La Mancha; and Huckleberry Finn, rafting down the heart-waters of America. After these four cardinal images—the very compass-points of my own narrative imagination—come a host of powerful but, to my mind, somewhat lesser ones: Dante touring the afterworld, Ahab chasing after his great white whale, Rip Winkle sleeping while the world turns upside down, Gregor Samsa waking to find himself metamorphosed into a big bug, Alice tumbling down the rabbit-hole or through the looking-glass on a Victorian summer afternoon. But in my personal pantheon, those first four are the regnant deities; there is no fifth, yet; and after calling your attention to the fact that what I said a minute ago applies to them (many, many more people know who Scheherazade and Don Quixote are than have actually read *The 1001 Nights* or Cervantes's novel, just as millions know the principal iconography of the passion of Jesus who have never actually read the gospel narratives, and millions know who Mickey Mouse is who have never seen the original Walt Disney cartoons and comic books, or don't remember them), I shall end this lecture by rubbing these four touchstones of mine against our subject: the limits of imagination.

First, without attempting to rank them, I cannot myself imagine more profound, multifaceted, transcendently appealing narrative icons than these four: Odysseus, Scheherazade, Don Quixote, Huckleberry Finn. For me, as I have declared, there is no fifth. Yet (this is my second point) though the creation of such transcendent icons is by no means the only literary virtue, and though numerous of my very favorite novels, for example, do not happen to contain such sublimely uncontainable images (*Tom Jones* doesn't, nor do *Bleak House* or *Ulysses* or *One Hundred Years of Solitude)*, nevertheless I cannot imagine a happier destiny for a storyteller than to add an item to that short list, or even to the somewhat longer one. I myself, after thirty years of professional storytelling, have not managed to do so; nor at my age am I now likely to. (Though it is not altogether unimaginable that I might; that consideration is among the things that keep me going, along with the cheering truth that most of the writers I most admire have not done so either. It is simply not given to the human imagination to come up with an Odysseus or a Scheherazade or a Don Quixote or a Huck Finn very often; 4,500 years of writing have produced—by my standards—only those four: about one every eleven centuries.)

But look here, I tell myself: If I had been a well-read citizen of thirteenth-century Persia—the Huntington Cairns of Baghdad or Basra—I guess I'd have thought there was only one such image, Homer's Odysseus, when in fact the second—Anonymous's Scheherazade—was being imagined right under my nose. And if I had lived in seventeenth-century Spain, I'd have said there are only two—Homer's Odysseus and Anonymous's Scheherazade—never imagining that my countryman Cervantes was about to prove me wrong. And had I been an American book reviewer in 1885, I might even have added my voice to the chorus of those who found Mr. Mark Twain's new novel mainly vulgar, not realizing that what I was hearing was the very voice of America.

And so here we are, at the close of the twentieth century, some of us imagining it to be unimaginable at this hour of the world that the human literary/mythopoeic imagination can dream up yet another image with the profundity and staying power of those great predecessors—when for all we know, the thing might be being done next door, right now, by someone too busy doing it to attend this lecture series. Or it might already have been done, but not yet recognized for what it is, like Odysseus in his beggar's rags, mocked by the bona fide beggars in his own house. Or it might imaginably be about to be done, by some hitherto not especially remarkable writer who, like late-middle-aged Cervantes, finds himself possessed by an image that he himself, till it possessed him, imaginably thought to be beyond the limits of imagination.

MANFRED PÜTZ

......

John Barth and the Challenges of the Imagination

In one of the introductory pieces to his most recent book-length work, *The Friday Book: Essays and Other Nonfiction* (1984), John Barth describes himself as "a habitual novelist and occasional short-storyteller who has also for three decades professed the reading and writing of fiction in American universities and along the way has entertained a couple of ideas at a time about literature."[1] He then proceeds to support this description of himself by presenting us with almost three hundred pages of wide-ranging observations, reflections, and ideas by the writer, teacher, and critic. In doing so, Barth avoids one of the pitfalls inherent in the enterprise of becoming an author-critic. It has been argued that all art is essentially mute, meaning that art can offer statements, but that it cannot interpret its own statements in terms other than those that fall within its own range as art. It may not be the place here to raise again the old question of whether a writer is infallibly his own best critic.[2] Suffice it to say that Barth avoids the dangers of literature enclosing itself in critical self-interpretations of dubious value by simply splitting up the two functions, author and critic, then joining the ranks of the literary critics on an equal footing. Far from claiming superior insights into the meaning of his own works, he enters a dialogue with other commentators which generally makes literature as such the issue at stake. As *The Friday Book* suggests, then, it is time to go beyond such questions as John Barth and the critics, and proceed to investigations of John Barth *as* a critic, or, perhaps, as a critic of the critics.[3]

Barth's essay on "The Limits of Imagination" appeared after *The Friday Book*, but its central questions fall within the scope of the book's major topics. The essay places Barth among the company of such author-critics as Poe, Coleridge, and James, for he shares one of their poetological preoccupations: the role, the function, and the achievements of the imagination. Barth has been called many names by contemporary commentators, ranging from "existentialist" and "absurdist" to "comic nihilist," "black humorist," "fabulator," "experimenter," "experimental traditionalist," and, of course, "postmodernist." (For the most part, he has borne this with good grace, only occasionally hitting back at the labeling industry.) But would it not be more accurate and justified to characterize him squarely as a proponent, a practitioner, and a philosopher of the imagination, literary or otherwise? Barth usually disclaims being a philosopher: "My principal line of work is making up and setting down stories, not holding forth upon subjects of a philosophical character."[4] But if he is not a philosopher in the narrow technical sense, he is surely the type of thinking novelist who would not argue an important issue of his trade without considerable deliberation on its depth and implications. And the nature of the imagination and the problems it poses is one such crucial issue of the trade that has haunted Barth throughout his career. Moreover, the subject of the literary imagination in conjunction with the problem of limits has rightly been considered, as Wolfgang Iser has noted, a perennial topic of literature and literary criticism: "Literature as a means of insight into the workings and functions of the imagination, and as a means of access to that uniquely human equipment which comes into operation when all our faculties have reached the limits of their capabilities—this is a subject with which literature itself is perennially concerned; and this no doubt is an area which the literary critic will also be bound to explore."[5]

There are many telling indications in Barth that point to his fascination with the literary imagination. For one, his admiration for the creative imagination is at the root of what he calls this "endless love affair of mine with one of the most splendid women and storytellers ever, Scheherazade."[6] His high regard for the imagination connects with his love for Borges, who habitually imagines hypothetical worlds and things into existence, including those which imagine themselves into being. Moreover, a specific concept of the imagination lies behind Barth's calling God a novelist,[7] and behind his description—in terms faintly reminiscent of Coleridge's view of the primary imagination—of his fellow writer, the human novelist, as "not finally a spectator, an imitator, or a purger of the public psyche, but a maker of universes: a demiurge."[8] Finally, an almost unlimited trust in the powers of the imagination lurks behind one of the most misunderstood statements of contemporary criticism, namely Barth's early statement on "exhaustion" as not only a pervasive condition of, but also a vital opportunity for, contemporary literature.[9]

The gist of all this seems to be that for Barth the imagination is a nearly omnipotent force without any definable limits or, rather, as he provocatively states it in his essay: "The human imagination is limited only by the limitations of our human imaginations." What, then, are the limitations of the human imagination?

Barth starts his essay with a reflection on what his topic could have been, or rather what it actually was before he discovered that the wording of the title was due to a technical error. He swiftly runs through a few optional topics, leading to what he calls "preliminary definitions" regarding "*limits* of imagination" versus "*limitations* of imagination" versus "*limited* imagination." This approach might appear to be somewhat playful at first, but the matter deserves careful consideration because it turns out that the depth and the range of the investigation depend to a large degree on which of the three problems is addressed. The question of the limited imagination is the least important because Barth sees it as a problem of mere deficiency or absence. One could indeed argue that since "limited imagination is a defect of the individual . . . not of the imaginative faculty as such," it poses only a minor problem, because—as Barth has noted in another context—individual lack of imagination or unimaginativeness "has no legitimate role in literature."[10] This is different, however, with the problem of the limits of the imagination and, even more so, with the problem of its limitations. Barth makes it clear that by *limits* he means the upper boundary of what can reasonably be expected as an achievement of the human imagination, whereas the limitations of the imagination would define "the shortcomings, even the hazards, of the faculty itself" or, we may say, the inherent, nontranscendable boundary beyond which the imagination somehow cannot go. In the field of literature the limits of what has been achieved by the human imagination are for Barth defined by "certain literary-artistic images . . . of such extraordinary imaginative power . . . as to be larger than the works that contain them." For him, such images are at the center of only four works of world literature, to which he returns time and again in his reflections: the *Odyssey*, Scheherazade's tales, *Don Quixote*, and *Huckleberry Finn*.[11] Barth deals with his preferences and the possible alternatives to them in the final sections of his essay. But this part of the discussion, and hence the whole question of the limits of the literary imagination, is not the most challenging one. What Barth considers here is his personal and somewhat debatable view of the major achievements of some four thousand years of world literature which, by the very token of being what and where they are, invite speculation as to whether they can be equaled, or perhaps surpassed. Barth is aware of this and, consequently, he closes his essay on a speculative and hopeful note: who knows? if the imagination was able to do it once, it might be able to do it again! In other words, the question of the limits of the imagination presupposes—besides changing judgments and personal preferences—the existence of an open scale of historically actualized achievements.

This is not necessarily so with the limitations of the imagination. And it is this problem which, I believe, becomes the most disquieting aspect of the whole matter for Barth. In his essay Barth couples the problem of the potentially inherent limitations of the imagination with the example of the Nazi genocide of European Jews. What can art be or offer in view of such atrocities? Is art rendered spurious in the face of the Holocaust? Can the imagination encompass and hope to comprehend such events, or are they, in principle, beyond its reach? Barth makes it clear that he feels deeply troubled over the implications of these questions. Like so many others, he recognizes the helplessness of the human imagination, standing on the brink of failure, when confronted by such events. But he is not very explicit about the reasons for such an assumed failure, reasons that are more or less apparent and that indeed seem to mark genuine limitations of the imagination. For one, the imagination meets its limitations when it calls its own role and value into question by *refusing* to function vis-à-vis that which is too appalling to be thought. And second, the imagination seems to fail in another important sense, when it is still willing to think something but unable to grasp an acceptable sense of what it is thinking. Whether or not these are self-imposed or necessary forms of failure is a question we will take up soon.

First, I would like to pursue a train of thought that seems to lead away from the issues at hand, but that actually leads directly to the heart of the matter. Considering Barth's work as a novelist and critical commentator, one could say that the question of the imagination has preoccupied him in a comprehensive way from the very beginning of his career. There is a cluster of ideas in his works that Barth circles time and again, and these ideas form a consistent though sometimes concealed argument on the function and the achievements of the imagination. This train of ideas leads him—not necessarily in chronological order—from the interconnected statements of the arbitrariness of language and the arbitrariness of facts, to defiant acts of the imagination as a response and potential antidote, and from there to the quandary of whether the imagination has thereby achieved its final triumph or rather met its final limitations. I would like to pursue this train of ideas step by step.

The idea of the arbitrariness of language is too obvious in Barth to warrant more than a few references. In his painfully self-reflective story "Title" it is said that "words are artificial to begin with, invented specifically to represent."[12] In *The End of the Road* Jake Horner aggressively holds that "the significances of words are arbitrary conventions, mostly; historical accidents." He underpins his statements with the observation: "Then the symbol *x* can represent anything we want it to represent, as long as it always represents the same thing in a given equation. But *horse* is just a symbol too—a noise that we make in our throats or some scratches on the blackboard. And theoretically we could make it stand for anything we wanted to also, couldn't we?"[13] In *Giles Goat-Boy* a sense of the arbitrariness of language and its significations is at the root of the extensive renaming program that outlines one of the central ambitions of the novel. It seems justified, then, when Tony Tanner as one of the earliest competent critics of Barth ascribes to him a "tendency to sport on lexical playfields," and when he concludes that in Barth's early works "signs tend to become more important than their referents, and the impresario of fictions, John Barth, plays with them in such a way that any established notions of the relationship between word and world are lost or called in doubt."[14]

The arbitrariness of facts is an equally fascinating and provocative subject for Barth. As an issue closely related to the arbitrariness of language and the arbitrariness of values, it appears frequently in his novels and in his poetological reflections. Quintessential sections of *The End of the Road* and *Giles Goat-Boy* are preoccupied with Wittgenstein's dictum, "The world is everything that is the case," a statement on which the doctor in *The End of the Road* elaborates: "There's no ultimate reason at all why the Cleveland Stadium should seat exactly seventy-seven thousand, seven hundred people, but it happens that it does. There's no reason in the long run why Italy shouldn't be shaped like a sausage instead of a boot, but that doesn't happen to be the case. *The world is everything that is the case*, and what the case is is not a matter of logic."[15] Concomitantly, the arbitrariness of given values is the starting position as much as the final result of Todd Andrews's ruminations in *The Floating Opera*. And the arbitrariness of facts and values intertwined form the philosophical premises on which rest the creation of the alternative worlds of *Giles Goat-Boy* and the provocative convictions and practices of one of the great comic characters of contemporary fiction, Henry Burlingame of *The Sot-Weed Factor*. (Incidentally, since these characters return together with their typical preoccupations in *Letters*, this novel, too, should be considered in the given context.) Almost as if to pull these ideas together, Barth has emphasized that the recognition of arbitrariness is a major driving force behind his own ventures as a novelist: "But a certain kind of sensibility can be made very uncomfortable by the recognition of the *arbitrariness* of physical facts and the inability to accept their *finality*. Take France, for example: France is shaped like a tea pot, and Italy is shaped like a boot. Well, okay. But the idea that that's the only way it's ever going to be, that they'll never be shaped like anything else—that can get to you after a while."[16] Barth the critic has also said, in another context, "that the general project of orientation . . . is my characteristic subject matter, my fictionary stock in trade."[17] I would hold that this is equally valid for Barth's own dealings with the world as he finds it before he turns to his fictions. So the subsequent question for Barth the writer becomes: how does the artist find, or impose, or create orientation in a world that predominantly consists of arbitrary givens and equally arbitrary change? Which brings us directly to the question of the role and function of the imagination.

The arbitrariness of facts, values, and language, one could argue, is an eminent provocation for the artist. And the artist answers this provocation by pitting the creative powers of the imagination—not merely the reproductive imagination—against it. Barth is fully aware of this motivational connection, and he confesses to its impact on his own works as a writer of fiction. In an interview he once coupled his diagnosis of arbitrariness with a programmatic statement:

> If you are a novelist of a certain type of temperament, then what you really want to do is re-invent the world. . . . And it seems to me that this emotion [being mad at the arbitrariness of facts], which is a kind of metaphysical emotion, goes almost to the heart of what art is, at least some kinds of art, and this impulse to imagine alternatives to the world can become a driving impulse for writers. I confess that it is for me. So that really what you want to do is re-invent philosophy and the rest—make up your own whole history of the world.[18]

Similarly, Barth has stated in another piece of early criticism: "But the artist, and in particular the novelist, in his essence wishes neither to explain nor to control nor to understand the universe: He wants to make one of his own, and may even aspire to make it more orderly, meaningful, beautiful, and interesting than the one God turned out."[19] Fiction, literature, and art are ideal instruments for the pursuit of this program, if we follow Barth's argument in the "Bellerophoniad": "*Butterflies* exist in our imaginations, along with *existence*, *imagination*, and the rest. Archimedeses, we lever reality by conceiving ourselves apart from its other things, them from one another, the whole from unreality. Thus Art is as natural an artifice as Nature; the truth of fiction is that Fact is fantasy; the made-up story is a model of the world."[20]

What this comes down to, then, is that in Barth's scheme the literary imagination frequently equals the power of reinvention; that it attempts, with a creatively defiant touch, to pit its own versions of things against the dictates of the given; that it wants to put to shame that which *is* by producing countless alternatives of that which is not; that, in a sense, it tries to transform the "world" by remaking it in the mind. In short, literature, in this context, still does what Shelley once ascribed to it in his "Defence of Poetry": "It creates anew the universe."[21] The world may be all that is the case, but Barth is not going to accept this. So his novels (at least some of them) become monuments to the alternative-making faculty of a "boundless imagination" (John Hawkes's expression)[22] that heaps versions upon versions and proliferates alternatives in a universe of the merely and allegedly given.

However, there are certain pitfalls in the program of replacing what is allegedly given with the alternatives of an imagination that deals in more than the given or the commonly accepted. One problem lies in the fact that the medium of the literary imagination for generating the "other" to that which the receptive faculties merely seem to register is language —and language itself functions (even according to Barth's own scheme) by producing arbitrary associations between referents and signs. The second, closely related problem in setting inventions against the arbitrariness of facts is, of course, that the inventions of the imagination are themselves patently arbitrary. Hence, there is what Tony Tanner has called a "sense of the arbitrariness of invention" in Barth, leading directly to the danger of the author's being "lost in the freedom of his inventions,"[23] reproducing, as it were, the joint quandaries of arbitrariness and freedom on a subsequent level. And finally, there is the problem of what exactly is meant when Barth speaks of the arbitrariness of facts. Arbitrariness is usually defined as a state in which chance rather than law or reason determines a decision or an event. And indeed, when Barth talks about the arbitrariness of facts, he is after the missing "ultimate reasons" for such phenomena as France's being shaped like a tea pot, and Italy like a boot. However, there are many reasons or causes for such facts—it is only that they are not the type of reasons or causes Barth so diligently seeks. What is brought into play in Barth's reflections on the absence of ultimate reason is a time-honored philosophical distinction, namely the distinction between *causa efficiens* and *causa finalis*. Barth never mentions this distinction explicitly, but his deliberations invariably hinge on it.

The example of France and Italy might serve to illustrate the point. There are, of course, many reasons that France and Italy are shaped the way they are, and these are reasons of a physical nature as part of a mechanical-physical chain of cause and effect, in short, what philosophers call *causa efficiens*. Yet this type of reason does not embrace purpose, *telos*, direction toward an aim, or the intentional correlation of means and ends, in sum, what philosophers call *causa finalis*. It is the lack of this dimension of *causa finalis*, the felt absence of a recognizable principle that arranges things according to meaningful design, that Barth complains about. And it is this complaint that stimulates his irritation and discontent when he addresses the problem of "arbitrary facts that make the world—devoid of ultimate meaning,"[24] or when he exclaims in comic anguish: "The final question is, Can nothing be made meaningful?"[25] More than this, it is the absence of *causa finalis* that becomes a motivational force behind the ambition of the literary imagination to supply the universe with what has been missing.

This is the context, then, in which the literary imagination sets out to invent its alternatives to worlds that are the case. In its course, it fights absence, reacts to deficiencies, and strives to give shape to the hitherto ineffable. More generally, as Wolfgang Iser has said, the literary imagination "brings the unavailable into view," adding, "This, in turn, is not a featureless entity, but is conditioned by the achievements through which the functional organizations of our reality have successfully patterned the intangible."[26] For Barth, such functional organizations are frequently marked by an arbitrariness that points to the absence of final meaning or ultimate sense. About his own philosophical orientation as a young novelist Barth has said in an interview: "When writing my first two novels it seemed to me that the notion of the world as absurd, of life as finally

mary and Annotated Secondary Bibliography (New York: Garland, 1976), pp. 65–69.

4 "The Limits of Imagination." Cf. also Barth's statements in "The Future of Literature and the Literature of the Future," *Friday Book*, p. 164, and "Tales Within Tales Within Tales," *ibid.*, p. 222. Also compare John J. Enck, "John Barth: An Interview," *Wisconsin Studies in Contemporary Literature* 6 (1965): 8; *First Person: Conversations on Writers & Writing*, ed. Gado, p. 116; and Glaser-Wöhrer, *An Analysis of John Barth's "Weltanschauung,"* p. 219.

5 Wolfgang Iser, "Changing Functions of Literature," *The Yearbook of Research in English and American Literature* 3 (1985): 20–21.

6 "Aspiration, Inspiration, Respiration, Expiration," *Friday Book*, p. 98. Cf. on the same subject: *Friday Book*, pp. 56–57, 135, 220.

7 For examples see "Tales Within Tales Within Tales," *Friday Book*, p. 219, and John J. Enck, "John Barth: An Interview," p. 8.

8 "More on the Same Subject," *Friday Book*, p. 29.

9 Cf. "The Literature of Exhaustion," *Friday Book*, pp. 62ff., and Barth's comments on the misunderstanding in "The Literature of Replenishment," *Friday Book*, pp. 193, 205f. Cf. also *Interviews with Contemporary Writers*, pp. 320f.

10 "The Role of the Prosaic in Fiction," *Friday Book*, p. 80.

11 For the same list of works, compare his essay "Tales Within Tales Within Tales," *Friday Book*, p. 220, and the interview with Charlie Reilly in *Interviews with Contemporary Writers*, p. 338.

12 *Lost in the Funhouse* (Garden City, N.Y.: Doubleday, 1968), p. 112.

13 *The End of the Road* (1958; rpt. New York: Bantam Books, 1969), p. 135.

14 Tony Tanner, *City of Words: American Fiction 1950–1970* (London: Jonathan Cape, 1971), p. 240.

15 *The End of the Road*, pp. 81–82. For further references to Wittgenstein's dictum, compare among others "Tales Within Tales Within Tales," *Friday Book*, p. 221.

16 Enck, "John Barth: An Interview," p. 8.

17 "Getting Oriented," *Friday Book*, p. 131.

18 See Enck, "John Barth: An Interview," p. 8. For Barth's differentiating comment on the project of reinventing the world in his fictions, see his interview with Glaser-Wöhrer in *An Analysis of John Barth's "Weltanschauung,"* pp. 213–14. As one of the most graphic examples in Barth's fiction of a writer figure actually inventing his own history of the world, see the "nameless minstrel" of the "Anonymiad" (*Lost in the Funhouse*, pp. 168ff.).

19 "How to Make a Universe," *Friday Book*, p. 17. Though this is from Barth's earliest public lecture (December 1960), he emphasizes in the reprint of the lecture that he continues to believe in its main tenets. Cf. *Friday Book*, p. 15.

20 *Chimera* (New York: Random House, 1972), p. 246.

21 "A Defence of Poetry," *The Complete Works of Percy Bysshe Shelley*, ed. Roger Ingpen and Walter E. Peck, vol. 7 (New York: Gordian Press, 1965), p. 137.

22 Cf. "Hawkes and Barth Talk About Fiction," *New York Times Book Review*, 1 April 1979, p. 7. Compare also Hawkes's later statement during the same conversation: "There is a risk in your work in creating enormous fictions that are self-contained. The voice, the language, the mentality involve considerable risk because they insist on creating their own reality" (p. 31).

23 Tony Tanner, *City of Words*, pp. 253 and 255.
24 "How to Make a Universe," *Friday Book*, p. 21.
25 "Title," *Lost in the Funhouse*, p. 105.
26 Wolfgang Iser, "Changing Functions of Literature," p. 19.
27 Glaser-Wöhrer, *An Analysis of John Barth's "Weltanschauung,"* pp. 219–20.

CONTRIBUTORS

Heide Ziegler is Professor of American and Recent English Literature at the University of Stuttgart. She has written a book on William Faulkner's short stories and one on John Barth. A study on irony in postmodernist American fiction is forthcoming. Together with Christopher Bigsby she has edited a book of interviews with contemporary British and American novelists.

Walter Abish received the PEN/Faulkner Award for his novel, *How German Is It?* His other books include *Alphabetical Africa*, *Minds Meet*, and *In the Future Perfect*. A recipient of a MacArthur fellowship, he recently spent six months in Berlin as guest of the DAAD, completing a novel entitled *As if*, of which "Is this really you?" is an excerpt. "I am the dust under your feet," also from *As if*, appeared in *Conjunctions* 10. He lives in New York, where he teaches writing at Columbia University.

John Barth is the author of seven novels: *The Floating Opera*, *The End of the Road*, *The Sot-Weed Factor*, *Giles GoatBoy*, *LETTERS*, *Sabbatical: A Romance*, and *The Tidewater Tales: A Novel*. He has also published *Lost in the Funhouse*, a series of short fictions for print, tape, and live voice, *Chimera*, a volume of novellas which won the National Book Award for Fiction in 1973, and *The Friday Book*, a collection of essays and other nonfiction. Mr. Barth has held professorships in the English departments of Pennsylvania State University, the State University of New York at Buffalo, and Boston University. Currently he is Alumni Centennial Professor of English and Creative Writing at Johns Hopkins. In 1974 he was elected to both the National Institute of Arts and Letters and the American Academy of Arts and Sciences. His latest novel, *The Tidewater Tales*, was published by Putnam in the spring of 1987.

Donald Barthelme teaches in the Creative Writing Program at the University of Houston. His most recent works include *Paradise*, *The Dead Father*, *Sixty Stories*, and *Forty Stories*.

Christopher Butler is a Fellow and Tutor in English Literature at Christ Church, Oxford. Among his publications are *After the Wake* (Oxford 1980) and *Interpretation, Deconstruction, and Ideology* (Oxford 1984). His current work is on early modernism in the arts and on theories of pleasure.

Marc Chénetier is Professor of American Literature at the Université d'Orléans. He runs the Groupe René Tadlov for Research on Contemporary American Fiction in Paris and edits the *Revue Française d'Etudes Américaines*. His publications include *Richard Brautigan* and

Critical Angles. His *Au-Delà du Soupçon* (American fiction, 1960–87) is forthcoming from Editions du Seuil.

Robert Coover was born in Iowa in 1932. His first novel, *Origin of the Brunists*, was the winner of the 1966 William Faulkner Award. His other works include *The Universal Baseball Association, J. Henry Waugh, Prop.*; *Pricksongs & Descants*; *A Theological Position*; *The Public Burning*; *A Political Fable*; *Spanking the Maid*; *Gerald's Party*; *A Night at the Movies*; and *Whatever Happened to Gloomy Gus and the Chicago Bears?* Coover lives with his wife, Pili, in Providence, Rhode Island, where he teaches at Brown University.

Guy Davenport, Alumni Distinguished Professor of English at the University of Kentucky, has, in addition to various critical works such as *The Geography of the Imagination*, *Every Force Evolves a Form*, and *Cities on Hills*, published five collections of short fiction: *Tatlin!*, *Da Vinci's Bicycle*, *Eclogues*, *Apples and Pears*, and *The Jules Verne Steam Balloon*. His collected poems appeared in 1987 as *Thasos and Ohio*.

Stanley Elkin's most recent novel is *The Rabbi of Lud*. Currently he is at work on a new novel, *The MacGuffin*. Mr. Elkin is Merle Kling Professor of Modern Letters at Washington University.

William H. Gass is the author of seven books of fiction and nonfiction, including *Omensetter's Luck*, *In the Heart of the Heart of the Country*, *On Being Blue*, and *The World Within the Word*. He is the David May Distinguished University Professor in the Humanities at Washington University in St. Louis.

John Hawkes is the author of such novels as *The Cannibal*, *The Lime Twig*, *Second Skin*, and *Adventures in the Alaskan Skin Trade*. His new novel, *Whistlejacket*, will be published in the spring of 1988. He teaches in the graduate writing program at Brown University.

Richard Howard is a poet, critic, and translator. He is the author of *Alone with America: Studies in the Art of Poetry in the United States since 1950*, and his ninth volume of verse, *No Traveller*, will be published next year.

Christine Laniel graduated from the Ecole Normale Supérieure in 1976 and has been teaching English in France for the last ten years. She is engaged in research on John Hawkes's fiction and has contributed to several publications on his work.

Joseph McElroy is the author of six novels—*A Smuggler's Bible*, *Hind's Kidnap*, *Ancient History*, *Lookout Cartridge*, *Plus*, and, most recently, *Women and Men*, from which "Choor Monster of the Long White Mountain" is taken.

Patrick O'Donnell is Associate Professor and Director of Graduate Studies in the English Department at the University of Arizona. He has published several books and articles on contemporary fiction and literary theory, including *John Hawkes* and *Passionate Doubts: Decisions of Interpretation in Contemporary American Fiction*. Recently he coedited *Intertextuality and Contemporary American Fiction* and is working on a book about the representation of "voice" in the modern novel.

Manfred Pütz holds the chair for American Literature at the University of Augsburg (Germany). He studied philosophy as well as English and American literature in Germany (Cologne), the United States (Berkeley), England (Cambridge), and Canada (British Columbia). His publications include works on Benjamin Franklin, Crèvecoeur, Max Weber, Emerson, Thoreau, Melville, Poe, and on modern American fiction and poetry.

Joseph C. Schöpp taught American literature at the John F. Kennedy Institute of North American Studies in West Berlin and at the universities of Mannheim, Stuttgart, and Tübingen before he was appointed Director of the German-American Institute in Freiburg. He is the author of a book on Allen Tate (1975) and postmodern American fiction (forthcoming) as well as a number of articles that have appeared in various German periodicals.

Among **Susan Sontag's** books are *The Benefactor* and *Death Kit* (novels), *I, etcetera* (stories), and five volumes of essays, including *Illness as Metaphor* and *Under the Sign of Saturn. A Susan Sontag Reader* was published in 1982. She is completing another novel.

Tony Tanner is Reader in American Literature at King's College, Cambridge University. He has held visiting professorships at Northwestern, Emory, and Stanford, has received a Harkness Fellowship and a fellowship from the American Council of Learned Societies. He is the author of *Conrad: Lord Jim, The Reign of Wonder: Naivety and Reality in American Literature, Saul Bellow, City of Words: American Fiction 1950–1970, Henry James: The Writer and His Work, Thomas Pynchon, Adultery in the Novel, Jane Austen*, and the forthcoming *Scenes of Nature, Signs of Men.*

Robert Walsh has been a member of the editorial staffs of the architecture quarterly *Oppositions* and *The New Yorker* and is now an editor of *Vanity Fair*. He has published art criticism in *Art in America* and *ArtNews* and is the main author of *The ICP Encyclopedia of Photography* (Crown, 1985). He is married to the writer Stephani Cook.

Alan Wilde is professor of English at the University of Pennsylvania. His most recent books include *Horizons of Assent: Modernism, Postmodernism, and the Ironic Imagination* (just reissued in paperback) and *Middle Grounds: Studies in Contemporary American Fiction.*

Library of Congress Cataloging-in-Publication Data
Facing texts.
Bibliography: p.
1. American fiction—20th century. 2. American fiction—20th century—History and criticism.
I. Ziegler, Heide.
PS659.F33 1988 813'.54'08 87-27541
ISBN 0-8223-0801-0
ISBN 0-8223-0818-5 (pbk.)

Praise for
Satan and His Friends

"Drawing on the ancient Near Eastern context, Second Temple Judaism, and early Christian interpretation, Edmon L. Gallagher unveils how disputed and uncertain many widely accepted views are. Gallagher walks us through the texts about the unseen realm and provides an account that is more restrained in his conclusions in contrast to what one might often hear from Christian pulpits. Reading this book is a healthy exercise in exegetical and theological caution. I appreciate where he ultimately lands—God is sovereign, Christ is victor, and we do not fear the unseen forces. I recommend the book as an alternative perspective to the dominant popular conceptions of the heavenly realm."

—**John Mark Hicks,** Professor of Theology, Lipscomb University

"'The world, the flesh, and the devil.' For decades (if not centuries), Christians have been warned to take all three antagonists seriously, or even to blame mishaps on one of the three members of this evil triumvirate. But what do we really know about the third? Enter Ed Gallagher's fascinating and readable study of the devil and all his friends. Journeying through a wide range of resources from the Dead Sea Scrolls to the *Book of Enoch* to *Paradise Lost*, Gallagher adeptly shows that many of our ideas about Satan—that he has a name (*Satan*), that he was an angel who fell from heaven, that he is locked in a cosmic battle against God, that he rules over hell with a pitchfork, and so on—are more features of interpretive imagination than they are clear teachings of the Old or New Testament. Gallagher lands on what he calls a minimalistic view of this ancient supernatural antagonist, but minimalistic in two ways: The Bible says less than we think about his origins and minions, and the scope of his power is far more limited than popularly thought. But the upshot of this book is not for us to take the *satan* less seriously (i.e., 'The greatest trick the devil ever pulled was convincing the world he didn't exist') but to provide comfort to all Christians, perhaps especially those who have an over-clocked fear of demons and the supernatural: Christ has defanged the devil and will one day punish him forever. Even if the reader disagrees with Gallagher at points, this book is still immensely valuable for those interested in digging deeply into scriptural teaching on the supernatural realm."

—**Gregory R. Lanier, PhD,** Professor of New Testament at Reformed Theological Seminary

"This book calls for us to seek those things which are above, to move away from an incessant focus on fear to an overwhelming confidence of faith. The central story of Scripture is about the faithfulness of God, seen in the finished work of Jesus Christ and the ongoing power of his Holy Spirit. What little may be gleaned concerning the dark powers pales in comparison with the One who dwells in unapproachable light. Gallagher writes with a pastor's heart, assuring us that the repeated refrain of Scripture is that Christ has won, is faithful to his promise, and empowers us to live in the light of God's glorious grace. May we heed the call of this important book, to avoid searching in the darkness for the shadowy vestiges of what is defeated in Christ, and, instead, give our attention to the One who deserves all our focus, love, and praise."

—**Nathan Guy, PhD,** Associate Professor of Philosophy, Theology, and Ethics; Director, David E. Smith Healthcare Ethics and Human Dignity Initiative, Harding University; Preaching Minister, West Side Church of Christ

"Devilishly good. Gallagher's treatment is critically astute, engagingly written, and pastorally sensitive. He argues that the Bible gives less importance to, and fewer details concerning, Satan and his minions than many Christians have traditionally wanted to affirm. Central to the biblical testimony is instead a principled minimalism, a decisive downgrade of the demonic realm."

—**Stephen B. Chapman,** Associate Professor of Old Testament, Duke Divinity School; Editor in Chief, *Journal of Theological Interpretation*

"In this engaging book, Edmon Gallagher explores how beliefs about Satan and evil spirits developed within Christian Scripture and tradition. Writing with both scholarly depth and pastoral sensitivity, Gallagher helps Christian readers see that Satan and his 'friends' play a surprisingly minor role in the biblical narrative. This welcome study invites Christians to reconsider their assumptions about evil and to refocus their attention on the sovereignty and centrality of God in the story of redemption."

—**H. Clay Smith,** Assistant Professor of Biblical Studies, Harding University